£ 37.50
1982

Water Resources Series

Volume 1

70 0176760 X

TELEPEN

Water Resources Management in Industrial Areas

WATER RESOURCES SERIES

Volume 1: **WATER RESOURCES MANAGEMENT IN INDUSTRIAL AREAS**
Selected papers from the International Symposium held by the International Water Resources Association (IWRA),
7–11 September 1981, Lisbon, Portugal

Editors: *Leo R. Beard and W.H.C. Maxwell*
Published for the International Water Resources Association
ISBN: Hardcover 0 907567 30 4
        Softcover 0 907567 31 2
Publication date: September 1982

Volume 2: **WATER FOR HUMAN CONSUMPTION**
Man and His Environment
A selection of papers prepared for the IVth World Congress of the International Water Resources Association (IWRA)
3–11 September 1982, Buenos Aires, Argentina

Published for the International Water Resources Association
ISBN: Hardcover 0 907567 61 4
        Softcover 0 907567 60 6
Publication date: August 1982

Volume 3: **LONG-DISTANCE WATER TRANSFER IN CHINA**
Editors: *Asit K. Biswas, Zuo Dakang, J. Nickum and Liu Changming*
Published for the United Nations University
ISBN: Hardcover 0 907567 52 5
        Softcover 0 907567 53 3
Publication date: October 1982

Water Resources Management in Industrial Areas

Selected Papers from the International Symposium held by the International Water Resources Association (IWRA), 7–11 September 1981, Lisbon, Portugal

Edited by:
Leo R. Beard and W.H.C. Maxwell

Symposium organized by
Portuguese Water Resources Association
International Water Resources Association

Sponsored by
United Nations
United Nations Industrial Development Organization
United Nations Environment Programme
International Institute for Applied Systems Analysis

Published by
TYCOOLY INTERNATIONAL PUBLISHING LIMITED
DUBLIN

Published by:
Tycooly International Publishing Ltd.,
6, Crofton Terrace,
Dun Laoghaire,
Co. Dublin, Ireland
Tel: (+ 353-1) 800245, 800246
Telex: 30547 SHCN EI

Typeset by Intercontinental Photocomposition Ltd., Dublin
Printed in Ireland by Mount Salus Press Ltd., Dublin 4.

ISBN 0 907567 30 4 Hardback
ISBN 0 907567 31 2 Softcover

Contents

Foreword

Close to five hundred persons from fifty-five countries attended the International Symposium on Water Resources Management in Industrial Areas at the Calouste Gulbenkian Foundation in Lisbon on 7–11 September 1981. Of the more than sixty technical papers presented, thirty-two have been selected by the editors with the advice of the rapporteurs, Professor Eloy Urroz and Dr. Blair Bower. These are published herein and are considered to constitute an outstanding representation of the state-of-the-art.

The collection is divided into papers on water quantity management and papers on water quality management. However, it is recognized that quantity without quality has little meaning and should be considered accordingly. Quantity refers to usable water and water is usable for any specific purpose only so long as its quality has not deteriorated beyond acceptable limits. Thus overall management of water resources should emphasize use and re-use in sequences of municipal, industrial and agricultural operations such that each operation can best tolerate effects of preceding operations. It is in this context that the papers presented in this volume should be viewed.

Leo R. Beard
Chairman, Publications Committee,
International Water
Resources Association

W.H.C. Maxwell
Technical Editor, WIN,
University of Illinois
at Urbana-Champaign

Organizing Committee

A. Eira Leitão
The Chairman, Portuguese Water Resources Association

Guillermo J. Cano
International Water Resources Association

Enzo Fano
United Nations

R. Olembo
United Nations Environment Programme

Gabriel Rezek
United Nations Industrial Development Organization

Janusz Kindler
International Institute for Applied Systems Analysis

L.J. Mostertman
International Water Resources Association

A. Caires Vila-Nova
Director, Office for Environment Studies, Portugal

A. Gonçalves
General-Subdirector for Hydraulic Resources and Uses, Portugal

A. Santos Gonçalves
General-Director for Quality

J. Correia da Cunha
President, National Commission for Environment, Portugal

J. Faria Ferreira
General Inspector, Council for Public Works and Transports, Portugal

J. Ferry Borges
President, National Laboratory for Civil Engineering, Portugal

J. Veiga Simão
Director, National Laboratory for Industrial Engineering and Technology, Portugal

L. Veiga da Cunha
Chairman, Executive Committee of the Symposium

Executive Committee

Luis Veiga da Cunha—*Chairman*
Artur Ascenso Pires
Jaime Melo Baptista
José Oliveira Raposo
João Bau

OPENING SESSION

Address by
Chairman of the Symposium Executive Committee
Dr. Eng. Luis Veiga da Cunha

Industrialization is the most relevant characteristic of the socio-economic development of the twentieth century. The development of the industrial sector, usually followed by population migrations from rural areas to urban areas, is generally considered as a conditioning aspect of economic development and also as a factor of environmental disturbances.

The available quantities of soil and water are factors of attraction for industries. So, the conservation of water resources and of other environmental elements require a combined action by those responsible for the planning and management of water and industrial resources in order to avoid the occurrence of undesirable situations, which are always difficult and expensive to control, if measures are not taken in due time.

Since water is a very important production factor, its use by industry constitutes a major problem within the framework of water resources management. Industrial impacts on water resources are reflected in water storage, by the effective consumption of water and by the pollution discharges in the receiving waters. Water may be used by industry mainly in four different ways, which are frequently associated: process water, cooling water, boiler water and water for general uses.

Although water is an important industrial production factor it is not usually a very significant factor from an economic point of view, as it only corresponds to a small part of the final product cost and, as a rule, does not reach 10 per cent of this cost. This means that it is not difficult to apply systems which condition industrial users to reach efficiency in the use of water resources and, particularly, to ensure control of the pollution they cause. As a matter of fact, this type of intervention will always be easier in the case of industrial water supply than in the cases of agricultural or domestic supply.

For an adequate forecast of water demand by industry it is necessary to analyse the development of the industrial sector. Usually this analysis is based on the consideration of alternative scenarios of development which correspond to the consideration of certain consistent combinations of the most relevant factors corresponding to future conditions of social and economic development, of technological progress and of life style.

The definition of alternative scenarios is based on a certain number of basic options related to growth rates, employment structure, consumption and production structures, degree of exposure to international trade, energy balance and environmental protection. This implies consideration of the role played by industrial development within the framework of the global strategy of development. The result of all this is that water demand for industry has to be linked, in a coherent way, with water demand for other uses, namely for agriculture and for domestic consumption.

Water demand for industry depends on numerous interrelated factors, including withdrawal and treatment costs, production technologies employed, the types and the costs of raw materials used, the kinds of final products, the conditions imposed on pollutant discharges, costs associated with waste treatment, the value of byproducts and the available existing capital.

Taking these factors into account, models have been established, which allow definition of industrial water demand. Users of these models to estimate future water demand should always consider that the existing political and economic conditions may change. Thus, there is a great need for analysis of the situation in terms of alternative scenarios as mentioned above.

The disaggregation of the water demand for industrial uses is usually done by regions, according to the size of the industrial units, the production technology and the nature of the final products. In each case one looks for the relationship between water demand and the variables that condition it, always considering the several possible alternatives for water use, mainly re-circulation, evolution of industrial technologies, reduction of the pollutant discharged and treatment of the water used in industry. So it is always important to specify the quality required for water in each one of the considered alternatives.

In the case of manufacturing industry, water consumption is frequently expressed according to the production value, the added value, the volume of employment, or the volume of the final product, and the defined relations are valid for certain conditions of industrial productivity and for certain production technologies. Whenever the productivity or the production technology is modified, this should be taken into consideration when one wishes to predict the evolution of water consumption by industry. So, it is expected that the unitary consumptions of water in a new industrial unit are different from those which occur in an equivalent unit already installed for some decades or even for some years.

Among the most important industrial sources concerning water pollution, mention should be made of extractive industries, several manufacturing industries, energy production either from fossil fuels or from radioactive substances, cleaning and maintenance of industrial units, transportation of people and goods by sea, leaching of pollutants from industrial wastes, absorption of gaseous wastes by water and, finally, the industry of drinking water or treated water production from natural, surface or groundwater.

The treatment of industrial effluents usually aims at withdrawing from wastewater the pollutants added to the water during the production process. So it seems obvious that the addition of such pollutants should be avoided in order not to have to remove them later on. This idea is the basis of the clean technologies to which increasing attention has been paid in recent years and which, in certain cases, have had excellent results and even sometimes unexpected ones.

In recent years, the pressures to reduce industrial water consumption have led to the introduction of technological changes to reduce either the quantity of water used in industry, its quality, or the pollutants discharged.

Changing industrial processes in order to achieve a reduction of the pollution discharged often includes good use of wastes which form the byproducts. So, the good use of these byproducts should be regarded not as a pollution control action but as a source of raw materials, whose reuse may, by itself, have an economic justification.

As a matter of fact pollution is, to a large degree, an indicator of an inefficiency of processes. Were that inefficiency reduced, pollution would also be reduced. We should keep in mind, for instance, that the total efficiency of the use of energy in industrialized countries is lower than 10 per cent, a great part of the non-used energy causing thermal pollution. It may also be pointed out that a lot of time and money are spent in building treatment systems for industrial wastes, when in many cases it would be possible to get a substantial reduction of the total costs simply by modifying the technological processes used or by replacing the raw materials.

Research and development of new industrial technologies and of new pollution control systems should be stimulated through grants to industrial users. Without this kind of incentive the users will prefer, in most cases, to invest in the already proved technologies rather than take the risk with new or non-conventional technologies. These grants would be reimbursed only in those cases where the new technologies, which would be the object of the research and development, proved to be efficient, and the results of the studies undertaken would be compulsorily published, whether or not the technologies proved to be efficient.

It is also important to point out that the existing wastewater treatment plants should be used as much as possible. A wastewater treatment system of an industrial unit is a productive unit whose operation in good condition is as important as the functioning of any other unit of the system referred to. To allow treatment units, whose installation is usually very expensive, to be out of action or to operate in bad condition is not acceptable. However, and somewhat paradoxically, it is in the developing countries, where the economic conditions are often more difficult, that this type of situation is frequently seen.

The industrialized countries have spent in recent years about 0.5 to 1.5

per cent of their Gross National Products on pollution control. On the other hand recent studies undertaken in different countries show that the damages caused by pollution, considering only the tangible aspects of these damages, vary between 1 and 3 per cent. As a result, pollution control appears as a feasible operation, even in pure economic terms.

Water resources management in industrial areas has to be considered within the framework of water resources management. In order to attain this aim, it implies the application of institutional and economic measures. The application of a set of measures of the same nature corresponds to the formulation of what is called a water resources management strategy. A wise combination of these strategies is called water resources management policy.

Water resources managers are supposed to promote the definition of a certain number of global policies, to analyse the economic, social and environmental impacts of these policies and to ensure that these impacts be explained in comparative terms in order to allow decision-makers to adopt the most advisable policy. Therefore a national water resources management policy should be defined in each country. Such a formulation was considered by the United Nations Water Conference (Mar del Plata, 1977) as a first step in implementing efficient water resources management.

Water resources management policy should be carried out with the participation of all the sectorial entities related to the water resources problems; it is essential to ensure the coordination of the actions undertaken by those different entities, through an institutional mechanism having an organization and power adequate to the functions to be carried out.

An adequate institutional framework for water resources management has already been implemented in several developed countries and is being launched in some developing countries. However, there is strong pressure to undertake these changes in many countries.

Water resources management problems frequently involve two or more countries. Portugal, which has 50 per cent of its water resources coming from Spain, is a typical case in which this situation of dependence may become highly inconvenient, if suitable agreements are not established in due time. Aware of the importance of a water resources management on an international scale, several countries have come to agreements in which the concept of an international hydrographic basin is an important basis for water resources management.

Besides the bilateral or multilateral agreements between countries sharing the same hydrographic basin, reference should be made to the intense activity in international cooperation concerning the problems of water resources. Special reference should be made to the activities undertaken through the agencies and programmes of the United Nations System and especially by UNIDO, UNEP, UNESCO, WMO, WHO, FAO, UNICEF, UNDP and the Regional Economic Commissions. I would like to make a reference to the United Nations Water Conference held in Mar del Plata in 1977 and the International Decade of Drinking Water Supply and Sanitation, which has been in progress since 1980. The sponsorship given to this Symposium by the United Nations, UNIDO and

UNEP should be considered as a clear demonstration of the great interest in resolving the above mentioned problems which concern all of us.

Besides the United Nations, several other international organizations include, among their main concerns, water resources problems. I refer to organizations with an active presence in this Symposium, the OECD, EEC and the IIASA.

Developing countries are in general characterised by an incipient industrialization and this leads quite often to considering the problems related to industrial use of water as not important, and to place major importance on water use for domestic water supply and irrigation. This attitude assumed in the developing countries sometimes dangerously neglects the damage caused to the environment and to the quality of life by uncontrolled use of water by industry.

In consequence of the severe restrictions existing in some industrialized countries regarding pollution control, these countries tend to negotiate the installation of highly polluting industrial units in developing countries, where there are no strict regulations on pollution control. Sometimes, these countries, fascinated by the apparent benefits to their economy by foreign investments, favour this situation. This happens because these countries forget the external costs caused by environmental pollution and do not calculate them when analysing the cost-benefit of the proposed investments. It is vital to react against this situation. Fortunately some reactions are already being felt. In fact, due to the alarm being given, situations of this type are being highlighted. Some developing countries recognise the importance of having legal and institutional tools capable of effectively protecting them against pollution caused by industrial units installed at foreign or national initiative. However, such tools have to be prepared before the potentially polluting industrial units are installed to become effective.

The fact of being less developed may actually have its advantages, such as making the best use of the experience of industrialized countries in order to avoid all the mistakes made in similar situations which developing countries are now facing. The presence of numerous representatives from developing countries at this Symposium clearly shows that these countries are in fact aware of the problems and are concerned with their resolution.

OPENING SESSION

Address by
The Minister of Industry and Energy
Professor Ricardo Bayão Horta

On behalf of the Portuguese Government I welcome the participants to this conference. In particular, I would like to thank the United Nations in the person of its delegate, Mr Enzo Fano, for its acceptance of my Government's invitation to hold this conference.

The United Nations has, for several years now, paid particular attention to the problem of water resources management either directly or through the United Nations Environment Programme (which is also a sponsor of this conference) or the International Institute of Applied Systems Analysis.

I would also like to note the important work of the Portuguese Water Resources Association which organized this symposium with the co-operation of the International Water Resources Association. In Portugal this organization has been developing dialogue and discussion on the subject of water resources. There now exists a real forum for the study and exchange of ideas relating to water resource problems. This has contributed to the identification of national problems and also to the choice of solutions.

An indispensable element of life, water can also prove a limiting factor in economic and social development. Although perhaps not so urgent as the search for solutions to the energy crisis, the problems of water resource management are equally important. Although it can be considered a renewable natural resource, water can still be scarce and expensive and a limiting factor in economic and social development.

Industrial development is the most important source of wealth in almost all countries and it is valid to study the important relationship between water and industrial activity. In Portugal, there are three major aspects to this question:

    (1) Analyzing the requirements of quality and quantity of water supply throughout various industrial sectors.

(2) Listing existing resources in terms of optimum usage and anticipated rates of demand with reference to the evolution of relevant science and technology.

(3) Assessing existing and proposed locations for industry in relation to the proper use and management of water resources.

In the Portuguese context it is important to realise that the connection between industrial activity and water resources is not a closed system. Besides its domestic and sanitary usage, water is also important from the viewpoint of:

(a) Electricity generation—hydropower represents 50 per cent of electricity production.

(b) Agriculture.

These must be regarded as factors in evaluating the integrated management of water resources for industrial purposes.

OPENING SESSION

Address by
President of Portuguese Water Resources Association
Eng. António Eira Leitão

Water is an essential element for life and a factor indispensable to economic and social development. The problems that have arisen in order to satisfy actual and future needs of the communities are quite complex. Such problems cannot be solved only by adoption of scientific and technological measures but also through the adoption of water resource management policies, on an interdisciplinary basis, within a broad economic perspective and a simultaneous and integrated consideration of its multiple purposes.

For several decades, water management has been a major problem for countries and international organizations with different domains of action, including economic communities. In fact, the perception that water is the major factor in the development of societies, either in quality and quantity, results frequently from hard realities experienced in rural or urban areas, in countries with different levels of development and in national or international river basins.

In fact, industrialization is one of the most determinant characteristics of economic growth of the last century. Countless industries collect and use large volumes of water, causing serious pollution in the neighbouring natural recipient bodies. It is also frequently observed that pollution effects are concentrated in reduced geographic areas. These facts imply that more attention should be paid to the technical, environmental, sociological, legal and institutional aspects related to water supply to industry as well as to rejection of its effluents, within the process of management of natural resources.

Therefore, it is becoming more stringent to control the process of industrialization, by planning its nature and location, forecasting the water requirements and polluting charges, developing new technologies of product transformation and implementing adequate and efficient administrative measures, mainly in areas with absolute or seasonal requirements of water.

Founded in August 1977 as a non-profit scientific and technical association, the APRH (Portuguese Water Resources Association) intends to promote multi-sectorial and interdisciplinary approaches to water resource problems, intending to be a forum for professionals from several organizations and sectors dealing with problems related to the field of water resources. Following the example of its international counterpart, the Association is not only concerned with the variety of specific aspects of water planning, use and control, but also with the pursuit of an integrated and optimised view of water problems. Its objectives are as follows:

(a) To further progress of knowledge at a national level, as well as the study and discussion of water resources problems, particularly in the fields of water management, planning, development, administration, science, technology, research and education;

(b) To obtain co-operation from interested individuals and entities in creating a suitable institutional framework and facilities for solving national water resources problems;

(c) To support and participate in the dissemination of the basic concepts of a suitable policy for water resources management in Portugal;

(d) To collaborate with similar foreign organizations and to promote Portuguese participation in international water resources programmes that may be of interest to Portugal.

The Association is developing an intensive cultural and editorial activity, through its Northern and Southern Regional Commissions and five Specialised Committees, and is participating in task force commissions and work groups, where APRH was invited to participate by the competent organisms of the Public Administration. The activities of the Association include:

Publication of a newsletter, the technical journal *Recursos Hídricos* (Water Resources) and a series of non-periodic publications, in Portuguese; Conferences, panels, seminars, symposia and study visits, which have already focussed on, among other subjects, the organizational aspects of water resources management, the multipurpose project of Alqueva, water supply and wastewater, the River Douro navigation project, hydroelectric production in Portugal, the use of water resources in Algarve and the drought of 1981; a symposium on the water resources planning of the basin of the River Tagus is in preparation.

The Association has been invited to participate in the organization of Environmental Departments and in the commission appointed by the Secretary of State for Planning for consideration of water resource problems in the four-year plan 1981/84.

The Association has more than 520 individual members and about 50 collective ones, including all the main organizations concerned with Portuguese water resource problems.

It is not our job to criticise the results reached so far and their consequences for the resolution of the problems which Portugal is facing including those related to the river basins shared with Spain, But unquestionably, the activity undertaken by APRH to date has given it a position, at a national and even at an international level, which cannot be denied. In the scientific and technical fields, where our activity is directed, we must and will keep on working for the harmonious development and welfare of the Portuguese community.

This International Symposium has 420 registered participants, from more than 55 countries of different continents. Within the main subjects "Water Resources Management in Industrial Areas Short of Water" and "Water Pollution Control in Industrial Areas", 60 papers will be presented, to be debated during successive technical sessions, the last one being dedicated to the presentation of the conclusions of the Symposium by the rapporteurs.

The programme also includes two special sessions on the following subjects: "Industrial Estates—A Better Water Resources Management?" and "Communitary Legislation concerning Water Resources", a bibliographic exposition, sessions of film and slide projection, a technical visit by ship to industrial plants located in the estuary of the River Tagus and a social programme for participants and accompanying persons.

For all the various countries at different stages of industrial and economic development, we have to find in each case the most appropriate method for the use of that precious resource which is water, either for human consumption, hygiene and recreation, the production of goods and services, or for controlling the damage that its scarcity or excess can provoke.

OPENING SESSION

Address by
President of the International Water Resources Association
Dr. Guillermo Cano

When I took the chair of the Association over which I have the honour to preside, I determined in a precise and definite way the policy of the activities to be undertaken. Three of these activities show clearly the role of this Association in this meeting. Firstly, I must say that it is not our intention to compete with other similar Associations concerned with water—national or international—but, on the contrary, we wish to cooperate with them, openly, being a forum for common activities and, whenever necessary, trying to fill the empty spaces left by others. A good example of this is our collaboration with the Portuguese Water Resources Association – a precedent which will remove any apprehensions of this kind that other Associations could have regarding us.

Although we had taken the initiative in promoting this Symposium and had undertaken actions in order to try to obtain the participation of the United Nations, it is a fact that the hard task of organizing this Symposium with such great success was due completely to the Portuguese responsibility and so, I wish to thank effusively our Portuguese friends and, most especially, Dr. Luis Veiga da Cunha, Chairman of the Executive Committee of the Symposium, who, and not by mere coincidence, is also the Chairman of the National Portuguese Committee of our Association.

In addition it is not mere coincidence that two of the invited authors and a great number of the participants are also members of our Association.

The second activity is that of complementing the action of the international governmental organizations, such as the United Nations agencies. We also provide, through our members all over the world, scientific collaboration with the university communities and the expertise of people in the private sector, who, without forgetting civil servants, belong to our long list of Associates.

It is not also mere coincidence that Enzo Fano—a well-known member of the staff of the United Nations and responsible for the participation of IWRA in this

11

Symposium – is a member of our Association, presiding over one of our Committees, which I hope, will shortly organize a meeting like this one in Sweden. This is the reason why we count on the active participation of the United Nations, the American States Organization, the World Bank and the Interamerican Development Bank in our Fourth World Congress to be held in Argentina (3rd to 11th September 1982), in the schedule of the International Decennium on Drinking Water Supply and Sanitation which was promulgated by the United Nations.

The aim of the third mentioned activity is to emphasise the interdisciplinary ways of the sciences of water. Our quarterly review *Water International*, published by Elsevier Sequoia has been revised and is now clearly interdisciplinary. I am pleased to greet its Editor-in-Chief, Mr. Leo Beard, who is here with us.

The subject matter of this symposium concerns both developed and developing countries and deals with aspects of water supply as well as water quality in relation to industrial use and pollution.

It is hoped that developing countries will learn from the experience of existing industrialized regions and avoid their costly mistakes through the proper application of pollution control technology.

Finally, I wish to sincerely thank the Portuguese authorities and the friendly Portuguese people for the welcoming hospitality that they have offered us.

Summary Report
on
Water Quantity Management

Eloy Urroz
ECO Inginiera S.A., Angel Urraza 414, Colonia del
Valle Mexico 12, DF, Mexico

DURING THE COURSE of the International Symposium on Water Resources Management in Industrial Areas, 20 papers were presented under Water Quantity Management and 40 papers were presented under Water Quality Management. Since the symposium was divided into these two large topics, it was necessary for the organizers to classify the various studies under management of water resources quantity and management of water resources quality. However, I would like to reaffirm that quantity and quality can never be treated separately, not even in 1981.

Here I would like to reiterate what I said during the presentation of my paper: The model of water resources management for industrial areas short of water is based on a simple assumption; water is clean and of quality suitable for industrial uses. Now we must conclude by saying that decline in water quality, or water pollution, is no more than another quantitative use of water; having a contaminated water resource is almost the same as having no resource.

Papers on water quantity were received from 10 countries and two international agencies, as follows: three from Hungary; two each from Portugal, Italy, the United States and Mexico; and one each from Canada, India, Sweden, the Netherlands and Venezuela. IIASA submitted two papers and UNEP one.

With respect to the conclusions of the Symposium, let me present them in two parts. First, the general conclusions include planning aspects and the socio-economic context. Second, the specific conclusions refer to the development and application of specific models for water resources management at a regional or industry-wide level. Aside from the conclusions, some recommendations which follow from the discussions are presented, even some which were not included in the papers presented.

It is important to note the fact that no papers were presented which combine the total concept of water resources management in industrial areas, since the symposium divided the theme.

General Conclusions

1. It has become essential in any region or country to introduce a system of development planning for water resources if good management of water resources in industrial areas is desired. (It is clear that this is valid in areas with both an excess and a scarcity of water.) In any society there are shortages, since a shortage means lack of economic resources.

2. National models of overall water resources management cannot be based on a single scheme. Each country, and in some cases each region, must be developed according to its historical background, culture and socio-political situation. Although in several countries water management is divided into supply and distribution, rational management can only be achieved when both water supply and use are considered as a conjunction whole, including management of supply, management within industry and control of pollution in all industrial estate areas.

3. Water resources planning must be pursued, having as its point of reference the river basin; nevertheless the majority of countries require regional and geopolitical units for planning water resources. This situation complicates management of the resource since it may be necessary to superimpose two plans at exactly the moment when political decisions are needed.

4. Hydraulic works for industry do not make sense if there are no industrial development plans; therefore, planning and management of water resources are the bases of economic and industrial development of a country or region.

Specific Conclusions

1. It seems that the lack of information and data on the use of water in industry and in other economic sectors make the development and application of mathematical models difficult.

2. The observations of data on the use of water in industry, which have been presented in the different studies of this symposium, permit us to conclude that there are two factors which directly regulate the demand for water in industry: the distribution of the resource and the technology used.

3. It can be concluded from some of the studies presented with the application of incentives, including high costs for water, that industrial technologies can be modified or developed for lower water consumption or consumption of lower quality water.

4. Finally, it is recommended that when the management of water resources in industrial areas is discussed in the future, the discussion should have as its point of departure a scheme or diagram of resources management (which includes quantity and quality), in order to accommodate and categorize all the studies and plans.

RECOMMENDATIONS

1. It is recommended that countries and international organizations increase awareness of the need for conservation of water resources and encourage education of users in the consequences of excessive use of resources as raw materials to industry.

2. It is recommended to countries that industries include environmental aspects, in particular water management, at the stage of their feasibility studies; this should include demand and requirements, as well as discharge of effluents.

3. It is considered essential to launch a technological and environmental movement of considerable scope toward industry and its processes with the objective of reducing the use of clear and potable water and increasing the use of brackish and residual water.

4. This symposium might recommend to some agency of the United Nations, that it make a concerted effort to look for formulae to make comparable the figures and data (including methods of collection) of surface and ground water volumes and the use of different qualities of water for different industrial processes. It is recommended that the agency prepare a manual of such criteria for use by planners and administrators.

5. It is important to take advantage of the experience of such countries as Sweden, the United Kingdom and the United States in the preparation of the most realistic predictions of water demand. The results obtained so far demonstrate that in all cases, the estimates are much higher than actual demand.

Summary Report
on
Water Quality Management

Blair T. Bower
3718-25th Street North, Arlington, Virginia 22207, USA

INTRODUCTION

THIS REPORT comprises an attempt to describe the major points and major issues in the discussions at the symposium, both those which were explicitly considered, and those which were only implied. To do so requires a short introduction to provide the setting.

By an industrial area was meant a geographic area in which industrial activities comprise the predominant source of water demands, in terms of water withdrawals, liquid residuals discharges, or both withdrawals and discharges. Such an area could be: an industrial park; an industrial section of a metropolitan area; a heavily industrialized section of an estuary; an industrialized river basin. Although industrial activities may predominate with respect to water withdrawals in such areas, they may not predominate with respect to discharges of all types of liquid residuals of interest having adverse effects on ambient water quality.

Having defined the type of area under consideration, the next step is to indicate the context of the discussions. At least four aspects of context can be identified. First, "management" implies decisions, so that the context of the discussion is a decision-making context. This is reflected in Figure 1, which was developed by an *ad hoc* committee during the symposium. The figure identifies many of the elements in water resources management, at least as related to planning and to the two themes of the symposium.

Fig. 1. Flow Chart of Decision Processes in Water Resources Management in Industrial Areas

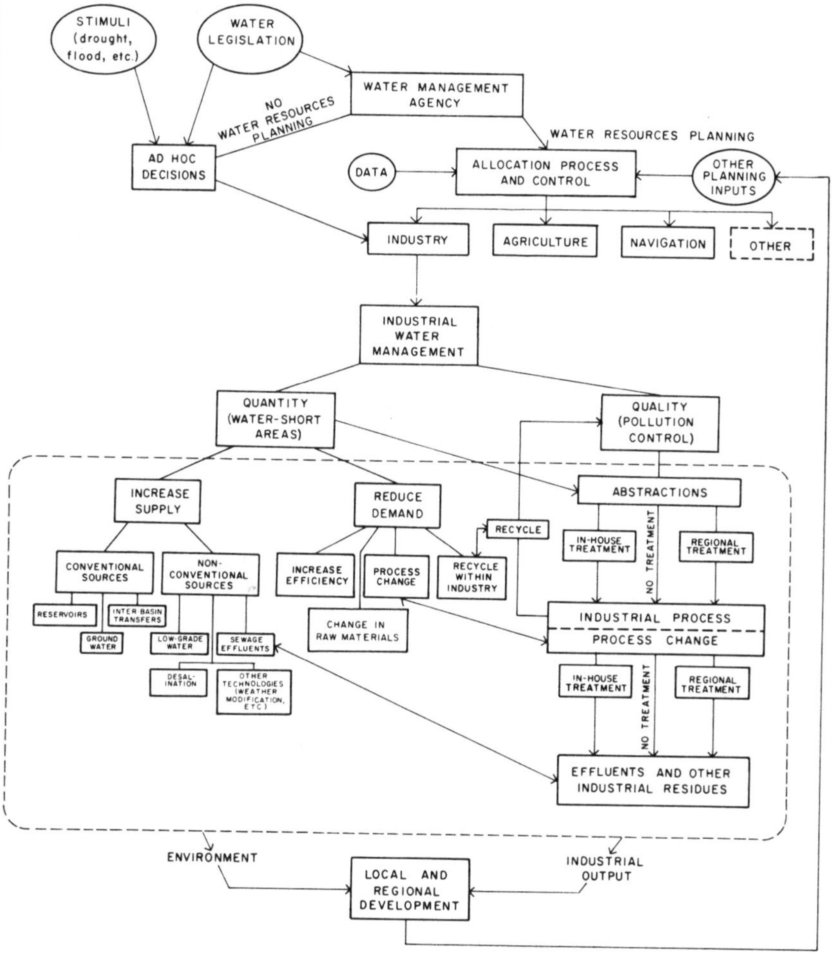

Source: *Ad Hoc* Committee at Lisbon Symposium, September 1981

Second, management also implies a set of tasks of which management, in this case water resources management, is comprised. The tasks of water quality management include: data collection; research; analysis to generate information for selection of water quality management strategies; planning, i.e., the process of selecting a strategy; design and construction of facilities; operation and maintenance of facilities; forecasting quantity and quality of streamflows; forecasting quality of lakes and group water bodies; monitoring water withdrawals, wastewater and residuals discharges, and ambient water quality; providing quality control of laboratory analyses; inspecting facilities; imposing implementation incentives on activities such as regulations, standards, charges, constraints on withdrawals and discharges; collecting fees and charges; imposing sanctions for non-compliance with standards/regulations/procedures; training operators, laboratory analysts, inspectors; and continual evaluation of performance of facilities and effectiveness of implementation incentives to feedback resulting information into analysis and the process of selecting a strategy. It is the carrying out of this total set of tasks which results in the desired output of ambient water quality. The papers for the symposium dealt primarily with: (a) analysis and planning; (b) forecasting quality of surface and ground waters; and (c) imposing and executing implementation incentives on activities.

The various papers presented under Water Quality Management can also be related to the following components of analysis for water quality management:
— analyzing activities;
— analyzing effects on aquatic systems, i.e., on ambient quality of terrestrial surface and ground waters and of coastal waters;
— analyzing the effects of changes in ambient water quality on various species, in both physical/chemical/biological and monetary terms; and
— developing strategies for water quality management in specified regions, including the implementation incentive systems and institutional arrangements associated with the physical measures.

(No papers were presented on the first component of analysis, i.e., estimating the levels and spatial pattern of activities at future points in time.)

Third, Figure 1 suggests a question which underlies, explicitly or implicitly, the subject matter of the symposium. That is:
— What are we trying to achieve in water quality management in industrial areas?
— What are the concerns, the goals?

Certainly one important goal is economic efficiency from society's point of view, given that all societies have limited resources. This means economic efficiency in terms of minimizing costs: (1) to achieve desired levels of outputs of products and services other than those related to water; and (2) to achieve desired levels of ambient water quality. Another goal is defined in terms of maintaining the long-run productivity of aquatic ecosystems, i.e., levels of quality which will enable continued use indefinitely of the water bodies for production of desired water-related outputs.

Achieving economic efficiency is generally a principal goal. But that goal may be constrained by various political, cultural, and administrative factors. Quantitative analysis can indicate what losses in economic efficiency, and hence in productive opportunities, can result from such constraints.

Fourth, how relevant were the discussions to developing countries, in contrast to developed countries, such as those of northern and north-western Europe? The tasks of water quality management in industrial areas are universal, and the basic principles for carrying out those tasks are universal. What differs among societies are: (1) goals and objectives; (2) commitment; and (3) resources. The second relates to the political commitment to achieve ambient water quality goals efficiently, effectively, and equitably. The third relates to human and monetary resources, the former in terms of analysts and operating personnel, the latter in terms of funds for analysis and for the capital and operating costs of execution. The basic problems, and approaches to those problems, are common to all countries, wherever they are on the scale of economic development and wherever they are on the planned-unplanned economy continuum.

MAJOR POINTS AND MAJOR ISSUES

Land Use Planning and Water Quality Management

The integral relationship between the planning and locating of activities in space and water quality management was emphasized. The spatial pattern of activities refers to the characteristics of the distribution of human activities over the landscape, e.g., dispersed/concentrated, linear/nodal, density, relationship between land capability and land use. The spatial pattern directly affects water demand at both "ends", e.g., losses in water distribution and wastewater collection via exfiltration and infiltration, and the pressure required to serve the periphery of the water distribution system. The lower the density of development, i.e., the more dispersed the activities, the greater the lengths of water and sewer pipes per capita, the higher the losses per capita, the higher the pressure and hence the higher the water demand per capita in the areas closer to the intake water treatment plants. The spatial pattern also indirectly affects water demands, for example, because of impact on energy demand, i.e., higher density results in lower energy demand per capita, and therefore lower water demand for cooling in energy generation.

The spatial pattern of activities also directly affects the economics of water quality management. For example, if major water-using industrial activities are concentrated, it is likely to be more possible to develop collective water management facilities than if the industrial activities are dispersed.

Particularly important with respect to the land use, water quality management relationship is the problem of sludge disposal. As constraints on wastewater discharges become more stringent, the quantities of sludge generated per unit of output increase substantially. Disposal, particularly in metropolitan areas, has become a major problem. Only by considering major water-demanding activities integrally in relation to land use (spatial) planning, can reasonably efficient economic land use and water quality management plans be achieved.

Industrial Estates

One increasingly common response to the multiple problems of water management in industrial areas is the establishment of "industrial estates". Such estates may be developed by public agencies, by quasi-public agencies under national (or provincial) government jurisdiction, or by private entities under government regulation. The rationale for establishing such estates is that, by concentrating industrial activities in a given area, the requisite infrastructural services, e.g., water supply and waste-water handling and disposal, can be provided at substantially lower costs than if the same industrial activities were located without planning, e.g., were located randomly in space.

An industrial estate is fundamentally analogous to a large plant, such as a major chemical manufacturing activity, in which multiple products are being produced in multiple production units. Each production unit has its own water demand, e.g., withdrawal, consumptive use, gross water applied, quantity and quality of wastewater discharge. Concentrating activities in a given area enables taking advantage of economies of scale and of interchanges of wastewater among the units, as illustrated in Figure 2. (This statement is valid for water supply, water quality management, and solid residuals management. The problems of air quality management may well be exacerbated by concentrating industrial activities in a given area such as an industrial estate.)

However, as in a large industrial plant, or as in a river basin in which multiple industrial water users are located in a series adjacent to a stream in the downstream direction, appropriate implementation incentive systems must be applied to each water user in the industrial estate in order to maximize economic efficiency for the industrial estate as a whole. Such systems are comprised of: (1) sets of incentives, e.g., abstraction charges, product standards, effluent charges, effluent standards; (2) indicators for measuring performance; (3) methods for monitoring performance, e.g., self-measuring and reporting, random checking; and (4) sanctions which can be applied for non-compliance. The objective is to minimize water costs for the industrial estate as a whole, while meeting specified output levels by each of the constituent units in the estate. This requires providing incentives to each production unit to induce explicit consideration of water intake, consumptive use of water, quantity and quality of wastewater discharge, and other residuals problems—solid and gaseous—in its production decisions, both investment and operating.

Operationally, each potential production unit (occupant) of the industrial estate should be presented with the unit water intake and unit wastewater

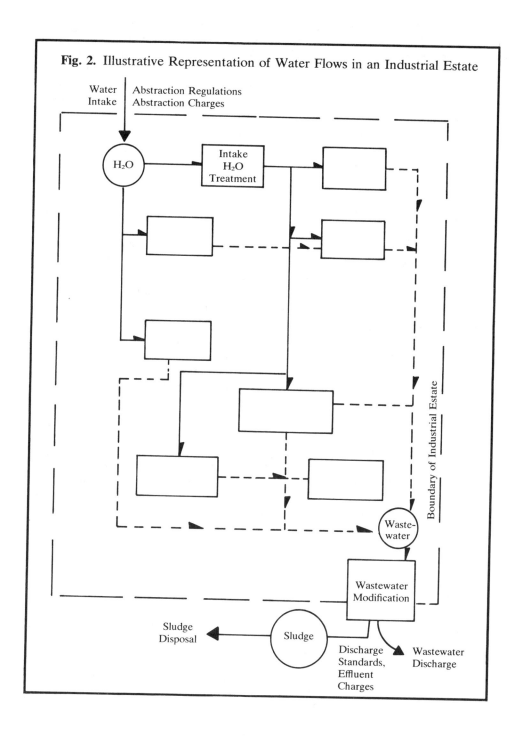

Fig. 2. Illustrative Representation of Water Flows in an Industrial Estate

charges, by season, by the agency operating the estate. Iteration between the agency and the activity should occur until the marginal cost of supply (intake charge) equals the marginal cost of wastewater handling and disposal (effluent charge) equals the marginal cost of the response by the activity. Only if, at a given point in time, there is excess capacity in the system at either end, should the marginal principle be foregone. (Although subsidies in terms of water supply and wastewater handling and disposal are common in many, if not most, countries, such subsidies typically result in a misallocation of scarce resources.) The cost of water utilization, as a proportion of total production costs, is so small, e.g., less than five percent even for heavy water-using industries, that adhering to marginal pricing will rarely, if ever, deter location in an industrial estate.

Estimating Water Demands

Whether or not the industrial water users are within an industrial estate, estimates must be made of the water demands of those users, which demands include the quantity and quality of wastewater discharge. As the discussion made clear, often there are few local data on water utilization by different categories of industrial activities. At the same time, it is known that there are many variables which affect industrial water demand, including: prices "at both ends"; nature of raw materials; type(s) of production process(es); product mix; product characteristics; prices of other raw materials such as energy and chemicals; costs of internal water recirculation. Given the lack of data, a typical procedure is to search for "numbers" from other countries for ostensibly the same activities. Several examples of this procedure were presented.

However, it was clear from the discussions that substantial care must be taken when considering transposing water use data from one country to another country or even to another region of the same country. Only if *both* exogenous variables, e.g., factor prices including effluent controls, and endogenous variables, e.g., production technology, raw materials, product mix, and product output characteristics, are approximately the same in both "exporting" and "importing" countries, are the coefficients likely to be valid.

Estimating Water Utilization Costs

One of the recurrent themes in the symposium was "cost". Unfortunately little of the discussion dealt with costs in explicit terms. Costs to whom—the supplier, the user? How are costs calculated? What components are included? Information with respect to costs is needed in order to estimate water demands and to estimate responses to implementation incentives. These in turn are essential to developing an efficient water management plan for an industrial estate, a river basin, a metropolitan area.

Whatever the region for which some agency (or set of agencies) has responsibility for water resources (and water quality) management, one major consideration in the decision process will be economic costs, i.e., the social costs of the resources required to construct and operate the regional water system. That system includes facilities and operations of *both* public and private entities, or—where all major water users are public—facilities and operations of both collective water management agencies or enterprises and individual water-using activities. It is critical to distinguish between economic costs and financial costs. The former refer to resource costs of the society, as noted above, regardless of how those costs are allocated, i.e., without subsidies. Financial costs relate to the actual costs borne by the regional water agency and by the individual water-using activities. If subsidies are significant, then the financial costs to a given water user may be substantially less than the resource costs to that user. In fact, what often occurs is that the subsidies provided by the government shift the choice of physical components of the individual or collective water systems away from the most efficient components.

To illustrate some of the problems in estimating costs, consider the industrial estate shown in Figure 2. Many of the likely components are not shown, such as modifications of discharges at some activities, additional intake water treatment at some activities, solid residuals generated by the activities and their disposal. The administrative arm of the industrial estate is the water utility, supplying water and disposing of wastewater. Its job is to do so efficiently. Consequently, it tries to determine what set of physical measures throughout the component parts of the estate will yield the most efficient water system. Its costs are those relating to: development of supply, e.g., wells, reservoirs, intake water treatment; wastewater modification; materials recovery; byproduct production; handling and disposal; distribution of water to and collection of wastewater from, individual activities; setting of charges and standards and monitoring of performance.

The agency must decide how it will cover its costs by charges on water supplied and wastewater handled. In addition to its capital and operating/maintenance/replacement costs, there are administrative costs. The agency must also decide how it is to induce the individual activities to adopt the physical measures which represent the most efficient system, e.g., by fiat, by charges, by some combination. In making that decision it needs to be able to estimate, approximately, the cost functions of the individual activities in the estate. That is, what is the cost to the individual activity of each increment in reducing water intake, e.g., by increasing water recirculation, and the cost of each increment of reduction in discharge of a given residual (undesired material). These costs are affected by the technology of production, the possibilities for material and energy recovery and for byproduct production, energy costs, to mention just a few factors.

Various problems arise in estimating costs to individual activities. One problem is that of separating water utilization costs to the activity from normal production costs of the activity. Some measures to reduce water intake and/or reduce discharge reduce other production costs at the same time; others increase production costs. A second problem is that of deciding what discount rate to use in translating future costs to be incurred to their present values (or what capital recovery factor or payout period to use). A third problem is how to price certain factor inputs, such as unemployed labor and capital limited by foreign exchange restrictions. A fourth problem is comprised of the effects of multimedia inter-relationships. Some measures to reduce discharges to water bodies result in increasing discharges to air and/or land. Similarly, imposing limits on the discharge of gaseous residuals, e.g., particulates, oxides of sulphur, may result in the installation of wet scrubbers, which in turn will increase the water demand of the activity. The water management agency needs to recognize both the effects of its decisions on the non-water media, and the effects of the decisions of air quality management agencies and of solid residuals management agencies on its costs.

Charges and Standards

One of the most important and difficult problems facing any country or region in developing a water resources management program is the determination of the "optimal" mix of charges and standards to impose on water users to achieve whatever are the socially selected goals. Four basic issues must be faced. One, what is (are) the objective(s) of imposing the charges and/or standards? Two, at what level(s) should they be set to achieve the specified objectives? Three, is sufficient known about the likely responses of different types of water users to different charges/standards imposed at different levels to be reasonably confident that the desired behavior by the activities will, in fact, be induced? Four, what are the costs of different implementation incentive systems involving charges and/or standards?

Before answering these questions it is important to indicate what is meant by the terms charges and standards. Charges may be imposed on: surface and ground water abstractions; water delivered to a user by some type of conveyance, e.g., pipe, channel, canal, ditch; consumptive use of water; inputs such as fertilizers and energy; wastewater volume discharged directly into a surface or ground water body or into a conveyance, e.g., pipe, ditch, canal; and quantities of residuals in the wastewater. Charges may be in terms of unit volume, unit flow rate, per unit of residuals discharged. Charges may be varied by time of year. Standards or limits may be imposed on: quantity and time pattern of water abstractions; volume of consumptive use of water; types of raw materials, production processes, residuals modification equipment, product characteristics; quantity/quality/time pattern of wastewater discharge; quantities and time patterns of residuals discharged in the wastewater.

With respect to standards, the objective of standards imposed on discharges from activities in water quality management is to achieve desired levels of ambient water quality to enable specified uses of the water body. Charges — on abstractions or discharges — are imposed primarily either to raise revenues to cover costs of water supply or wastewater handling and disposal, or to induce reductions in withdrawals or discharges. In reality, if the charges are sufficiently high, they will induce some reductions even though the primary objective is to raise revenues. But it is very important to be clear about the objective(s), because of the differences in implications and procedures stemming from the two objectives.

Typically, with respect to wastewater discharges, both standards and charges are imposed. Thus, the two objectives, i.e., achieving ambient water quality and raising revenues are presumably jointly achieved.

Determining at what levels to set the standards and charges involves analyses both of the natural systems involved and of the water utilization systems of at least the major water users. For any given residual it is possible to allocate the available assimilative capacity. Standards then can be tailored, assuming perfect knowledge, to each discharge. Charges, on the other hand, are set based on knowledge of the cost-reduction functions of the major dischargers, such that sufficient reduction will be induced to meet the ambient water quality goals.

The responses of the water users will be based on their costs as they see them, including whatever subsidies may be available. Thus, in the case of charges, if the cost-reduction functions are not calculated in terms of the costs to the individual dischargers, rather than in terms of resource costs to society, then the responses will likely be different than anticipated. With respect to standards, probably the primary factors resulting in positive responses on the part of dischargers are: the fear of sanctions; their perception of the reasonableness of the standards, e.g., in terms of costs to them and of benefits from discharge reduction; the amount of technical information available to the discharger; and the history of cooperation with the water quality management agency.

The costs of any given implementation incentive system, excluding the original costs of "designing" the system, include: depreciation on monitoring equipment, e.g., meters and samplers; labour costs for laboratory analyses and inspections; administrative costs for applying sanctions. Labor costs increase with the frequency of inspections and the degree of detail in each inspection, e.g., "walk-through", 24-hour sampling, 1 week sampling. Then the question becomes, how does the degree of compliance, in the case of standards, relate to the frequency of inspection? (In the case of charges, there is no question of compliance or noncompliance, in that the discharger simply pays for whatever he discharges. The monitoring and inspection are to determine the actual basis for the charges.)

Basically the same problem of monitoring performance exists for both charges and standards. What differs is that standards require the application of sanctions to be effective. Where this involves the judicial process, long delays can result.

Several points concerning standards and charges were made during the symposium discussions. One, it is important to retain flexibility in setting standards and/or charges, to allow for local/regional conditions. Establishing uniform standards or charges throughout a country is likely to result in considerable economic inefficiency, and often in a disregard of standards because they are considered unreasonable. However, to vary standards and charges by subarea of a country requires adequate professional personnel, both to design and to administer. In the early stage of developing a water quality management programme, limited resources may make more uniformity a logical procedure. The danger is that, once set in place, it will be difficult to switch to a more flexible system.

Two, variability in abstractions and discharges from day-to-day and by season is a "fact of life". That variability, plus the variability in water supply, e.g., streamflow, makes designing a set of standards and/or charges much more difficult than if such variability did not exist. Nonetheless, such variability must be explicitly considered if the water management objectives are to be achieved.

Three, mixed systems of standards and charges seem to achieve better results than either standards or charges alone. Charges on discharges have been observed to induce more consistent adherence to discharge standards than is achieved by the standards themselves.

Four, that system of standards and/or charges which is considered to be effective in inducing original compliance may not be effective in inducing continuing compliance, and the reverse. Experience demonstrates that achieving day-to-day adherence to standards is often considerably more difficult than inducing original installation of the physical measures deemed necessary.

SOME RELEVANT BUT ESSENTIALLY UNDISCUSSED PROBLEMS

Some problems of water management were only alluded to during the symposium. Several of these merit attention.

System Operation

Planning and constructing efficient water management systems are necessary, but not sufficient, to achieve ambient water quality goals. Once constructed, the facilities must be operated at, at least, the efficiencies for which they were designed.

The "operating function" is particularly critical in water quality management in industrial areas. That is, at any point in time in a given management area, a system of physical facilities exists, such as surface water reservoirs, well fields, intake structures and raw water treatment facilities, waste treatment plants, in-stream aerators, spray irrigation systems for disposal of wastewater. Associated with this system of facilities and with the ultimate users of water and water-related products and services produced by the system is an "operating procedure". An operating procedure is a set of rules for: withholding water in and releasing water from surface and ground water reservoirs, operating in-stream aerators, closing and opening valves/gates/diversion structures, cleaning debris basins, and prescribing/proscribing behavior of water users under various sets of stream flow, weather, and other conditions. Thus, operating procedures must be specified for four types of conditions: (1) "normal" water; (2) excess water (flooding); (3) shortage of water; and (4) spills, e.g., spill of toxic material into a stream as a result of faulty valve, incorrect procedure, accident. Developing and executing an efficient and effective operating procedure requires: high quality staff, both in the overall management agency and in the individual activities; an effective communications system; and effective incentives to induce the desired behaviors.

Too often efforts are expanded on developing a plan with little effort being expended on how the plan will be executed and operated.

Organization for Water Resources Management

The most efficient water resources management plan will go no further than the nearest file cabinet if an adequte institutional arrangement does not exist for carrying out the management tasks. The form which the institutional arrangement will take is a function of a country's culture and history. However, in most — if not all — cases, a number of agencies will have responsibilities for one or more of the tasks. Thus, a fundamental question in all countries is how to organize for water resources management and water quality management, i.e., how to allocate responsibilities among governmental agencies, and between governmental agencies and the private sector.

Three other points with respect to institutional arrangements merit mention. One, political boundaries often will not coincide with water quality problem areas, with river basins, or with economic regions. However, experience indicates that it is less important that the boundaries of the water quality management region include all of the residuals dischargers and all those affected by changes in ambient water quality, than it is that the boundaries represent some area for which there is an institutional arrangement which is directly responsible for water quality management.

Two, obtaining adherence to specified abstraction conditions and/or discharge standards may be made more difficult, rather than less difficult by nationalizing an industrial activity in a mixed economy. For example, maximizing profits or minimizing costs often has less importance for a public enterprise than for a private enterprise. Also, the public enterprise is often a monopoly, so that it can simply "pass on" additional costs imposed to achieve ambient water quality standards, without having to investigate possible alternatives which could have achieved the same objective at less cost. The problem is identical in socialistic and non-socialistic economies. Devising an institutional arrangement which is effective, not to mention efficient, is a difficult, and as yet unsolved, problem.

Three, even where an adequate institutional arrangement exists, its operations may be constrained by political considerations. This is particularly true where it is perceived, correctly or incorrectly, that there will be a loss of jobs if the specified standards are enforced.

Level of Detail of Analysis

Several symposium papers described studies to develop regional water quality management plans. But there was no discussion of: how many resources should be allocated to such an activity; what level of detail is justified under what circumstances/conditions; how the available analytical resources should be allocated to the different segments of the analysis. In all cases the regional analyses must be done with limited resources in a finite time period. A critical part of continuing water management is the allocation of resources to, and within, the analysis activity, in relation to the information needed to answer the questions specified.

Administration of Water Resources in Industrial Areas with Limited Water Supplies

Eloy Urroz
Director General of Eco-Engineering Ltd.
Consulting Engineers, Mexico

SYNOPSIS

This paper presents an integrated planning model for water management in industrial areas short of water. The model includes a brief explanation of the interaction of five components (Inventory, Constraints, Planning Projections, Programming and Action) which can be the focus of a system for water development and administration in predominantly industrialized zones.

Special emphasis has been given to the extrapolation of internal factors and to predictions of demand in relation to the supply of water. All of this is presented in the context of goals and specific objectives for each region or country. Furthermore, the constraints of the system which obviously affect the direction of socio-economic development toward the set goals are discussed.

Finally, particular emphasis has been given to water use in industry, the possibilities of reuse and recirculation, and the costs associated with the reuse of water.

29

RÉSUMÉ

La présente communication propose un schéma intégré de planification pour la gestion de l'eau dans les zones industrielles où les ressources en ce domaine sont limitées.

Ce modèle comprend une brève explication de l'interaction de cinq facteurs (Inventaires, Planification prospective, Restrictions, Programmation et Action), ce qui permet d'appliquer le schéma de systèmes de développement et d'administration des eaux en zones éminemment industrielles.

On a insisté sur les aspects liés à l'extrapolation des facteurs inhérents et sur la prédiction des demandes par rapport à l'eau disponible; tout ceci est placé dans un contexte de buts et objectifs spécifiques pour chaque région ou pays. De plus, les restrictions du système qui affectent de façon évidente la direction du développement socio-industriel vers les buts préétablis, sont indiquées.

Finalement, on place une emphase toute particulière sur les usages de l'eau dans l'industrie, et sur les possibilités de réutilisation et/ou récirculation de l'eau ainsi que sur le coût de cette réutilisation.

RESUMEN

En el presente trabajo se propone un esquema integrado de planeación para el manejo del agua en áreas industriales con poca disponibilidad de este recurso.

El modelo incluye una breve explicación de la interacción de 5 bloques conceptuales (Inventarios, Planeación Prospectiva, Restricciones, Programación y Acción), lo que permite aplicar el enfoque de sistemas de desarrollo y administración del agua en zonas eminentemente industriales.

Se hace especial énfasis en los aspectos de extrapolación de los factores inherentes y en la predicción de demandas, en relación con la oferta de agua; todo ésto dentro de un contexto de metas y objetivos específicos para cada región o país. Además, se mencionan las restricciones del sistema, que obviamente afectan la dirección del desarrollo socio-industrial hacia las metas preestablecidas.

Por último, se hace particular énfasis en los usos del agua en la industria, en las posibilidades del reuso 6/o recirculación del agua así como el costo asociado a este reuso.

GENERAL MODEL

THE CONTINUED GROWTH of the world's population, and especially that of developing countries, has created an increasing demand for goods that are mass-produced by industries in response to such a demand. An industry is nothing more than a mechanism to transform natural resources into products required by human beings.

Without doubt, water is the most important of all our natural resources. Unfortunately, water is a limited resource, subject to pollution and rapid deterioration. It will not be too long before fresh water becomes the limiting factor in biological, economic and social growth throughout the world. Therefore, it behoves us to seek methods, systems and policies to improve global administration of water resources. A summary of the most important considerations that must be included in any model is given in Figure 1. It will be noted that such considerations have been grouped into five categories comprising: inventory, regulations, planning, programming and action (implementation). We shall proceed by reviewing each of these categories.

Inventory

The feasibility of urban, industrial or agricultural development must be initially based on an inventory of water resources. These include surface water (fresh and salt), groundwater (fresh and salt), wastewater (municipal and industrial) and precipitation. The availability of water must also be examined in the light of the technologies that are currently available. In addition to increasing our present inventory of water, we must also study the availability of water in space and over a time period.

Highly sophisticated techniques are available for determining the flow of a given water source over time, and for planning multiple-use water systems, i.e. simulated models using random hydrographic variables; optimization of water use in view of pre-established economic goals that take into account the physical, political or social restrictions pertinent to each region or country.

It is likely that the concept of the availibility of water resources is much more meaningful in highly developed nations than in less developed countries. However, even though a developing country may initially save money by deciding not to use advanced technologies in industry or in the development of hydro projects, in the long run the cost of repairing damage to the ecology and the environment caused by inappropriate technologies (plus the risk of not being able to rectify the harm done) may be higher than if the best technology compatible with the characteristics of a given nation were to have been adopted in the first place.

As shown in the "inventory block" in Figure 1, once the available resources are known, it becomes indispensable to obtain detailed information on the location and types of industry, classifying them by product, raw materials used,

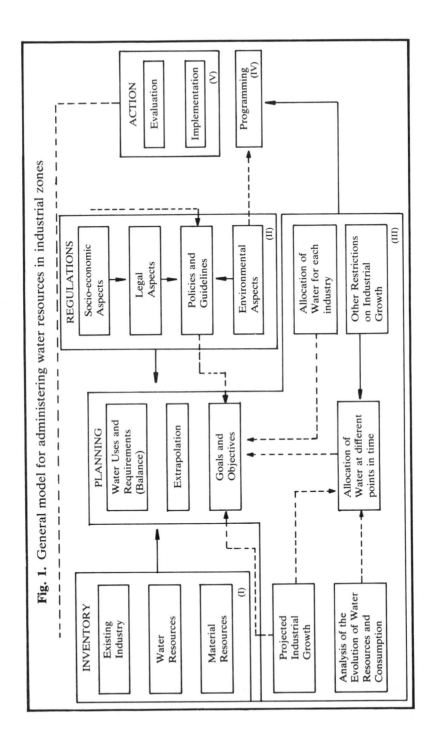

Fig. 1. General model for administering water resources in industrial zones

and even according to the efficiency with which they use water. The latter idea is relevant when we speak of the final allocation of this resource to each industry.

It is also necessary to know the state of the art of the technology used in each industrial process, in the light of how much water each requires. Industries using technologies that result in zero wastewater will be ideally efficient, economically speaking; industries that are unable to reduce their volume of wastewater will encounter serious problems, since they will continually come under attack and criticism from local residents, with the resulting political and social consequences.

Therefore, research on new technologies that can be applied to water use and wastewater in each industrial sector will become increasingly necessary. This type of research will require the greatest possible amount of information regarding water, such as:

(a) Quality of water required for different industrial uses;
(b) Production of wastewater in the area;
(c) Quality of wastewater per industry and product;
(d) Location of discharge points, topography and general hydrology;
(e) Possibility of treating wastewater;
(f) Feasibility of direct recycling or large-scale reuse of treated water;
(g) Feasibility of substituting treated industrial wastewater for drinking water or water used for other purposes;
(h) Cost competitiveness between using pure water for agriculture and other industries and the cost of using treated water in a given industrial zone, not necessarily for drinking purposes.

Lastly, there can be no disagreement as to the fact that, without a complete inventory of the material resources available in a given industrial zone, few or none of the plans for the future can be implemented.

The application of models will require detailed information on the sources of supply; the characteristics of the hydraulic control in a given watershed; the prevailing pollution control in the watershed; pumping stations; and water purification plants. For this purpose, it will be necessary to prepare charts showing the length of time such equipment and structures have been in use, their useful life, their capacity and their costs. Such information will facilitate the integration of the production goals and objectives of the industry in a given area with that region's socio-economic and ecological goals and objectives.

Regulations

Certain restrictions exist in each industrial zone and will obviously affect its economic development, e.g., general national guidelines and policies, legal, socio-economic and ecological-environmental concerns. These restrictions will most likely have been expressed in laws, the most common of which are aimed at guiding economic and environmental development. Other major restrictions involve the educational and technological levels of a given region or of an entire country. This implies the competitiveness of salaries and wages in a given zone, as compared with other industrial zones having similar standards of living.

In all types of society, legislation becomes the basic element for regulating the use and development of water resources, and therefore, industrial development. In Mexico all water uses are basically regulated by law. Under the Constitution, water resources are the property of the nation, but the State, through the Department of Agriculture and Water Resources, is empowered to 'guarantee' (cities and towns) or 'concede' (to private parties) the water they require for their legitimate uses. In allocating the resource, human consumption is, and must continue to be, the first priority. Agriculture comes in second place and industry is third. Other countries assign different priorities to water allocation, as Mexico itself has done in the past. It is likely that agricultural and industrial priorities may be reversed, depending on the area, the scarcity of water, and the ecological characteristics of the region. It is in this regard that the idea of efficiency-effectiveness is most relevant. In most cases, neither industry nor agriculture require pure, unrecycled, or drinking water. Legislators must realize that the only way to determine the order and magnitude in which water can and should be used in agriculture and/or industry is through financial, technological and environmental analysis. Such analysis should take into account the fact that wastewater from towns or urban centres in the region can be recycled.

The above necessitates laws and regulations that will make it compulsory for the officials responsible for managing the resource to conduct detailed studies of the "efficiency in space and time" of water use in industrial or urban-industrial zones (Figure 1, Block III). The priority must be given to preserving the quality of water and air, as well as protecting cultural and historical heritages, within the general framework of the quality of life, when planning and implementing projects for economic development. Traditionally, industrial zones have been polluted, simply because the historical goal has been "cheap production". Mankind has now learned, however, that economic development does not automatically lead to a better standard of living.

Future technological developments should take into account the socio-ecological impact of industry and be compatible with environmental requirements. We could add that in our time public opinion has become the greatest restriction on the misuse of and failure to protect natural resources, including water.

Planning

It is this part of the model that clearly requires the greatest amount of thought and experience on the part of those individuals responsible for making final decisions. There are three determining factors in this stage of water management: goals and objectives; balance between water use and requirements; and projections of general growth.

All actions must be taken within the framework of goals and objectives. The nation's general objectives must be taken into account, but it is also indispensable to determine private and local objectives. Without the latter, it is not possible to plan efficient and effective industrial development.

There are many techniques for determining the balance between water use and requirements. Once the inventory is known, we must discover the demand. This is not an easy task and requires a detailed analysis in space and time of the way in which the region's technology and economy will evolve. This information will be used to project the scaling-up of demand, either through deterministic or probabilistic processes, in such a way that development potential and the size of plants and investments can be determined.

Although economic growth has been the traditional goal of development, more modern approaches tend to look towards 'human' development. In this context, many nations have established priorities for the use of natural resources. Certain countries have assigned lower priority to industrial uses than to municipal and agricultural uses.

In regions with limited water resources and where planning is governed by the guidelines mentioned above, very little pure water is available for industrial uses. In such cases, classic models for the optimum allocation of water for different uses are virtually unworkable, due to the obvious difficulty of introducing into them social variables, which in most cases, are valued according to subjective processes. A situation like this requires the use of more flexible models, such as those that simulate dynamic systems. In this case, the purpose of applying them is to determine future allocations of water to industry, considering all the sources that it is technologically feasible to exploit. Under these circumstances, the allocation of pure water for industry will tend to decrease over time, and therefore other measures (such as importing water from other regions, the recycling of wastewater from industry itself and the reuse of municipal sewage and agricultural residues) will tend to increase.

Future projections will be based on those variables that reflect the growth of industry and its water requirements. Restrictions will be determined in advance, based on the availability of water at a given point in time. Allocations of water by type of industry at different times can later be defined by applying any of the classic models for allocation that will permit the cost/benefit ratio, for example, to be optimized. By approaching the problem in this way, the important variables in the model will be technical and economic in nature, and will have been reduced to a minimum. The goals and objectives of industrial growth must be guided by the availibility of water at the pertinent moment in time and space, and the values of the variables at each point can be applied to the model for allocation of water by type of industry.

Programming

Once the goals and objectives have been defined and the water sources to be developed have been decided upon (surface water, groundwater, recycled water, etc.) within the different time parameters, it should be an easy task to programme and implement activities and investments.

It is likely that synchronization of activities will become the important task to oversee, since if the work is to be effective, the different components of the hydro-economic system must come into operation simultaneously, just as they were provided for in the planning stage. In developing countries, it is often the case that good industrial development plans are drawn up, which include both internal and external factors and even environmental factors, but due to the lack of financial capacity it becomes very unlikely that they will actually be implemented. In addition, in the programming stage, the problem of limited financial resources is re-encountered, which makes it necessary to programme implementation of the work in question in a fashion that is different from the original plans. Obviously, the results are not those which were originally expected.

Thus, it is clear that the financial aspects of a development plan must be programmed by a single agency or at least be prepared with close cooperation between the respective projects' planning office and the financial planning office.

Action

The two most relevant aspects in this stage are implementation and evaluation. If no systems or programmes for ongoing evaluation exist, we cannot know whether all the earlier work was productive and profitable, or if the pre-established social and environmental standards were complied with. Evaluations should be made by the agency or body responsible for authorizing expenditures. The premise that "one cannot act as both judge and plaintiff" is important. The agency responsible for implementing a project for water supplies and allocation should not be responsible for evaluating it.

It is likely that the models pre-established in the planning stage will be most effective for distributing water in zones where this resource is scarce. If these models, which must be mathematical, are designed in the planning stage, they will automatically be budgeted for, and the pertinent activities will be regulated.

The nature of this presentation obviously does not permit specific references to all the factors that must be considered in the process of planning how water should be administered, nor does it allow discussion of the interrelationships among these factors. The system shown in Figure 1 (which does not claim to cover all the possibilities) is intended only as an invitation to think about the complexity of the problem.

WATER USES IN INDUSTRY

UP TO THE Second World War, the two main uses of water were for domestic requirements and crop irrigation. However, the technological progress achieved during the War considerably accelerated worldwide industrial development, which had begun in the middle of the 19th century with the invention of the first steam engine.

In the last decade, much of the socio-economic growth of many nations has been based on the industrial sector, which involves the production of goods to meet man's needs. As a dynamic factor in the development of a country, industry has demanded an increasing share of the water resource to meet its production and service requirements. In Mexico, industrial demand for water occupies third place, as shown in Table 1.

Table 1. Water Consumption in Mexico from 1950 to 2000[1]

Use	Consumption (millions of m³/year)		
	1950	1975	2000[2]
Agriculture	23 600	38 000	71 300
Domestic service	200	1100	4200
Industrial	100	971	3400
Power generation	0	100	1600
Total	23 900	40 171	80 500

[1] National Water Plan Commission. Department of Agriculture and Water Resources. 1976.
[2] Estimated.

Although there has been a tremendous increase in the demand for water for domestic consumption in Mexico in recent years, this demand is low in comparison with the United States (as can be seen in Table 2), which is a highly industrialized nation.

Table 2. Per Capita Industrial Demand for Water

Country	Demand (l/cit./day)			
	1965	1980	2000	2020
Mexico[1,2]	30	46	85[3]	235[4]
United States[2]	136	150	162	631

[1] National Water Plan Commission. Department of Agriculture and Water Resources. 1976.
[2] Department of Water Resources. *Water Use in Cities*, 1974.
[3] Population estimated at 110,000,000.
[4] Population estimated at 140,000,000.

Table 3. Demand for Water for Various Uses in the Main Mexican Industrial Sectors (1980)[1]

Industrial Sector	Cooling ($10^6/m^3$ year)	%	Processes ($10^6/m^3$ year)	%	Boilers ($10^6/m^3$ year)	%	Others ($10^6/m^3$ year)	%	Total ($10^6/m^3$ year)	%
Food	1551	51.1	1227	40.4	121	4.0	137	4.5	3036	100
Chemical	692	76.5	158	17.5	21	2.3	33	3.7	905	100
Metal	619	85.2	52	7.1	7	1.0	49	6.7	727	100
Pulp & Paper	136	34.2	249	62.9	7	1.8	4	1.0	396	100
Petroleum	97	90.2	4	3.7	5	4.8	1	1.3	107	100
Total[2]	3095 (98.1)		1690 (53.6)		161 (5.1)		224 (7.1)		5171 (164.0)	

[1] *Reuse of water in agriculture, industry, municipalities, and in groundwater recharging.* Undersecretariat of Planning, Department of Water Resources, 1975. (Based on the study *Use of water industry, evaluation of the current regional situation and estimated demand in 1980, for transforming industries.* National Water Plan, DWR, 1973.)

[2] The figures in brackets represent demand in m^3/sec.

Based on the total volume of water needed for various industrial processes, it is possible to determine which industrial sectors have the highest consumption, and which sectors produce most wastewater. This information can be used to implement measures that reduce costs and increase the rate of recycling.

The main uses of water in industry are to generate steam or power, as in boilers for cooling, through closed cycles in which the coolant does not come into contact with the product being cooled and through open cycles in which the cooling water comes into direct contact with the product; for processing, including water used as part of the finished product, water used as the transportation medium and as an aid in manufacturing the product; and lastly, water for general purposes, including cleaning, toilet facilities, and in some cases, sprinkling factory grounds. Table 3 shows water use in the main Mexican industrial sectors.

The industrial sectors in Mexico that are most important from the viewpoints of economics, the type of product manufactured, the size of the plants, the demand for water, and the quantity and makeup of wastewaters include: the pulp and paper industry, iron and steel, textiles, tanning, metal finishing, chemicals, coffee processing, and the sugar, food and petroleum industries. The two industries that require the largest amounts of water are the sugar industry, with a demand of 294 m^3 of water per ton of finished product, and the pulp and paper industry, with a demand of 160 m^3 of water per ton produced. It should be noted that the

Table 4. Demand for Water by Different Industries in Various Countries

	Water Required per Unit Produced (m^3/ton)			
Industry	Mexico[1]	African Technology[2]	Italy[3]	United States[4]
Pulp	159.97	50–150		250–800
Paper	36.49	200–1000	184.6	120–160
Iron and Steel	14.67	10–50	52.2	
Textiles	0.354 m^3/m^2		272.6	200–300
Tanning	73.04		443.5	
Chemicals	32.50	10–500	84.3	7–800
Petroleum	0.321 m^3/barrel	10–30 m^3/ton crude oil		

[1] Bonilla, D.U. and Contreras M.R.J., Mexico.
[2] Adapted from the Department of Economy and Social Well-Being, United Nations. 1965. (Data taken from the study *The Role of Water Resources Development in Industrial Development: A Perspective for Africa* by Kenneth M. Strzepek.)
[3] Merli, C. *et al. Water Use in Industry.* Rome, 1973. (Data taken from the study *Assessment of Industrial Water Demand: Some Regional Survey Experiences* by Faust Maria Spaziani.)
[4] Metcalf and Eddy, Inc. *Wastewater Engineering: Treatment/Disposal/Reuse,* 1979.

discharge of wastewater from these two industries, like most other industries, is more than 80 per cent of the water initially used.

As can be seen from the above, water requirements for each industrial sector vary widely, and even the demand by sister industries in a single country can vary. For example, there are three large Mexican iron and steel industrial complexes. The first, Fundidora Monterrey, is located in the state of Nuevo Leon in an area where water is scarce, and consumes $166 \, m^3$ per ton produced. The second, Hojalata y Lamina, Ltd. (HYLSA) is located in the state of Puebla and consumes $139 \, m^3$ per ton produced; the third, Siderurgica Lazaro Cardenas-las Truchas (SICARTSA), located in the state of Michoacan, at the mouth of the Balsas River, one of the most abundant rivers in the country, consumes $105 \, m^3$ per ton produced. The differences in the demand for water by these industrial complexes are mainly due to the efficiency of their cooling systems, since this is the operation that requires the largest amount of water. When we compare the demand for water by different industries in various countries (see Table 4), we can note considerable variations, mainly due to the type of technology used, the abundance of water in the area where the industry is located, the type of product manufactured and so on.

WATER RECYCLING AND REUSE

IN SOME AREAS of the world, the relative scarcity of water, due to the population growth rate and the different industrial and commercial activities conducted, has led in recent years to considering wastewater as an additional source of supply, above all for uses that do not require high-quality water—although in the near future it will become necessary to use wastewater for domestic purposes as well.

It is feasible to reuse water in industry, since the demand for water by the industrial sector remains constant over the year. There are various treatments that permit different qualities of water to be obtained for industrial operations, and in certain industrial processes, wastewater may be used as a replacement for better quality water, mainly in areas where water is scarce and most of the higher quality water is used for domestic purposes.

In recent years in Mexico, water has been mainly reused in urban-industrial areas, where drinking water is reserved for domestic supplies only. One of these areas is the Valley of Mexico, approximately 2400 m above sea level, which has the largest urban-industrial complex in both the nation and the world, with a current population of almost 16 million, and over 40,000 industries, representing 48 per cent of total national production.

In 1974, the Valley of Mexico required almost 1356 million m^3 of water: 725 million m^3 of this (approximately 52 per cent) was used for domestic purposes and 480.8 million for industrial uses, 444.9 million of which was discharged as wastewater. The investment required to bring one m³/sec of water to the city of Mexico, using the sources of supply available in 1974, was estimated at 150 million pesos, a figure that rose to 350 million in 1980. The Valley of Mexico, where the nation's capital is located, is probably the site that has the most unfavourable balance between industrial demand for water and availability.

The cost of supplying water to an industrial area such as the Valley of Mexico makes it necessary to implement every workable programme for the optimum management of the resource. Reuse and direct recycling, in addition to treatment for certain processes, permit large amounts of drinking water to be set aside for human consumption at the regional level.

Surveys and studies of this area showed that it was possible to obtain volumes of 2.0 m³/sec for immediate (direct) reuse at a cost of 200 million pesos per m³/sec, including the costs of intake, conduits, treatment and distribution systems. This programme resulted in net savings of from 400 to 600 million pesos, plus 2.0 m³/sec of drinking water for other uses that require high-quality water. However, the total volume of reused and recycled water could reach figures of from 6.0 to 10 m³/sec. Figure 2 shows the increase in the reuse of water for industrial purposes and the related savings achieved.

It is estimated that there will be a considerable increase in the reuse of water in industry when the habit of using high-quality water indiscriminately for all

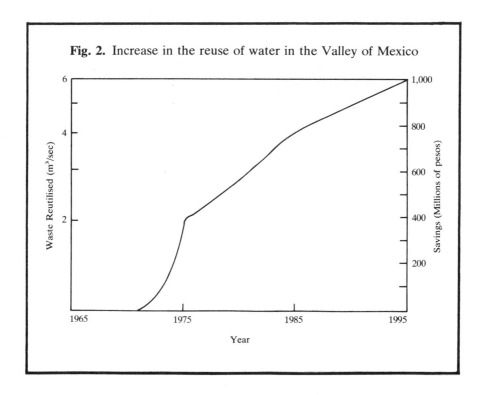

Fig. 2. Increase in the reuse of water in the Valley of Mexico

kinds of industrial processes has been eradicated. Rational use of available water resources and its recycling will require careful balancing of the following factors: cost of treatment plants; demand and consumption of water per industry; the availability of water resources; technological, socio-political and economic conditions; and the desired development models.

Economic Incentives for a Rational Water Use in Industry

L.V. da Cunha

Head of Hydrology and River Hydraulics Division,
Laboratório Nacional de Engenharia Civil, Lisbon, Portugal

SYNOPSIS

The different aspects related to the application of economic incentives to industrial water uses are analysed, mainly from a pragmatic point of view. Economic incentives are compared with other instruments for a rational industrial water use. The main features of abstraction charges and pollution charges are described, based on actual examples of economic incentive systems that are in use in France, the Netherlands, the Federal Republic of Germany and Czechoslovakia.

Legal, financial and administrative aspects of the implementation of economic incentives are described, and public and user participation in this implementation is also analysed.

The effectiveness of abstraction and pollution charges as economic incentives is questioned and the factors that condition this effectiveness are referred to.

Taking into consideration the different aspects referred to, it can be concluded that abstraction charges and pollution charges may be effective as economic incentives for a rational water use, particularly as regards industrial water use. The experience of application of abstraction and pollution charges in some countries that have adopted them shows that this effectiveness depends largely on the actual values of the charges and on the existence of a water management framework that is able to correctly implement the

43

charges policies in their legal, financial and administrative aspects and to ensure an adequate participation of the public and of the industrial water users.

RÉSUMÉ

Les différents aspects de l'application d'instruments d'incitation en ce qui concerne l'usage de l'eau dans l'industrie sont analysés, surtout du point de vue pragmatique, en faisant la comparaison avec d'autres instruments pour rationaliser l'usage de l'eau.

On décrit les principales caractéristiques des redevances de prélèvement d'eau et de pollution prenant pour base des exemples réels de systèmes d'incitations économiques employés en France, dans les Pays Bas, République Fédérale d'Allemagne et Tchécoslovaquie.

On décrit les aspects légal, financier et administratif de l'application des instruments d'incitation, et on analyse la participation du public et des usagers dans ce procédé.

L'efficacité des redevances de prélèvement et de pollution en tant qu'incitations économiques est analysée et les facteurs qui conditionnent cette efficacité sont mentionnés.

Tenant compte des différents aspects mentionnés on peut conclure que les redevances de prélèvement et de pollution peuvent être efficaces pour stimuler l'usage rationnel de l'eau, en particuler en ce qui concerne l'utilisation de l'eau dans l'industrie.

L'expérience d'application des redevances dans les pays où elles ont été adoptées montre que leur efficacité dépend largement de la valeur de ces redevances et de l'existence d'un système institutionnel d'administration de l'eau capable de promouvoir la politique d'application de redevances dans leurs aspects légaux, financiers et administratifs et d'assurer la participation effective du public et des usagers industriels de l'eau dans cette politique.

RESUMEN

Los diferentes aspectos de la aplicación de medidas de estímulo en lo que se refiere a la utilización de água en la industria son analizados, sobretodo de un punto de vista pragmático, haciéndose la comparación con otros instrumentos para racionalizar la utilización de la água.

Se describen las principales características de las tasas de toma de água y de polución tomando como base ejemplos reales de sistemas de estímulos económicos empleados en Francia, en los Países Bajos, en la República Federal de Alemania y en Checoslovaquia.

Se describen los aspectos legales, financieros y administrativos de la aplicación de instrumentos de estímulo y se analiza la participación del público y de los usuarios en este proceso.

Se analiza la eficacia de las tasas de toma y de polución en su calidad de estímulos económicos y se hace mención a los factores que condicionan esta eficacia.

Teniendo en cuenta los diferentes aspectos mencionados se puede concluir que las tasas de toma y de polución pueden ser eficaces para estimular la utilización racional del água, en particular en lo que se refiere a la utilización de água en la industria.

La experiencia de aplicación de tasas en los países en que han sido adoptadas pone en evidencia que su eficacia depende fuertemente del valor de dichas tasas y de la existencia de un sistema institucional de administración del água capaz de promover la política de aplicación de tasas en su aspecto legal, financiero y administrativo y de garantizar la participación efectiva del público y de los usuarios industriales del água en esta política.

INTRODUCTION

ECONOMIC INCENTIVES have been adopted by an increasing number of countries as an instrument for application of environmental policies. Economic incentives usually concern different kinds of environmental problems related to water, air and land, including water withdrawal and pollution, air pollution, solid wastes, land use, traffic congestion, noise and energy conservation.

As regards water, economic incentives concern the different water uses in the framework of natural water management policies.

The purpose of this paper is to analyse the different aspects related to the application of economic incentives to industrial water uses. The presentation will be focused mainly on the pragmatic aspects, leaving out the theoretical fundamentals of economic incentives that have been the object of considerable attention [see References 1, 2, 3 and 4].

The most common type of economic incentives that are presently applied in relation to industrial water use are charges applied to water withdrawal, currently called abstraction charges, and charges for waste water discharge, currently called pollution charges. These charges are based on the payment, by the user, of an amount that is proportional to the quantity of water withdrawn or pollution discharged. The reason charges act as economic incentives is very simple: the obligation to pay for harm caused to other water users or to the environment provides an incentive to reduce this harm. Therefore, if a charge is to act as an economic incentive it must have values that are high enough to effectively condition the user.

Ideally, the purpose of economic incentives is to ensure that the different polluters are made to withdraw water or to treat waste water in measures that benefit the overall interests of the community, ensuring the interiorization of external costs caused by water withdrawal and, chiefly, by water pollution. In practice it is not possible to attain this ideal aim completely and one is led to be somewhat less ambitious. Thus, for instance, as regards pollution charges, some countries establish as the goal of the application of charges the respect for certain water quality standards of receiving water bodies. In other cases the charges fixed are aimed at creating an income for financing the control of residual pollution. Charges may also contribute to make up a fund to pay damages to the entities affected by pollution. These different aims are frequently combined in some of the charge systems put into practice.

Such actions as government loans at low interest or the reduction or exemption of taxes for the installation of treatment systems are sometimes also considered as economic incentives to the control of industrial pollution. However, these actions are not in fact true economic incentives, because, although they stimulate investment in pollution control equipment, they do not correspond to efficient forms of reducing pollution. After all, they are merely grants awarded to the polluting entities or to the consumers of the goods produced by these entities. Besides, this type of grant, which is awarded in many countries, is usually only given to finance treatment units, which are also no means of encouraging economic efficiency, since it is often preferable to spend additional amounts in changing the production process or in recuperating by-products than in the improvement of treatment systems.

In what concerns pollution control, some countries have adopted direct regulation systems instead of pollution charge systems. These are based on the setting of standards defining the maximum limits for pollution load in the effluents. These systems may be called regulatory systems and together with the economic incentive systems referred to above they may be considered as economic instruments for favouring a water management policy.

It is generally assumed that charges are more cost effective than standards, costs being therefore smaller for the community. Actually it would in principle be possible to reach the same degree of efficacy with standards as with charges but only at the cost of extremely high administrative expenses which would have to be supported by the community. The system of charges is also more easy to implement than the standards, since with the charge system the polluter has every advantage in installing his pollution control system quickly so as to stop paying the charge. This is not so with the standards, for in this case the polluter will benefit from trying to drag out the discussion about the best system to be installed.

Disregard for a standard must be punished with a fine the amount of which must be on the basis of the degree of infringement. The fine is usually proportional to the pollution load discharged in excess of the value laid down by the standard.

A combination of both charges and standards is often resorted to. This is for instance the case with problems such as the control of toxic substances, which must be governed by strict standards. Also the maximum pollution levels are sometimes limited by standards and then charges only apply to lesser pollution.

Attention should also be called to the difference between pollution charges and the fees for sewage collecting, usually called user fees.

The charges are intended to change the behaviour of the users and to control water pollution and at the same time to provide some compensation for inconvenience that cannot be avoided. They are calculated on the basis of social costs, of the marginal benefits they provide or of the marginal costs of treatment.

User fees are usually considered as the price to be paid for a public service or for the use of resources. They are calculated on the basis of the services rendered with pollution control.

The differences, in conceptual terms, between charges and fees are important. The object of the charges is to reduce pollution, while the object of the fees is reimbursement for services rendered. Revenue is the principal object of fees and only a secondary object of charges.

Abstraction and pollution charges, as other environment related charges, should be both effective and equitable.

Effectiveness presumes that the charge systems are simple and clear so as to be easily understood and applied, and provide an incentive that in fact induces water users to change their behaviour in order to approach the economic and social objects of the water management policy, and also provide the funds necessary for the implementation of this policy.

Equity presumes that the charge systems are fair, give equal treatment to equal situations and are socially acceptable.

The interest taken in economic incentives for industrial water use has not finished growing both in developing countries that are establishing their water management systems for the first time, and in developed countries that are shifting from standard systems to charge systems. The interest in these problems shown by international organizations such as the United Nations [5, 6, 7, 8] or the Organization for Economic Co-operation and Development [3, 9, 10, 11, 12 and 13] has also been considerable.

ABSTRACTION CHARGES

ABSTRACTION CHARGES consist of a payment per unit volume of water with-drawn. In some systems of charges it is accepted that the user may receive a bonus per unit volume of water returned.

The unit charge may be constant, i.e. independent of the volume of water withdrawn, or else increase or decrease with the degree of water use. If it increases we have progressive charging schemes that in principle are more effective as an economic incentive for saving water. If the value of unit charge decreases with consumption we have regressive charging schemes that may be recommended only in special cases when water is not scarce and consumption must be encouraged in order to achieve economies of scale.

Abstraction charges are only used in certain countries, licensing systems which do not involve payment for water consumption being more widely used. Abstraction charges are less frequent for ground water than for surface water.

The simplest and most traditional form of conditioning water abstraction is through water property regulations. However, when water is scarce these regula-tions, either following the riparian rights doctrine or the appropriative rights doctrine, have proved to be inefficient as automatic instruments for a rational use of water. It is to respond to this inefficiency that abstraction charges have been introduced.

The criteria adopted in some Basin Agencies in France to estimate ab-straction charges are good reference criteria for this purpose.

In the Loire-Bretagne River Basin Agency [14, Appendix 9] the charges for withdrawal of surface waters are determined according to the formula:

$$T = T_g - B$$

with

$$T_g = T_f \text{ for } V < V_0$$

$$T_g = T_f + (V - V_0)t \text{ for } V > V_0$$

$$B = \sum_i (V_i t_{B_i})C_r$$

in which:

T—yearly net charge (francs);

T_g—yearly gross charge (francs);

B—yearly bonus for recirculation of water withdrawn (francs);

T_f—fixed charge corresponding to withdrawal volumes $V < V_0$ (francs);

V—total volume withdrawn (m^3);

t—unit charge (francs/m^3);

V_i—volumes of water withdrawn in the i consumption class (m^3);

t_{B_i}—bonus unit charge corresponding to the i class (francs/m^3);

C_r—coefficient of recirculation given by the ratio between volume recir-culated and volume withdrawn.

The unit charges t and t_{B_i} may have different values according to the region and time of the year. In some months t or t_{B_i} may be zero, which means that the abstraction charges are not applied in these months but only in the part of the year in which water is more scarce.

The volume V_0 establishes the value below which there is a fixed charge independent of the amount withdrawn. If V_0 is null the abstraction charge is always variable with the amount withdrawn.

The coefficient C_r may have different values according to the type of water use. For industrial water use values of C_r are as follows: without recirculation $C_r = 0$; with recirculation by spreading $C_r = 0.3$; with direct recirculation $C_r = 0.993$.

The values of unit charges t and t_{B_i} are periodically updated, the rationale for establishing their values being the optimization of water users or simply the reimbursement of the costs of making water available to users. In this last case the abstraction charge is usually called a user charge.

These criteria of estimating abstraction charges are only applied in France for surface water. In the case of groundwater use there is no bonus for recirculation, the charge being calculated only by the first term of the above presented equation.

Payment of charges per volume unit of water withdrawn, and the possible institution of a bonus per volume unit of water returned, calls for measurement of the quantities of water withdrawn and returned. Though such measurement does not, in principle, raise special problems, it may be accepted that in the case of some small consumers the volume of water should not be measured but fixed on the basis, for example, of the maximum withdrawal capacity, the industrial output of the consumer, or the number of workers of the industrial plant.

The actual values of the abstraction charges vary very much from country to country. Based on a comparative study of seven river basins in different countries OECD [13] gives values of surface water abstraction charges between 2.5 and 0.08 US$ per thousand m^3 per year respectively in Seine-Normandy (France) and Severn-Trent (United Kingdom) river basins, with intermediate values found in basins studied in Australia, Japan and the USA. The conversion of currency is made according to the rates of exchange in May 1981.

POLLUTION CHARGES

THE SYSTEMS of charges so far applied in practice have two distinct aims:

(a) to induce polluters to reduce the pollution loads discharged, down to levels that are low enough to allow meeting the legally established quality standards for the water of the receiving water bodies.

(b) To raise funds that make it possible to finance actions of water pollution control at regional and local levels.

The system of charges adopted in Czechoslovakia, which will be mentioned later on in this section, is a typical example of situation a. A good example of situation b is the system of charges which has long been used in the Ruhr, in the Federal Republic of Germany. The systems that have been used for some years in France and in the Netherlands, and which have also been adopted by the Federal Republic of Germany in 1981, are an attempt to fulfil both a and b. These systems are also briefly described later.

Pollution charges must be paid per unit of pollution load discharged, and must, in principle, be established according to the nature of type of pollutant. In the case of industrial users the range of pollutant substances to be considered is very wide, and in order to simplify the charge systems, it may be of interest to define sets of representative pollution parameters or criteria allowing the conversion of the pollution caused, into terms of an equivalent pollution, expressed, for example, in population-equivalents.

Examples of these two different procedures are given by the systems of pollution charges adopted respectively in France and in the Netherlands, which are presented later on in this paper.

The parameters taken as a basis for establishing pollution charges are usually selected from the biochemical oxygen demand (BOD), the chemical oxygen demand (COD), nitrogen, suspended matter, salinity, temperature and toxicity.

In principle the charge must be established on the basis of the damage caused by the pollutant activity, but assessment of such damage may be hampered in many cases, due not only to the complex analysis of a system in which there may be various pollutants and various polluted users, but also due to the difficulty in establishing criteria for an objective definition of the damage.

One current assumption is to consider that there is a linear variation of the charge with the pollution load, which corresponds to accepting a linear relationship as well between the pollution load and the damage to third parties. This assumption of linearity is accepted as an advantageous and sufficiently accurate simplification, provided that the three following conditions simultaneously occur:

— damage is proportional to the concentration of pollutant matter in the water;
— pollutions caused by various pollutants are cumulative;
— there is no advantage in using treatment procedures that simultaneously treat pollutant matter of different origins.

Should any of these conditions be missing, the particular circumstances of each must be examined, in order to establish a suitable criterion for establishing charges. If, for example, the first condition is lacking, it is necessary to define the nonlinear concentration-damage relationship for each pollutant element and each injured user. If, moreover, the pollutions caused by the various pollutants are not cumulative, the definition referred to above must be made for various combinations of pollutants.

In these cases it is impossible to provide users with very precise information as regards the variation in charges in terms of the streamflow. Provisional charges must be established on the basis of a certain number of initial assumptions, and adjustments progressively made.

Any significant changes in the streamflow of the receiving watercourses may have great influence on the damage caused by effluent discharge. Not only do pollution load concentrations increase when the flow is low, but also the self-purification capacity per unit discharge of the watercourse generally tends to diminish. In fact, low-flow periods often coincide with periods of high temperatures that reduce the saturation level of dissolved oxygen in the water.

Waste water discharge is therefore more harmful in periods of low streamflow and consequently unit values of pollution charges must be correspondingly higher. This increase in the unit value of the pollution charge, in order to act as an optimizing factor, must aim at reducing the effluent discharge by offering an incentive to interrupt or limit the industrial activity, or temporarily to raise the degree of treatment or store the waste. Obviously solutions of this kind can only be considered if they involve costs which are lower than the savings in charges that are not being paid and some of them would only be feasible if the low-flow period is not too long.

This system of charges that increase as the streamflow decreases is, actually, an incentive to use the natural self-purification potential of the watercourse when its values are higher.

A system of charges varying with the streamflow naturally requires knowledge of streamflow variations. This requirement means that the monitoring system, which would be needed in any case, must be extended to the streamflow of the receiving watercourse. There is thus the risk of having to set up a control system that is economically unjustifiable.

Pollution charges must be set according to the characteristics of the effluent, and it may be accepted that the charge shall depend only on the quantity of the effluent or also on its nature.

Charges based only on effluent quantity, for example in terms of volume discharged, do not seem adequate since the pollution load concentration is more significant than the volume of waste. In order to reduce the charge due, a user might concentrate the waste, thus reducing the volume but maintaining the quantity of pollution load discharged.

This system in which charges are a function of the quantity and the nature of the pollution load discharged seems the most rational. This system calls for measurement of volumes discharged and monitoring of the water quality parameters that are considered most important. Usually, in order to simplify the inspection procedure, the observations are made as simple as possible, as referred to in the following section.

To illustrate the application of systems of charges, three examples of pollution charges adopted in France, the Netherlands and Czechoslovakia are presented below. These systems of pollution charges only concern surface water and they do not apply to groundwater pollution.

France: Loire-Bretagne [14, Appendix 10]

The gross pollution charge is based on the pollution load of the effluent, and this can be arrived at by direct measurement of the pollution load discharged into the receiving waters and/or public sewers, or else fixed on a lump sum basis.

In the case of direct measurement, the pollution load relates to one day of normal effluent discharge during the course of the month of greatest discharges, and is defined by the amounts of suspended solids M_s (kg), of oxidizable matter M_0 (kg) and, of inhibiting matter M_i (kg equitox). Both the oxidizable matter and inhibiting matter are determined after separation of solids settleable in two hours.

The amount of oxidizable matter is determined by the formula:

$$M_0 = \frac{M_{COD} + 2M_{BOD5}}{3}$$

in which M_{COD} and M_{BOD5} are the oxidizable material corresponding to the chemical oxygen demand (kg) and to biochemical oxygen demand in 5 days at 20°C (kg).

In the case of the pollution load being fixed on a lump sum basis, use is made of tables relating such loads to characteristic parameters (number of workers, amount of raw materials consumed or of products manufactured, etc.).

The pollution loads determined by direct measurement or fixed on a lump sum basis are multiplied by the corresponding yearly unit charges and also by a coefficient of zone with which an attempt is made to take into consideration, for the various discharge points, the particular conditions of the receiving waters.

If the effluents are treated and the treatment facilities meet certain standard requirements of design and operation, the gross pollution charge can be reduced by application of suitable coefficients of bonus.

The yearly net pollution charge is given by

$$T = T_g - B$$

with

$$T_g = (M_s t_s + M_0 t_0)C_{z_1} + M_i t_i C_{z_2}$$

$$B = m_s t_s C_{b_s} + m_0 t_0 C_{b_0} + m_i t_i C_{b_i}$$

in which:
    T—yearly net pollution charge (francs);
    T_g—yearly gross pollution charge (francs);
    B—yearly bonus (francs);

M_s, M_0, M_i—quantities of suspended solids, oxidizable and inhibiting matter, calculated by direct measurement or defined on a lump sum basis;

m_s, m_0, m_i—quantities of suspended solids and oxidizable and inhibiting matter entering the treatment facilities (kg);

t_s, t_0, t_i—yearly unit charges, for suspended solids, oxidizable and inhibiting matter (francs/year);

C_{b_s}, C_{b_0}, C_{b_i}—coefficients of bonus for suspended solids, oxidizable and inhibiting matter;

C_{z_1}, C_{z_2}—coefficients of zone.

The Netherlands [14, 15]

The estimation of pollution charges is based on the determination of the pollution load expressed by the number of population-equivalents.

The number of population-equivalents P_e corresponding to raw sewage is given by the formula

$$P_e = \frac{(COD + 4.57N)Q}{180} + A.$$

In this case of biologically treated wastewater, the pollution load is given by the formula

$$P_e = \frac{(2.5 BOD_5 + 4.57N)Q}{180}.$$

COD is the chemical oxygen demand (mg/l), BOD_5 the biochemical oxygen demand (mg/l), N the nitrogen, A the weight of toxic substances discharged and Q the waste water discharge (m³/day).

In the case of small industries with a population-equivalent lower than 1000 and without wastewater treatment systems, where it is not economical to carry out measurements, the incidence basis of the charge, in population equivalents, may be calculated by the formula.

$$p_e = cn_1$$

in which c is a coefficient and n_1 may be, according to the type of industry, one of the following values: number of workers; number of units produced yearly; annual volume of water consumed; number of livestock.

The coefficients are established for use by industries that operate during the whole year (250 working days), and their reduction is envisaged for seasonal industries. If a firm covers different sections of activity, the basis of overall incidence is calculated by adding the bases of partial incidence.

Czechoslovakia [14, Appendix 16]

Under Czechoslovakian legislation, the charges payable for effluents are divided into two parts: the basic charge and the surcharge.

The basic charge is calculated on the basis of the treatment costs of the discharged waste, by means of formulae of the type shown below, relating to biochemical oxygen demand (BOD) and suspended solids (SS):

$$T = tM$$

where
T is the basic charge relating to BOD or SS (crowns/year);
t the unit charge relating to BOD or SS (crowns/t); and
M the quantity of BOD or SS in the effluent (t/year);

The unit charge for each of the two parameters referred to is determined by two processes, according to whether there exist or not preliminary technical-economic studies, or treatment plant designs that make it possible to calculate the yearly operation costs of the plants for eliminating the biochemical oxygen demand and suspended solids. In the first case, the unit charge is obtained by dividing, respectively, the yearly operation expenses by the yearly quantities of eliminated biochemical oxygen demand and suspended solids. In the second case, the unit charges are obtained by the formulae:

$$t_{BOD} = 5 - \log X$$

$$t_{SS} = 2.75 - 0.25 \log Y$$

where
X is the yearly quantity of BOD discharged into the watercourse (t) and
Y is the yearly quantity of SS discharged into the watercourse (t);

The surcharge is calculated, in percentage of the basic charge, by:

$$S = \frac{D}{U_d}$$

where
S – is the surcharge relating to BOD or SS in percentage of the basic charges
D the degree of deterioration caused in a watercourse by the discharge of wastewater (mg/l) and
U_d the basic unit of deterioration (mg/l).

Calculation of the degree of deterioration is done by considering the quantity of pollutant discharged (BOD or SS) and the streamflow of the watercourse which in an average year is guaranteed for 355 days. By dividing the quantity of pollutant matter by this flow the degree of deterioration (BOD or SS) is obtained.

The basic unit of deterioration is 0.25 mg/l for BOD and 0.50 mg/l for SS values which represent, respectively, fractions of the difference of standards between the quality characteristics of the waters of two consecutive categories in the water classification in force.

Besides these three examples of pollution charges systems that have been applied for a number of years, the new system applied since January 1981 in the Federal Republic of Germany, deserves a reference. In this country pollution charges were not implemented before on a national basis, but only in the Ruhr region.

In this system the charges levied depend on the harmfulness of the effluent, one unit of harmfulness being equivalent to approximately the pollution load of untreated water produced by one person in one year. The harmfulness is calculated on the basis of the volume of waste water, suspended solids, oxydisable substances and toxicity.

The law on which the charge system recently implemented in the Federal Republic of Germany is based was passed in 1976 to give dischargers enough time to build adequate waste water treatment works. The law includes a clause, which has caused some controversy, that establishes that the charges will be reduced by 50% if legal minimum standards for the waste water discharges are met.

In the European Economic Community some thought has been given to the study of the introduction throughout the community of a system of pollution charges, that so far have been the object of expert group discussions without any submission of proposals to the Council.

For establishing the pollution charges the pollution load must be determined, measurement being the most efficient method. This, however raises problems and leads to costs that are not always justifiable, especially in the case of users with a relatively low pollution potential. In such cases it is best to fix the pollution loads on the basis of parameters such as the discharge of water withdrawn, the number of units produced or the number of workers employed.

Broadly speaking, the system should make it possible to determine with sufficient accuracy the volumes of water withdrawn and effectively consumed and the pollution loads discharged, but it must be simple enough not to make it too costly.

In principle the charges are a function of space and time, i.e. they may vary from one river basin to another or even within the same river basin, and may evolve in time. Variability of charges in space is justified by the fact that it is necessary in the optimization processes to take into account the variations in the economic value of water from region to region and the characteristics required of the water in every watercourse, according to the quality goals set by law for watercourses. Variation of charges in time is due to the fact that the economic value of the water grows as the water becomes scarcer, a rise in the cost of water use being thus justified regardless of any inflationary trends.

In practice, for easy application of the system, there should be charging schemes that are not too diversified, and revision of the charge values should be carried out yearly or at least every two years.

A forecast should be made of the evolution of charges over a period of five or ten years, in order to give consumers an idea of the amount of the expenditure for which, in principle, they must budget. However, it should be noted that although charges may increase over the years with the increase in the use of water, the overall amounts received by the river basin agencies may not increase, since the increasing value of the charges will, after a certain time, lead to a reduction in the volumes of water withdrawn and of pollution loads discharged.

The variation of charges in space is usually based on the establishment of constant values for each water management region as is the case in the Netherlands. However, in cases where the regions are comparatively large, the charges may vary within each region in order to protect certain parts of the water management region, as happens in certain Basin Agencies in France.

The values of pollution charges vary widely from one region to the other and also with time.

In the Netherlands, for instance, the maximum, minimum and average values were about 29, 70 and 17 US\$ (May 1981 conversion rate) per population equivalent in 1980. In France in the same year the corresponding values of the charges were 2.2, 1.2 and 1.7 US\$ per population equivalent.

This shows a large disproportion between the values of the charges in the two countries, which may suggest that the values adopted in France are too low to act effectively as economic incentives.

The evolution of average values of pollution charges with time in recent years is shown for the two countries in the following table (also in US\$).

	The Netherlands		France	
	charge	rate of growth	charge	rate of growth
1977	12.9		1.22	
1978	13.0	8%	1.45	18%
1979	15.1	17%	1.60	10%
1980	17.2	14%	1.68	5%

This shows that in spite of the fact that the values of the charges are much lower in France than in the Netherlands the rate of growth is also smaller in France and shows a definite decreasing trend.

The values of the table above correspond to current prices. A comparison based on constant prices, taking into account inflation would of course show a much smaller growth in both cases.

IMPLEMENTATION OF ECONOMIC INCENTIVES

THE IMPLEMENTATION of systems of economic incentives involves some important problems of a legal, financial and administrative nature. Adequate public and user participation is also a condition for the success of the implementation. The purpose of this section is to present some comments related to these aspects.

Legal Aspects of the Implementation of Economic Incentives

The legal definition of the concepts of abstraction and pollution charges is one essential aspect of the implementation of economic incentives related with water resources management.

Sometimes abstraction and pollution charges are compared to taxes. However, they are quite distinct legal instruments. In fact, taxes are mainly expected to collect a revenue to support governmental activities, whereas charges are expected to stimulate an optimal use of water and/or to finance water supply works and water pollution control.

The differences between charge systems and regulatory systems based on pollution standards, whose disregard is punished with fines, have already been pointed out.

There is sometimes a tendency to consider charges and fines as instruments with similar effects, both comparable to criminal penalties intended to punish infractions of a given law. However, this idea is not true. Charges are by no means criminal penalties whereas fines are. As remarked by Anderson et al [16]: "the behaviour for which charges are carried is not evil in itself, as for example, are robbery and homicide"; the conduct "charged" is socially desirable and the conduct "penalized" is not, since in fact the application of charges may imply considerable social benefits, which is not the case with fines.

There are also differences in the application of charges and fines. Whereas fines are applied on an individual basis, case by case, and only attain a small number of transgressors, charges are applicable as a routine, to all water users.

The assessment of the value of the charges is usually done inside the water management framework and eventually approved by the government, this usually being preceeded by the hearing of legislative or advisory councils that are part of the water management framework at the regional level.

In the implementation of the charging schemes that have recently been established a conciliatory attitude has prevailed over very rigid or technocratic positions. Enquiries, consultations and public hearings should be considered in order to smooth out possible difficulties in the application of the law, which should be applied wisely and only in the case of consistently serious infringements.

Financial Aspects of the Implementation of Economic Incentives

As previously referred to, one of the aims of pollution charges is to raise funds for financing water supply and pollution control activities.

This financing can be made through different types of measures such as payment for construction of collective works by the water management authorities, compensation to polluters, grants to regional or local authorities, and support of research and development programmes or education and training programmes.

The construction of collective works such as treatment plants that jointly handle the waste of various polluters, reservoirs for regulating the discharge of the watercourses receiving the effluents, reservoirs for storing the effluents of several polluters or works for watercourse aeration will obviously redound in benefit for the water users.

Compensations to polluters may be due to those that are not expected to be able to support entirely the cost of pollution charges. In view of the adoption of different pollution charges for different regions, equity may not be ensured to all polluters and this may be corrected by compensations.

The attribution of grants to regional or local authorities is intended to help to support the expenses related to water supply or waste water discharge systems that are the responsibility of these authorities. These grants may be in the form of subsidies, loans or advances.

Finally, an indirect type of financing is achieved through the support by the governments of research and development programmes or of education and training programmes in the area of pollution control, whose results are expected to benefit the polluters in the medium or long term.

In some cases subsidies may be granted to encourage industries to develop new industrial processes and new systems of pollution control. Without this the users would prefer to invest in well-proved technologies and not in new or non-traditional technologies. Special subsidies for testing new technologies should be available, these subsidies being only reimbursable if the new technology proves to be efficient. The results of these subsidized experiences should always be publicized, whether the new technology proves efficient or not.

Administrative Aspects of the Implementation of Economic Incentives

The authorities responsible for enforcing abstraction and pollution charges are usually placed at the national, regional and local levels.

At the national level the general principles for the implementation of charge systems and some regulatory instruments are usually defined. At the regional level (with regions ideally based on river basins), the charges are defined and applied for the whole region, in order to ensure an integrated regional water management policy. At the local level there may be some regulations established by the municipalities, within the framework of the legislation established at the regional level.

For a smooth operation of the whole system, an effective coordination among the three levels is essential. In particular the establishment of charges and the distribution of aid is often carried out in cooperation between the central and regional authorities.

An adequate system of monitoring of water consumption and pollution is very important for the implementation of economic incentives. In fact, as previously mentioned, the application of both systems of abstraction charges and pollution charges entails the measurement of the rates of flow of water withdrawn or waste water discharged. In the case of pollution charges it is also necessary to measure the concentration of some pollutants or the level of some pollution parameters.

Flow measurements are inexpensive and easily made. It is also easy to apply proportional sampling techniques that make it possible to collect a composite sample representative of the average characteristics of the effluents. The determination of the concentration of pollutants and of the level of pollution parameters is far more difficult.

The Biochemical Oxygen Demand (BOD) is the most frequently used measure of the reduction of oxygen caused by most pollutants discharged in water courses. The BOD is a parameter difficult to measure and not suited for continuous monitoring, because its determination implies the observation of the reduction of dissolved oxygen in a sample of pollution after five days under controlled conditions in the laboratory.

To avoid these difficulties it is possible to do continuous monitoring of the Total Organic Carbon (TOC) and Chemical Oxygen Demand (COD) parameters, that are related to BOD. However, continuous measurements of TOC and COD are also expensive.

The amount of suspended solids (SS) is another important parameter to be measured when establishing charges. The standard procedure for the determination of SS is also carried out in laboratory but it does involve a delay as does the BOD. For continuous monitoring of SS, it is possible to measure the turbidity of water using comparatively inexpensive techniques, but the correlation of this parameter with SS is not always very accurate.

Other parameters of water pollution can also be the object of monitoring, some of them easily, such as temperature and salinity (by measuring conductance), others, such as several inorganic and organic compounds, through more difficult and expensive procedures including automatic laboratory analysis based on special techniques such as colorimetric and spectrographic techniques.

The effectiveness of any charge system is definitely conditioned by the accuracy of the measurements of the pollution loads discharged.

The direct measurement of these loads by the agency in charge of water management would be extremely expensive and consequently impractical. The solution usually adopted is to ensure that the polluters measure and report their discharges, and the agency only intervenes by means of surprise inspections. The agency should also specify the methods used for monitoring and approve the performance of the equipment installed.

The above solution is however adopted only in the case of major polluters.

As was previously mentioned in the case of minor polluters it is currently admitted that pollution charges are proportional to the volume of water withdrawn, the number of employees or the volume of industrial output.

Public and Users Participation in the Implementation of Economic Incentives

Up to a short time ago, decisions regarding the problems of water resources were taken chiefly by the public administration based on the judgement of its technical staff. Participation of the public in the decisions, when there was any, would only take place at an advanced stage of the procedure, after the fundamental decisions had all been taken. The only possibility left to citizens when they disagreed with a water resources project was to try and prevent it from being implemented. Frequent conflicts were thus created whose solution was in certain countries left to the courts.

This procedure has been very much criticized lately because of the delays it causes and consequent inconvenience. Therefore, as water resources problems are getting more serious and citizens are becoming more aware of these problems, there is a tendency to give the public a chance to intervene in the decision-making process, from the beginning.

Public participation in the decisions concerning water resources problems, particularly as regards economic incentives, entails actions to ensure that this participation is carried out in a way that ensures the effective protection of public interest.

Educational institutions may play a very active part in the public education process. As regards the actions to be carried out for senior citizens, public education may be achieved along several lines. The distribution of written information or the presentation of audio-visual information spread directly through official channels, different kinds of associations, or the press, are among the more passive actions.

As regards education techniques of a more active kind, we may quote those in which the population actually takes part in the decisions made in connection with specific cases, by means of meetings, public discussions, committees with the participation of the public, etc.

The most direct type of participation as regards the establishing of charges consists in discussing the standards and criteria related to charges between the authorities and the users.

Other possible solutions consist in discussions, in meetings of representatives of water management authorities, users, citizens, regional bodies, and local interests affected by water use or pollution. Public hearings are also possible as wider forms of public participation.

A few instances of public participation referred to by the OECD [13] are:
— required formation and use of advisory committees to make inputs in the water quality management planning process;

— required publication and dissemination of water quality management plans for comment and discussion at public hearings;

— required publication (notice) of applications for permits to abstract or discharge, with specified time period for comments and objections;

— required publication of discharge standards for various industrial and other types of dischargers with specified time period for comments;

— permission for private individuals or groups to file court suits with respect to discharge standards, behaviour of specific dischargers, individual permits.

EFFECTIVENESS OF ABSTRACTION AND POLLUTION CHARGES AS ECONOMIC INCENTIVES

ABSTRACTION AND POLLUTION charges will only be effective as economic incentives if their value is high enough.

The value of the charges must reflect not only the cost of pollution control measures but also the harm to other water users and to the environment. This involves some difficulties as it is often not easy or even possible to evaluate harm to the environment. As a consequence, the consideration of this harm tends to be neglected when establishing the charges, which may, for this reason, be fixed at too low values.

When establishing the charges, the consideration of the harm to other water users (quantified by external costs) induces allocation effects that consist of the modification in production and consumption patterns as a response to the modified price structure. The consideration of the harm to the environment creates regulatory effects that correspond to a reduction of certain types of pollution as a consequence of the modification of production and consumption patterns.

Werner [17], reasoning on the effects and implications of economic incentives in the countries of the Economic Commission for Europe (ECE), states:

— In the economic field, among others, such effects can be stated, e.g.: economic returns and benefit of investments for water distribution, supply and treatment; development of valuable cost-benefit procedures and standard systems of calculation; higher production results per unit of water; use of more efficient technologies in industry and agriculture with higher profit and in this connexion lesser water demand and costs; a better function of the interaction between the state of the pollution of water resources and their rational use; better and more comprehensive management in water resources.

— In the social field such important problems are influenced as, for example, the state of pollution of water resources and their use for human consumption; growth of unemployment caused by difficulties for certain industries which use too much water; a rise in the level of prices by added costs resulting from the control of pollution.

— The application of economic incentives and instruments involved in the ECE countries have facilitated higher efficiency of capital investments in water management. Thanks to this application, it has become possible to compare the alternatives, to distribute investments between the consumers involved, to establish discounting norms, etc. That means also, the right application of economic incentives and instruments in time and space gives the opportunity to influence industrial technological processes under special consideration of rational utilization of water resources.

It is often claimed that the application of economic incentives may create difficulties to some industries which depend very much on the water use, and contribute to the growth of inflation by raising the level of prices. As previously referred to in some cases compensations or aids are used to solve these problems, in an attempt to ensure equity among the different users. These aids are of particular importance during transition periods in the first years after abstraction or pollution charges have been established.

In each country the effectiveness of charges as economic incentives should be periodically analysed through an adequate statistical analysis of the pertinent economic, social and environmental data, the results of this analysis influencing essentially the policy of charges to be implemented in the future.

One interesting aspect which conditions the effectiveness of application of economic incentives are the individual and collective reactions to the implementation of these incentives. These reactions may come mainly from the industry and the public agencies involved with water management.

The opposition of affected industries to the introduction of economic incentives is well known. The rationale for this opposition is that the industry will be better off without the introduction of such incentives.

As Anderson et al [16] state "under a charge system, a firm is almost certain to have to pay the charge, or spend money to abate in order to reduce its charge payments. Under direct regulation, however, an industry might conclude that because the enforcement mechanism is so cumbersome and ineffective, it either will not have to pay for the most expensive kinds of abatement techniques, or will be able to gain the monetary advantages of years of delay past the official deadlines. Thus, all other factors being equal, the firm, in rational self-interest, would prefer the present system to an effective charge system".

The reaction from public agencies comes from the fact that public administration usually tends to react to innovation. This reaction has been very strong in several countries that have adopted charge systems to replace standard systems. Anderson et al [16] also explain this situation, stating that "agency personnel are used to working with standards enforced by direct regulation, while effluent charges are a new and uncertain program. The agency people usually have had a difficult time achieving whatever they have accomplished and are understandably reluctant to start the process over again under different ground rules. They think that a charge system will require more stringent monitoring procedures than are now in use, and doubt their feasibility. Even when examining the monitoring procedures that might be used under different charge proposals, they tend to search for ways to "play the regulatory game"—to seek accommodations that would keep the regulated firms pacified and thus make life easier for the agency."

References

1. Kneese, A.V. and Bower, B.T. *Managing Water Quality: Economics, Technology, Institutions*. The Johns Hopkins Press, Baltimore, 1968.
2. Kneese, A.V. and Schultze, C.L. *Pollution Prices and Public Policy*. The Brookings Institution, Washington D.C., 1975.
3. OECD. *The Polluter Pays Principle*. Organization for Economic Co-operation and Development, Paris, 1975.
4. Baumol, W.J. and Oates, W.E. *Economics, Environmental Policy and the Quality of Life*. Prentice-Hall, Englewood Cliffs, N.J., 1979.
5. UN. *Principles and Methods for the Provisions of Economic Incentives in Water Supply and Waste Water Disposal Systems Including the Fixing of Charges*. United Nations, New York, 1976.
6. UN. *Report of the United Nations Water Conference (Mar del Plata 1977)*. United Nations, New York, 1977.
7. UN. *Seminar on Rational Utilization of Water (Leipzig)*. United Nations Committee on Water Problems, Economic Commission for Europe, 1979.
8. UN. *Seminar on Economic Instruments for Rational Utilization of Water Resources (Veldhonen)*. Committee on Water Problems Economic Commission for Europe, United Nations, 1980.
9. OECD. *Economic Implications of Pollution Control*. Organization for Economic Co-operation and Development, Paris, 1974.
10. OECD. *Studies on Economic and Policy Instruments for Water Management (several countries' monographs)*. Organization for Economic Co-operation and Development, Paris, 1980.
11. OECD. *Water Management Policies and Instruments*. Organization for Economic Co-operation and Development, Paris, 1977.
12. OECD. *Pollution Charges in Practice*. Organization for Economic Co-operation and Development, Paris, 1980.
13. OECD. *Water Management in Industrialised River Basins*. Organization for Economic Co-operation and Development, Paris, 1980.
14. Cunha *et al*. *Management and Law for Water Resources*. Water Resources Publications, Fort Collins, CO, 1977.
15. Geuze, E.C. and van de Wetering, B.G. *Charging Policy in the Protection of Surface Water Against Pollution in the Catchments of the Rivers Dommel and AA*. Seminar on Economic Instruments for Rational Utilization of Water Resources (Veldhonen). Committee on Water Problems, Economic Commission for Europe, United Nations, 1980.
16. Anderson, F.R. *et al*. *Environmental Improvement Through Economic Incentives*. Johns Hopkins University Press, Baltimore, 1977.
17. Werner, F. *Evaluation of the Effects of Economic Instruments and Economic Incentives and the Implication of their Introduction in Water Resources Management*. Introductions Report to Topic IV. In Seminar on Economic Instruments for Rational Utilization of Water Resources (Veldhonen). Committee on Water Problems, Economic Commission for Europe, United Nations, 1980.

The Need for a Rational Water Management Policy

G. Dorin*

Environment Directorate, Water Section
OECD, Paris

SYNOPSIS

The task of water management in industrialized river basins is usually a highly complex one because of the wide variety of activities and constraints involved.

In most countries of the world, water resources are the limiting factor as regards regional, economic and social development. Moreover, wastage of such resources leads to disamenities and costs for the community.

A sound water management policy requires a modern institutional framework based on river basins, public ownership of water resources and a single authority at government level.

The establishment of an order of priorities for different uses, particularly from the quality standpoint, must invariably result in a progressive re-allocation of water resources giving priority to drinking water supply; too often low quality raw waters (containing toxic micropollutants) are used for this purpose.

Recycling and re-use of water should become the rule wherever the resource is limited, with drinking water taking first

---

* Responsibility for the views expressed in this paper rests solely with the author.

place in the cycle, followed by industry and, lastly, irrigation (where the water is used up).

The improper use of the drinking water supply network to satisfy all needs (industrial, urban, agricultural) often leads to a lowering in the quality of drinking water because frequently low quality raw waters have to be abstracted in order to satisfy the increased demand.

In order to limit the wastage and pollution of water resources, it is essential that there should be a permanent system of incentives based on appropriate regulations and economic measures and a rational and effective pricing system.

Regulations and standards should be framed in a practical and flexible way, so that they are easy to amend and adjust (in line with scientific, technical and economic developments).

In conclusion, modern water management should be based on sound socio-economic considerations (in addition to the purely technical aspects) and water resources should be allocated on a rational basis, particularly in terms of quality, not only quantity.

RÉSUMÉ

La Gestion des Eaux dans les Bassins Industrialisés présente généralement un maximum de complexité en raison de la multiplicité des activités et des contraintes.

Les ressources en eau représentent, dans la plupart des pays du monde, le facteur limitatif du développement régional, économique et social. Et de toute façon le gaspillage de ces ressources mène à des dommages, et des coûts pour la communauté.

Une politique sérieuse de Gestion des Eaux exige un cadre institutionnel de type moderne s'appuyant sur une structure de bassins, la propriété publique de l'eau et une autorité unique au niveau gouvernemental.

La hiérarchie des différentes utilisations, spécialement du point de vue qualitatif doit absolument mener à une réallocation progressive des eaux donnant priorité à l'eau potable, car trop souvent des eaux de basse qualité sont utilisées pour cet usage et contiennent des micropolluants toxiques.

Un recyclage et une réutilisation systèmatiques de l'eau doivent être institués d'autorité quand les ressources sont limitées:

l'eau potable étant en début de cycle, l'industrie en position inter-mediaire et l'irrigation en fin de cycle—l'eau disparaissant.

L'utilisation abusive du seul réseau d'eau potable pour cou-vrir tous les usages (industriels, urbains, agricoles) mène à une détérioration de la qualité de l'eau potable; une distribution plus rationnelle est nécessaire.

Un système d'incitation permanente est indispensable pour limiter le gaspillage et la pollution des eaux et doit être basé sur les instruments réglementaires et économiques adéquates et un système de tarification rationnel et efficace.

Les réglementations et normes doivent être établies d'une manière pratique, dynamique, et facile à amender et réajuster (en fonction de l'évolution scientifique, technique, économique . . . .).

En conclusion, d'une part, la gestion moderne des eaux, doit être fondée sur des considérations socio-économiques solides (en plus des aspects purement techniques) et de l'autre part, les ressources en eau doivent être assignées sur une base rationelle, non seulement en ce qui concerne la quantité mais, également, la qualité.

RESUMEN

El trabajo de la administración de agua en las cuencas fluviales industrializadas es normalmente de alta complejidad por la gran variedad de actividades y restricciones implicadas.

En la mayoría de los países del mundo, los recursos de agua son el factor restrictivo en cuanto al desarrollo regional económico y social. Además, la pérdida de tales recursos causa la falta de amenidades y un gasto mayor para la comunidad.

Una política sana de administración de agua requiere una estructura institucional moderna basada en las cuencas de ríos, la propiedad pública de los recursos de agua y una sóla autoridad a nivel de gobierno.

El establecimiento de una orden de prioridades para diferentes usos, en particular desde el punto de vista de calidad, debe ser, sin excepción, el resultado de una relocalización de los recursos de agua dando prioridad al suministro de agua potable; es demasiado frecuente la utilización de aguas crudas de baja calidad para este propósito (agua que contiene microcontaminantes tóxicos).

El reciclo y la re-utilización de agua debe ser la regla donde los recursos de agua sean limitados, con el agua potable tomando el primer sitio en el reciclo, seguido por la industria y, en último lugar, la irrigación (aquí se termina con el agua).

La utilización impropia de la red de suministro de agua potable para satisfacer a todas las necesidades (industriales, urbanas, agrícolas) causa una reducción en la calidad del agua potable porque a menudo deben ser abstraidos aguas crudas de calidad baja para satisfacer la demanda creciente.

Con el fin de limitar el desperdicio y la contaminación de agua, es imprescindible que haya un sistema permanente de incentivos, basado en regulaciones apropiadas y medidas económicas con un sistema de precio racional y efectivo.

Las regulaciones y las normas deben ser formadas de una forma flexible y práctica, para que sean fáciles de enmendar y ajustar (en linea con los desarrollos científicos, técnicos y económicos).

Para concluir, la administración moderna de agua debe barse en consideraciones socio-económicas sanas (aparte de los aspectos puramente técnicos) y los recursos de agua deben ser distribuidos en una base racional, en particular en términos de calidad, no cantidad.

INTRODUCTION

THE TASK of water management in industrialized river basins is usually a highly complex one because of the vast number of factors which have to be taken into account simultaneously, e.g. competition between domestic, industrial and agricultural uses; concurrent and conflicting problems of quality and quantity; political and socio-economic constraints etc. The only means of reconciling as far as possible these diverse uses and constraints, in the interests of the community as a whole, is by rational and equitable management and public ownership of water resources, with the exclusion of any special privileges. But to achieve this, it is absolutely essential that there exist the necessary political will and determination.

THE REASONS FOR A RATIONAL USE OF WATER

IN MOST COUNTRIES, investment in water resources far exceeds investment in any other environmental resource and the question of water supply is one of major importance. It should not be necessary to insist on the advantages of conserving a resource which, in many parts of the world, is scarce and, in many cases, is the factor which limits regional, economic and social development. In the competition for the use of water resources, wastage in one sector will often mean shortage in another. What must not be forgotten is that, whatever their degree of scarcity, the use of water resources leads almost invariably to a corresponding deterioration in the quality of these resources and of the environment. The new resources required to satisfy the growing demand will generally be increasingly difficult and costly to exploit and require a greater input of energy.

Water is not only an ecological and environmental medium of vital importance, but also by far the most widely used raw material in all forms of human activity. The conflict between the two is a constant dilemma of water resource management.

Clearly, in regions where water is scarce its wastage is dramatic; but even in countries where water is not scarce, wastage leads to additional costs for the community and has serious direct and indirect effects on the environment, e.g.

—a drop in river flows, with its consequent effects in terms of the environment and the diluting of pollution (particularly in summer);

—reduction and depletion of underground waters;

—the need to carry out major construction work (dams, reservoirs, etc.) to cope with increased demand and the negative impact of this on the environment;

—the higher the offtake of water (e.g. by industry), the greater is the volume of effluent, its treatment becomes more costly and the elimination of pollutants less effective as the result of their dilution;

—excessive irrigation leads to the runoff and leaching of fertilizers and mineral salts, involving a loss for agriculture, a danger of eutrophication of waters and, in many cases, irreversible pollution of underground waters (nitrates, salinity).

THE NEED FOR A RATIONAL BASIS FOR A SOUND WATER MANAGEMENT POLICY

UNDERGROUND and surface waters constitute a closely interrelated hydrologic system which has to be managed on a long-term basis, using an integrated approach combining under one authority all the aspects of water quality and quantity, offtake and discharge, supply and conservation. The split of these various functions between the different ministries and departments is a legacy of the past and is gradually giving way to integrated management under a single authority.

The ideal operational structure for water resource management is one based on a hydrological river basin system, because the resource being managed has rationally defined hydrological boundaries; water supply and demand can be more realistically matched and pollution controlled more effectively. Such systems have already been adopted successfully in an increasing number of countries. The national water management structure should therefore consist of a limited number of sizeable regions which should be large enough to justify the hiring of the multi-disciplinary skills required for effective modern management. However, certain countries, either for geographical, historical or administrative reasons, could find it difficult to make the radical changeover to such a system and may need to develop flexible systems which adapt the pre-existing administrative framework to an overall river basin concept.

In order to co-ordinate regional river basin management authorities and harmonise their policies, there should be a co-ordinating body responsible for water policy at national level. Further, in order to match water policies with other national priorities and resolve potential conflicts, this body should be in close liaison with the various ministries concerned with water resources. It would also play an effective part in harmonising water management policies at international level. As is already the case in several countries, the minister in charge of the environment could be responsible for running this body.

A RATIONAL ORDER OF PRIORITIES FOR THE USE OF WATER RESOURCES (Based on needs in terms of quality and quantity)

AUTHORITIES should endeavour to promote a rational and equitable allocation of water resources among all users based on real needs in terms of quality and quantity, and taking into account possible priorities as well as the effects on the environment. In some countries, traditional practices and structures such as private ownership of surface and underground waters, water rights and similar privileges have created situations which are often not consistent with a modern and rational water policy and should therefore be progressively revised. The first and absolutely indispensable step towards modern rational water resources management involves legal measures to re-establish ownership by the State or Provinces of all water resources, including underground waters.

When there is a high demand for water resources, some order of priority needs to be established at the regional level as regards the volumes and especially the qualities required. Such a rational allocation of water demands good knowledge of the qualitative and quantitative requirements for the different uses as well as the environmental role of the resource. Current water allocation procedures are still frequently far from rational. Pre-existing uses and different forms of water rights virtually confer on certain users the right or possibility to abstract and use at will precious water resources at the expense of other users. Furthermore, high quality waters, such as underground waters, are frequently abstracted in large quantities for purposes (industry, agriculture) which do not need water of this quality, whereas for the very exacting requirements of drinking water, for example, low quality raw waters have often to be used. Such irrational use of limited water resources is clearly unacceptable. The solution to these problems is primarily a legal and institutional one and often requires drastic and radical action.

A case in point is the increasing use, particularly in major industrial and urban areas, of what is often highly polluted raw water for the production of drinking water. Not only is the treatment of such water becoming increasingly costly but in addition, the quality of this water even after treatment is frequently unsatisfactory from the standpoint of taste, odour and health. This is generally due to the large number of trace pollutants which pass in solution or fine particulate form through treatment plants and which cannot be removed. New and often dangerous pollutants are also formed during treatment of this low quality raw water since, in many cases, chlorine is used in massive doses at every stage: (1) during the conveyance of the raw water, (2) the treatment process itself, (3) the final disinfection phase and (4) the residual chlorine in the supply system. This chlorine naturally reacts with the numerous organic compounds usually present in this type of water to form a variety of organochlorines, which are now generally regarded as a danger to health (potentially carcinogenic). Under present technological and financial operating conditions at treatment plants, the situation is not likely to be substantially improved unless special efforts are made to enhance adequately the quality of the raw water itself. Since, in many cases, it would probably be unrealistic to expect that all the polluted waters used can be improved sufficiently quickly and extensively, a major effort needs to be made to re-allocate water resources on a regional basis, using the best quality resources for the drinking water supply.

Another disturbing problem threatening a number of countries' best quality water resources, and underground waters in particular, is the presence of nitrates. High concentrations of nitrates are toxic (particularly in the case of young children—"methaemoglobinaemia"). They also tend to stimulate the potentially carcinogenic chain: nitrates/nitrites/nitrosamines. This is a relatively recent problem; it has become prevalent mostly since the 1960s and has assumed alarming proportions over the past 3–5 years in many regions which are densely populated and intensively cultivated. Agriculture and stock breeding now also use industrial methods on an increasing scale, and are a significant cause of pollution. The high nitrate content in raw water is constantly increasing and affecting a wider area, and this contamination will continue to get worse because the main factors causing it are also becoming more acute. The fact is that, generally speaking, no adequate control is exercised over agricultural pollution.

THE REUSE, SERIES-USE AND RECYCLING OF WATER

In a number of its uses, the water itself is not consumed (or only to a slight extent) but is returned usually in a deteriorated form, i.e. after being subject to certain forms of pollution. However, in some cases (irrigation for example), it is almost entirely consumed (by evapo-transpiration) and in many countries, irrigation is the main user and consumer of water.

From a quality standpoint, however, some uses generate moderate pollution whilst others cause heavy pollution. As regards the overall strategy for a region or river basin, the existence on the upper reaches of a river of activities which are polluting or are heavy consumers of water can have a highly negative effect on other activities downstream. A rational water resource management policy would endeavour to formulate an optimum strategy for the different uses, particularly when water is a limiting factor on the development of that particular region.

Reuse/Series-Use

At this point, it may be useful to illustrate this by an instructive and typical example of a serious problem common to many regions bordering on the Mediterranean and other regions where water is scarce. The water resources have traditionally been used, in the main, for irrigation, which is indispensable for agriculture in climates such as these. However, over the past 20 years, the demand for water has risen substantially as the result of the tourist, urban and industrial development in these coastal regions, and this has led to the harnessing of all the region's available resources. Further development then becomes impossible without some rational policy of recycling water.

A surprising fact is that, in the vast majority of cases, water is used only once (by the towns, tourist centres, industries) and the waste waters discharged directly into the sea (usually without treatment) where they cause a serious problem of coastal pollution, particularly since the coast is a major tourist area.

It is quite obvious that, in this case, a rational use of water could easily satisfy the requirements of all these activities and avoid serious pollution of coastal waters. Water resources should first be used for drinking water supply and then the urban effluent, after treatment, reused for industry and other activities which do not need high quality water; and then finally, this water, after treatment if necessary, could be used for agriculture, which will inevitably be the end user. It would seem that, in many cases, the obstacle to this kind of series-use of water is not so much the infrastructures that would be needed (e.g. mains, storage basins, treatment and pumping equipment), but rather the usual structural, legal or administrative constraints (e.g. reluctance on the part of local authorities, industries or farmers to co-operate in a joint system; reluctance too on the part of the various administrative services dealing with agricultural, urban and industrial matters, which come under different ministries; the problem of ownership of the water, sharing the costs etc.). However, increasing water resources say two-fold in this way would open up very substantial possibilities for the social and economic development of these regions.

This is an example of the potential benefits to be derived from rational reuse of water at a regional level; however, reuse and recycling, which are central to a modern rational system of management (not only for water but for other resources), are methods which must be employed at all levels. Recycling generally involves reutilising a resource for the same purpose within a closed circuit, whereas reuse, in principle, has a much wider meaning and involves successive uses for a number of different purposes.

Recycling

The systematic recycling of waste water is the principle used in the new industrial technologies which cause little or no pollution. It is usually applied to individual processes and not to mixed effluent. The discharge of polluted effluent means an outright loss for industry of potentially recoverable matter (i.e. raw materials, reagents, finished products and water); their recovery means a gain for industry and, of course, for the environment! In addition to systematic recycling, a modern industrial complex may also incorporate a system of series-reuse of water and residues for other purposes. As a result, total water consumption can be reduced to a substantial extent — sometimes to as little as 1/10 or 1/50 of that consumed by older traditional processes (e.g. pulp and paper manufacturing, sugar refining, electroplating, etc.).

In principle, out-of-date technologies, which are heavy consumers of water and cause considerable pollution, should on no account be used in new industries or when existing industries are modernised or expanded. Although the new technologies already available, incorporating full effluent recycling, are slightly more expensive to install, this outlay is rapidly recouped by way of substantial savings in water and raw materials, particularly if one takes into account the pollution levies or charges which are thus avoided.

Where drinking water is concerned, recent studies have shown that direct effluent recycling is to be avoided since the effluents generally contain large numbers of trace pollutants which pass in solution or fine particulate form through treatment plants without being sufficiently eliminated (e.g. nitrates). What is more, it is often the case that massive doses of chlorine are used because of the high concentrations of pathogenic micro-organisms (bacteria, viruses, parasite eggs or larvae) and also to eliminate organic or ammonium compounds. However, chlorination of water which still contains a large number of organic substances inevitably results in the formation of large amounts of organochlorines, which are dangerous. It is therefore advisable to use good quality "virgin" water for the drinking water supply and then to reuse domestic waste water, after suitable treatment, for other purposes (industry, agriculture). It is necessary of course to have the requisite supply systems for these different uses and grades of water.

A RATIONAL SYSTEM OF WATER DISTRIBUTION

DISTRIBUTION is a key factor, which can determine whether or not it is possible to arrive at a rational and intelligent use of water based on needs and on qualities available. First of all, let it be said that in regions where there is sufficient high quality raw water for all purposes, in theory there is no problem, and any type of distribution system would probably be acceptable; however, only a very small minority of countries in the world have water resources in such abundance.

Thus, in regions where the supply of high quality raw water is scarce, this water should obviously be primarily reserved for the drinking water supply on the basis of an appropriate order of priority of uses. If this principle were strictly followed, there would in general be no problem. However, the present growing tendency to use the drinking water supply for the widest possible range of uses is a serious matter and one which, generally, has fairly negative effects on the drinking water supply itself. It is obvious, that in many cases, a substantial increase in the amount of "drinking" water distributed for a wide variety of other uses, via a single supply network, necessitates an ever-increasing offtake of low quality raw water. Instances of this are sufficiently numerous and telling for it to be unnecessary to stress the drawbacks of such a policy, based on short-term technical, commercial and financial considerations, with little regard for the social and health aspects.

A dual distribution network

The pattern of water distribution needs to be geared to the scarcity of water resources (and of high quality water in particular) and planned at a local and regional level in relation to different users' requirements in terms of quality and quantity (the reuse of water for purposes where a high grade supply is not necessary can be of great assistance in easing the problem as regards quantities). This, of course, implies that there should be more than one distribution network. Generally speaking, it is sufficient to have one distribution network of high quality water for drinking and other domestic uses and a second network supplying standard water for other purposes (industrial, urban, watering, etc.); this standard water would of course be disinfected so as to eliminate the risk of accident. In particularly difficult situations where there is insufficient high quality water for all domestic uses, essential requirements (kitchen, bathroom) would have to be supplied with high grade water whereas disinfected "standard" water would serve for other purposes (e.g. toilets, laundering, garage, gardens, etc.). Many countries and regions are, in fact, using dual systems (i.e. domestic use plus other uses) with success and it is to be hoped that effective steps will be taken to remedy the wasteful use of the drinking water supply for all purposes—admittedly, convenient for certain users but, in most cases, incompatible with the interests of the community as a whole and contrary to an optimum and rational utilisation of water resources.

WAYS OF PROMOTING RATIONAL USE OF WATER RESOURCES

EVEN WHEN the most advanced techniques are used, if water resources are limited and have to be safeguarded and carefully managed, it is absolutely essential that users should have a permanent incentive to reduce pollution and wastage of water. A point which bears repeating is that the qualitative and quantitative aspects of water resources are closely linked and constantly affecting each other.

Regulatory and economic instruments

There is permanent conflict between the competing requirements of the various water users and also between maximum utilisation of the resource and its conservation in view of its essential ecological role within the environment. It is unlikely that a single instrument will, on its own, be able to provide a satisfactory solution for all the complex management problems involved, particularly in densely populated and industrialized river basins.

On the other hand, a judicious use of complementary instruments (regulatory and economic) will, in most cases, make for more efficient operation of the management system and better control by the authorities responsible at minimum cost to the community. These instruments need to be used together so that they are mutually supporting; it is usually advisable to adopt a gradual, phased approach in introducing these regulatory and economic instruments so that the desired level of control can be achieved, without causing economic disruption.

Economic and regulatory instruments should therefore be designed to provide a permanent incentive for more rational utilisation of the resource (by saving on consumption and reducing pollution); this is an essential element in any dynamic water management policy. It would also constitute a permanent incentive to progress in water technology and research.

As a general rule, the application of flat-rate charges should be avoided since, in practice, this often serves to encourage over-consumption and pollution. When charges are fixed at a sufficient rate, they act as a good incentive and can serve as an extremely useful adjunct to regulations (permits, standards) by making these more effective and by providing greater overall flexibility. Charges, moreover, generate a substantial revenue, which provides the authorities with the additional income required to promote whatever water resource development and pollution control projects they feel to be the most appropriate and most urgent in the interests of the community as a whole. In practice, regulatory and economic instruments are being used to an increasing extent, particularly in Europe, by the authorities responsible for water resource management and there is now a wealth of information on this subject.

Pricing policy

One aspect, however, needs special attention, since it would seem that so far it has not been given sufficient emphasis — the question of the price and a scale of charges for water. The situations and systems which exist at present vary considerably, not only from one country to another but even from one village to the next as well as in relation to the resources available and the different purposes for which they are used. In some countries, water resources (underground or surface) may still be privately owned, which is completely incompatible with rational management of this public resource. In many countries water is used (by industry, agriculture) free of charge: all that is required is an authorization either for a stated (but generally non-verifiable) volume or for an unstated volume — which obviously tends to encourage waste.

However, a growing number of countries are introducing more rational systems where the consumer, as in the case of any other limited resource, has to pay for what he uses. In some systems of a rudimentary (or temporary) nature, the consumer pays a flat charge, either for a stated maximum amount or for an unlimited quantity; since such systems have little or no incentive element, their sole virtue is simplicity and they are workable only when there are abundant resources for the community as a whole.

With the more elaborate systems, which are gradually tending to replace the others, the consumer pays in accordance with the quantity used, either on the basis of a fixed price per unit volume or on a sliding scale, which may be either degressive (which is frequent, but not to be recommended, because it provides no incentive to reduce consumption) or progressive (a system which is still uncommon, but extremely valid because of its incentive element).

In most cases, the price of water is low or even very low, compared with the price for other widely used resources. Subsidised or not, either directly or indirectly (as is often the case for 'public services' type of supply), in many regions the current price of water would seem to provide very little in the way of an incentive for numerous categories of user.

The elasticity of the demand for water in relation to its price (in other words, the degree of consumer response) can vary substantially depending on the purpose for which it is used. For example, industry on the whole has a greater elasticity i.e. it is able to reduce its consumption to a substantial extent if necessary, although water generally represents only a small part of its budget. By contrast, elasticity is less in the case of agriculture and the upper limit as regards price is soon reached. The case of the domestic consumer is different again: a household's consumption is relatively stable and a fairly substantial increase in the price of water seems often to make little difference since, being still low, it generally does not reach the level where it becomes a deterrent; what is more, the system in many cases does not lend itself to this kind of incentive approach e.g. the absence of individual meters, flat-rate charges, water charges included in the overall charges for the building, etc. There is still a great deal of progress to be made in this area, since the aim of rational management must be to have an equitable price structure for water, having regard to consumption (meters), type of use, type and quality of the resource and, of course, local operating conditions.

MORE EFFECTIVE USE OF STANDARDS AND REGULATIONS IN INDUSTRIAL RIVER BASINS

EXPERIENCE has shown that static regulations may gradually lose their initial effectiveness and lead to a progressive reduction in the level of environmental protection. This weakening and erosion of regulations is a well-known fact and the result of a combination of several factors such as:
—continuing changes in industry and other polluting activities;
—the growth and expansion of these activities;
—the tendency of the polluter to find ways round legislation;
—the transfer or evacuation of pollution into other media or other forms;
—inflation and falling money values (rates, fines).

It would be wise to change the static nature of some of the legislation based on fixed regulations and standards so as to allow greater flexibility and easier updating when necessary. For instance, when a permit is granted, it is essential to provide for subsequent alteration by means of a regular review procedure.

The protection of water resources and the environment has often been seriously hindered by the lack of regulations and quality standards (with respect to effluent, the natural environment, drinking water, etc.) and the overly rigid and formal manner in which these are drawn up and applied. Too often, this will lead to a situation of stalemate i.e. (i) it is argued wrongly, that current scientific and technical knowledge is insufficient to enable any standards to be fixed; accordingly, (ii) no standards or regulations, even provisional ones, are drawn up; with the result that (iii) polluters are not compelled to reduce pollution levels and the authorities are deprived of an essential means of action.

In order to make standards and regulations more effective, the authorities concerned should see to it that they:
—exist for a wider range of sectors and parameters (even if only on a provisional basis);
—are based on information currently available and formulated, if necessary, on a short-term basis.
—are updated frequently and progressively strengthened as the result of: better information, the progressive adjustment of industry and the improvement of technologies and processes.

It is essential that regulations should embody a sufficiently attractive incentive element so that it is always in the user's interest to restrict his consumption and the pollution he causes. Measures of an economic kind are likely to prove the most successful in this respect. When standards are drawn up, they should be accompanied by a clearly defined programme for their application and by deadlines for achieving the various objectives.

Water and the Industrial Environment

D. Larré

Director, Industry and Environment Office, United Nations Environment Programme, 17 rue Margueritte, 75017 Paris

and

J.C. Noel

Consultant, United Nations Environment Programme

SYNOPSIS

Industry, which still uses water in an undisciplined manner in many countries, without bothering about the consequences arising from both a fall in available resources and a lowering of quality, is beginning to take this element into account in its overall economic strategy.

Governments have recently begun to include the question of water resources in their national and regional development policies. It is evident that industrial activities can have a very great influence on the social and economic life of a given region; the various requirements for water are sometimes incompatible.

International organizations, and in particular the United Nations, have felt the need for very close co-operation on this subject and have initiated a certain number of measures aimed at pooling the experiences of each country on this question and at promoting, in particular, various training programmes.

For the pursuit of industrial development in harmony with

man's environment, it is essential to launch a vigorous campaign covering several areas of reflection and action: new industrial technology, reduced water consumption, recycling and recuperation of waste products, new purification methods, information and training.

RÉSUMÉ

L'industrie, qui utilise l'eau de manière encore anarchique dans de nombreux pays, sans se préoccuper des conséquences que présentent à la fois la diminution de la ressource disponible et la dégradation de la qualité, commence à prendre en compte cet élément dans la stratégie économique globale.

Depuis peu de temps les gouvernements intègrent la notion de ressource en eau dans les politiques d'aménagement du territoire. En effet, les conséquences d'une activité industrielle peuvent influencer de manière très importante la vie sociale et économique d'une région donnée; les divers usages de l'eau sont quelquefois difficilement compatibles.

Les organismes internationaux, et au premier chef les Nations Unies, ont senti la nécessité d'une coopération très étroite sur ce sujet et ont développé un certain nombre d'actions visant à la mise en commun des expériences de chaque pays en la matière et la promotion d'un certain nombre d'actions de formation en particulier.

Pour la poursuite d'un développement industriel en harmonie avec la vie des hommes, il est essentiel de se lancer vigoureusement dans plusieurs axes de réflexion et d'action: nouvelles technologies industrielles, faibles consommations d'eau, recyclage et récupération de déchets, nouvelles méthodes d'épuration, formation des hommes.

RESUMEN

La industria, que en numerosos países aún utiliza el agua de manera anárquica, sin preocuparse de las consecuéncias que presentan a la vez la disminución de los recursos disponibles y la degradación de la calidad, empieza a tomar en cuenta este elemento en su estrategia económica global.

Recientemente los gobiernos han empezado a integrar la noción de recursos de agua en las políticas de fomento nacional. En efecto, las consecuéncias de una actividad industrial pueden influenciar de manera muy importante la vida social y económica de una región dada; los diversos usos del agua son a veces dificilmente compatibles.

Los organismos internacionales y principalmente las Naciones Unidas, han sentido la necesidad de una cooperación muy estrecha a este respecto y han dessarrollado ciertas acciones para poner en común las experiencias de cada país y promover un cierto número de acciones, de formación en particular.

Para proseguir un desarrollo industrial en armonía con la vida humana es esencial reflexionar vigorósamente y actuar en várias direcciones: nuevas tecnologías industriales, poco consumo de agua, recuperación y reutilización de los residuos, nuevos métodos de depuración y, formación de personal.

INTRODUCTION

WATER IS VERY CLOSELY involved in the life of industry, large and small, i.e. in all human activities designed to produce a product which can be used by man either directly, from a natural raw material (minerals, agricultural produce) or indirectly, following a series of more or less elaborate manufacturing processes. For several centuries, few people reflected on the overwhelming importance of this particular "raw material" in the human life cycle. The main reason was its widespread availability:

—water was found everywhere in most of the older industrial countries (18th–19th centuries)

—it was free

—modification of its main characteristics after use had no effect on the consumer, who had a ready supply of all he needed

—there was no "supplier", except nature; with air, water was practically the only product available on demand without, in general, the need to request supplies from another person.

Except for some very remarkable special cases, this situation continued until the end of the first half of the 20th century, when the enormous population explosion demonstrated that nature had its limits. Even though the total amount of water available in the world more than covers requirements, it would be necessary for each cubic metre of river water to be usable and, in many regions, this is not the case.

INDUSTRY AND WATER

An inexhaustible supply

How is it that the situation in certain regions has become catastrophic as far as the quality of surface water is concerned? Very often, because industry has drawn enormous quantities of clean water from the groundwater table, polluted it during production processes and afterwards discharged it, untreated, into the surface water. Before 1970, in industrialized countries, even those traditionally concerned with protection of the environment (e.g. the Scandinavian countries, Switzerland, Canada), hardly any success was achieved in reducing the wasteful use of water by industry. Everywhere, whether locally or over the whole drainage area of certain large rivers, it was observed that the imbalance in the aquatic environment had reached such a point that it was practically impossible to use the water in its natural state.

It was only during the nineteen-seventies, by the use of all available means, technical as well as administrative and financial, that the rapid deterioration in the quality of surface water was slowed down. Although the considerable pollution due to the modern way of life (increased domestic use of water without the installation of required purification plants) should not be neglected, there is no denying that industrial activity, in industrialized regions, is responsible for the greater part of the deterioration in the quality of water.

Unmanaged potential

It was only very late in the day that industry started to concern itself with possible problems arising from its use of water; for many years, it considered any other user of water to be an enemy who had to be either fought or ignored. It is interesting, for example, to note the different fundamental reactions that industrial enterprises may have when faced with fishermen in various countries:
—in Europe, where freshwater fishing has become a sport, the economic weight represented by a local angling club, in the face of a powerful industry employing thousands of people but destroying all aquatic life downstream, is almost negligible; no consideration will be given to angling activities in competition with industrial life.
—in Southeast Asia, where fishing is often very closely linked to basic human food requirements, any degradation of the watercourses, leading to scarcity of aquatic life, would have considerable economic and social

consequences; here, the weight carried by the fishermen could be as important as that of industry.

Awareness of the problem came the day when, in many countries, water was no longer available at an acceptable price, which meant just above zero for the industrialized world; this awareness of the problem was increased when many companies found themselves in the situation of having no more water available (e.g. Northern France).

For industry, water is an element of unquestioned importance. In industrialized countries, even today, a company wishing to expand by building a new factory rarely considers the question of whether enough water will be available for its activities and whether it will be able to discharge its waste; power supplies (electricity, gas) are basic necessities, road and rail links are important, telecommunications essential, but water is not considered to be a problem. Nevertheless, its presence, its availability and the preservation of its quality are of overriding importance. It is imperative that the industrialization of any region should take this element into account: an industry using and polluting water cannot be set up just anywhere, unless it is prepared to pay the costs arising from its choice. Certain examples are worth citing:

—a factory processing 1,200 tonnes of potatoes per day to make frozen chips was only able to be sited in an area of rich agricultural soil on condition that it used over 12 per cent of the investment for the building of a purification plant. This company was obliged to make important changes to the siting of its factory to take account of available water supplies and the possibility of discharging polluted waste-water. These important questions had been completely ignored by the company's management, who had come to their decision without taking them into account.

—an industrial estate was created by a large town to attract companies in the primary manufacturing sector; the local authority was responsible for laying on all mains service and for providing a rail link to the estate. This estate is still unoccupied, in spite of several inquiries; negotiations have always failed, due, on the one hand, to lack of water resources in sufficient quantity to satisfy the needs of large consumers and, on the other hand, to the very low volume of polluted waste-water able to be received by the receiving waters. This imposed the use of large purification plants for which the very high investment costs were unacceptable to the companies.

These actual cases are not rare, and similar circumstances can dramatically endanger the economic activities of a country or region.

Rationalizing resources

These monumental errors of management are happily becoming rare in many countries, following the policies introduced more or less vigorously by regions. Two concomitant methods are currently used and would appear to be necessary: regulation and financial pressure. The first is most widely used the world over, even though its effectiveness has not been universally demonstrated. The fact that governments lay down certain standards to be followed by various branches of industry does not, in itself, solve all the problems. Respecting these standards necessarily imposes on companies more or less onerous investments which may or may not be acceptable within the economic strategy of the company, or even of the country; the idea of competition to keep cost prices down then becomes reality and there is a veritable "blackmail" to avoid applying the laid-down standards.

This notion of industrial competition is most widely prevalent in those cases, still fairly rare (as the Netherlands, France, Great Britain, Czechoslovakia, certain areas of the United States and West Germany), where water is paid for. This policy, stated to be based on the principle of "he who pollutes, pays" is often criticized for distorting free market forces when the charges represented by the various taxes reach certain levels; in actual fact, in countries where this principle is applied, it does not appear that it really has any harmful effect on company competitiveness, except in special cases (wool-washing, distilleries, paper-pulp) which of course represent industrial activities which are high-polluting and which therefore greatly contribute to the destruction of water resources. From an institutional point of view, it is therefore necessary for governments to carry out a dual economic/regulatory policy. This is the only sure way to make the industrial world aware of the necessity to protect the quality of water.

It is also imperative that national and regional development policies take into account this idea of protecting water resources. It is illogical, for example, to wish to industrialize, at all costs, the high drainage areas of rivers, unless extremely strict anti-pollution measures can be imposed and permanently sustained. It is imperative that the headwaters of a watercourse be used only for non-polluting industries; it is true that this is perhaps not compatible with the fact that river basins upstream are often rural and therefore favourable for the development of high-polluting agricultural processing industries, but it is only by paying this price that there is a good chance of successful water management. Downstream, the problem arises of protecting marine life.

Industry must not be allowed to set up anywhere and do anything. Before any decision is taken on industrial development, a very serious in-depth examination must be made of water requirements, the pollution generated, the means to be made available to stop it, the financial outlay required for investment and operation.

WATER IS UNIVERSAL

IT IS OFTEN the case that a watercourse does not run over just one national territory and any degradation by one country affects the use that can be made of it by another: this is the case, for example, for several watercourses in Western Europe but this situation is also found in North and South America and in the Middle East. To some extent, it was this type of situation which led to international action in the field of industry and the environment; cooperative international action developed from this and is currently underway, particularly in the technical field under the aegis of the United Nations and its specialized agencies, OECD, the European Community and other international institutions. There have been some very rare examples of international management of hydraulic potential, as far as the preservation of quality is concerned, but without complete success: the problems of the Great Lakes of North America, the Rhine, the Danube, the Mediterranean. In general, industrial pollution was the main problem and attempts were made to introduce catching-up programmes by standardizing the efforts of each country. Unfortunately, progress has been slow because of lack of action by governments concerned; the fear of no longer having competitive industrial enterprises weakened their good intentions and led to nothing very much being done. This problem of a universal awareness of water as a fundamental raw material in economic development no doubt stems from the very different points of view of various countries concerning priorities for its use.

In many countries, competition is very strong between various possible consumers and the choices made at the individual level may be incoherent, in spite of a will to co-operate. An example is the enormous crop-irrigation requirement of some countries. This essential requirement to satisfy food needs has, however, the great inconvenience of removing water from its surface cycle. A country using a large volume of water from a watercourse for crop irrigation may be depriving a neighbouring country, sharing the same watercourse, of an essential raw material. It is evident that such a situation cannot continue without causing serious disruption.

From the strictly industrial point of view, production activities which do not require the use of water are rare; even certain transformation activities in the field of high technology (electronics and aeronautics, for example) often need water for cooling certain manufacturing equipment.

The industrial technology developed about a century ago, and which has since spread throughout the world, has evolved very little in this field. This is the likely cause of some very serious situations in certain countries. Where the opinion was shared that water posed no problem, some countries experienced the creation of industrial technology which was a heavy user of water and highly polluting, when the available resources were very small and already widely used for other purposes (public water supply); unless new technology is introduced, the development of such industrial activities will inevitably be throttled. For certain developing countries, it is indispensable that this be taken into account when industrial development is decided. Through international co-operation, appropriate technology selection should permit the introduction of certain industries in countries able to assimilate them, and the development of new technology in countries where water resources prevent the use of traditional methods.

Action by organs of the United Nations system

In support of their main objective of peace and friendship, governments of countries which together formed the United Nations co-operate to solve international economic and social development problems. Specialized agencies are each responsible for one of the essential aspects of development: FAO, food and agriculture; ILO, improvement in working conditions and productivity; WHO, the health of mankind; UNESCO, education and culture.... Industrialization, an essential tool of progress, is the main concern of UNIDO. Each of these institutions is responsible for assessing the relationship between water resources and its development sector and for drawing the right conclusions.

A new understanding of the relationship of interdependence between man's activities and the environment has encouraged the representatives of one hundred and twelve countries to lay the foundations of a common programme of action. The United Nations Conference on the Human Environment, which was convened in Stockholm in 1972, approved a plan of action including 109 recommendations calling on governments, specialized agencies of the United Nations and international organizations, governmental or not, to co-operate in taking specific measures to solve environmental problems, while taking into consideration their great diversity; and a resolution concerning the corresponding institutional and financial steps to be taken. Rather than forming a new agency to cover environment, the General Assembly decided to create a small institution the United Nations Environment Programme. The Secretariat, established for the first time in a developing country—Nairobi, Kenya—today co-ordinates environmental matters amongst the various United Nations bodies. An Under-Secretary-General of the United Nations, elected by the General Assembly for a four year term, serves as Executive Director of UNEP. This post has been held, since 1978, by Mostafa Kamal Tolba (Egypt), a microbiologist and former President of the Egyptian Academy of Scientific Research.

A Governing Council of UNEP, composed of fifty-eight member states elected by the General Assembly, defines priorities in a programme that concerns the whole United Nations family. An environment fund, financed by voluntary contributions from member states, eases UNEP's task promoting this large programme. It is an essential support for the organization's role as a "catalyst" and co-ordinator, an organization that has sometimes been called the "environmental conscience" of the United Nations. The fund has authorized a 1980–81 spending programme of approximately 68 million dollars. On the industry and environment issue, UNEP has taken as its short-term target the preparation of the main guidelines and recommendations that government and industry can use to reduce the harmful impact on the environment of certain industrial practices. Guidelines have been published, particularly concerning consideration of the natural environment in the choice of industrial sites. A special office in Paris runs consultations, sector by sector, leading to the establishment of overviews, technical reviews, manuals and guidelines. Information acquired is made available, on request, using a computerized data base. Files are available on pollution abatement and control technologies and on the discharge standards and ambient quality standards in specific countries. A quarterly newsletter, *Industry and Environment*, is published in English and French and is available to specialists.

The following two examples, from the European region, attempt to show how countries can co-operate to improve water management in relation to industrial development. Many other examples of co-operation could be given in Asia, Africa and Latin America.

Action of the United Nations Economic Commission for Europe

Within the framework of the United Nations Economic Commission for Europe (ECE), a vast programme of co-operation has been launched, much of which addresses water pollution problems. Among many significant activities, one is of special interest. The ECE has decided to promote, in all fields, the rational use of natural resources by encouraging low-pollution and low-waste production techniques, permitting the re-use and recycling of by-products. This decision entails the promotion of a certain number of methods based on:

  —reduction in waste production and in the emission of polluting matter: use of improved industrial processes, development of products with a longer life-span or that can be easily separated and possibly re-used

  —waste recovery

  —re-use of a maximum proportion of wastes as basic products for other production processes.

A certain number of recommendations have been made to implement the declaration adopted in this respect. One relates to the need for international exchange of information, training of specialists at all levels and evaluation of the financial impact of these new technologies, in order to optimize the use of raw materials and energy. This international initiative is of deep significance and should permit greatly increased and innovative development of new technology.

Action of the European Community

Very close to each other in their economic environment, the countries of the European Community find themselves confronted by an acute environmental problem, particularly where water is concerned, given that several water-courses are common to several countries. European industry is, indeed, very concerned that there should be a common policy in this field, as firms in different countries become direct competitors in various markets. Although the situation is far from being the same in every country, the different themes of present co-operation can be underlined. In the framework of the community policy towards sound management of water resources, as an increasingly important economic asset, and to introduce qualitative preoccupations in the initiation and organization of the economic and social development, principles have been laid down, the most important of which are the following:

— the "polluter pays principle", which makes the polluter financially responsible for making good the environmental damage he has caused

— the principle of priority being given to a preventive policy, more rational and less costly than a curative policy

— the principle according to which each type of action undertaken should be addressed to the most appropriate geographical level (local, regional, national, community or international). More precisely, the Community will only become involved once action has been carried out at national level: in order to have full effect, it needs to be included in a much wider context; or when it concerns common interests (e.g. protection of waters); or when the adoption of different national measures would lead to widespread economic or social disruption.

Community policy assumes several functions in relation to that carried out by member states:

— it contributes to the definition of a joint concept of environmental policy, objectives and common principles

— it harmonizes these policies when, if taken in isolation, they are likely to create economic difficulties (obstacles to trade or unfair competition) or when they cannot be really effective because of the very nature of the problems addressed

— it provokes, by its very existence, incentive and impetus. It creates a structure of dialogue and enables regular meetings and exchanges of views and experiences between national representatives from all levels; civil servants, members of parliament, businessmen, ecologists, etc.

The "information agreement" signed in March 1973 plays an important role in this respect. The member states undertook, through that agreement, to submit to the Commission, at the discussion stage, projects for national regulations concerning the environment. This procedure therefore ensures that preliminary information is forthcoming. But the agreement goes above and beyond this because it gives the Commission the possiblity of requesting member states to postpone adoption of their projects until, rapidly, Community measures in the field concerned are proposed by the Commission and adopted by the Council. In this way, a sort of osmosis takes place between the different national regulations, through Community regulations aimed at disseminating, throughout the Community, national initiatives favourable to the environment.

— it provides the best geographical and political dimension to certain measures. This is the case for action aimed at reducing cross-border pollution, co-ordinating research, making the public aware of the problems. The same is true when measures taken to protect the environment affect international trade.

INDUSTRY'S FUTURE ROAD

THE TERMS USED above could lead one to believe that the situation has dramatically deteriorated in 1981 and that the fight for improved protection of natural resources has been lost for good. Fortunately, the industrial world has realized that it was on the way to great difficulties if no serious effort was made in this matter. In certain countries (Great Britain, the Netherlands, Japan), with the vigorous backing of government, spectacular progress has been made, at least in certain areas, by the introduction of policies that are sometimes radically different; in certain cases pressure was exercised just through the use of regulations imposing the respect of very strict standards, to be attained within varying deadlines; in other cases this policy was accompanied by important financial incentives in the form of both sanctions (pollution charges) and grants (investment aid). It is still too early to decide which of these two methods it is best to apply but it is absolutely certain that, if industry does not have the will to act, both will fail.

In a market economy, unwelcome distortions might take place if regulations were applied imposing considerable investment on the part of some companies, thus raising their costs, when the same charges were not levied on others; economic reality and the existing competitive market have to be taken into account when catching-up plans are defined and the necessary financial means have to be found at national level or, perhaps, at international level. In planned economies, individual costs are not normally taken into consideration. Over the last ten years considerable investment has been made in industry, often with success; however, what has been done represents the easiest part of the work. In most cases, firms have been content to carry out a curative policy using fairly rustic means, not technically sophisticated and costing relatively little: for example, traditional methods of biological effluent treatment are based on ideas and research some of which goes back to the beginning of the 20th century, with fewer later technical improvements, even though technology (automation, regulation, performance) has evolved. Given the current industrial situation regarding energy, raw materials and general economic trends, the following guidelines may serve for reference in defining a rational policy for industrial water use.

Prevention is better than cure

The creation of polluted industrial effluents usually results from a decision to use water in industry to evacuate unwanted waste. To reduce environmental pollution, once an effluent is created, one has to take out from the water what has just been added to it on purpose. This absurd process appears even more absurd when comparing an easy act (adding waste to the water) to a difficult, technically complex and very costly act (removing, from that same water, the waste, transformed, diluted but still present). A case-study in absurdity was that of a paper pulp mill which invested heavily in an enormous effluent treatment plant which it never used because the operating costs were too high to be added to the manufacturing costs. It was nevertheless in this way that industry, and administrations operated over several decades.

Reviewing the many unsuccessful experiences in the fight against pollution, an increasing number of people concerned realized that water pollution arose through mechanical evacuation of more or less useful but costly products and that it would be better not to mix them with water in the first place, in order not to be obliged to spend a lot of effort and good money to remove them. In this way, about ten years ago, was born the idea of:

—low- and non-waste technology
—clean technology.

This idea is fundamental for the future.

It is absolutely indispensable to focus research and development studies on a calling into question of industrial processes which have existed for years. All managers, specialists, engineers, must have as a key work theme the idea of *"technology without environmental nuisance"*. In those sectors where this idea has already been put into practice (canning factories, metal surfacing, paper mills), fascinating results have been obtained, sometimes by chance. *Existing industrial processes must be called into question at all levels*: production managers, manufacturers of production equipment and engineering designers must regroup and direct their efforts towards the same goal. Energy savings and "pollution savings" must be used as arguments and criteria for selection of production equipment. Some examples are worth citing:

—The mechanical transformation of steel billets, for the manufacture of sheet metal or household articles (stainless steel sink units, for example), requires that they be previously descaled to remove the iron oxide. This process traditionally consisted of carrying out an acid bath stage to dissolve the oxide, followed by numerous rinsings leading to considerable pollution by acid and iron salts and to extremely high pollution control costs. The introduction of shot-blasting to remove the iron-oxide layer completely replaced the use of water and hence its pollution.

—The canning of certain vegetables entails preliminary superficial peeling which was traditionally carried out using a chemical process to dissolve the peelings, the vegetable afterwards being thoroughly rinsed; the water used contained very large quantities of both chemical reagents (soda, generally very poisonous for aquatic life) and organic matter. In addition, purification of this water was technically very difficult and costly. The introduction of peeling using a technique of mechanical abrasion enabled all pollution to be avoided and, in addition, offered the possibility of using the residue for animal feed.

—The manufacture of ammonium nitrate, a widely-used fertilizer, gave rise to the production of fumes charged with nitrogen which were traditionally washed in a strong current of water which was afterwards discharged into the surface water, creating widespread poisonous pollution, practically impossible to purify. These fumes being produced at high temperature, it was decided to condense them in a condenser cooled externally by water, without any contact being possible; the condensates are recycled during the manufacturing process and there is no longer any water pollution.

These new technologies, which have hardly started to develop in all industrial sectors, must be actively encouraged; it should be noted that, in many cases, it is not a question of a "technological revolution" but the introduction of technical modifications following reflection by the manufacturer on the interest he has in using water for a purpose which is not obviously justified.

It is absolutely indispensable that all countries should be fully informed about these techniques. The initiatives taken by the United Nations are of great importance in this respect and should be followed by all governments. The future, to a great extent, lies in this course of action.

Do not throw out what is useful

These possibilities of industrial production without waste, and therefore without pollution, may be thought by some to be somewhat utopian. Another family of environmentally significant industrial processes are those which generate wastes that can be re-used, recycled and used as raw material for other products.

The possibility of recycling paper, glass, scrap iron, etc. will be just mentioned. These processes are well known and simply require the political will to carry them out. More important is the multitude of possible uses in everyday life, in agriculture, in industry, of a whole range of products commonly called "residues": serums from cheese-making plants, used as animal feed in the place of precious cereals; blood from slaughterhouses as a source of protein in all food, including that for human consumption; metallic hydroxide as a source of metal; spent lubricating oil which can be regenerated and thus re-used. In tropical regions fertilizer, animal feed and oil have been produced from waste-water from palm-oil extraction.

It is essential that industrial residues should no longer be considered as waste matter but as potential raw materials. Recycling what otherwise would be mixed with water is, in many cases, a technically feasible and cost-effective industrial operation.

Finding new waste disposal and effluent treatment methods

Given that not all problems can be solved by the introduction of clean technology or by total recycling of all residues, it will probably always be necessary to use more or less traditional waste treatment processes. If new methods cannot be found, those in existence must be improved, both from performance and profitability points of view.

For some years, hopes have been set in "biomass", which may one day deliver mankind from its energy straightjacket. Although some very interesting developments can be expected from this technology, particularly concerning anaerobic purification of waste-waters polluted by natural organic matter, with considerable energy saving, it nevertheless requires more in-depth study.

This idea increases in importance as energy costs rise. The industrial world is showing a distinct lack of enthusiasm for traditional energy-intensive technology. At the very moment when physical energy restrictions could be imposed, industry has a definite tendency to close down old fashioned effluent treatment plants before production units. The best way of saving energy is by not having a need for it.

Ensuring continuous plant operation

"Fish only die once". These four words sum up perfectly the difficult situation faced by the person responsible for water quality. In the same way as an aircraft out of fuel will fall 26,000 feet, causing the death of 200 to 300 people, so an industrial pollution control plant which is no longer working will cause such degradation of a watercourse that all previous efforts will be reduced to nought.

It is therefore necessary to obtain full value from the capital represented by existing plants. This is of the utmost importance. A company's effluent treatment plant is not a marginal installation but an essential tool, linked to production and therefore just as fragile, to which every attention should be given. The "clean technology" concept which links good production to pollution prevention, ensures almost total system security. In existing "end of the pipe" pollution control plants, such safety would require absolute reliability of the plant system, which cannot exist.

Correct siting

Improvement of technology, whether in pollution control or production, should not prevent deep reflection on the part of those responsible for the siting of industrial plants. A factory with high pollution risk must not be sited in the upper drainage area of a watercourse and even less on lakesides or in fairly closed and heavily populated bays; industry should be sited according to the capacity of the local aquatic environment to accept residual pollution while maintaining its balance. These factors concerning the impact on the physical environment must be weighed against the other socio-economic impacts of the creation of industrial activity. In the same way, it does not appear reasonable to site, on the banks of a small watercourse, an industrial unit consuming large quantities of water, although discharging little pollution, but causing gradual disappearance of the water resource: water recycling should be insisted on. In every country, whether water rich or not, environmental criteria for industrial siting must be one of the main considerations when dealing with questions of physical planning and regional development.

FINALLY, MAN

UNTIL NOW one of the main causes of the present situation has been ignored. If man, in industry or not, is unaware of the consequences which result from the undisciplined use of water and degradation in its quality, the battle is lost in advance. It is shocking that so little serious training is given in environmental matters; few engineers complete their studies with even a vague concept of what pollution is, except maybe something to amuse "poets" or underworked civil servants. Later it is difficult to modify their attitudes, and to convince them that pollution prevention is a significant element of industrial design and operations.

Increasingly, training in the saving of energy and raw materials represents an essential asset for the manufacturer, as a key to production and financial profitability. Training in the problems of environmental nuisances is practically unknown in the majority of countries. One of the key aspects in industry/water relations, therefore, is man.

Everything should be done to ensure that water becomes an important criterion in technical and economic considerations of all concerned with industry, whether private enterprise or states developing their economic structures. Men must be educated to have this idea of their environment and of its importance, failing which national or international policies will be doomed to failure. This is the hardest task of all and it is in front of us.

The Role of Water Resource Development in Industrial Development: A Perspective for Africa

Kenneth M. Strzepek

Research Scholar, International Institute for Applied
Systems Analysis (IIASA), Laxenburg, Austria

SYNOPSIS

The role of water resources in industrial development and the relationship of water to overall regional development is outlined, including the description of the direct and indirect benefits to industrial development of water use in other economic sectors. The concept of the river basin as the basis for integrated regional development is presented. The present and future role of water resources for industrial development in Africa is described. The international nature of Africa's water resources is illustrated and the potential of international river basin commissions or authorities as a catalyst for industrial development through integrated regional development for the efficient use and allocation of the region's water and other natural resources is proposed.

RÉSUMÉ

L'article met en évidence le rôle des ressources hydrauliques dans le développement industriel et le rapport entre l'eau et le développe-

ment régional total. Il décrit les avantages directs et indirects que le développement industriel peut tirer de l'usage de l'eau dans d'autres secteurs industriels. Il présente le concept de basin fluvial comme base d'un développement régional intégré. Il décrit également le rôle présent et futur des ressources hydrauliques dans le développement industriel de l'Afrique. Il montre la nature internationale des ressources hydrauliques africaines et propose la possibilité de commissions ou autorités internationales des basins fluveaux comme point de départ du développement industriel à travers le développement regional intégré pour l'utilization et l'allocation efficace des eaux régionales et des autres ressources naturelles.

RESUMEN

Se destaca el papel de los recursos hidráulicos en el desarrollo industrial así como la relación del agua con el desarrollo regional. Se describen los beneficios directos e indirectos para el desarrollo industrial con referencia al uso del agua en otros sectores económicos. Se presenta el concepto de cuenca de río como base para el desarrollo regional integrado. Se describe el papel del presente y el futuro de los aprovechamientos hidráulicos para el desarrollo industrial en Africa. Se ilustra la naturaleza internacional de los recursos hidráulicos del Africa y se sugiere el potencial de las comisiones o autoridades internacionales de cuencas de ríos como puntos de partida para el desarrollo industrial a través del desarrollo regional integrado con miras al uso y asignación eficaz de aguas regionales y otros recursos naturales.

INTRODUCTION

WATER CAN BECOME a constraint to industrial development when any of the following four conditions exist alone or in combination [1]:

(1) water inputs into important production processes are fixed in relation to output;

(2) water supplies are fixed or only capable of slow and/or costly expansion;
(3) supplies are rigidly allocated among uses over time;
(4) water is a controlling factor in human health and productivity.

This paper will outline the relationship between water and industrial development. The management of water resources to allow for the efficient allocation among all uses in balance with increased industrial development will be presented. The relationship and allocation of water from the perspective of African industrial development will be discussed. The role of integrated international river basin development will be discussed and examples from Africa will be presented.

THE ROLE OF WATER IN INDUSTRIAL DEVELOPMENT

THE NEED for water for industrial development is not limited to use of water in the production process. Water has a wide variety of activities in any economy and the interaction between the uses and industrial development occur directly and indirectly. Table 1 outlines these interactions. It is necessary, therefore, when planning water resource development for industrial development to look at an integrated development of all water resources activities. In the following sections the water use of each activity is described to give the reader a better understanding of the interaction outlined in Table 1.

INDUSTRIAL WATER DEMAND

WATER is but one factor input to industrial production. As such, there is no fixed water demand for each industry but rather a range of values due to the

Table 1. Interaction among Water Use Activities and Industrial Development

	Industrial	Waste Disposal	Hydropower	Agriculture	Navigation	Water Quality	Flood Control
Direct Benefit	x	x	x			x	x
Indirect Benefit		x	x	x	x	x	x

substitution effects of different technologies. Even with alternative technologies, some industries such as petro-chemical, pulp and paper, and steam electric power generation demand large quantities of water in their production processes. The demand and use of water in industry is a complex process which requires clarification. There are four parameters: water intake, consumptive use, effluent quantity and effluent quality, and two processes: production process and waste treatment that characterize the technical aspects of industrial water demand. This is schematically illustrated in Figure 1.

The intake water is the amount of water that is withdrawn from the waterbody that is needed for the production process to operate. A list of intake water demands for various industries and technologies appropriate for development in Africa are found in Table 2. In certain industries, the quality of water intake is important.

A certain portion of intake water is consumed during the production process; this is called consumptive use. Consumptive use may be the direct use in the output of the industrial product (e.g., beverage industry) or evaporated in a cooling process (e.g., petro-chemical industry). Table 3 lists typical consumptive use percentages of water intake for various industries.

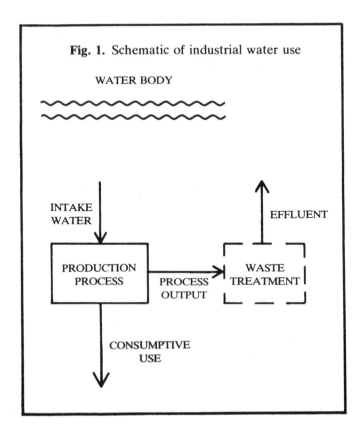

Fig. 1. Schematic of industrial water use

Table 2. Industrial water demand (range of demand for appropriate African technologies)*

Product	Unit of Production	Water Required per Unit (liters)
Food Products		
Canned Vegetables and Fruits	Ton	10 000 to 50 000
Meat Packing	Ton	8 000 to 30 000
Fish, Canning	Ton	16 000 to 20 000
Poultry	Ton	6 000 to 43 000
Milk	1 000 liters	2 000 to 5 000
Sugar	Ton of sugarbeets	2 000 to 20 000
Beer	1 000 liters	6 000 to 30 000
Pulp	Ton	50 000 to 150 000
Paper	Ton	200 000 to 1 000 000
Petroleum Refining	Ton of crude petroleum	10 000 to 30 000
Fertilizers	Ton (saltpetre)	270 000
Chemicals	Ton	10 000 to 500 000
Textiles		
Scouring, Wool	Ton	200 000 to 250 000
Dyeing and Finishing	Ton	60 000 to 200 000
Milling	Ton	50 000 to 350 000
Mining	Ton	1 000 to 12 000
Iron and Steel	Ton	10 000 to 50 000
Electric Power	Kilowatt-Hour	200
Automobiles	Ton	38 000

* Adapted from the Department of Economic and Social Affairs, United Nations, 1969.

The remaining intake water of the consumptive use plus any liquidified by-products from other inputs to the production process are combined into process waste. If process waste is not treated it becomes directly industrial effluent and is discharged to a receiving waterbody. Process waste is often passed through a waste treatment process before being discharged to the receiving waterbody. The effluent then is the output of the waste treatment process and can vary in quantity and quality (content of pollution) depending upon the technology of treatment. Table 4 is a list of the range of biological and chemical effluents from various industries to demonstrate their relative pollution potential.

As demonstrated above, when discussing industrial water use, one must look at the entire system and not focus on any one single parameter as a measure of industrial water demand. When locating more than one industry on a waterbody, it requires a careful planning of the effect of one industry effluent on the intake

Table 3. Percentage of water intake consumed
by selected industries in the United States

Industry	% Consumption of Intake Water
Automobile	6.2
Beet Sugar	10.5
Chemicals	5.9
Coal Preparation	18.2
Corn & Wheat Milling	20.6
Distillery	10.4
Food Processing	33.6
Machinery	21.4
Meat	3.2
Petroleum	7.2
Poultry Processing	5.3
Pulp & Paper	4.3
Salt	27.6
Soap & Detergents	8.5
Steel	7.3
Sugar Cane	15.9
Textiles	6.7

Source: National Association of Manufacturers, 1959.

Table 4. Bio-chemical pollution content of
various industry effluents

Source of Waste	5-Day, 20°C BOD Mg/liter
Beet Sugar Refining	450 – 2 000
Brewery	500 – 1 200
Cannery	300 – 4 000
Meat Packing	600 – 2 000
Milk Processing	300 – 2 000
Pulp and Paper	16 000 – 25 000
Tannery	500 – 5 000
Textiles	
Cotton Processing	50 – 1 750
Wool Scouring	200 – 10 000

Source: McGauhey, *Engineering Management of Water
Quality*, McGraw-Hill, 1968.

water of another industry. This requires in many cases the planning of industrial water use on a regional basis rather than on industry-by-industry basis, to allow for industry-environment and industry-interaction to be analyzed and their harmful effects minimized to make full utilization of the water resources of a region for industrial development.

An example of the need to consider the entire industrial water system is the Steam Electric Industry (Fossil Fuel or Nuclear). For a 500 megawatt power station, the water intake requirement for once-through cooling is 227,000 liters per second, but the consumptive use is only 2770 liters per second, one per cent of water intake. The effluent that is discharged has little biological or chemical pollution since it was used only for cooling but the effluent is approximately 10°C hotter than the intake water passing through the cooling process. This large amount of heated water is discharged to a waterbody causing thermal pollution. Thermal pollution can have both negative and positive effects to a water ecology and likewise may enhance or decrease the possible use for other industries. If the thermal pollution was found to be detrimental or the large volume of intake water needed was not available, it is possible to install cooling towers or a cooling pond which recycles the water in the cooling process. This water intake is reduced to approximately 2% of once-through cooling and the effluent is reduced to about 1% of once-through cooling, but is at a higher temperature. This demonstrates the effect of alternative technologies; however, the addition of cooling towers or ponds add about 10% to the capital cost of the plant and require higher operating costs.

This example has shown that one needs to review the entire system of industrial water use as opposed to focusing on any one parameter of water use which would have given a distorted view, possibly leading to a situation constraining rather than enhancing further industrial development.

Water Disposal

Waterbodies have a natural ability to assimilate waste material from industrial processes through a self-purification procedure. However, each waterbody has a limit to the amount of waste that it can accept before the self-purification mechanism becomes overloaded. In this event, the quality of the waterbody begins to degrade and loses the ability to perform other functions as listed in Table 1, thus limiting the amount of industrial development. In some cases, the amount of industrial use of the water for disposal can increase, if the industrial effluents are first treated by a waste treatment process thus reducing the quantity or concentration of pollutant in the effluent, and allowing for more effluents in total.

If the water quality due to waste disposal degrades and loses the ability to perform certain functions, it can have a direct effect upon industrial development as will be outlined below.

Hydropower

Water use for hydropower can be viewed as a direct industrial use as part of the electric power industry, or as an indirect use as part of an essential infra-structure necessary for industrial development. In either case, water for hydropower use has some special characteristics.

Hydropower does not consume water directly in the generation of electricity. However, if an artificial reservoir is created to store water for power generation there can be an increase in evaporation due to the large surface area of the reservoir. This is particularly a problem in arid regions. For example in Egypt, 10% of the average yearly flow of the Nile River past Aswan evaporates from the Lake Nasser Reservoir behind the High Aswan Dam. Most hydropower is used as "peaking power" on a daily basis since fossil plants are expensive to start and stop, and cannot respond as efficiently as hydropower to changes in demand. However, on a seasonal or annual basis, it is beneficial to the electrical power system output when the releases of water are as uniform as possible over the year. This unified release will provide firm daily "peaking capacity power" to the electric power system. This firm peaking capacity will reduce the need for fossil plant capacity to make up the daily load when the reservoir releases are low. However, for multipurpose reservoirs, uniform releases are not consistent with other uses such as agriculture and flood control, and conflict results and release rules must be developed that weight the benefits of each purpose to the regional development. An example for the High Aswan Dam is given in [2].

Agricultural Water Use

Agricultural water use is an indirect benefit to industrial development. In many strategies for African industrial development, agro-industry is stressed for areas where irrigated agriculture is needed. Water is an important input then, to provide sufficient agricultural production as an input to industry. Secondly, if the output of irrigated agriculture is exported, the foreign exchange generated will be important to allow for the importation of capital goods necessary for industrial development. The increased income generated by increased agricultural production will also provide a greater market for industrial products.

Navigation

The use of water for navigation is an indirect benefit for industrial development. Navigation is part of the transportation infrastructure so important to development. It can be substituted by rail or truck but it allows for cheap transport of bulk commodities. This is important to keep costs down on industrial inputs.

Municipal Water Use

Municipal water supply is part of the infrastructure necessary to foster industrial development. The direct benefit of a good municipal supply system is that for small industries, the municipal supply system is the source of water intake for industrial production. As industries get larger, they tend to develop their own water supplies due to lower costs. Thus, a good municipal water system with low water rates can attract industrial development. Secondly, industrial development requires a viable labour force. A good municipal supply which is related to better public health will attract good workers and increase their efficiency through better health leading to increased industrial production.

Water Quality

Water is sometimes used as a measure of increasing the self-purification potential of waterbodies. By increasing flow, it allows for the water quality to be improved. A high water quality level is important for uses such as municipal supply, fishery, and recreation, which are indirect benefits to industrial development.

Flood Control

The damage caused to life and property each year as a result of floods is enormous. With many of the best locations for industrial development in river valleys near to the source of water and main transport routes, it becomes important to protect these large investments from floods. At the same time, labour's reaction of living in a high risk flood zone may make it hard for industry to attract good and adequate labour. How these activities relate to the industrial development of Africa will be presented in the next section.

The Link Between Industrial Development and Water in Africa

In a report on long-term development strategies for the Sahel-Sudan area of West Africa [3], the following statements were made about the link between water and industrial development in West African nations:

Chad: "The possibility of constructing a hydroelectric power plant . . . in southwest Chad . . . is listed in the development plan as essential to industrialization."

Mali: "There is also a plan to establish an iron and steel works, but depends on a firm agreement with neighboring countries and the *building of the barrage (dam)* at Gorena."

Mauritania: "Manufacturing industry is limited because of the small
                   domestic market, lack of transport, scarcity of raw
                   material, *deficient supply of water* and electric power . . ."
                   "*Insufficient water* is one of the serious problems facing the
                   towns and villages in Mauritania."
Niger: "*Scarcity of water resources* is the greatest impediment to
                   economic development."
Senegal: "River traffic on the Senegal River into Mali [is limited]
                   from July to September." [Due to low flows.]
Upper Volta: "Industrial activity in Upper Volta has also been affected
                   by the limitations of *natural resources* and skilled labour."

The above statements show how lack of adequate water resources can limit
industrial development. Following, a few African examples of how water resources
development directly contributes to industrial development will be given.

(1) Egypt: The completion of the High Aswan Dam and hydropower station
    provided conditions for increased industrial development in Egypt. With a
    cheap source of electricity, fertilizer and aluminium industries, both heavy
    electrical users, were established near Aswan; irrigated cotton production
    was able to continue (despite growing demand for foodstuffs) to supply raw
    materials for the textile industry; navigation was available year round from
    the Mediterranean to Aswan; and a fishery industry has developed in the
    Lake Nasser reservoir.
(2) Ghana: The Volta Dam Project in 1969 provided enough hydroelectric
    power to allow the construction of a huge aluminium factory and
    aluminium smelter in Ghana as well as export power to Togo and Benin to
    aid in their infrastructure development [4].
(3) Zambia/Zimbabwe: The Kariba Dam and power plant on the Zambezi
    River (first stage 1960) allowed expansion of copper mining and refining in
    Zambia; growth of manufacturing in Zimbabwe and the construction of an
    electrolyte ferrochrome plant, possible only with cheap power from Kariba
    [4]. Cheap hydropower alone is not sufficient for industrial development.
    The Owen Falls Hydroelectric Project is an example.
(4) Uganda: When the Owen Falls Project was completed in 1954, it was not
    until 1957 that a copper smelter was established. The small industries which
    comprised most of Uganda's growth were not power-oriented and widely
    dispersed. Thus, it was necessary to make a 50 year agreement with Kenya
    to export electricity to make the project financially stable [1].

As these last examples have shown, energy is an important input to
industrial growth. With current high cost of oil and the lack of coal in Africa, the
full utilization of African hydroelectric potential is necessary. The greatest
hydroelectric potential in Africa is in Zaire (500 billion Kilowatt hours annually—
KwhA); Angola (200 billion KwhA); Malagasy Republic (100 billion KwhA); and
Cameroon (100 billion KwhA). Congo, Central African Republic, Gabon, and

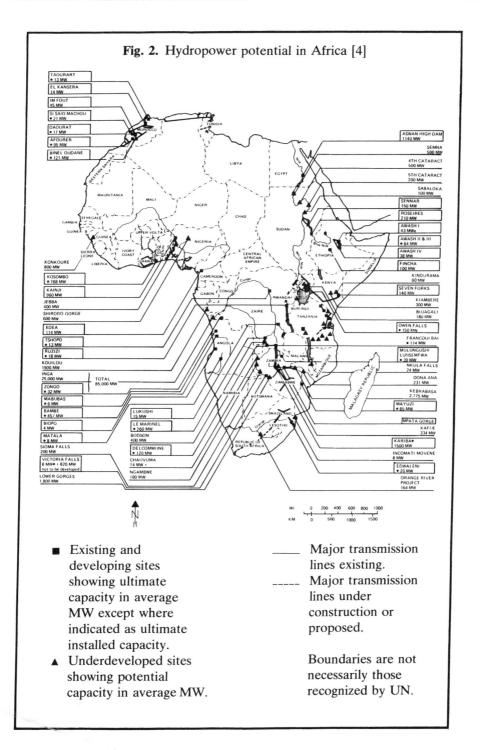

Fig. 2. Hydropower potential in Africa [4]

■ Existing and developing sites showing ultimate capacity in average MW except where indicated as ultimate installed capacity.

▲ Underdeveloped sites showing potential capacity in average MW.

_____ Major transmission lines existing.

----- Major transmission lines under construction or proposed.

Boundaries are not necessarily those recognized by UN.

Liberia also have significant potential [4]. Figure 2 shows the location of major hydropower sites in Africa.

Large scale irrigation schemes can prove quite successful in arid and semi-arid regions in Africa. Egyptian agriculture and the Gezira scheme in Sudan have proven successful. Other schemes successful to varying degrees are the Office du Niger scheme in Mali; the Richard Todd scheme in Senegal [4]; the Accra Plans Project in Ghana; the Kafue Flats in Zambia; and the Cunene River scheme in Namibia [4, 5]. *Village Water Supply* [6] and *Drawers of Water* [7] are both good references for the role of municipal water supply to public health and productivity in Africa.

The important aspect about water quality management in Africa is the false notion that environmental protection is only a luxury affordable by the developed nations. The costs of environmental degradation are enormous and may not reveal themselves till many years later, when it is too late to address the problem. This is quite true of groundwater contamination, and groundwater is the main source of water in many parts of Africa. An important feature of maintaining environmental quality at the initial stage of industrial development is that it is vastly cheaper to provide environmental protection in the construction stage than to retrofit waste treatment after production is underway. Africa is in a unique position to be able to learn from the mistakes of the developed nations and benefit from the new environmental protection technologies that have been recently developed. The question is not whether Africans can afford to protect the environment, but whether they can afford not to.

The water resources uses that have been outlined above do not exist independent of each other, but are rather linked in complex physical, economic, and political networks. Thus, when analyzing industrial water use, one must analyze all the links in an integrated fashion. The next section will provide a mechanism for that type of analysis.

THE ROLE OF INTERNATIONAL BASIN PLANNING IN AFRICAN INDUSTRIAL DEVELOPMENT

THE DEMAND for industrial water use cannot be analyzed separately from the other activities of water use due to the interaction that takes place within the waterbody, economy, and across political borders. Therefore, industrial water demand must be analyzed systematically within a regional framework. Since water is the key to the analysis, the most appropriate regional framework is the river basin or lake basin. (The river basin will be discussed in detail, but the discussion is equally applicable to lake systems.) The river basin includes the area into which water falls and through which water drains, generally flowing to a common terminal point. Thus, the implications of development can be traced throughout the basin, indicating sources of conflict and collective opportunity [8]. Many political institutions share jurisdiction over river basins, nations, provinces, municipalities.

A river basin that lies within the territories of two or more nations is called an international river basin. Although each country has control over the resources flowing within its territory, (subject to general rules of international law), a nation cannot exercise such control until the water reaches its territory; and control is relinquished once these waters leave its territory [8]. Conflict over the control of international water is a major issue in international affairs. "Few issues between nations and people generate greater controversy and, on occasion, even hostility, than those involving competing interests in the use of water of international rivers" [9].

Africa contains 64 first-order (linked directly to the sea or to inland lakes) international drainage basins [10]. With this in mind, water for African industrial development is an international river basin planning problem.

The need exists for an international agency such as the UN or its branch agencies, to aid in the efficient utilization of international water resources. A few examples of UN participation in this area are found in References 8 and 11, which discuss a UNDP project for the allocation of the waters of the Vardar/Axios rivers between Yugoslavia and Greece, and Reference 5, which presents the WMO study of the hydrometeorology of the ten-nation Nile basin. The question arises as to how to analyze the water reservoirs in this complex setting.

Analysis of International River Basins

The international river basin is such a complex physical, economical, and political system, that many times, standard engineering analysis is not sufficient to analyze the system interactions. This problem requires a modern system analysis approach that can address the interactions between economic, political, and hydrologic systems [12].

References 8 and 11 present state-of-the-art water resource system analysis techniques for the analysis of an international river basin. These methods address the problems of variation in streamflow, economic costs and benefits and constraints imposed by international agreements. Not all techniques are directly transferable from one basin to another and thus methods must be chosen or developed that are appropriate for the major problems confronting a river basin.

Need for International Cooperation

In the development of water resources for African industrial development, an agency such as UNIDO, or the Economic Community for Africa (ECA), should play a major role in developing and cataloging a method for the planning of international multipurpose river basin systems. It is also essential that an agency coordinating African industrial development cooperate with the UN agencies that deal with the other water resource activities, such as the FAO, the UNEP, the UNDP, the WMO, and the WHO, to develop the proper institutional framework in which to perform effective river basin planning. There exists a great need to develop international commissions for the planning of international rivers, such as the Permanent Joint Technical Committee for the Nile (Sudan–Egypt); the four-nation Inter-State Committee for the Senegal River; the Niger River Basin Development Committee; and the Lake Chad Basin Commission, for example. Each river basin has specific hydrologic, economic, and political problems which are best addressed by the nations involved, using their expertise on local hydrology, institutions, and economics. It is important to develop extensive cooperation and information transfer among member nations. This communication will help legitimize any recommendations that result from such a commission as truly the best for the development of the basin as a whole. In this way, all nations will benefit from the optimal utilization of a natural resource, such as water.

The planning of any river basin is a major undertaking requiring a large well-trained inter-disciplinary team. The efforts required in collecting data, developing methods of analysis and formulating development scenarios to be analyzed are great. With such a task, it is important that as much as possible be done to foster the transfer of information and technologies about river basin planning between the various river basin commissions. This exchange of information will allow planners to learn from successes and failures, and to avoid the unnecessary duplication by other commissions of existing tools, expecially when the size of the task is great and there are very few skilled personnel. It is also advisable to use international experts whenever needed, to help train and advise river basin commissions on the new and powerful tool for river basin planning. These international experts can also play an important role as an impartial observer to avoid any single national domination in the planning process.

Lepawsky [13] stresses the need of international experts in international river basin planning: "What cannot be accomplished solely by national statesmen in the realm of (international) river basin development may yet be wrought by international administrators . . . , and by a new breed of professional and technical experts concerned with the planning and development of international river resources."

CONCLUSION

THIS PAPER has attempted to show the important link between industrial development and water resources development. It is not meant to imply that water alone is responsible for development, but rather that together with the proper economic, political, and social conditions, it is an essential ingredient to the process. It has shown the importance of water in African industrial development and the need to analyze water resources development for industrial use in a systematic regional framework. It was illustrated that for Africa, the international river basin was the most important regional framework for which water resources planning should take place. The need to develop international commissions for systematic river basin planning was stressed. The role of water resources in the economic development of Africa has a multi-objective, multi-purpose character. The interaction between the various activities of water resources can best be analyzed at the river basin level. It is at this level that the best opportunity exists for the efficient allocation of water resources between the different sections of the economy to foster balance of economic growth.

References

1. Howe, C.W. (1978) The effects of water resources development on economic growth: the conditions for success. In: *Water in a Developing World*, edited by A.E. Utton and L. Teclaff. Boulder, CO: Westview Press.
2. Alarcon, L.F., and Marks, D.H. (1980) A stochastic dynamic programming model for the operation of the High Aswan Dam. *Ralph M. Parsons Technical Report No. 246.* Cambridge, MA: Massachusetts Institute of Technology.
3. Seifert, W.W., and Kamvany, N.M. (1974) A framework for evaluating long-term development strategies for the Sahel-Sudan area. Cambridge, MA: *Interim Report, Centre for Policy Alternative*, Massachusetts Institute of Technology.
4. Kamarck, A.M. (1972) *The economics of African development.* New York, NY: Praeger Publishers.
5. Balek, J. (1977) *Hydrology and water resources in tropical Africa.* Amsterdam: Elsevier Scientific Publishing Company.
6. Saunders, R.J., and Warford, J.J. (1976) *Village water supply: economics and policy in the developing world.* Cambridge, MA, Johns Hopkins University Press.
7. White, G.F., Bradley, D.J. and White, A.V. (1962) *Drawers of water: domestic water use in East Africa.* Chicago, ILL: University of Chicago Press.
8. Stone, P.J. (1977) A methodology to provide analytical information for coordinated water resource use in international river basin development. *Unpublished Ph.D. Thesis*, Department of Civil Engineering, Massachusetts Institute of Technology, Cambridge, MA.
9. Garretson, A.H., Hayton, R.D. and Olmstead, C.J., editors. (1967) *The law of international drainage basins.* New York, NY: Oceana Publications.
10. Sand, P. (1973) Development of international water law in the Lake Chad basin. In: *Water for the Human Environment*, edited by V.T. Chow, S.C. Csallany, R.J. Kriszek, and H.C. Preul.
11. Strzepek, K.M., and Lenton, R.L. (1978) Analysis of multipurpose river basin systems: guidelines for simulation modeling. Cambridge, MA: *Ralph M. Parsons Technical Report No. 236*, Massachusetts Institute of Technology.
12. Miser, H.J. (1980) *What is systems analysis?* PP-80-09. Laxenburg, Austria: International Institute for Applied Systems Analysis.
13. Lepawsky, A. (1963) *International development of river resources.* International Affairs 39: 533–550.

Systems Approach to Planning Interplant Water Management in Industry

L. Kelemen

Head of Research Section, Research Centre for Water Resources "VITUKI", Budapest, Hungary

SYNOPSIS

The fundamental requirement which any interplant water management system is expected to meet is that water of the volume, quality and pressure required for the water using processes should be available reliably and efficiently at specific points and times. The two basic (flow-through and recirculation) models of supply can be connected to each other parallel, or in series. The alternative systems composed of the basic models are examined by the flow-rate, quality and pressure equations. The same equations form the mathematical models for formulating the computer programmes of the systems. The balance equations for the two basic models are derived.

RÉSUMÉ

L'exigence fondamentale envers le système d'aménagement en eaux d'une usine industrielle est d'assurer en lieu et en temps bien determinés la quantité, qualité et pression par une solution optimale et fiable pour les besoins des processus nécessitant l'eau. La solution possible consiste d'employer l'un des deux modèles de base de l'utilization d'eau (traversant ou recirculatif) et pour chacun, d'utiliser l'un des deux méthodes de raccordement [parallèle ou successif]. Les différentes variations de systéme établies à partir des modèles de base peuvent être éxaminées à l'aide des équations quantitatives, qualitatives et d'équilibre de pression. Ces équations peuvent servir également comme base pour les programmes d'ordinateur des variations. L'étude fournit une analyse des équations d'équilibre pour les deux modèles de base de l'utilisation d'eau.

RESUMEN

El requísito básico, al que debe responder el suministro de agua de una planta industrial es que el agua pedida para los procesos industriales debe ser garantizada en cantidad, en calidad y con la presión deseada, en punto y tiempo definido, con seguridad de servicio y con la solución óptima. La solución es posible con ayuda de dos modelos básicos [con agua pasada y con agua recirculada] y cada uno con dos tipos de conexiones [paralela y en sucesión]. Los tipos diferentes de las sistemas formados de los modelos básicos pueden ser investigados con ayuda de ecuaciones de equilíbrio referentes a la calidad, cantidad y presión del agua. Estas ecuaciones dan la base del modelo matemático necesário para la programación por computadora. El estudio hace conocer las ecuaciones de equilibrio para los dos modelos básicos de suministro de agua.

INTRODUCTION

VIEWED ON THE AVERAGE, the water resources of Hungary would be sufficient to meet the present and anticipated future demands, were it not for the fact that over 90 per cent of these supplies are available along the three major rivers, namely the Danube, Tisza and Dráva. This is the reason why the supplies are short in several regions. The water demands of advanced agricultural production, accelerating rates of industrial development and rising living standards of the population have exhausted the local supplies in several regions already. Moreover, unless the current techniques of using water are improved, the supplies needed for the development of industry, or any other sector of economy will be impossible to procure at reasonable cost in the majority of the regions. Of the total withdrawal from natural supplies by all sectors of economy, the share of industry is almost 60 per cent (3 thousand million m^3/year) and three-quarters of the pollutants detrimental to water are discharged by industrial plants to the recipient streams and lakes. A development programme has therefore been initiated to achieve the balance of demands and supplies over long perspectives. The two main objectives of the programme are as follows:

    a. Controlling the runoff of surface waters to augment the supplies (storage) and the distribution thereof by regional networks (long-distance pipe-lines).

    b. Controlling the demands (reduction of the demands, or at least slowing down considerably their growth rate).

Economic opportunities for effectively controlling withdrawals from supplies and discharges of harmful pollutants exist primarily in the sector of the economy using the largest volumes of water, namely industry. In the overwhelming majority of industrial plants, no more than 3 to 5 per cent of the total technological water demand must, or can economically be met from freshwater resources. (On the average for the entire industrial sector this proportion is estimated at 8–10%.) The present freshwater consumption of industry in Hungary is, however, 43 to 45 per cent on average and 28 to 30 per cent if the power industry is neglected.

Evidently, the rate of reuse at industrial plants is a question of economics alone, as long as fresh water can be procured at reasonable costs. Beyond this limit, reuse becomes an emergency measure, i.e., the plant must be kept operating with the fresh water supply that can be made available, insofar as this solution remains at all within the margin of profitability. Another possibility consists of reducing the overall water demand of the individual operations (or eliminating the demand entirely) by modifying the technology of production.

Even greater attention must be devoted to water pollution caused by industry. The losses resulting therefrom are in the majority of cases heavier than those due to wasteful consumption. This is why the controls imposed upon discharge of industrial wastes to the recipients present a much more severe constraint than the former, the potential solutions requiring often considerable engineering efforts and high costs (treatment of wastewaters, modification of production technologies, etc.). Rational designs for interplant water management systems in industry will be examined subsequently.

DESIGNING RATIONAL WATER MANAGEMENT SYSTEMS FOR INDUSTRIAL PLANTS

THE FUNDAMENTAL requirement which any interplant water management system is expected to satisfy is that water of the volume, quality and pressure required for the water using processes of the plant should be available reliably at specific points and times. It should ensure, moreover, the safe removal of the effluents produced. At the same time, the system should be efficient from the engineering and economic aspects alike.

The first step of designing consists of checking the water demands specified by the technologist for their quantity and quality, further of estimating the pollutant emission by each of the individual water using operations and equipment performing these, taking into account all potential conditions of operation. In the next step the supplies available in the surroundings of the proposed plant site should be explored, identifying their geographical position, quantity, quality and water level elevation. The potential recipients should also be explored for their position, actual level of pollution and the amount of pollutants that may be discharged into them without violating the relevant quality criteria. Once reliable figures have been established on the demands and effluent parameters pertaining to different operating conditions of the plant, further with accurate information available on environmental criteria and particulars, work can be started on designing the interplant water management system. The alternative supplies to the individual consumption points within the plant are determined by examining the flow-, quality- and pressure balances for the two basic water management models adopted for industrial plants, viz.

—the open (flow-through) system and
—the closed (recirculation) system.

Both basic water management models can be connected to each other, either parallel or in series.

The symbols used in the figures are explained as follows:

Q_F freshwater demand (m³/h)
Q_P compensation water demand (m³/h)
Q_T total technological water demand (m³/h)
Q_H total flow used (m³/h)
Q_R flow recirculated (m³/h)
Q'_{Hh} reuse from interplant effluent (m³/h)
Q''_{Hh} reuse from external effluent (m³/h)
Q_L effluent from the recycling circle (m³/h)
Q_{Sz} plant effluent (wastewater discharge) (m³/h)
Q_{Vp} evaporation from the system (m³/h)
Q_V total loss from the system (m³/h)
Sz_n pollutants entering and leaving the system (kg/h)
Sz_{ki} permissible water pollutant discharge from the plant (kg/h)

K_n symbol of water and wastewater treatment facilities
c_n pollutant concentration (mg/l)
p_n water pressure (Pa, metre water column, El. above sea level)

Balance analysis of open (flow-through) water management model (ref. Fig. 1)

The magnitude, quality and pressure of the water demand needed for the production technology:

$$Q_T, c_T, p_T$$

The magnitude and quality of the supplies available in the area:

$$Q, c, p$$

where $Q \geqslant Q_T$, $c = c_F$, $p = p_T$.

The amount of pollutants (Sz_1) to be removed at the fresh water treatment plant K_1 is thus

$$\text{if } c_F > c_T$$

$$Sz_1 = Q_F(c_F - c_T)$$

$$Q_F \cong Q_T$$

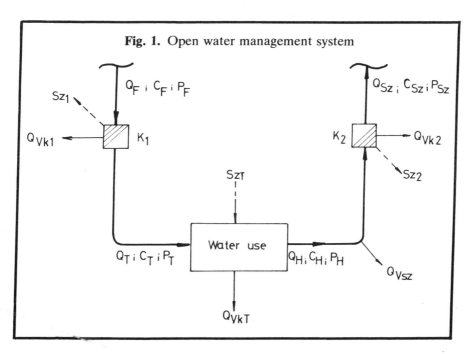

Fig. 1. Open water management system

The amount of pollutant which the recipient is capable of assimilating

$$Sz_{ki} = Q_{sz}c_{sz}$$

The amount of pollutant which must be removed by treatment

$$Sz_2 \cong Q_Tc_T + Sz_T - Q_{sz}c_{sz} = Q_H(c_H - c_{Sz})$$

The water losses caused by using the water

$$\Sigma Q_V = Q_F - Q_{Sz} = Q_{V_1} + Q_{V_T} + Q_{V_2}$$

The balance analysis for two, or more open water management systems connected in series is performed in a similar manner following logically the same approach.

Balance analysis of a closed (recirculation) water management model (ref. Fig. 2)

The parameters of the water demand needed for the production technology are

$$Q_T, c_T, p_T$$

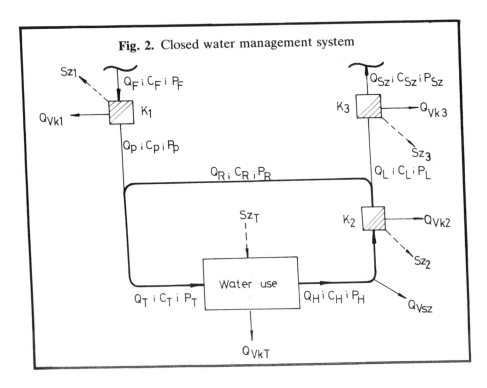

Fig. 2. Closed water management system

The magnitude, quality and pressure of the freshwater supplies available in the area:

$$Q, c, p$$

where $Q < Q_T$, $Q \geqslant Q_F$, $c = c_F$, $p = p_F$.

The amount of pollutants which the recipient is capable of assimilating

$$Sz_{ki} = Q_{sz}c_{sz}$$

The kind of treatment (K_1), the flow of compensation water (Q_p), the kind of effluent (wastewater) treatment (K_2, K_3, K_4) and the effluent release (Q_L) in the case of recirculation can be determined by examining the balance conditions.

Consider thus the flow and water quality balance conditions of the system. The *flow balance* in the recirculation loop is

$$Q_p = \Sigma Q_{V_R} + Q_L$$

The water quality balance (by polluting component) is

$$Q_p c_p + Sz_T = (\Sigma Q_{V_R} - Q_{V_p})c_R + Q_L c_R + Sz_2$$

Once the basic criterion Sz_T is established, the water losses are determined, further the water and wastewater treatment technologies are decided upon, the values of Q_V, Sz_n and c are known. The two unknowns Q_p and Q_L can be found from the two balance equations.

If $Q_p + Q_{V_1} = Q_F$ and $Q_F > Q$, then it is necessary to reduce Q_p, which can be achieved by improving the quality of compensation water, thus the level of water treatment must be raised and this will decrease Q_L at the same time.

If $Q_L c_L > Q_{sz}c_{sz}$ then additional wastewater treatment (K_3) must be introduced, or Q_L, Q_P and c_p must be reduced. A third alternative is to reduce Sz_T (changing the technology of water use).

General model of interplant water management system

By the different combinations of the following parameters, any particular water management system model can be derived from the general system illustrated in Fig. 3.

With $Q_R = 0$ and $Q_{Hh} = 0$—open system
With $Q_R = 0$ and $Q'_{Hh1} = A$ m³/h—series-connected system
With $Q_R = A$ m³/h and $Q'_{Hh1} = 0$—recirculation system
With $Q_R = A$ m³/h   and $Q'_{Hh1} = B$ m³/h—series-connected   recirculation system.

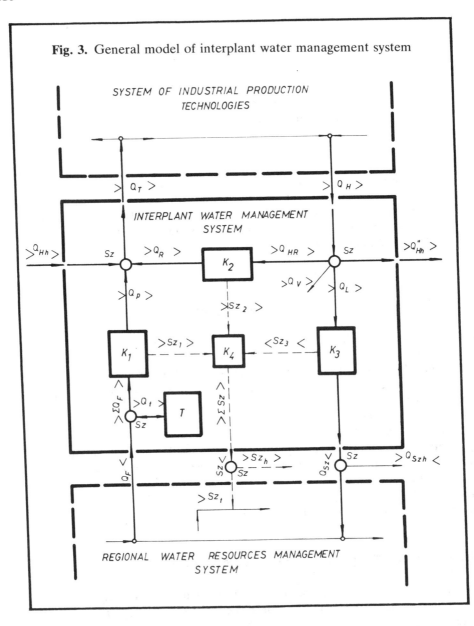

Fig. 3. General model of interplant water management system

The operation of the interplant water management system can be represented visually by indicating the elements and subsystems, as well as the technological-functional relations thereof. The pattern of the system thus produced is the ikonographic model thereof. By describing the interrelations between the elements of the resulting model (Fig. 3) further the effects of various outputs and inputs with the help of exact, or approximate mathematical expressions, i.e., by describing the operation of the system in analytical terms, the mathematical model of the system is obtained.

The balance equations of pressure conditions can also be written with the help of the corresponding familiar relationships.

The approach outlined in the foregoing is suited to the examination of interrelations between the elements of interplant water management models and to select the model applicable in particular cases.

The water management system in most industrial plants, particularly in the large ones, is composed of several of the aforementioned basic water management models in different parallel, or series arrangements, which are in simple, or multiple functional connection with each other.

OPTIMIZATION OF INTERPLANT WATER MANAGEMENT SYSTEMS

OWING TO THE WIDE engineering varieties of the elements and subsystems composing the water management system, as well as to the wide range of requirements imposed on the production technological system of the consumer, to the broad spectrum of different supplies and water quality criteria of the regional system, a number of potential alternatives are conceivable for the interplant water management system of an industrial plant. Of these, the most efficient can be selected by setting a definite objective, e.g., the water demand of a production technology must be met in a reliable manner and at the lowest possible cost

—with the lowest freshwater demand, or

—with the lowest power consumption, or

—with the lowest pollutant discharge, etc.

The target function to be optimized is in symbolic form:

$$K_V + K_a + K_{Tt} \to \text{minimum}$$

under the constraints

$$Q_{T\min} \leq Q_T \leq Q_{T\max}$$

$$Q_F \leq Q_K$$

$$Q_{Sz} c_{Sz} \leq Sz_{e1}$$

$$I_{Sz} \leq Sz_{e2}$$

Notation:

Sz_{e1} the amount of pollutants that can be discharged to the recipient with the waste water Q_{Sz}

Sz_{e2} the amount of pollutants that can be disposed of in the environment with the sludge I_{Sz}

K_V the total cost associated with the freshwater and the effluent

K_{Cs} the total cost associated with the waste water and the sludge

K_{Tt} the additional cost of modifying the production technology for improved
         water management.
         A graphical plot of the symbolic cost function of the system is shown in Fig.
4. The symbols used in Fig. 4 are explained as follows:
a_1, a_2 Construction costs of water supply-sewerage for the same plant at
         different sites
b additional costs of modifying the production technology and equipment
         for improved water management, as well as for water reuses.

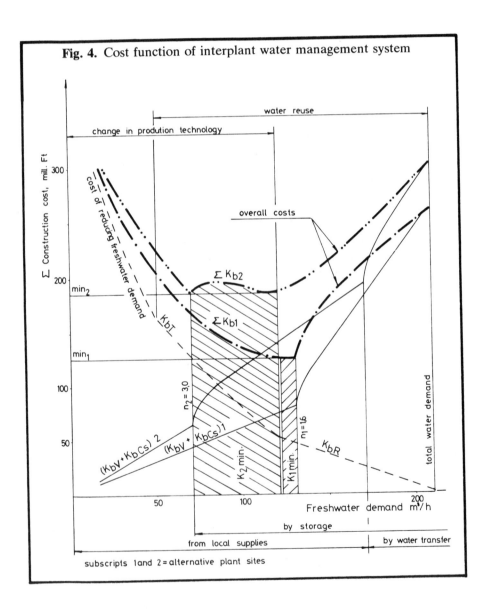

Fig. 4. Cost function of interplant water management system

Rational and more careful management of water supplies has become a problem of growing economic importance in Hungary. Several industrial regions face already serious water shortages and pollution increases rapidly in the main sources of supply, viz. in the surface waters. Since industries play a decisive role in water management, effective controls on water demands and water pollution in this field present a key problem. The systems approach outlined in the foregoing to water management planning for industrial plants would offer the possibility of effective control at least in the case of new plants, or such contemplated for expansion, reconstruction or modernization.

Multiobjective Decision-making as a Tool for Industrial Water Management

Istvan Bogardi
*Senior Scientific Researcher, Mining Development
Institute, Budapest, Hungary,*

and

Lucien Duckstein and Martin Fogel
Professors, University of Arizona, Tucson, Arizona, USA

SYNOPSIS

*Two practical applications of multiobjective decision making
(MODM) to regional industrial water management are presented.
Regional development often results in conflicting objectives such as
the satisfaction of various water requirements (industrial, agricultural and domestic) under limited resources or else, the maximiza-
tion of economic benefits versus minimization of environmental
disruption caused by industry. When the above objectives are
measured in non-commensurate units, MODM provides an approach to select the "best" industrial water management scheme.
The two case studies illustrating the methodology are as follows:*

1. *The Eocene region in Hungary has considerable industrial
   potential (mining and metallurgy). However, the regional
   water resources system has to satisfy not only industrial water
   demands but also domestic water requirements and
   environmental objectives. Among various available MODM
   techniques, compromise programming has been used to find
   the most satisfactory solution.*
2. *The Bakony region in Hungary has wide potential for*

mining, agriculture and tourism. The regional water resources system, principally a karstic aquifer, has to satisfy conflicting interests (industrial, environmental). MODM has again been applied to find a trade-off.

RÉSUMÉ

La décision multicritère [DMC] est appliquée à deux cas d'espèce de gestion régionale des eaux à usage industriel. Lorsque la demande en eau pour divers secteurs [industriel, agricole, domestique] est supérieure à l'approvisionnement, il s'ensuit des conflits. Il en est de même lorsque l'on cherche à maximiser une fonction économique et, en même temps, à minimiser les effects négatifs du développement industriel sur l'environnement. Si les objectifs se mesurent en unités non commensurables—ce qui est le cas général—, la DMC permet de trouver une solution de compromis. Les deux cas d'espèce présentés ont les caractéristiques suivantes:

1. *La région éocene hongroise possède un potentiel industriel considérable [mines et métallurgie]. Le système de ressources en eau régional doit répondre aux exigences de la consommation industrielle, domestique et de protection de l'environnement. La technique de DMC "copromise programming" est choisie, parmi d'autres possibles, afin de trouver un "satisfactum".*
2. *La région de Bakony en Hongrie occidentale est en cours de développement minier, agricole et touristique. La gestion des eaux de la région, provenant en majeure partie d'une nappe karstique, est sujette aux conflits de ces trois intérèts. Comme précédemment, on fait appel à la DMC pour parvenir à une solution de compromis.*

RESUMEN

Aquí quiere presentarse dos aplicaciones prácticas del análisis de fin multiple para la economia regional de agua industrial. El desarrollo regional esta motivado frecuentemente por intereses contradictorios. En el caso de que estos fines fuesen medidos por unidades incompatibles, se puede seleccionar la "mejor" política de economía de agua industrial por el análisis de fin multiple. Los métodos se presentan por dos estudios de caso:

1. *La región eocena en Hungria tiene un potencial industrial importante [para la mineria e industría de metales]. Pero el sistema de economia regional de agua tiene que satisfacer los fines no solo de la industría, sino los de la población misma y de la protección del ambiente. Entre los métodos posibles se fue utilizado el programa de compromiso.*

2. *La región de loma de Bakony en Hungria sirve así mismo para la minería, agricultura y turismo. La base de la economía regional de agua esta formada por una albuhera cárstica, la cual tiene que servir intereses contradictorios [desarrollo industrial así como protección del ambiente] así mismo. Se ha seleccionado la solución en este caso también por el análisis de fin multiple.*

INTRODUCTION

THE PURPOSE of this paper is to show how conflicting interests related to industrial water management can be accounted for by multiobjective decision making (MODM). The specific problem addressed is the selection of such a strategy for one or more industrial complexes. This selection is made by trading off economic objectives and environmental protection. The set of goals related to industrial economy and environmental protection is acknowledged to be non-commensurable (monetary versus physical units) and, as such, an optimum solution cannot be found so that a "satisfactum" is sought [1]. In the sections that follow, the problem of industrial development versus environmental protection is defined. Then, elements of a dynamic model available to MODM are introduced, followed by a presentation of two examples taken from regional industrial analyses in Hungary. Finally, conclusions are drawn in the last section.

INDUSTRIAL DEVELOPMENT VERSUS ENVIRONMENTAL DISRUPTION

THERE IS WORLDWIDE concern that industrial development leads to environmental disruption. There are three general possibilities that will tend to maintain harmony between industry and environment [2]:

   a. The control of technology and emissions

   b. Modification of the assimilation capacity of the environment

   c. Utilization of the residuals.

The above general problem is now specified for the case of water related technology and water related environment. Note, however, that the methodology can be used for other effects of industry on the environment, such as effect on air and land use.

   Typical examples of the above three groups of control actions:

   a. water recirculation, underwater mining, wastewater treatment

   b. wastewater storage, modification of aquifer properties by grouting

   c. extraction of metals or generation of gas from sludge.

   Depending on the technology, the industrial plant(s) may require given amounts, quality and levels or stage of water. Water level requirement is pertinent, for instance, to the case of a surface intake or mining operation under a water hazard. Industrial production and related economic performance measures such as benefit-cost are strongly connected to the technology, and thus, to the required water. On the other hand, environmental impact is caused by fulfilling water requirements (e.g., less water downstream) and by discharge of used and polluted waters. The usual approach is to set limits for environmental impact in the form of regulations and seek maximum industrial economy of performance under such constraints. Or else, under a prescribed industrial production level, one may seek to minimize environmental impact. In this paper, a simultaneous consideration of both factors is envisioned. Regardless of the type of problem, a model of both industrial production and environmental effects is required. The production model yields economic performance and emission data as related to the technology and, thus, to water use. The environmental model calculates the spatial environmental impact as caused by meeting water requirements and disposal of wastewater. The next section shows how these elements can be embedded in a general dynamic model amenable to MODM.

MODEL ELEMENTS

FIVE MODEL ELEMENTS—input, state, state transition function, output and output function—are defined [3, 4, 5] for time $t = 0, 1, \ldots, T$, where T is the total planning horizon.

   (a) The input $I(t)$ comprises

      i. natural elements (wind, rainfall, evaporation, . . .)

      ii. physical properties of the region (area, soil, topography, mineral resources, . . .)

      iii. non-controllable economic, social and environmental elements (capital, machine, manpower and water requirements, environmental standards, . . .)

iv. control actions of decisions (capacity increase, technology, wastewater treatment, effluent charges, . . .)

(b) The state $S(t)$ includes the production characteristics such as the level of industrial development, and the environmental elements such as "downstream hydrology" (flow, level, quality)

(c) The state transition function Φ calculates the state at time $(t + 1)$ as a function of state and input at t:

$$S(t + 1) = \Phi(S(t), I(t)) \tag{1}$$

The production state can be calculated by the production model; for instance, capacity at time $(t + 1)$ can be determined from capacity at time t and inputs such as capacity increase at t. The environmental state transition function is represented by the environmental model. Typical examples are the partial differential equations describing the movement of water and solid material in surface or underground waters. Note that the numerical solutions of such equations are generally calculated for discrete time steps as in Eq. (1).

(d) The output, $R(t)$ also has economic and environmental elements. Economic output can be loss, cost or benefit risk. Usually, total period economic output such as discounted net benefit is considered. The environmental output may include elements of the state vector itself, say quantity and quality downstream flow.

(e) The output function Ψ calculates the output vector as function $S(t)$ and $I(t)$:

$$R(t) = \Psi(S(t), I(t)) \tag{2}$$

Examples for the output function are the calculation of discounted net benefit by well known formulas or of downstream flow by the state transition function. Given the above model elements, one may select one output to be optimized, leading to a classical optimization problem or, several outputs may be considered jointly, leading to a multiobjective problem. The level of remaining outputs constitutes constraints. In the next section, MODM is applied to regional problems that have been defined within the above systems framework.

EXAMPLES OF APPLICATION

TWO CASE STUDIES are briefly described. Both deal with regional (multiplant) industrial development (mining and electricity generation and bauxite extraction) interacting with a large-scale aquifer.

Mining in the Hungarian Eocene Region

Large-scale mining development for electricity generation is being planned in the Eocene region of Hungary over the next 50 years (Fig. 1). Coal resources are located below the underground (karstic) water level; thus, mining activity necessarily includes water control of the underground water. At the same time, the principal water supply source of the region is provided by the karstic water, which is to be delivered to a rapidly growing number of municipal and industrial users. A falling water level would have adverse environmental effects, because, for example, the thermal waters of Budapest receive their natural recharge from this karstic aquifer. Three non-commensurate objectives are associated with these three aspects of water control, supply and recharge. Three alternative mine water control technologies are available: a) artificial sealing which reduces the total yield of mine water that has to be pumped to the surface; b) INSTANTAN protection [6] which lets water inrushes occur in special cuts and holes instead of active workplaces; c) passive protection, in which inrush activity follows its natural course and disturbs the mining operation in a random manner. The mining industrial objective is total discounted economic benefit to be maximized over the mine lifetime. Since annual production and mining technology are given, maximizing benefit is equivalent to minimizing water-related costs.

A simple technological model is as follows:

The volume of minewater $X(i, t)$ withdrawn from mine i at stage t consists of the sum of the water amount $XM(i, t)$ entering workings and that amount $XD(i, t)$ appearing in the INSTANTAN system:

$$XM(i, t) + XD(i, t) = X(i, t) \qquad (3)$$

The sum of minewater volume withdrawn from mine i and volume $XG(i, t)$ sealed in mine i at stage t equals the total amount of minewater available $A(i, t)$:

$$X(i, t) + XG(i, t) = A(i, t) \qquad (4)$$

Another expression for $A(i, t)$ is $A(i, t) = \Sigma_{e=1}^{t} a(i, e)$ where $a(i, e)$ is the minewater increment given from the planned production schedule [7].

The objective of regional industrial water supply is to minimize the disutility of water shortage. This disutility can be measured as water volume, a water shortage index, or monetary loss. In the present study, it is assumed that water requirements must be fully satisfied, and thus, the proxy of supply cost is used to represent the second objective. The environmental objective is to maintain the existing flow of Budapest thermal waters. Two alternative courses of action are available for reaching this environmental goal. The first one consists in controlling the withdrawal of karstic water for both mining and industrial water supply, so that sufficient natural recharge for Budapest thermal waters are maintained along the edge of the aquifer. The second course consists in providing artificial recharge of the aquifer at proper sites so as to compensate for the effect of large water withdrawals.

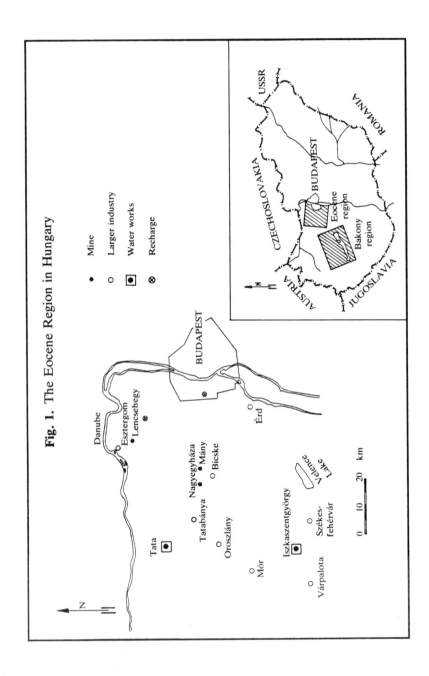

Fig. 1. The Eocene Region in Hungary

Elements of the regional model are given in Fig. 2. The vector $d(i, j, k, t)$ of decision variables (inputs) is defined at stage t by means of the following incremental elements:

$x(i, t)$ = withdrawal from mine i

$xm(i, t)$ = inrush yield allowed in workings

$xd(i, t)$ = inrush yield allowed into INSTANTAN cuts and drillings

$xg(i, t)$ = yield of water prevented from entering the mine by sealing or grouting

$v(i, k, t)$ = yield of water conveyed from mine i to recharge point k

$y(i, j, t)$ = yield of water supplied from mine or other intake i to water requirement point j

With the above decision vector, the following state variable vector referring to the level of development at stage t is defined as:

$$S(i, j, k, t) = \sum_{e=1}^{t} d(i, j, k, e) \tag{5}$$

The production state transition function shows how the level of development, that is, the state of stage $t + 1$ depends on the state at stage t and the decision on incremental development at t:

$$S(i, j, k, t + 1) = S(i, j, k, t) + d(i, j, k, t) \tag{6}$$

The environmental state transition function calculates the underground recharge to Budapest thermal levels:

$$g(t) = h[X(t), Y(t), V(t)] \tag{7}$$

where $X(t)$ is the yield vector of mining withdrawals, $Y(t)$ that of water supply withdrawals, and $V(t)$ is the vector of artificial recharge.

To estimate the relationship in Eq. (7), sample sets of values of X, Y, V are selected at random and, for each set of values, a computer-simulation groundwater model is used to calculate the discharge q [8]. These calculated values have been fitted by least squares to a linear function [9].

Now, the three objective functions, to be minimized, are:

$$f_1 = \sum_{i=1}^{n_1} \sum_{t=1}^{T} D(t) \left[\sum_{u=1}^{4} CA(i, j, k, u, t, S(t-1), d(t)) + OP(i, k, u, t, S(t)) \right.$$
$$\left. + L(i, t, u, d(t)) \right] \tag{8}$$

where

n = number of mines

$D(t)$ = discount factor

u = serial number of decision vector elements

$u = 1$ refers to withdrawals x, $u = 2$ to workings mine water yield xm, $u = 3$ to INSTANTAN yield, $u = 4$ to sealed mine water yield xa, $u = 5$ to water conveyed v and $u = 6$ to amount of water supplied y

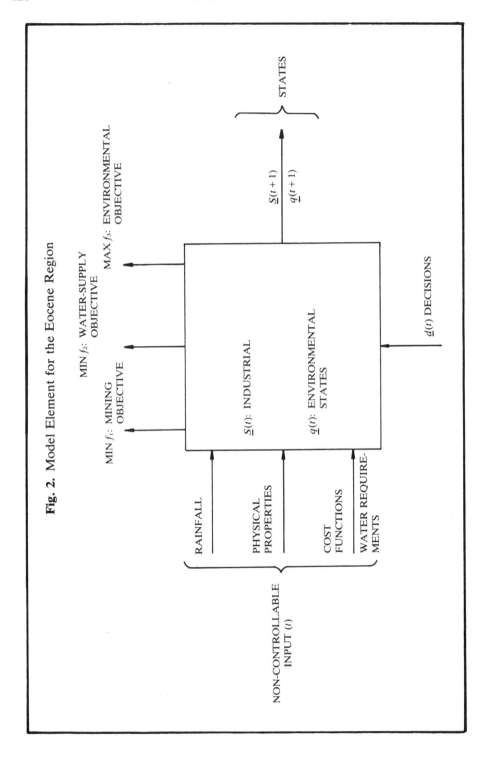

Fig. 2. Model Element for the Eocene Region

CA = capital cost function
OP = operation cost function
L = loss function, $L(u = 1, 3, 4, 5, 6) = 0$

$$f_2 = \sum_{i=1}^{n_1+n_2} \sum_{y=1}^{m} \sum_{t=1}^{T} D(t)[CA(i, j, t, u = 6, S(t-1), d(t)) + OP(i, j, t, u = 6, S(t))] \qquad (9)$$

where n_2 is the number of water intakes other than mine sites, and m is the number of water requirement points.

$$-f_3 = -q(t) \qquad (10)$$

Multiobjective techniques that can be used to solve the above problem include compromise programming [10, 11], cooperative game theory [12], and many others as discussed in Gershon [13] or Goicoechea et al [14]. A linear version of the compromise programming technique leads to the results shown in Fig. 2.

Though depending on the preference structure, compromise solutions such as the one shown in Fig. 2 are always superior to optimal solutions found stage by stage. In fact, separate mining or water-supply optima are not feasible since they would correspond to insufficient recharge for the Budapest thermal baths. Compromise solutions are characterized by a) large-scale sealing in mines; b) development of water works at sites 5, 6 affecting natural underground recharge in a minimal way; c) a moderate amount of artificial recharge at site 2, which is the closest to Budapest.

Bauxite Extraction in the Bakony Region, Hungary

In the Bakony region, there are several existing and planned sites for surface or underground mining (Fig. 3). In a number of sites, the groundwater level is higher than the bauxite deposits. For such cases, the allowable groundwater levels have an upper limit which are a function of the bauxite amount to be extracted. Two main technological options available for mining under a water hazard, are water level lowering and decrease of local transmissivity by grouting.

The economic objective is to allocate production rates among mines at minimum total discounted cost. Other formulations of the economic objective are also possible as shown in Vizy et al [15]. Among environmental factors, the impact of bauxite mining on the regional groundwater system is of greatest concern. The groundwater system is basically part of a large-scale karstic aquifer [16]. As a result of bauxite mining, the original state of the groundwater system has changed, such that a) the regional karstic water level has dropped and, b) the flow of several springs and thermal baths has become smaller or disappeared altogether. The environmental objective is, therefore, to minimize the deteriora-

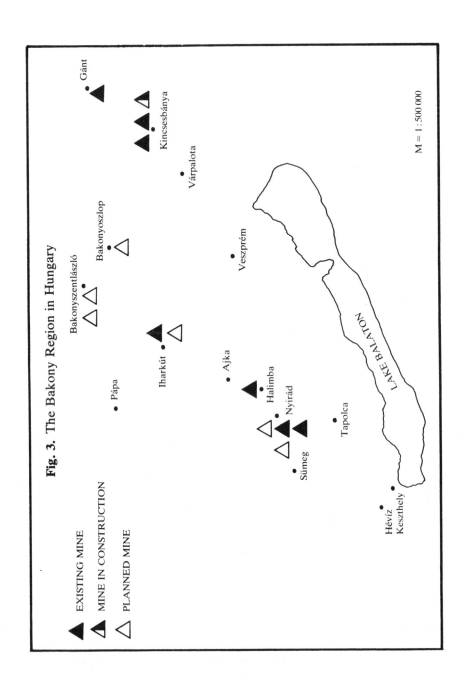

Fig. 3. The Bakony Region in Hungary

EXISTING MINE

MINE IN CONSTRUCTION

PLANNED MINE

M = 1 : 500 000

tion of the environmental state. Since there is much discussion on which given values of flows represent a "sound" groundwater system, we have not assigned such fixed values but have taken two alternative approaches to the problem. First, a multiobjective approach is taken in which environmental flows are maximized as in the problem treated in the first part of this paper; second, a single objective approach is used in which environmental constraints are taken as fuzzy as in Bogardi et al. [17]. Environmental protection may be provided by various combinations of mine water withdrawal control, decrease of local transmissivity and artificial recharge.

Elements of the regional model are shown in Fig. 4. Production state transition functions deal with

a. total quantity of bauxite extracted from mine i

$$X(i, t+1) = X(i, t) + x(i, t) \tag{11}$$

where x is the annual production and
b. groundwater level in mine i

$$Z(i, t+1) = \Phi[Z(i, t), Tr(j, t), q(i, t), v(k, t), tr(j, t)] \tag{12}$$
$$i = 1, \ldots, M; j = 1, \ldots, J; k = 1, \ldots, K$$

where the state variable is: Tr = transmissivity and the decision variables are: q = withdrawal, v = recharge, and tr = transmissivity change.

Environmental state transition function Φ_e calculates the underground flow $H(u, t+1)$ at control points $n = 1, \ldots, N$ as a function of those variables shown in Eq. (12).

State transition functions Φ_p and Φ_e have been estimated by a multivariate fitting of the finite difference solution of the partial differential equation describing regional groundwater movement [8, 17]. The economic objective is to minimize total discounted costs:

$$\underset{(q, v, tr)}{\text{Min}} \sum_{t=1}^{T} D(t) \left\{ \sum_{i=1}^{M} [f(i, t, x(i, t) + f_q(i, t, q(i, t))] \right.$$
$$\left. + \sum_{k=1}^{K} fv(k, t, v(k, t)) + \sum_{j=1}^{J} fg(j, t, tr(j, t)) \right\} \tag{13}$$

where $D(t)$ is the discount factor and f, fq, fv and fg are cost functions for mining, withdrawal, recharge and grouting, respectively. The environmental objective is to minimize the maximum deviation of underground control flows from given ideal values:

$$\min_{t} \max_{n} [HI(n, t) = H(n, t)] \tag{14}$$

for $t = 0, \ldots, T$ and $n = 1, \ldots, N$, under a set of natural, economic and tech-

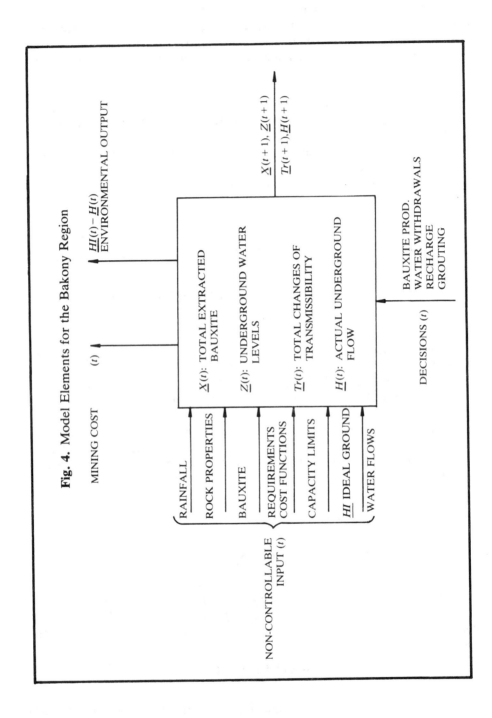

Fig. 4. Model Elements for the Bakony Region

nological constraints. The MODM technique selected here is based on compromise programming and fuzzy set theory [18]. A solution algorithm based on discrete dynamic programming has been developed for the general nonlinear case in Gershon et al [19]. Sample numerical results referring to a simplified example are given next. In this example, $T = 20$ years, divided into four stages, $M = 3$ (including one mine underwater hazard), $K = J = N = 1$.

Bauxite requirements, capacity units and ideal groundwater flow can be found in Table 1. Unit costs are: $f(1) = 100$, $f(2) = 320$ and $f(3) = 300$, all in Ft/ton, and $fg = 880$, $fv = 700 \cdot 10^3$, both in Ft/m³/min/stage. The state transition function for groundwater level is:

$$Z(3, t+1) = Z(3, t) - 0.127(1 + Tr(1)q(3) + 0.039(1 - Tr(1)V(1) + 7.28 \quad (15)$$

and for groundwater control flow:

$$H(t+1) = 36 - 0.041(1 - Tr(1))q(3) + 0.13(1 + Tr(1))V(1) \quad (16)$$

Results of compromise programming application are given in Table 2. As demonstrated in Bogardi et al [17], the compromise solution is much preferable to a

Table 1. Data for Bauxite Example

	Stages, years			
	1	2	3	4
Bauxite Requirements				
Amount, 10³ tons	2500	3800	4400	4700
Module	7.2	7.0	6.8	7.0
Mining capacity limits, 10³ tons				
mine 1	1000	1600	1600	1600
2	900	2000	2900	2900
3	1800	2700	3200	3200
Minewater withdrawal capacity limits, mine 3, m³/min	310	350	400	400
Recharge capacity limits, m³/min	10	30	50	50
Grouting capacity, relative trans- missivity	0.4	0.4	0.4	0.4
Ideal groundwater flow, m³/min	30	30	30	30

Table 2. Results of Linear Compromise Programming.
Range of Weights 0.4 – 0.6, Medium Grouting

Activity	Stages in four-year units			
	1	2	3.	4
Mine 1 production	1000	1600	400	0
Mine 2 production	900	2000	2272	2128
Mine 3 production	600	200	1728	2572
Water withdrawal	0	45	328	364
Recharge	0	0	42	50
Grouting	0	0.1	0.1	0
Underground control flow	36	31	30	30

Total discounted costs: 3.103×10^9 Ft.*
*Ft = Forint, Hungarian currency, worth about $0.04 U.S.

purely economic optimum, which would result in the disruption of the thermal baths after 10 years. Naturally, if a realistic cost function could have been assigned to disruption of thermal baths, then a single objective optimization may have led to an acceptable solution. However, as mentioned before, no agreement could be obtained as to what constitutes "good" groundwater flow.

CONCLUSIONS

Results of this paper lead to the following conclusions:
  a. Industrial water management may have, in addition to economic consequences for the industry, substantial environmental impacts which themselves result in economic consequences at a later date.
  b. A water management scheme is to be sought which results in a trade-off between economic efficiency and environmental protection.
  c. MODM may be a useful tool to define a model and then to find a satisfactory solution.
  d. A discrete dynamic model with five elements provides a good basis for an MODM approach.
  e. Two examples of MODM application include regional industrial development interacting with a large-scale aquifer. In both cases, a compromise solution enables one to examine more meaningfully trade-offs than a strictly economic optimum would allow.

ACKNOWLEDGEMENTS

This research was supported in part by funds provided by the Hungarian Mining Development Institute and by the U.S. National Science Foundation, under grant #INT 78-12184 titled "Decision-Making in Natural Resources Management". Furthermore, the substantial contributions of F. Szidarovszky and A. Bardossy to both modeling and computational phases of this study are gratefully acknowledged.

References

1. Simon, H. (1957) *Models of Man: Social and Rational*, John Wiley, New York, NY, USA.
2. Kneese, A. and Bower, B. (eds.) (1972) *Environmental Quality Analysis: Theory and Method in the Social Sciences*, Johns Hopkins Press, Baltimore, MA, USA.
3. Booth, T.L. *Sequential Machines and Automata Theory*, John Wiley & Sons, New York, NY, USA, 1967.
4. Wymore, A. (1976) *Systems Engineering Methodology for Interdisciplinary Teams*, Wiley-Interscience, New York, NY, USA.
5. Duckstein, L. and Bogardi, I. (1978) "Uncertainties in lake management," *Proceedings, Int'l. Symp. on Risk & Reliability in Water Resources*, University of Waterloo, Ontario, Canada, June 26–28, pp. 697–712.
6. Kapolyi, L. (1976) "New trends and researches in protection against mine water," *Proceedings, 7th Conference on Mine Water Management*, Mining Research Institute, Budapest, Hungary.
7. Schmieder, A., Kesseru, Zs., Juhasz, J., Willems, T., and Martos, F. (1975) *Water Hazard and Water Management in Mining* (in Hungarian), Muszaki Konyvkiado, Budapest, Hungary.
8. Szilagyi, G., Heinemann, Z. and Bogardi, I. (1978) "Application of a simulation model for a large-scale aquifer," *Int'l. Symp., SIAMOS*, Granada, Spain.
9. Szidarovszky, F. and Bogardi, I. (1980) "Dynamic multiobjective control of mining, water-supply and environmental effects," *Proceedings, 17th APCOM Conf.*, Moscow, USSR.
10. Zeleny, M. (1973) "Compromise programming," in *Multiple Criteria Decision Making*, J.L. Cochrane and M. Zeleny (eds.), University of South Carolina Press, Columbia, SC, USA, pp. 262–301.
11. Duckstein, L. and Opricovic, S. (1980) "Multiobjective optimization in river basin development," *Water Resources Research*, Vol. 16, No. 1, pp. 14–20.
12. Szidarovszky, F., Bogardi, I., and Duckstein, L. (1978) "Use of cooperative games in a multiobjective analysis of mining and environment," *Proceedings, 2nd Int'l. Conf. on Applied Numerical Modeling*, Sept. 11–15, Madrid, Spain.
13. Gershon, M. (1981) "Model choice in multiobjective decision making in water and mineral resource systems," *Natural Resource Systems Technical Report Series #37*, Department of Hydrology & Water Resources, University of Arizona, Tucson, AZ 85721, USA.
14. Goicoechea, A., Hansen, D., and Duckstein, L. (1981) *Introduction to Multiobjective Analysis with Engineering and Business Applications*, to appear, John Wiley & Sons, New York, NY, USA.
15. Vizy, B., I. Bogardi and Bardossy, A. (1981) "Modeling of factors influencing bauxite mining development," (in Hungarian), BKL Banyaszat, Hungary, to appear.
16. Szilagyi, G. (ed.) "Investigation into the effect of mining activity on the karstic waters in the Transdanubian Mountain," (in Hungarian) *Research Report, Hungarian Mining Research Institute (MRI)*, 13-9/75, Budapest, Hungary.
17. Bogardi, I., Duckstein, L., and Bardossy, A. (1981) "Multiobjective analysis of regional bauxite mining under water hazard," *Working paper, Department of Systems & Industrial Engineering*, University of Arizona, Tucson, AZ 85721, USA.

18. Zadeh, L., Fu, K., Tanaka, K., and Shimura, M. (eds.) (1975) *Fuzzy Sets and Their Applications to Cognitive and Decision Processes*, Academic Press, New York, NY, USA.
19. Gershon, M., Duckstein, L., and Bardossy, A. (1981) "Differential dynamic programming: Application to multiobjective decision making," presented, *CORS/ORSA/TIMS Joint Mtg.*, May 3–6, Toronto, Ontario, Canada. Available as *paper #81-8, Department of Systems & Industrial Engineering*, University of Arizona, Tucson, AZ 85721, USA.

Modelling of Industrial Water Demands

Janusz Kindler
Area Chairman, Resources & Environment Area,
International Institute for Applied Systems Analysis,
Laxenburg, Austria, (on leave from the Institute of
Environmental Engineering, Warsaw Polytechnic
University, Warsaw, Poland),

and

Clifford S. Russell
Director, Quality of the Environmental Program
Resources for the Future, Inc., Washington, DC, USA

SYNOPSIS

This paper is based on the forthcoming IIASA book on "Modelling of Water Demands". Following introduction of industrial water use, requirements, and demands, the dimensions of industrial water demand and its determinants are briefly presented. Two broad approaches to modelling water demands are introduced, one of which is called statistical, the other, engineering. Examples of application of these approaches to modelling the water demands of individual industrial activities are supplemented by discussion of water-demand modelling at the regional and national levels. At the end, the possible ways of making water-demand models more useful in the future are discussed.

RÉSUMÉ

Cet article est inspiré du livre de l'IIASA à paraître sur "La Modélisation des Demandes en Eau". Après une introduction concernant l'utilisation, les besoins, et les demandes de l'eau industrielle, l'ampleur des demandes en eau industrielle et ses composantes sont présentées succinctement. Deux approches générales de la modélisation des demandes en eau sont abordées, l'une de caractère statistique, l'autre orientée vers l'ingénierie. Des exemples d'application de ces approches vis-à-vis de la modélisation des demandes en eau de differentes activités industrielles sont complétés en examinant la modélisation de la demande en eau au niveau régional et national. En conclusion sont discutées les possibilités de rendre les modèles de demande en eau plus utiles dans l'avenir.

RESUMEN

Este trabajo esta basado en el próximo libro titulado "Modelaje de demandas de agua". Después de la introducción del uso del agua industrial, restricciones y demandas, se presentan brevemente las dimensiones y determinantes de la demanda de agua industrial. Dos maneras generales de modelación son presentadas, una es la estadística y la otra la ingenieril. Ejemplos de aplicación de demandas de agua en actividades industriales son complementados por medio de una discusión de modelación a niveles regional y nacional. Al final son discutidas las posibles formas en que los modelos de demanda de agua pueden ser de más utilidad.

INTRODUCTION

WHENEVER INVESTMENT in a water resources project is under consideration or new water policy is contemplated, several important questions relating to water demand usually arise. Typically they are concerned with how much water will be used, where, and for what purposes at various points of time. The amounts of water actually demanded depend on many time-related variables such as government policies, population levels and distribution, energy use, cost of energy, per capita disposal income, technological development, pricing of water withdrawals and waste water disposal, consumer habits and lifestyles. It is only with the aid of analytical approaches that relationships among these variables can be developed, and alternative levels of water demand then estimated for different sets of possible conditions.

This paper is based on the forthcoming IIASA book: "Modelling of Water Demands" edited by J. Kindler and C.S. Russell, in collaboration with B.T. Bower, I. Gouevsky, D.R. Maidment, and W.R.D. Sewell. Focusing on modelling of industrial water demands, this paper presents an overview of the forthcoming book based on water-demand studies carried out during the years 1976–1980 at IIASA. In addition, some general reflections on the role of industrial water-demand modelling, its limitations, and further research needs are presented.

INDUSTRIAL WATER USE, REQUIREMENTS, AND DEMANDS

MOST INDUSTRIAL PROCESSES use water as an input, though the purposes to which the water is put vary widely. In some cases, water is an input in the classic sense and forms part of the product. The beverage industry is an obvious example. But water or steam is also used as feedstock or processing agent in numerous chemical and pharmaceutical processes. In other plants, it is used to convey the product from one stage of production to another. For example, in paper-making, pulp is carried in slurry from the pulping operation to bleaching and paper-making. In the canning industry, fruits and vegetables are often transported through the production process in a water stream.

Where excess or unwanted heat is generated by a mechanical process or chemical or nuclear reaction, water is the obvious choice as the heat-removal medium. This use is nearly universal, but is on an especially grand scale in the steam-electric power generating industry.

Water is used for washing and cleaning throughout industrial facilities. In the canning industry, fruits and vegetables are washed with water at the beginning of the production process. Hydraulic debarking in the pulp and paper industry is a standard method for removing the bark and cleaning the dirt from incoming logs. Water is also used to wash final products. Water is, of course, used for personal and plant hygiene and for other overhead purposes such as lawn watering, vehicle washing and fire protection. Steam may be used for space heating. Moreover, an examination of the water utilization system of an industrial plant may show that water is actually a net output of some stages of the production process as when liquid residuals result from the production of some dry foods. Non-product residuals other than energy are also commonly removed from industrial processes in water streams, and treatment and disposal of the resulting "waste-waters" is a major concern of public policy in most industrial nations.

The discussion so far has referred rather generally to the multiplicity of different uses of water by individual plants. However, industrial water-users should not be implicitly, or explicitly, assumed to have inflexible requirements for water (per unit of output, per employee, or whatever). While all these activities may have certain irreducible requirements for water, for the most part, analysis goes on and policies are made concerning quantities of use above these requirements. At these higher use levels, as price or cost rises, it is possible for the activities to substitute more of some other input or inputs for water. It should be recognized that, all else being equal, industrial enterprises will choose to use less water when the price or cost per unit is high than they will when that cost is low. Thus, the 'requirement approach' should be abandoned and the economic concept of water demand substituted for it.

THE DIMENSIONS OF INDUSTRIAL WATER DEMAND AND ITS DETERMINANTS

AS INDICATED EARLIER, the water use of an industrial activity is a multidimensional phenomenon and consequently, some separate dimensions of water demand can also be distinguished. These are:

(1) quantity of water withdrawn at the intake(s) of a given activity (withdrawals);
(2) total quantity of water used, including any recirculation (gross water applied);
(3) quantity of water evaporated, incorporated in a product or otherwise lost before discharge (consumptive use);
(4) quantity of water discharged (discharge);
(5) quality of water discharged (waste-water disposal services demanded);
(6) the time patterns of each of the above dimensions.

At a given point in time, industrial water demands with respect to all six dimensions set out above are determined by the following inter-related factors:

(i) production technology;
(ii) product mix and quality specifications;
(iii) qualities and prices of raw materials, including fuel and electrical energy;
(iv) unit values of recoverable non-product materials and energy;
(v) price of purchased water of given quality at the intake to the plant;
(vi) costs of different amounts of self-supplied intake water, e.g. costs of intake facilities, treatment and recirculation;
(vii) limitations, standards or unit fees imposed on the discharge of liquid,

gaseous and solid residuals from the plant, either directly to the environment or to some collection and disposal system;

(viii) costs of different degrees of in-plant residuals modification;

(ix) capital availability;

(x) climate.

DEMAND MODELLING

THE PRECEDING SECTION immediately suggests that planners at all levels should take into account the responsiveness of quantity demanded to price (as well as to other factors and policy instruments), whether setting out to analyze the effects of new policy initiatives on water resources or deciding about the desirability of new supply and transmission capacity increments in a region. The technique for doing this generally involves the production of water-demand relations using either of two approaches: statistical or engineering. The first of these tries to infer from observations on many users at a point in time (or the same user over a period of time, or from a combination of both types of observations) the structure of water-demand relation producing the observations. The second attempts to construct the relation from fairly detailed engineering knowledge of the production or consumption unit processes, and the associated substitution possibilities, carried out by the activity.

Some of the complications and extensions relevant to these two approaches should be mentioned. In particular, for the statistical approach, there is a lack of appropriate data in sufficient quantity, and the difficulties posed by simultaneous determination of prices (or costs) and quantities. In connection with the engineering approach, the potential complexity of the resulting model, seen as all possible combinations of the relevant unit processes, and the great practical difficulty of finding solutions to particular problems (such as finding the lowest cost reaction by an industrial plant to an increase in the cost of water withdrawals) are to be mentioned. Into this breach is thrust mathematical (usually linear) programming. This technique was shown to be a means of organizing the information developed in the engineering approach in such a way that a well-developed and quite efficient algorithm is available for finding optimal paths through the set of all possible unit process combinations, for different specifications of the policy instruments, such as price or waste-discharge standards.

The basic concepts and techniques of water-demand modelling have been illustrated by IIASA through case studies undertaken in cooperation with several institutions from the IIASA National Member Organization countries. Regarding industrial water demand, both major techniques—statistical and engineering programming—were applied within the framework of these case studies. The first is a small-scale attempt to develop a statistical water-demand equation for Dutch paper mills, using available data on water use and effective price, plant size, product and type technology. The results of the exercise are disappointing, primarily because of the ubiquitous problem of data poverty.

The second application deals with modelling the water-demand relations for a fossil-fuel, thermal-electric power plant, the particular plant being a Polish project located on the Vistula River. The engineering realities of the electricity production process have been combined with the principles of programming model design to determine the structure of the constraint matrix for the plant model. Examples of the output available from the model include the derived demand function for cooling withdrawals and the shifts in that function due to changes in other parameter values.

The problems of water-demand modelling, however, go beyond the level of individual industrial activities. Aggregated analysis of regional demand for shared water resources—either as a source for withdrawals or as a sink for waste-water discharges—is required. The emphasis here must be on the constraints that reflect the sharing problem in the context of a regional resource, with the overall objective being to maximize the net benefits from all the activities (industrial as well as agricultural, municipal and other). These constraints may arise from a policy of maintaining streamflow in the shared river in the face of water withdrawals and consumptive uses. Even a regional water-quantity model can become large and complicated rather quickly.

The additional complications necessary both in the individual activity models and in the regional constraints, in order to reflect standards for regional water quality, may be illustrated by existing regional, water-quality models. One of the best examples in this respect, is the Lower Delaware River Valley model constructed at Resources for the Future, largely for research rather than actual planning or policy implementation purposes. The dimensions of this model (about 3,200 rows and 7,900 columns) give the point made about potential model size a certain reality. (It should be noted that the Lower Delaware model dealt with air as well as water pollution.) A major lesson obtained from this model seemed to be that introducing non-linearities is asking for trouble—both in the area of computational difficulty and cost, and in the matter of the reliability of the results.

The next level of aggregation beyond the region is the nation. It is not, however, symmetric with regional aggregation, not because one could not imagine building a national water-demand model by bringing together the required set of regional models (as by including interbasin water transfer activities and a national economic model), but because it seems that this sort of national model does not exist. What does seem to exist in fairly great number are studies of projected national water use, often based on the aggregations across industrial and household sectors, and with almost no reflection either of the role of price or cost in affecting water demand, or of the importance of natural recirculation via water courses. While true national water-demand models, constructed as aggregations of regional models, could be very large and complex, the decisions made at the national level may involve extremely large and costly undertakings, such as interregional water transfer projects or sea-coast desalting installations. It is not clear, therefore that national models are 'too expensive,' for they might point policy-makers away from truly enormous mistakes.

THOUGHTS FOR THE FUTURE

If one takes seriously the proposition that models of water-demand relations can be useful additions to the armories of water-resource management agencies and other concerned institutions, it is tempting to ask as a final question: Are there ways to make these models more useful in the future? In particular, are there developments to be sought or areas of application to be opened or expanded?

Four suggestions seem appropriate as a partial answer to the question. First, the reader will have noticed that even brief discussions of approaches and applications presented herein have been dominated by data problems. Quite often it is necessary to favor an engineering approach because of its relative independence of historical data. But statistical modelling has considerable appeal, particularly because a well done statistical demand relation may mimic the important behavior of a very complex linear programme while being itself compact and easy to use once estimated [1]. Therefore, the potential social payoff to more and better data on activity-level water use and related variables is large. Whether that social payoff could be translated into individual rewards (for data collection can be thankless work) or whether it could be used to outweigh the negative aspects of confidentiality claims, agency inertia, and hostility to further forms and questionnaires, is doubtful. On the other hand, data gathering required by existing laws, especially those laws governing environmental policy, already produces an enormous quantity of data, and a systematic exploration of these would be valuable.

Another subject worthy of more attention than it has historically received is that of the costs and benefits of model simplification. In approaching a water-demand (or any other) policy problem, the first impulse of the modeller(s) is often to try to capture every detail of the situation: that is, to include every conceivable variable instead of thinking about and even testing which ones make little difference; to introduce non-linearities when linear approximations are or can be made available; to use the newest and most abstruse computational packages though it is unclear whether any gain is obtained; or to imbed the water-demand model in a general equilibrium context without analyzing the importance of doing so. Each such decision is likely to be approved by the disciplinary colleagues of the modellers. Indeed, the choice of a simple technique over a complex and sophisticated one is likely to be greeted in seminars and informal conversation with a "But don't you know about the problem of . . .?", or "But haven't you seen the latest paper by . . . where he develops a technique that allows for . . . .?" Professional pride, in other words, is not the ally of simplicity. But each complicating step also tends to make the resulting model more inflexible, idiosyncratic in operation, and opaque to the planners and decision-makers who ultimately should be the ones to benefit from the exercise.

These planners and decision-makers are not, however, blameless in the matter. Their preference for a detailed, regulatory approach to achieving public policy goals in such a field as water-resource management leads to a need for quite specific and detailed prescriptions. Thus, if one must tell refinery X exactly what to do about water withdrawals, consumption, or waste water discharge, a simple model is not likely to be considered particularly useful, since it will be easy for the refiner to claim that his real refinery is so much more complex, contains so many more processes and so many more interconnections, uses such a variety of crude oils, etc., that the simple model's results cannot be applied. Detailed regulation demands detailed knowledge. At the same time it tends to reduce the need for optimizing models aimed at, for example, minimizing the cost of achieving some regional or plant-wide result. Thus, the allowable waste-water discharges for an industrial enterprise might be calculated on the basis of the application of specified treatment devices to raw waste loads. There is really no response model required (though someone, somewhere, might be interested in asking whether the specified loads could be achieved more cheaply via another method). Thus, it might be said that certain regulatory practices create situations in which either models are hardly necessary or only very specific and complex models will do.

On the other hand, it must be admitted that we do not know much about the costs of using simpler models, in terms of information and accuracy lost, nor about the benefits in terms of the costs of model construction and of subsequent computation avoided. This is perhaps because it is difficult to find the time or money to support the analysis of various levels of modelling complexity aimed at a particular problem; usually one round of analysis exhausts budget, time, and researchers. One water-demand model that was eventually subjected to this kind of investigation was a linear-programming model of steel production and associated water use and pollution [2]. Vaughan subsequently constructed two other, simpler and smaller models covering the same steel production processes and, with only a few exceptions, the same array of water use options and of water- (and air-) borne residuals. One of these models was derived from the full Russell-Vaughan LP by averaging over some input options to get 'typical' inputs, removing some activity vectors almost never chosen under a wide variety of imposed conditions, and reducing the product mix complexity. This model was about 45 per cent as large as the full model (size being measured by number of rows). The third model was developed by an entirely different route: by adding residuals generation, treatment and discharge, and some additional detail on heat balances to a previously published steel-production LP [3], which in turn was based on aggregate average data on input use per ton at the several stages of integrated steel-making. This model was about 80 per cent as large, in terms of row numbers, as the second, or about 35 per cent as large as the full LP [4].

Smith and Vaughan have provided estimates of the cost of developing and operating the largest and smallest of the three models. These figures indicate diseconomies of scale, with both development and operating costs growing faster than row size. Development costs go up by a factor of more than five as row size goes up by a factor of slightly less than three. And cost per run, based on experiments and cost curve fitting, would vary as the square of row size—or by a factor of 9 as row size triples.

Unfortunately, however, the results of the Smith-Vaughan analysis do not allow us to say that the smaller model would serve 'just as well as' the larger. First, because the authors have no measures of objective reality against which to compare the various models' responses to such stimuli as changes in discharge constraints and in factor input prices, it is impossible for them to say which of the models does best at mimicking real steel mills. Moreover, the models give different results, whether measured informally via graphs or the marginal and average costs of various discharge reducing requirements; or statistically via tests for the equality of Cobb-Douglas cost functions estimated from data points based on repeated runs of the models across different input price sets and residuals discharge constraints. As Smith and Vaughan say:

"The level of process detail can lead to quite different patterns of firm (or plant) responses that are depicted by these models. These differences can have direct and indirect effects on outputs of the models that are of central interest to policy-makers."

Thus, what little we know about model simplification reinforces the old adage that model-building is an art and that one of the most important talents needed by the artist is a feeling for where to make cuts. Simpler may always be cheaper, but is also different, though not necessarily worse, in terms of outputs generated. More work on this question would be very valuable.

Specific attention ought also to be given to improving the analytical basis for short-run, water management decisions, especially on how to cope with the threat of water shortages. While there exist quite sophisticated reservoir-operating models, and while hydrological prediction capabilities seem to be improving, knowledge of short-run demand phenomena is, it seems, vestigial. Yet it is such knowledge that will allow more intelligent choice among alternative rules for reacting to particular combinations of storage and use levels and extended weather forecasts. This is true even though the rules may not involve short-term price changes but rather regulations, such as prohibition of lawn-sprinkling and car-washing. For in order to evaluate the true costs of such regulations and to balance them against the possible costs of not taking action (that is, the expected value of losses over all possible future precipitation patterns), it is necessary to have the demand curves for the water uses to be regulated and for those that will be affected by actual shortage. A discussion of research and policy needs in this area may be found in Russell [5] and examples of the methodology of loss estimation are given by Russell, Arey and Kates [6] and Young, Taylor and Hanks [7]. Again, there is considerable scope for useful work in this area—in the measurement of the relevant demands, the study of response to regulations, and the development of (nearly optimal) rules of thumb for water-system managers.

Finally, modelling water demands provides an important part of the information required for water-demand forecasting. It does not by itself, however, yield estimates of future demands. The latter are conditioned by a variety of considerations exogenous to the water management itself. Important in this connection are such factors as the future state of the economy, shifts in various political situations, the likelihood of technological breakthroughs, alterations in government policies which might affect either management of water resources or the demand for goods and services in which water is an input—changes in levels of support for housing programmes, policies for regional economic expansion and the alteration of water quality standards are germane in this connection. Because each of these can take various paths of development, none of which can be foreseen with complete accuracy, the fundamental step upon which all water-demand forecasting is based involves examination and quantification of 'alternative futures'. Building consistent scenarios of 'alternative futures' is one of the most complex undertakings and much remains to be done to supplement this concept with the sound guidelines of an operational value.

In speculating on future developments in water-demand forecasting, it is important to note that the improvements brought about by modelling water-demand relations can only be useful to the extent that the structure of these relations, based on the historical and existing conditions, endure into the future. If the structure changes in some unanticipated way, the most technically sophisticated and elaborate model will be little better than the crudest sort of extrapolation [8]. There is plenty of empirical evidence that the likelihood of structural changes in the long-run, (i.e., 10 years or more) is very high; therefore, the water-demand models discussed in this paper seem to be more suited for application within the framework of short-run policy analyses in water resources management. Such applications, however, may yield several insights concerning sensitivity of water demand to different demand-generating factors. Such information, if used with proper care, can certainly improve our long-term policy choices.

References

1. Hazilla, M., Kopp, R.J. and Smith, V.K. (1980) *The Performance of Neoclassical Econometric Models in Measuring Natural Resources Substitution with Environmental Constraints.* RFF Discussion Paper D-70, October.
2. Russell, C.S. and Vaughan, W.J. (1976) *Steel Production: Processes, Products, and Residuals.* (Baltimore, MD: Johns Hopkins Univ. Press for RFF).
3. Tsao, C.S. and Day, R.H. (1971) *A Process Analysis Model of the US Steel Industry.* Management Science, vol. 17, pp. 588–608.
4. Smith, V.K. and Vaughan, W.J. (1980) *The Implications of Model Complexity for Environmental Management.* Journal of Environmental Economics and Management, vol. 7, no. 3, (September), pp. 184–208.
5. Russell, C.S. (1979) Water Deficit Planning, in J.R. Wallace and B. Kahn, eds., *Water Conservation and Alternative Water Supplies.* (Baltimore, MD: Johns Hopkins Univ. Press for Resources for the Future).
6. Russell, C.S., Arey, D.G. and Kates, R.W. (1970) *Drought and Water Supply.* (Baltimore, MD: Johns Hopkins Univ. Press for Resources for the Future).
7. Young, G.K., Taylor, R.S. and Hanks, J.J. (1972) *A Methodology for Assessing Economic Risk of Water Supply Shortages.* (Alexandria, VA: Inst. of Water Resources, US Army Corps of Engineers), IWR 72-7.
8. Ascher, W. (1978) *Forecasting: An Appraisal for Policy-Makers and Planners.* The Johns Hopkins University Press.

Industrial Water Demand in the Netherlands: Some Forecasts and a few factors which affect Industrial Water Consumption

R.J. Lahr

Ministry of Health and Environmental Protection,
Domestic and Industrial Water Supplies Branch,
Leidschendam, The Netherlands

SYNOPSIS

Industrial water consumption in the Netherlands amounts to about 4,000 million cubic metres per annum. Many industrial plants are sited in places where there is little or no fresh groundwater. There are also many problems associated with supplies from surface-water sources because of the pollution of the Rhine. Research on industrial water consumption and the factors which affect it began in 1974. The results of the research and the forecasts for water demand, made with the aid of economic growth predictions, are summarised. The changes in economic activity and legislation which, the research shows, have affected industrial water consumption are discussed.

RÉSUMÉ

Aux Pays-Bas, l'industrie consomme environ 4 milliards de m³ d'eau. Une grande partie de l'industrie est établie dans des régions où il n'y a pas, ou guère, d'eaux souterraines. L'approvisionnement en eau de surface est également difficile en raison de la pollution du Rhin. Depuis 1974, la consommation d'eau par l'industrie et les facteurs qui l'influencent ont été étudiés. Les résultats de cette étude et les prévisions qui ont été établies à l'aide des prévisions de croissance économique sont résumés. On expose les modifications de l'activité et de la législation économiques qui semblent avoir influencé la consommation d'eau par l'industrie.

RESUMEN

En nuestro país el consumo de agua por la industria asciende a unos 4 mil millones de m³. Una gran parte de la industria se encuentra establecida en lugares donde no hay o escasean las aguas dulces freáticas. Debido a la contaminación del Rin, el suministro de agua de la superficie implica también serios problemas. Desde 1974 se tiene en estudio el consumo de agua por la industria y los factores que en él influyen. Se recogen los resultados de dicho estudio y los pronósticos hasta ahora hechos partiendo de las predicciones sobre el desarrollo económico. Se examinan los cambios operados en la actividad económica y legislación que, según las prospecciones, han repercutido en el consumo de agua por la industria.

WATER SUPPLIES IN THE NETHERLANDS

IN THE NETHERLANDS, as in other West-European countries, industrial development has played an important role throughout the century, changing the country from an agricultural to an industrial one. Dutch industry is concentrated around the ports of Rotterdam and Amsterdam in the west of the country because of the good communications they provide. There is an agglomeration of oil refineries and chemical industries at the "Europoort", in the immediate vicinity of Rotterdam. As Fig. 1 shows, it is in those very areas in the western Netherlands, with the greatest concentration of industry and the highest population density, that fresh groundwater is scarce or non-existent.

The Rhine could be an ideal source of fresh water, as it is both rain-fed and

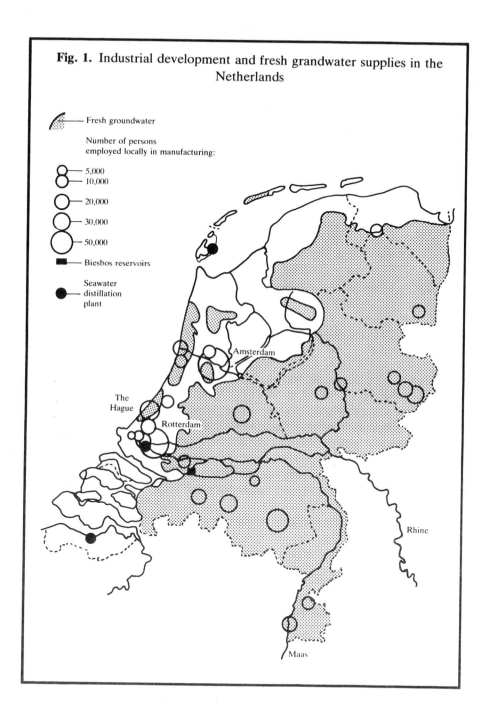

Fig. 1. Industrial development and fresh grandwater supplies in the Netherlands

Fresh groundwater

Number of persons
employed locally in manufacturing:

5,000
10,000
20,000
30,000
50,000

Biesbos reservoirs

Seawater
distillation
plant

Amsterdam

The
Hague

Rotterdam

Rhine

Maas

glacial and has a fairly regular flow determined by rainfall and evaporation and the amount of snow in its basin. The Rhine's rate of flow at the Netherlands border, averaged over many years, is about 2,200 m³/sec, the lowest recorded rate being 620 m³/sec. Unfortunately, industrial development has turned the Rhine into the sewer of Western Europe. The contents of the 80×10^9 m³ of Rhine water which flowed into the Netherlands in 1979 contained, amongst other substances, 13×10^6 tonnes chloride, 156×10^3 tonnes phosphate, 80 tonnes cadmium, 6×10^6 tonnes sulphate, 960 tonnes chromium, 24 tonnes mercury, 27×10^3 tonnes nitrite, 1200 tonnes copper, 1200 tonnes lead, 1×10^6 tonnes nitrate and 7200 tonnes zinc.

Amsterdam and the coastal province to the north of the city use Rhine water as the raw material for their domestic water supply. However, before it is fit for human consumption, it has to undergo a lengthy and expensive purification process. Artificial infiltation into the dunes along the coast plays an important role in this process. In 1974 and 1976 respectively, the cites of Rotterdam and The Hague turned from the Rhine to the better-quality Maas water for their supplies. The Maas, however, is a pluvial river and its volume therefore depends on the rainfall in the river basin. The rate of flow at the Dutch border, averaged over many years, is about 260 m³/sec, dropping to a minimum daily rate of only a few cubic metres per second.

The fluctuating level of the Maas, and the need to bridge periods in which disaster makes Maas water temporarily unuseable, made it necessary to construct reservoirs. The dunes are used for water-storage for The Hague, as for Amsterdam, and three reservoirs have been built in the Biesbos to supply the extensive industrial estates of Rotterdam. They are situated about 25 km to the south of the city and have a total capacity of 81×10^6 m³, which, given a bridging period of four months, can supply a draft of 250 million m³ per year.

Water is supplied in the Netherlands by some 100 water works which together produced 1053×10^6 m³ in 1979—688×10^6 m³ from fresh groundwater, 144×10^6 m³ from surface water infiltration and 221×10^6 m³ direct from surface waters. In areas where there is insufficient fresh water of a reasonable quality, a limited amount of brackish surface water and sea water is distilled. Two of the three plants (Fig. 1) make use of waste heat from power stations while the other uses waste heat from a refuse incineration plant. A total of 14.2×10^6 m³ of distilled water was produced in 1979, of which 0.7×10^6 m³ was added to the fresh water supplies for potable water production; the rest was supplied direct to industry as feed water for boilers. In addition, 41×10^6 m³ of water was supplied to industry as a semi-finished product: surface water which has undergone a preliminary purification and which is otherwise further purified for potable water.

Only rough figures are available on the distribution of potable water consumption over industry, households and all other users since 1976. Precise data on industrial consumption is obtained every five years from a national survey on industrial water consumption carried out by the Central Bureau of Statistics. Table 1 summarises the latest available figures which date from 1976. About 72 per cent of the total amount of water used was consumed in the two western provinces where industry is most concentrated. Because of its limited availability in these

Table 1. Industrial water consumption in 1976
(quantities in $10^6 \, m^3$)

	total	amount of total used for cooling
Public water supply	200.4	54.2
including: potable water	149.3	
distilled water	8.6	
partially purified water	42.2	
Own supply	3701.7	3428.3
including: fresh groundwater		
(<300 mg/l Cl⁻)	354.9	173.8
salt groundwater		
(>300 mg/l Cl⁻)	78.5	76.5
surface water		
(excluding sea water)	3268.3	3176.0
Total water consumption	3902.1	3482.5

provinces, fresh groundwater constituted only about 5 per cent of the national figure.

FORECASTS FOR INDUSTRIAL WATER DEMAND

A STUDY OF industrial water consumption was begun in 1974 with the cooperation of Dutch industry. By means of sample surveys at a few firms in a particular branch, or written questionnaires for a whole branch of industry, a correlation was sought between water consumption and a factor determining production. In many cases this factor was the tangible output of a firm or the quantity of raw materials processed. It was concluded that the level of specific water consumption (i.e. consumption per unit of output or raw material) has dropped considerably in the past few years. The amount varies according to the branch of industry and very large deviations can be observed within a single branch. A national scenario for the development of specific water demand was made on the basis of the data for each branch of industry and additional figures from the Central Bureau of Statistics. In order to combine the figures, it was necessary to convert the forecast for water demand in each branch to water demand per unit of gross added value in 1970 prices.

The study disregarded the quantities of surface water used for industrial cooling purposes because these abstractions do not affect the scope of present or future infrastructural works of the water system. The study devoted much attention to the expectations within each branch with regard to specific water demand in the future. Table 2 summarises the results of the study; figures are given for specific water consumption in the past and the expectations for each branch up to the year 2000.

Table 3 shows production by Dutch industry in guilders in gross added value and in fixed prices (1970). The forecasts are based on studies conducted by the Central Bureau of Statistics, the Ministry of Economic Affairs and the Advisory Council on Government Policy. There are two possible scenarios according to the last forecast; one based on continuous economic growth and a satisfactory level of employment and a second one based on stunted economic growth and a growing awareness that nature and the environment must not be subject to any further harm. A forecast for the water demand for the various branches of industry and for industry as a whole is obtained by multiplying the figures for specific water demand (Table 2) by those for production (Table 3). This forecast is shown in Table 4.

FACTORS AFFECTING INDUSTRIAL WATER CONSUMPTION

Economic activity

The production forecast in the previous section was based on economic expectations from 1975. At that time 4.4 per cent annual growth was expected in total industrial production between 1976 and 1980. For the 1980 to 1985 period 5 per cent annual growth was predicted in the optimistic forecast and 2.7 per cent annual growth in the pessimistic one. The predictions were wrong; we now know that the average annual growth for industry from 1976 to 1978 was 1.1 per cent. In 1979 it was 3.1 per cent and in 1980 0.6 per cent. The present forecast for annual growth between 1980 and 1985 is about 1.5 per cent. Figure 2 shows how this will be reflected in production figures of industry and mining materials.

What effect this will have on industrial water consumption is not yet known. Detailed figures on industrial water consumption will not be published until 1982 when the Central Bureau of Statistics will have processed the results of its 1981 survey. Differences arise in economic growth and growth in the demand for water as a result of differences in the specific water demand of the various branches of industry and the uneven distribution of the growth in production in the various branches of industry. Rough estimates for 1979 showed that the 2 per cent growth in the economy could mean a growth of about 3.8 per cent in industrial water demand because the branches of industry which require large amounts of water were expanding faster than branches with low specific water requirements.

Figures are now available for total water consumption (fresh water, excluding surface water for cooling purposes) in the Netherlands, i.e. industrial water consumption plus domestic, commercial, government, agricultural and recrea-

Table 2. Specific water demand of Dutch industry in m^3 per 1,000 guilders added value

Branches of industry	industrial classification	specific water demand								
		1957	1962	1967	1972	1976	1980	1985	1990	2000
Food, beverages and meat processing, including: animal products	20/21	70.7	67.6	60.2	47.3	32.3	22.9	19.8	17.3	14.6
other food products	201/203	·	·	94.2	91.8	63.5	41.5	35.0	29.1	23.2
drink and tobacco	204/213	·	·	53.4	35.7	23.9	18.0	15.7	14.3	12.6
	214/217	·	·	28.4	19.6	14.0	11.0	10.1	9.2	8.4
Textile and clothing (excluding footwear)	22/23	·	·	36.8	16.0	15.6	15.6	16.4	16.7	16.7
Footwear and other leather products excluding clothing; rubber and plastic products	24, 31	·	·		12.0	17.7	21.5	23.3	24.2	26.6
Paper, paper products, printing, publishing and allied industries	26/27	·	·	19.6	34.8	21.4	31.2	34.6	36.6	38.6
Chemical industries, man-made and synthetic fibres (except glass)	29/30	69.4	60.2	48.8	37.0	30.6	22.5	17.5	12.8	7.9
Petroleum industry	28	·	·	43.2	39.9	25.8	19.2	16.1	15.0	13.5
Metal Industries	33	23.5	24.5	49.9	27.6	31.8	21.5	30.3	29.1	27.2
Manufacture metal products excluding machinery; transport equipment, mechanical engineering, electrical engineering	34/36			21.3	8.1	32.8	29.6	29.9	29.9	30.2
Other manufacturing industries	25, 32 37/39			13.3	6.4	5.4 5.5 5.8	5.3	5.1	4.9	4.7
Total manufacturing industry excluding construction	2/3	39.4	34.6	30.4	23.1	18.1	14.7	13.0	12.0	10.8
Mining and quarrying	1	63.3	59.9	80.4	38.3	45.9	37.9	39.9	41.0	41.6
Total excluding natural gas	1/3	41.1	36.2	32.3	23.4	18.4	14.9	13.2	12.2	11.0

Table 3. Production forecast for Dutch industry in 10^6 guilders added value (1970 prices). Figures up to 1976 based on data the Central Bureau of Statistics (CBS)

Branches of industry	industrial classification	(CBS) 1957	1962	1967	1972	1976	optimistic forecast 1980	1985	1990	2000	pessimistic forecast 1980	1985	1990	2000
Food, beverages and meat processing, including:	20/21	2829	3551	4362	5381	6211	6749	7490			6749			
animal products	201/203	752	976	1161	1398	1622	1791	2026			1791			
other food products	204/213	1695	2084	2501	2974	3307	3538	3849			3538			
drink and tobacco	214/217	382	491	700	1009	1282	1420	1615			1420			
Textile and clothing (excluding footwear)	22/23	.	.	1765	1860	1381								
Footwear and other leather products excluding clothing: rubber and plastic products	24, 31	.	.	811	864	838	2369	2579			2369			
Paper, paper products, printing, publishing and allied industries	26/27	1124	1610	2121	2606	2690	3087	3667			3087			
Chemical industries, man-made and synthetic fibres (except glass)	29/30	.	.	2466	4659	5755	8035	12193			8035			
Petroleum industries	28	276	368	438	813	785	950	1207			950			
Metal industries	33	426	694	1105	1830	1728	1983	2355			1983			
Manufacture metal products excluding machinery: transport equipment, mechanical engineering, electrical engineering	34/36	.	.	6442	9054	10273	18752	24254			18752			
Other manufacturing industries	25, 32 37/39	.	.	3975	5140	5070								
Total manufacturing industry excluding construction	2/3	13871	18395	23521	32266	35281	41925	53745			41925	48100	54400	63900
Mining and quarrying	1	1106	1235	850	520	220	270	300			270			
Total excluding natural gas	1/3	14977	19630	24371	32766	35501	42195	54045	64070	94270	42195			

Table 4. Forecast water demand Dutch industry

Branches of industry	industrial classification	water demand in 10^6 m³					optimistic forecast					pessimistic forecast				
		1957	1962	1967	1972[2]	1976[2]	1980	1985	1990	2000	2010	1980	1985	1990	2000	2010
Food, beverages and meat processing, including: animal products	20/21	200[1]	240[1]	262.8	254.4	200.8	154.6	148.3				154.6				
other food products	201/203	·	·	109	128	103	75	71				75				
drink and tobacco	204/213	·	·	134	106	79	64	61				64				
	214/217	·	·	20	20	18	16	16				16				
Textile and clothing (excluding footwear)	22/23	70[1]	70[1]	64.9	29.8	21.6	50.9	60.1				50.9				
Footwear and other leather products excluding clothing: rubber and plastic products	24, 31	15[1]	11[1]	15.9	10.4	17.9										
Paper, paper products, printing, publishing and allied industries	26/27	78[1]	97[1]	103.4	90.7	82.4	69.5	64.2				69.2				
Chemical industries, man-made and synthetic fibres (except glass)	29/30	·	·	106.6	172.2	148.7	154.3	196.3				154.3				
Petroleum industry	28	·	·	21.9	32.5	25.0	30.9	36.6				30.9				
Metal industries	33	10[1]	17[1]	23.5	50.5	56.7	58.7	70.4				58.7				
Manufacture metal products excluding machinery: transport equipment, mechanical engineering, electrical engineering	34/36	40[1]	55[1]	85.5	73.3	55.3	99.4	123.7				99.4				
Other manufacturing industries	25, 32 37/39	·	·	31.5	33.1	29.4										
Total manufacturing industry excluding construction	2/3	546.1	637.1	716.0	746.8	637.8	618.3	699.6	781.7	1037.0	1290	618.3				
Mining and quarrying	1	70[1]	74[1]	68.4	20.0	10.1	10.2	12.0				10.2				
Total excluding natural gas	1/3	616.1	711.1	784.4	766.8	647.9	628.5	711.6				628.5	634.9	663.7	702.9	742

· no figures available
[1] estimated figure
[2] adjusted CBS-figures

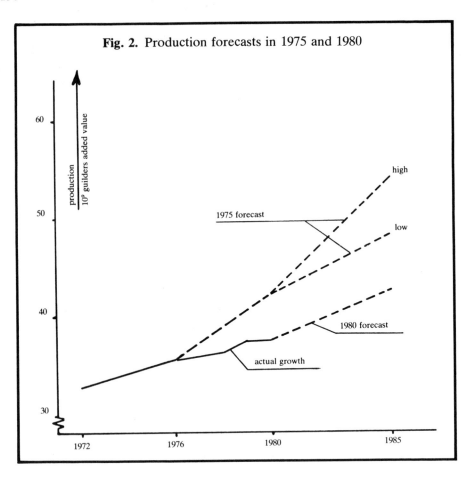

Fig. 2. Production forecasts in 1975 and 1980

tional requirements. Figure 3 shows the 1975 forecast for total water demand against actual consumption up to 1979. Actual consumption has been extrapolated on basis of current data on water demand and an economic growth of about 1.5 per cent per year, to show that water consumption will be considerably lower in 1985 than was forecast in 1975. The difference in the forecasts is largely due to economic stagnation.

The Pollution of Surface Waters Act

Under the Pollution of Surface Waters Act, which came into force in 1970, levies can be imposed on the principle that "the polluter pays". The levies are linked primarily to the degree of pollution, expressed in population equivalents (p.e.) but the volume correction is also very important as surcharges can be imposed or reductions granted according to the volume of waste discharged.

These levies meant a considerable rise in costs for industry. Figure 4 shows

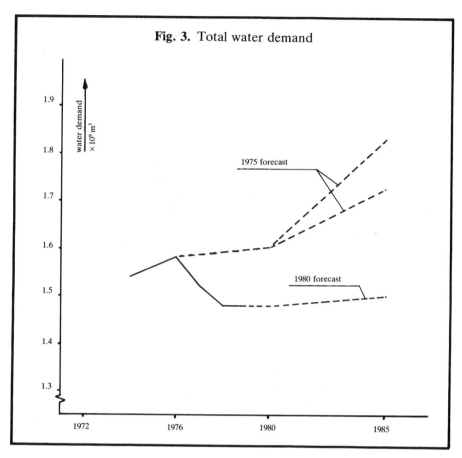

Fig. 3. Total water demand

the costs that have to be met in 12 regions in the Netherlands by an average firm, requiring 2×10^6 kWh of electricity, 1×10^6 m^3 of natural gas and 50,000 m^3 of water annually, discharging waste water with a degree of pollution of 4,000 p.e. It is clear from this figure that the cost of water alone is of little significance but that the cost of water combined with waste water levies, as gas and electricity charges, are high enough to make the firms concerned aim to reduce these overheads. Efforts by firms to limit costs by discharging as little waste as possible, or by purifying the waste water themselves, resulted in a reorganization of all aspects of industrial water management. This produced an automatic reduction in consumption, as shown in Figure 5.

It is difficult to produce scientific proof of the connection between the levies and reduced consumption. Specific water demand did decrease more sharply after 1970 than before but there is only circumstantial evidence as to whether the decrease was due solely to the Pollution of Surface Waters Act or whether other factors were involved. It is a fact, however, that when interviewed, managerial staff in industrial concerns have always cited the Act as the major reason for economising as much as possible on water consumption.

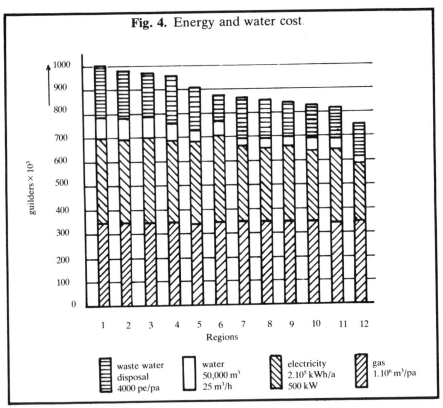

Fig. 4. Energy and water cost.

Legend:
- waste water disposal 4000 pe/pa
- water 50,000 m³ 25 m³/h
- electricity 2.10⁵ kWh/a 500 kW
- gas 1.10⁶ m³/pa

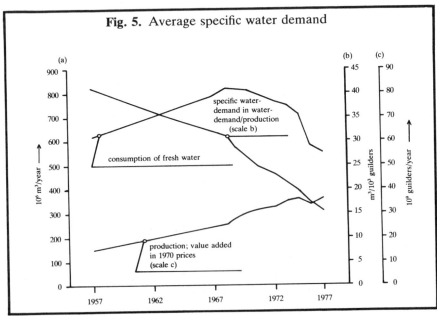

Fig. 5. Average specific water demand

Legislation governing the use of Groundwater

Groundwater management is at present regulated by:
(1) the Water Supply Undertakings (Groundwater) Act which governs the abstraction of groundwater for the public drinking water supply;
(2) the Provincial Ordinances which govern the abstraction of groundwater for all other purposes.

At present a Groundwater Bill is under discussion in Parliament. It will replace the legislation referred to above and will govern the abstraction of groundwater for all purposes. The present Provincial Ordinances contain regulations on the registration of groundwater abstractions and the issuing of licences. Compulsory registration was introduced in the various provinces between 1966 and 1974 and in general applies to abstractions of more than $10^3 \, m^3$ per hour, though some provinces register all abstractions. Licences became compulsory between 1966 and 1977 and, depending on the province, were required for abstractions exceeding 2 to 30 m^3 per hour with a total abstraction of over 200 to 20,000 m^3 per month. There are separate regulations for well-pointing, test pumping and sprinkling in the agricultural sector. Licence and registration regulations may vary from province to province, as the local availability of groundwater is taken into account. Conditions may be attached to licences, for instance in cases where abstractions by water works would suffer or where industrial abstractions could cause environmental or agricultural damage. The abstraction registers are open to the public.

It is also difficult to demonstrate a direct link between the reduction in the amount of groundwater abstracted by industry and compulsory registration and licensing. However, investigations into industrial water demand have shown that compulsory licensing has contributed to a reduction in industrial groundwater demand while industrial activity has increased.

Figure 6 shows the total registered amount of groundwater. In 1974 the last two of the twelve provinces introduced compulsory registration and since then the total amount of groundwater abstracted per concern has decreased. Remarkably, this is largely due to the decrease in the amount of groundwater abstracted for cooling purposes.

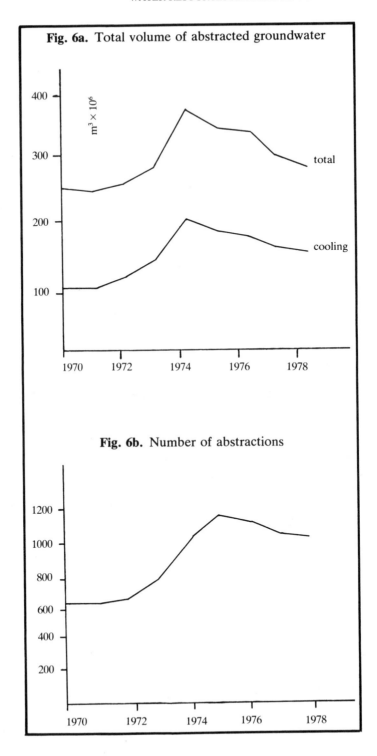

Fig. 6a. Total volume of abstracted groundwater

Fig. 6b. Number of abstractions

Use of High-TDS Water for Cooling at Thermal Electric Generating Plants

Trevor C. Hughes

Research Scientist at the International Institute for Applied Systems Analysis, Laxenburg, Austria

J. Clair Batty

Professor of Mechanical Engineering at Utah State University, Logan, Utah, USA,

and

C. Earl Israelsen

Research Scientist at the Utah Water Research Laboratory, Logan, Utah, USA

SYNOPSIS

Major increases in the fraction of water resources allocated to cooling of thermal electric plants is presently occurring and this trend is projected to accelerate during the next few decades. As the freshwater resources in energy-rich regions become fully allocated, additional cooling water is being acquired by transfer from other sectors, principally agriculture. One possibility for extending regional, water-resource bases is to use brackish or saline water in place of fresh water. Increases in cost of operating thermal electric recirculating cooling systems as salinity of make-up water increases are modeled. The example used is a hypothetical 1,000 MW power plant located in the Upper Colorado River Basin in Western US. The parameters modelled include changes in input and output quantities of cooling water and resulting increases in the size of zero-discharge effluent disposal ponds. The increased treatment costs for three operating modes are calculated. Specifically, the options modeled include: (1) no treatment other than biocide (causing large waste streams and related disposal costs); (2) water softening to prevent scaling; and (3) a combination of softening, desalination, and brine concentration. In addition to the increased treatment and disposal costs (as functions of salinity) a relative value scale for saline water is presented. The concept involves calculation of costs one should be willing to pay for water of any level of salinity, given an assumed delivery cost for water of lower (higher) salinity.

Conclusions are that it is technically feasible to operate recirculating tower-type cooling systems with high salinity water (examples already exist) and indeed, innovative cooling tower designs allow salinities as high as 150,000 mg/l of total dissolved solids. The economic feasibility of using low quality, make-up water depends upon relative costs of saline and fresh water and/or quantification of social benefits resulting from maintaining fresh water allocations to agricultural and environmental uses.

RÉSUMÉ

Actuellement, on assiste à une forte augmentation de la part des ressources hydrauliques consacrèes à la réfrigération des centrales thermiques et on prévoit que cette tendance va encore s'accéler au cours des prochaines décennies. Une possibilité pour accroître les ressources hydrauliques consacrées à la réfrigération des centrales eaux saumâtres ou salées à la place d'eau douce. L'augmentation des coûts opératoires des systèmes de réfrigeration en circuit ferme en fonction de la salinité de l'eau est modelisé. Les paramètres modelisées comprennent les variations des quantités d'eau captées et rejetées par le systéme de réfrigeration ce qui se traduit par une modification de la taille des installations d'épuration des eaux rejetées. Les calculs de l'augmentation des coûts de traitement a été fait pour les modes opératoires suivants: (1) traitement exclusivement chimique (ou chlore, ce qui entraine des pertes et des coûts importants); (2) adoucissement de l'eau pour éviter la formation de tartre; (3) une combinaison d'adoucissement, de desalement et de concentration de saumure. En conclusion, on montre qu'il est techniquement possible d'utiliser des eaux fortement salées dans des systèmes de réfrigeration en circuit fermé (des exemples e istent déjà) de plus des nouvelles conception de systemes de refroidisse-ment autorisent des concentrations de l'ordre de 150,000 mg/l de matières dissoutes. La faisabilité économique de l'utilisation des eaux de mediocre composition dépend du cout relatif entre eau salie et eau douce et/ou de la quantification du gain social obtenu en reservant l'eau douce a l'agriculture et l'environement.

RESUMEN

Un mayor aumento en la proporción de recursos hidráulicos para enfriamiento de plantas de generación electrica esta actualmente occurriendo y esta tendencia esta proyectada para aumentar durante las próximas decadas. Una posibilidad para extender las bases regionales esta de recursos hidráulicos es utilizando salobre o aguas salinas en lugar de agua dulce. Los aumentos en los gastos de operación de un sistema de enfriamiento de reciclo de generación electrica conforme la salinidad de abastecimiento de agua es modelado. Las entradas y resultados de los parametros modelados incluyen cambios en las cantidades de agua para enfriamiento, resultando aumentos en el tamaño de descargo-zero de las aguas residuales. El aumento de costos es calculado de la siguiente manera: (1) Ningun tratamiento fuera del de biocido (causando grande corriente de desperdicion y causando grandes gastos de disposición. Llegamos a la conclusión que es posible recircular tecnicamente el sistema de enfriamiento con aguas de alto porcentage de salinidad (ejemplos y a existen) y en realidad diseños de torres de enfriamiento permiten que salinidades tan altas como 150,000 mg/l a un total de solidos desueltos. La posibilidad economica de usar baja calidad de abastecimientos de agua depende de los costo relativos de aguas dulce y salinas y/o los beneficios sociales resultando del mantenimiento de aguas dulces con distribución para uso de agricultura y de ambiente.

INTRODUCTION

DURING THE SHIFT from oil-based energy to renewable energy sources in the next few decades, there will inevitably be a period of heavy reliance upon coal and synfuels. This transition period will be associated with very large increases in water resource inputs to energy development and various environmental impact outputs within the regions where the fossil fuels are extracted and converted to a useable energy form. Unfortunately, much of these fossil fuel resources are located in areas which are semi-arid and where high quality water resources are already completely allocated. There are, however, in many such regions, very significant quantities of water which are so high in total dissolved solids (TDS) as to be unuseable for municipal or agricultural purposes. Sources of such water can include pumped groundwater from shale and other soluble formations, artesian flow from oil and gas exploration testholes, return flows from agricultural land, effluent from coal mines, geothermal development wastewater, and even seawater. Usually the actual quantities of high TDS water are unknown because most surface and groundwater data-gathering efforts have ignored this water (it is usually classified as a potential contaminant rather than a resource). In this paper high TDS water will be considered to include brackish water (1 to 10 thousand mg/l) and saline water (10 to 35 thousand mg/l).

The occurrence of large quantities of high-TDS water is, of course, not limited to semi-arid regions. For example, in Poland (certainly not an arid region) serious coal-related, saline water disposal problems exist in at least 3 river basins; the opening of additional coal mines in the Vistula River Basin depends upon protecting the Vistula and its tributaries against additional drainage of saline groundwater from coal mines [1, 2].

There are two possible approaches to increasing the water supply available to regions short of water, thereby meeting demands for energy without eliminating or greatly decreasing irrigated agriculture. One solution is to import the water needed from other water-rich regions. Major importation projects are now being discussed in Canada, the USA, Mexico, Australia, India and the USSR [3]. Importation projects usually are associated with significant negative environmental impacts in the exporting basins and, therefore, should not be implemented before all possible management concepts for local water resources have been exhausted.

The second approach for increasing the supply of water available for energy demands is the use of high-TDS water. This concept is not feasible for irrigation users since it would require treatment costs which greatly exceed the value of irrigation water, except in very unusual circumstances (very high-valued crops). However, the energy industry experiences no such constraint. Even if the additional treatment costs due to using high-TDS water were $0.40 per m^3, the marginal increase in cost of operating a thermal electric power plant would be only 2.6 per cent [4]. If the plants were designed specifically for use of such water, the increase in cost should be considerably less.

The remainder of this paper will summarize research on the economic feasibility of using high-TDS water for cooling of thermal electric power plants, which has been done at Utah State University, and will outline continued work on this topic which is being undertaken at both USU and the International Institute for Applied Systems Analysis (IIASA).

UPPER COLORADO CASE STUDY

THE RESEARCH PROJECT at USU focused upon use of high-TDS water for energy development within the Upper Colorado River basin. This basin has several characteristics which make the TDS water-use concept attractive, as follows:

(1) Total water demand is rapidly approaching total supply.

(2) Very large energy-related water demands are projected for the near future.

(3) The Colorado River already has a serious salinity problem. Its magnitude is suggested by the fact that various studies which attempted to quantify the value of reducing its salinity (actually the measure of damages to downstream water users) have calculated it as $230,000 to $320,000 for each mg/l of change [5].

A thermal electric power plant with multiple circulation through cooling towers can be conceptualized for our purposes as a black box which requires water and fossil fuel as inputs and which outputs a much smaller quantity of water (having evaporated some 90 per cent of the make-up water). Once-through cooling will not be considered because of the immense water diversion quantities required. Of particular interest is the fact that, essentially, the entire quantity of input minerals is returned in the concentrated blowdown (cooling tower waste) stream. Consider a hypothetical 1,000 MW power plant operating at 35 per cent thermal efficiency and an 80 per cent load factor which has average cooling water cycle flows (using high quality water), as shown in Figure 1. The actual Rankine power cycle water system is not shown since its make-up water requirement is extremely small and it has essentially no effluent. We will be concerned only with the cooling cycle which rejects the huge quantities of waste heat to the atmos-

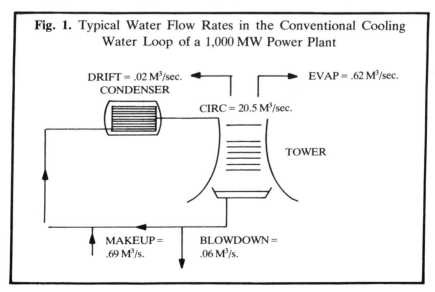

Fig. 1. Typical Water Flow Rates in the Conventional Cooling Water Loop of a 1,000 MW Power Plant

DRIFT = .02 M³/sec.
CONDENSER
EVAP = .62 M³/sec.
CIRC = 20.5 M³/sec.
TOWER
MAKEUP = .69 M³/s.
BLOWDOWN = .06 M³/s.

Table 1. Concentration of Constituents in Cooling Tower Make-up Waters

Constituent	Sample 1 TDS = 1000 to 3000 mg/l	Sample 2 TDS = 3000 to 10,000 mg/l	Sample 3 TDS = >10,000 mg/l
Al	0.25	0.72	1.14
B	0.1	0.5	0.7
Ca	156	343	312
CO_3	117	361	550
Cl	592	138	4880
F	0.17	0.68	0.46
Fe	<0.02	<0.02	<0.02
Mg	48	267	109
Mn	<0.01	0.25	0.50
NO_3-N	<0.04	0.50	1.02
$O-PO_4$	0.71	0.72	0.98
K	4	20	102
SiO_2	11	22	35
Na	458	620	4300
SO_4	700	2740	2770
TDS	2220	4640	13180
pH	7.6	8.3	7.8

phere. The number of cycles through cooling towers, and the water treatment and disposal costs, are all functions of salinity of the make-up water. Therefore, the focus of the following discussion on the cooling water system modeling will be upon calculating changes on these costs, as salinity is varied.

The added costs for operating a cooling system as salinity increases depend, in part, on the particular ions making up the salinity. Since this study could not look at all possible combinations, the wide variety of water chemistries which might be encountered in the geographical study area was represented by obtaining analyses of typical waters from the region. The particular analyses used are shown in Table 1. The broad implications of using these kinds of waters in conventional power plant cooling are examined.

Mass Balance Equations

The follow mass balance equations necessary to calculate the cooling tower system input/output relationships are the following:

$$\text{Make-up Water} = \text{drift loss} + \text{Evap. Loss} + \text{Blowdown} \qquad (1)$$

$$\text{Make-up Salt} = \text{drift salt} + \text{Blowdown salt} \qquad (2)$$

An energy balance for the cooling tower is:

$$\dot{Q} = \dot{M}_1 h_1 - \dot{M}_2 h_2 \tag{3}$$

where the $\dot{M}_1$ and h_1 terms are mass flow rates and specific enthalpy respectively, of the water entering and leaving the tower, and $\dot{Q}$ is the rate of heat rejection from the 1,000 MW plant, as shown in Figure 2. The bd and mu notation refers to blowdown and make-up.

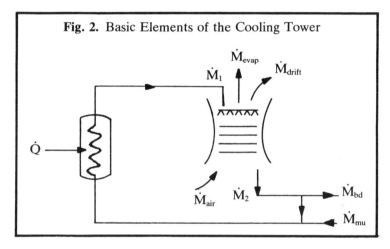

Fig. 2. Basic Elements of the Cooling Tower

$\dot{Q}$ can be calculated as (note that waste heat from a plant with 35 per cent efficiency and 80 per cent load factor can be approximated as 40 per cent efficiency at 100 per cent load):

$$\dot{Q} = 1000\ (1.0 - 0.4)/0.4 = 1500\ \text{MW} = 5.12(10^9)\ \text{BTU/hr}. \tag{4}$$

By assuming temperatures entering and leaving the tower of 43.3°C and 26.7°C and an evaporation rate of 1 per cent of the circulating water per 5.5°C (10°F) reduction in temperature, we have:

$$\dot{M}_{evap} = 0.01\ \dot{M}_1 (\Delta T)/5.5 = 0.03\ \dot{M}_1 \tag{5}$$

Also drift will be estimated to 0.1 per cent of $\dot{M}_1$. From these simple equations, the make-up and blowdown water flow rates can be calculated as a function of their salt concentrations if no water treatment (other than a biocide to prevent organic growth on surfaces) is used. The results of such calculations are displayed in Figure 3 for a single upper limit of circulating water salinity.

The actual upper limit on salinity (and more importantly the type of salinity) that is permitted is a function of the design and type of materials used in the cooling system and/or the extent and type of water treatment provided. The additional investment costs for corrosion and deposition-prevention materials in

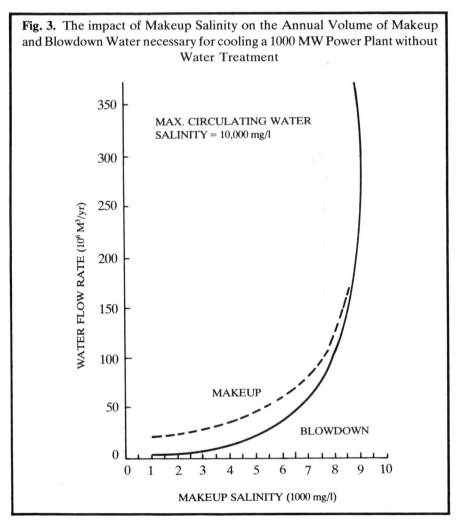

Fig. 3. The impact of Makeup Salinity on the Annual Volume of Makeup and Blowdown Water necessary for cooling a 1000 MW Power Plant without Water Treatment

the cooling system are not modeled in this paper. However, water treatment costs will be included and treatment, such as softening, is to a large extent an alternative to more expensive materials. As Figure 3 shows, the quantity of both make-up and blowdown water increases with salinity of make-up and as the make-up salinity approaches the circulating water limit, the quantity of blowdown approaches the quantity of make-up (thereby approaching the unfeasible domain of once-through cooling).

Water Treatment and Disposal Costs

From the large array of possible make-up and/or recirculating water-treatment methods, only three will be evaluated here.

Option 1. *No treatment—Disposal in Evaporation Ponds.* The mass balance equations already presented provide a means of calculating water and salt inflows and outflows from the cooling loop. The only treatment cost assumed will be the relatively minor cost of biocide.

The disposal costs are essentially those for constructing an evaporation pond designed for zero discharge during a critical (high precipitation/low evaporation) year. The calculation of required pond volume and area as a function of salinity, and therefore volume of inflow (blowdown), is difficult since evaporation rate depends upon wind, radiation, temperature of water and air, precipitation, relative humidity, salinity and, most important, the pond area itself. Therefore, an iterative computer programme was developed to calculate pond sizes, given climatic data for an average and a critical year in the case study area. The related construction costs were then estimated by assuming flat topography, a plastic lining and allowance for mineral deposition at the bottom for 40 years plus 1 meter of brine depth. The cost per unit of pond area is somewhat dependent on size but generally in the $85,000 to $100,000/hectare range. The pond size model and cost functions are detailed in Israelsen *et al* [4].

Option 2. *Softening of Make-up Water plus Sidestream Treatment (and Disposal).* This option requires cold-process softening (addition of lime to precipitate Mg^{++}, Ca^{++} and SiO_2) for both the make-up water and recirculation sidestream to keep hardness below 400 mg/l and prevent scaling (Figure 4). Lime quantities were calculated as a function of Ca and Mg in the make-up water.

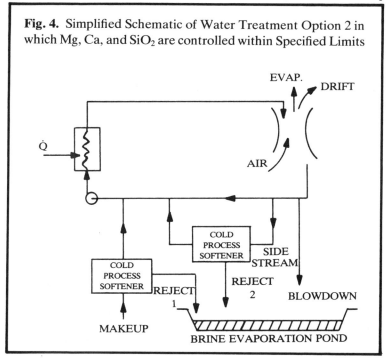

Fig. 4. Simplified Schematic of Water Treatment Option 2 in which Mg, Ca, and SiO_2 are controlled within Specified Limits

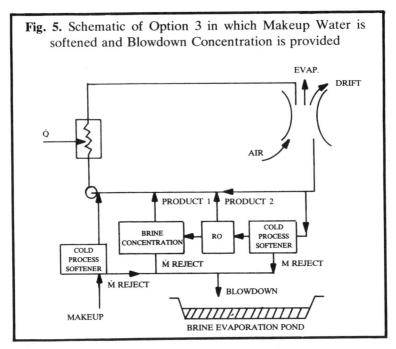

Fig. 5. Schematic of Option 3 in which Makeup Water is softened and Blowdown Concentration is provided

Capital costs and cost of lime were estimated at 1980 US levels. Disposal costs were calculated as described for Option 1.

Option 3. Make-up Water Softening plus Desalination and Brine Concentration of Blowdown (and Disposal). This option replaces sidestream softening with both reverse osmosis (r.o.) and brine concentration of the r.o. waste stream. The assumed brine concentration (b.c.) design has been used in several recently constructed plants in the Colorado Basin. It has a waste stream of only 7 per cent of inflow and the only external energy required is that to drive a compressor (24 Kwh/M^3 of feed). The tandem operation of the r.o. and b.c. units (Figure 5) appears to be efficient since the r.o. unit produces a large reject stream of about 48 per cent of feed. The costs and details of operation are given in Israelsen et al. [4]. Disposal costs were calculated as previously described.

Results

The water treatment and disposal costs for the three options, and a range of make-up water and circulating water salinity, are given in Figures 6, 7 and 8.

Option 1 is not realistic both because of scaling problems (no softening is provided) and because of the large evaporation ponds required. It is included here only to show the reduction in disposal costs which results from proper treatment (it consists of only disposal costs plus a small biocide cost). Disposal costs are greatly reduced as the circulating salinity is allowed to increase, as indicated by

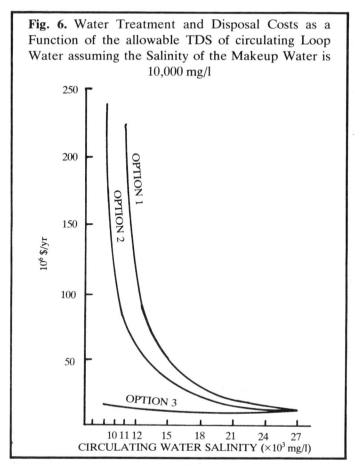

Fig. 6. Water Treatment and Disposal Costs as a Function of the allowable TDS of circulating Loop Water assuming the Salinity of the Makeup Water is 10,000 mg/l

Figure 6. However, some increase in capital cost of the cooling system would also occur as allowable circulating salinity is increased (due to changes in materials for corrosion protection), and these costs are not included. Figures 7 and 8 show a clear advantage for Option 3 (softening, desalination and brine concentration) as compared to Option 2 (softening only).

Relative Value of Water as a Function of Salinity

With the information provided in the previous section, it is possible to present the concept of a relative value scale for waters of various salinities. The rationale for the development of this scale is as follows: Suppose lower-quality water (for example TDS = 5,000 mg/l) is available and can be delivered to the plant at a cost of $0.08/M³, and better quality water (for example TDS = 1,000 mg/l) is available but the delivery cost to the plant is $0.40/M³. While the lower-quality water costs less per unit volume, a greater volume will be required and treatment and

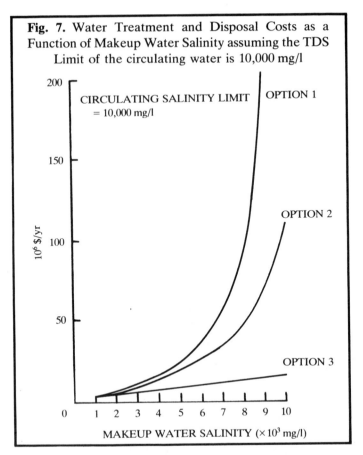

Fig. 7. Water Treatment and Disposal Costs as a Function of Makeup Water Salinity assuming the TDS Limit of the circulating water is 10,000 mg/l

disposal costs are greater. All other factors being equal, which water is economically preferable for cooling purposes?

To establish a relative value scale for 5,000 mg/l make-up water, consider the following equations:

$$MU_i \times VALUE_i + COST_i = MU_5 \times VALUE_5 + COST_5 \qquad (6)$$

where the MU_i and MU_5 are quantities of make-up water of salinity i and 5,000 mg/l respectively; $VALUE_i$ and $VALUE_5$ are the value (in the case of MU_i) and the price (in the case of MU_5) of make-up water delivered to the plant. $COST_i$ and $COST_5$ are the water treatment and disposal costs as described previously. By assuming a price for 5,000 mg/l water, and calculating the costs and quantities via equations already given, one could calculate $VALUE_i$ which should be interpreted as the highest cost one should pay for water of salinity i. The results of such calculations, for assumed allowable circulating salinities of 10,000 and 24,000 respectively, are displayed graphically in Figures 9 and 10. For example, if circulating water at 10,000 mg/l is allowed in a system using Option 2

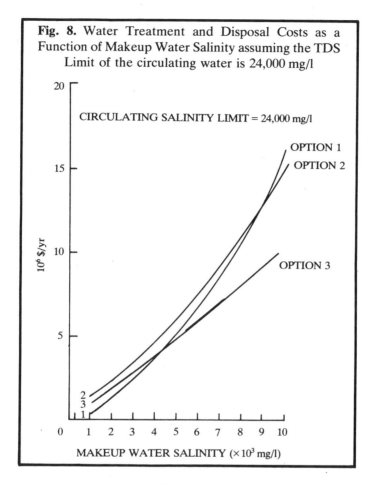

Fig. 8. Water Treatment and Disposal Costs as a Function of Makeup Water Salinity assuming the TDS Limit of the circulating water is 24,000 mg/l

treatment, and make-up water of 5,000 mg/l is deliverable at $0.08/M³, one should pay as much as $0.80/M³ for water of 1,000 mg/l. If, however, the circulating limit is relaxed to 24,000 mg/l, then no more than $0.32/M³ should be paid for the better quality water.

DISCUSSION

THE POTENTIAL for utilizing high-TDS water in energy-related uses includes other applications, such as transport media for coal slurry lines (with recycling as cooling water at the destination), cooling for coal gasification and other syn-fuel conversion processes, materials handling and dust control at mines. The summary of the economic modeling effort reported here was limited to only a single

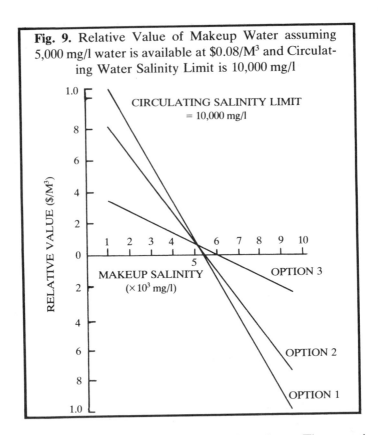

Fig. 9. Relative Value of Makeup Water assuming 5,000 mg/l water is available at $0.08/M³ and Circulating Water Salinity Limit is 10,000 mg/l

application—cooling of thermal electric generating plants. The equations allow calculation of variations in both input and output quantities of water and treatment and disposal costs as a function of make-up water TDS. Some of the costs and the evaporation pond sizes are specific to the Upper Colorado River Basin but the methodology should be useful in other climates and economies.

There is no question that cooling systems can be designed for successful operation with highly saline water. Examples of existing plants which use circulating water varying from brackish to seawater (7,800 to 45,000 mg/l TDS) are Chalk Point (Washington, D.C.), Turkey Point (Florida), and Forked River (New Jersey). Also, there is considerable current activity related to developing innovative cooling-tower designs specifically for operating at very high salinities. An example which appears very promising is the Binary Cooling Tower (BCT) concept which is being proposed in the US. The BCT approach uses a closed loop of high-quality water with heat exchange to a secondary fluid through a thin membrane in the cooling tower. The secondary fluid (which rejects the heat by evaporation) can be at salinities as high as 150,000 TDS.

The economic aspects of make-up quality selection can be reduced to questions of:

(1) cost of delivering low-quality water relative to the cost of higher-quality

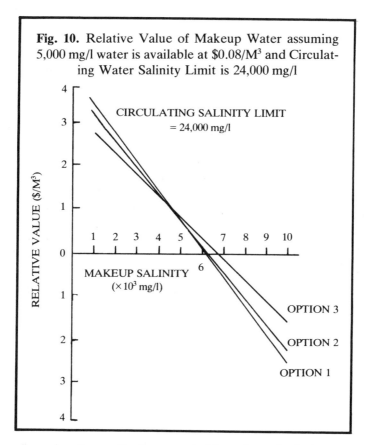

Fig. 10. Relative Value of Makeup Water assuming 5,000 mg/l water is available at $0.08/M³ and Circulating Water Salinity Limit is 24,000 mg/l

alternatives (by using the methods presented here for calculating treatment and disposal costs);

(2) increases in cooling system investment cost as a function of circulating water salinity and the trade-offs between treatment and investment costs which are possible (which are not included in this paper but will be the subject of future research). As demonstrated here, increasing the make-up water salinity causes significant increases in both the quantities of required supply and waste streams and treatment and disposal costs. This implies that so long as fresh water is available at a cost less than the positive value levels indicated by Figures 9 and 10 (and adjusted for other climates), the power producers will continue to seek high-quality water (usually by purchases from agriculture). If sufficient social and/or environmental benefits can be identified for maintaining the high-quality water, either in a stream or for diversion by users which cannot use the available low-quality sources, then governmental incentives, such as tax allowances for using the low-quality water for cooling, may be appropriate.

Space limitations prevent a discussion of possible environmental benefits which such low-quality water use could create. The basic notion, however, is that it is possible to convert a power plant from a salt concentrator to a salt remover by both evaporating saline rather than good-quality water, and by disposing of minerals on pond bottoms rather than returning them to the river. In this context, pond life (based upon mineral storage volume) equal to the life of the power plant becomes important unless commercial recovery of minerals is feasible—which is currently doubtful.

Another topic which is not addressed here, but is of importance, is the problem of mineral disposal in climates where zero-discharge holding ponds are not feasible. In that situation, one can envision small brine pipelines to deliver water to large rivers and seas or to more arid regions. The International Institute for Applied Systems Analysis of Laxenburg, Austria, is currently planning research on this topic as part of their ongoing regional water management task. The objectives will include extending the modeling effort begun at Utah State University, addressing the question of disposal in non-arid climates, identifying case studies in both planned and market economies and assessing the potential benefits of desalinating municipal water supply with waste heat from thermal generating plants. IIASA collaborators will include, but certainly not be limited to, USU where research is also continuing. A current topic of interest at USU is use of the inverse thermal gradient in solar ponds (ponds created for power plant effluent waste disposal) for supplementing energy production.

References

1. Bojarski, Z. and Skinderowicz, B. (1980) *Problems of Environmental Protection in the Polish Coal Mining Industry*. Szczyrk Conference Papers—Paper II Coal: Issues for the Eighties, Collaborative Paper CP-80-24, International Institute for Applied Systems Analysis, Laxenburg, Austria.
2. Stone, John C., Gadkowsky, M., Salewicz, A., Sikorski, W. and Singleton, Jr., F. Dail. *Mathematical Programming Approach to Modelling Industrial Water Demand Relationships: Water Demand for Electric Energy Generation in Poland*. (Forthcoming Research Report). International Institute for Applied Systems Analysis, Laxenburg, Austria. November 1981.
3. Voropaev, G.V. (1979) *The Hydrological and Engineering Aspects of the Interregional Water Transfer Problem in the USSR*. Proceedings (Volume 2) of the International Association for Hydraulic Research XVIII Congress, Cagliari, Italy.
4. Israelsen, C. Earl, Adams, V. Dean, Batty, J. Clair, George, Dennis B., Hughes, Trevor C., Seierstad, Alberta J., Wang, H.C. and Kuo, H.P. (1980) *Use of Saline Water in Energy Development*. Water Resources Planning Series UWRL/P-80/04, Utah Water Research Laboratory, Logan, UT.
5. Narayanan, Rangesan, Sumol Padungchai and Bishop, A. Bruce (1979) *Economic Evaluation of the Salinity Impacts from Energy Development: The Case of the Upper Colorado River Basin*. Water Resources Planning Series UWRL/P-79/07, Utah Water Research Laboratory, Logan, UT.

Multicriteria Planning of Water Resources-Demand Equilibrium in Industrial Areas

László Dávid

Director, State Office for Technical Development,
Budapest, Hungary

SYNOPSIS

The comprehensive planning of water resources-demand equilibrium in industrial areas is a complicated problem. The paper provides a multicriteria planning methodology for accomplishment of equilibrium by a comprehensive development of the most reasonable, multipurpose water management system. The approach is based on the general process-control model for regulation of equilibrium, which involves three basic regulation elements and five regulation factors. The alternative systems are evaluated by a multicriteria goal function, which involves ten economic, social, water management, environmental and natural resource criteria. The selection of alternatives can be solved by one of the multicriteria-ranking methods. The application of the methodology is shown in a realistic example.

RÉSUMÉ

L'étude complexe de l'équilibre ressources-besoins en eau est une tâche composée. Le mémoire présente un procédé d'études à plusieurs critères pour la mise en pratique de l'équilibre par le développement général du système d'économie hydraulique le plus rationnel a buts multiples. L'approche se repose sur le modèle de direction de cours général de la régulation d'équilibre, qui comprend trois éléments de régulation de fond et cinq facteurs de réglage. Les systèmes alternatifs sont évalueés par une fonction de but à plusieurs critères, qui renferme dix critères exprimant des ressources économiques, sociales, d'économie hydraulique, d'environnement et naturelles. Le choix des alternatives peut se faire une méthode de classement quelconque à plusieurs critères. L'application du procédé est illustrée par un exemple réel.

RESUMEN

La planificación complexo del equilibrio, entre la demanda y los recursos hidráulicos es una tarea compleja. En el estudio se presenta un método de planificación de policriterio, para realizar el equilibrio, con el desarollo complejo de un sistema de recursos hidráulicos, con varios objetos y de modo que es el más razonable. La base de la aproximación es el modelo general de la orientación del proceso de la regulación del equilibrio, que contiene tres elementos básicos de regulación y cinco factores de regulación. Los sistemas alternativas son evaluados por una función de policriterio, que contiene diez criterios, respecto los recursos de: económicos, sociales, hidráulicos, ambientales y natural. Se puede realizar la selección de las alternavivas con la ayuda de alguno método de graduación de policriterio. Un ejemplo práctico muestra la aplicación del método.

INTRODUCTION

THE PURPOSE of this paper is to provide a multicriteria planning methodology for accomplishment of equilibrium between natural water resources and demands for water in industrial areas with water shortages, by a comprehensive development of the most reasonable multipurpose water management system (WMS).

A multicriteria model for basin-wide regulation of general water resources-demand equilibrium in river basins, considering the river basin development

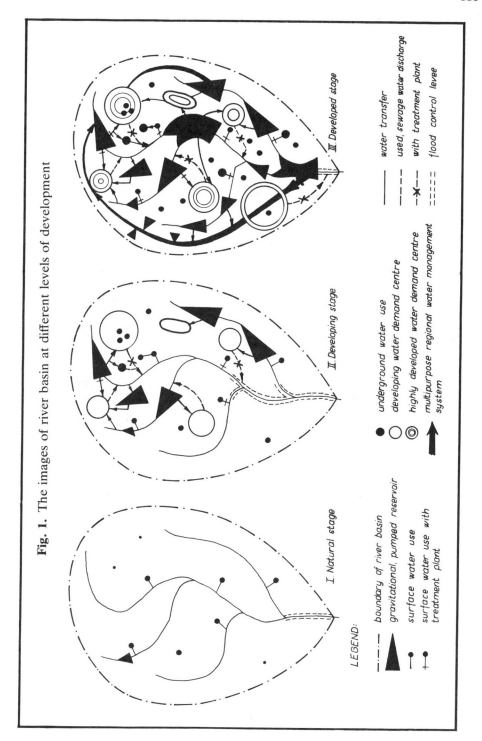

Fig. 1. The images of river basin at different levels of development

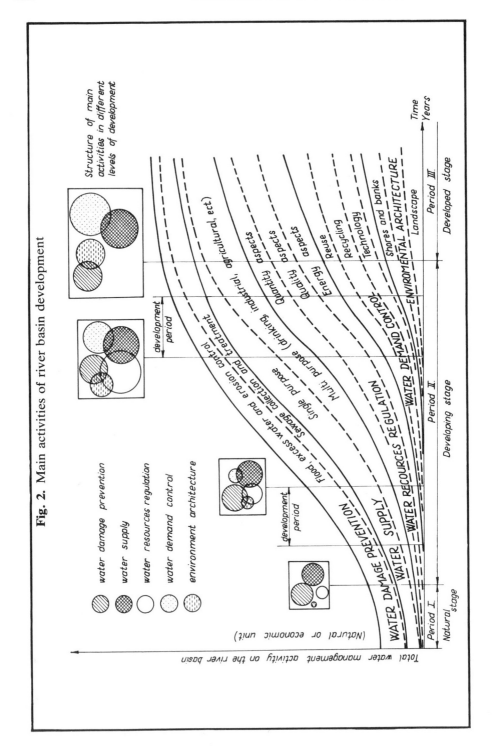

Fig. 2. Main activities of river basin development

process (Figs. 1 and 2), has been developed by Dávid [1]. It is based on the process-control theory of the long-term river basin development and it considers the river basin as a hierarchical system (Fig. 3). Among others, the optimum water resources system planning has been investigated in Reference 2, in which the problem is analyzed from a stochastic viewpoint. Multiobjective planning of runoff regulation under uncertain water demands has been studied in References 3 and 4. Greenberg and Hordon [5] investigated the deterministic equilibrium between resources, demand and capacity for a domestic water supply problem. Further aspects of such equilibrium in river basin planning have been reported by the United Nations [6]. Moss and Dawdy [7] have investigated economic optimization under stochastic supply and demand. The basin-wide aspects of a planning system have been reported by Kuzin [8]. The trade-off between increase of water availability by runoff regulation and by water quality control has been examined in Reference 9.

The present paper also describes a multicriteria study on comprehensive planning of industrial WMS in river basins with water supply shortages. It can be used for the development of both new and existing industrial areas. The WMS is considered as a bridge between natural water resources and the water demands.

The paper is constructed as follows. First, the characterization of equilibrium

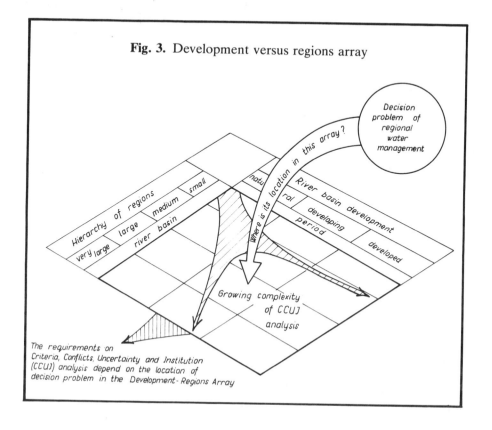

Fig. 3. Development versus regions array

and the goals of its regulation are presented; secondly, the multicriteria model for ranking of alternatives is described. And finally, a simplified example reporting an experiment on application of the model illustrates how the most reasonable WMS for making an equilibrium can be selected.

REGULATION OF RESOURCE-DEMAND EQUILIBRIUM

THE CONCEPT AND SYSTEM of regulation (Fig. 4) is described in detail in Reference 10. Referring to this presentation, the regulation of water resource-demand equilibrium in industrial areas can be considered as follows

$$\mathbf{A}(t) + \max \mathbf{CM}(\Delta t) = \mathbf{A}(t + \Delta t) \tag{1}$$

in which $\mathbf{A}(i) =$ indicator matrix to describe the existing resource-demand situation in time t and it is assumed that $\mathbf{A}(t) \neq \mathbf{Ao}$, in which $\mathbf{Ao} =$ indicator matrix for the equilibrium in an industrial area. Therefore, $\mathbf{A}(t)$ describes here an unbalanced situation which needs planning and development; $\max \mathbf{CM}(\Delta t) =$ the control matrix to describe the most reasonable system of control systems needed to achieve a new equilibrium, during time Δt; $\mathbf{A}(t + \Delta t) =$ indicator matrix of the planned resource-demand situation in time $t + \Delta t$ for which $\mathbf{A}(t + \Delta t) = \mathbf{Ao}$, therefore it indicates an equilibrium.

The state variables form two groups, namely the basic regulation elements: natural water supply (resource)—S; water demand—D; system capacity of WMS—SC; and the regulation factors: space—s; time unit—t; quantity or volume—v; quality—q; energy content—e.

The indicator matrix, $\mathbf{A}$, can be composed of these variables, where the basic elements form the rows, while the regulation factors form the columns of the matrix, as follows

$$\mathbf{A}(t) = \begin{bmatrix} Ss, & St, & Sv, & Sq, & Se \\ SCs, & SCt, & SCv, & SCq, & SCe \\ Ds, & Dt, & Dv, & Dq, & De \end{bmatrix} \tag{2}$$

This 3×5 matrix describes the resource-demand situation in a general form. Each of the 15 elements of the matrix can be specified by one or more positive figures, not less than 0. For example the Sv, SCv and Dv elements indicate the quantitative character of S, SC and D, respectively as random variables. Each of the elements, for example, can be specified by two, three or more components of the basic elements. The system of D for all of v, q and e factors can be specified by the freshwater demand (DFW), the water consumption (DCU), the total water use (DTU), the reuse (DRU), the waste water produced (WWP), the treated

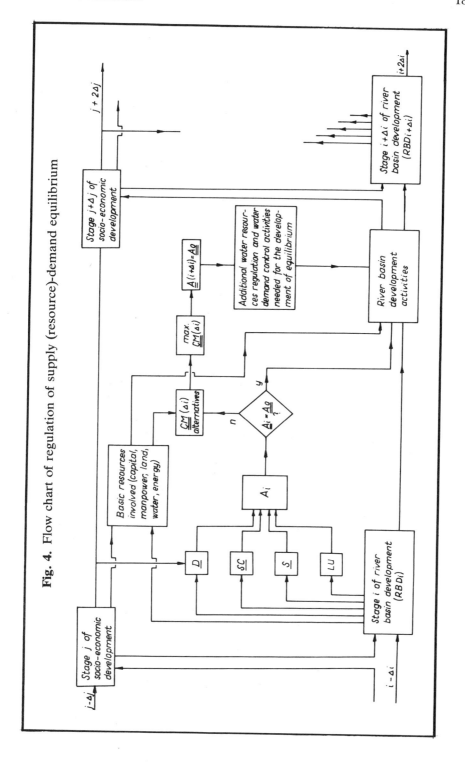

Fig. 4. Flow chart of regulation of supply (resource)-demand equilibrium

waste water (*TWW*) and by the need for waste water disposal (*WWD*), consider-ing the connections among these elements and their random characters [3]. The *St, SCt, Dt* elements indicate the time unit of the process control elements (e.g. year, month, ten-days, day, hour, second, etc.). The *Sq, SCq* and *Dq* indicate the qualitative character of *S, SC* and *D* respectively, also as random variables. Summarizing, the indicator matrix can be developed to a multi-dimensional matrix by the specification of general elements according to the planning circum-stances and it can provide a basis for the planning of equilibrium.

The **A**(*t*) matrix describes an equilibrium situation only if the following system of constraints is completely realized: [**A**(*t*) = **A**o]:

$$
\begin{array}{llll}
1.\ Ss = SCs = Ds & 3.\ Sv \geq SCv \geq Dv & 6.\ Uv \leq LUv & (3)\\
2.\ St = SCt = Dt & 4.\ Sq \geq SCq \geq Dq & 7.\ Uq \leq LUq\\
& 5.\ Se \geq SCe \geq De & 8.\ Ue \leq LUe
\end{array}
$$

Constraints 1 and 2 prescribe that the evaluation and the process control should be made for the same territory and for the same time unit by all basic regulation elements. Constraint 3 denotes the quantitative, Constraint 4 the qualitative, equilibrium of the basic elements, respectively. For example Con-straint 4 prescribes that the quality of the available water resources and/or the quality of the water delivered by the treatment capacity of the WMS should be better, or equal with, the water quality needed by the water demand. Considering the random character of *S, SC* and *D*, the Constraints 3, 4 and 5 can be performed only with certain uncertainty. Therefore, Constraints 6, 7 and 8 denote that the uncertainties of equilibrium according to the quantity, quality and energy aspects (*Uv, Uq, Ue*) should be less than the acceptable limit uncertainties (*LUv, LUq, LEe*), respectively.

The two other matrices in Eq. (1) are formed in the same structure as **A**(*t*). They are also 3×5 matrices. To achieve the equilibrium, a set of alternative industrial WMSs, each indicated by a control matrix, should be planned. In case of planning of a new industrial area, the first element of Eq. (1) cannot be considered. The alternative systems should meet the following goals:

(a) the constraint system of equilibrium (Eq. 3) should be accomplished;
(b) the utilization of natural, economic and social resources needed for the development should be kept to a minimum;
(c) a harmonized connection between the industrial water management system and its natural and regional environment should be provided;
(d) the selected WMS should be flexible enough to meet a broad spectrum of future requirements, most of which cannot be foreseen at the time of planning.

The selection of the most reasonable WMS (**CM**(*t*)$_y \to$ max, in which $y = 1, 2, \ldots, Y$ denotes the specific WMS) can be performed by a multicriteria analysis, according to the large number of variables, purposes and constraints involved in this planning problem.

MULTICRITERIA RANKING OF ALTERNATIVE SYSTEMS

LET US ASSUME that the specified variables, state transition functions and constraints are known for each alternative WMS on the basis of the specification of the control model (Eq. 1). These systems involve the different combination of the three basic control actions, namely the run-off regulation, the water demand regulation and the increase of the delivering system capacity. The next task is the formulation of the criteria as goal functions to evaluate alternative systems. The following ten criteria have been selected to measure how well a given system performs with respect to meeting the listed goals.

(1) Total annual monetary expenditures (total costs—TC) which involve both the investment and operation costs (C) of the three basic control actions to perform the equilibrium from quantity, quality and energy aspects altogether:

$$TC = C[Sv, Sq, Se, SCv, SCq, SCe, Dv, Dq, De]\qquad(4)$$

(2) Total annual monetary(economic) losses (L) which are expected in consequence of the random character of D and S the deterministic character of SC, and of the uncertainties of the planned equilibrium:

$$TL = L[Sv < SCv < Dv; Sq < SCq < Dq; Se < SCe < De; Uv; Uq; Ue]\qquad(5)$$

(3) Probability of fresh water shortage (PS) which evaluate the social, non-monetary impacts of quantitative uncertainties involved in the planned equilibrium, considering water resources availability:

$$PS = P[Sv, SCv, Dv(DFW), Uv]\qquad(6)$$

This criterion involves the evaluation of Constraints 3 and 6 in Eq. (3).

(4) Extent of the reuse of water resources in the industrial WMS which evaluates the water demand regulation from water resources management aspect:

$$RF = \frac{\text{average amount of reused water } (DRU)}{\text{average amount of waste water produced } (WWP)} 100\qquad(7)$$

(5) Extent of water consumption in the industrial WMS which evaluates the water demand regulation from a technological aspect:

$$WC = \frac{\text{average amount of consumed water } (DCU)}{\text{average amount of fresh water demand } (DFW)} 100\qquad(8)$$

(6) The fulfilment of water quality requirements (WQ) to evaluate the

environmental and social, non-monetary qualitative impacts of the planned equilibrium by the WMS including the impacts of waste water treatment and disposal. It integrates the evaluation of Constraints 4 and 7. It can be expressed by both measurable and subjective, non-measurable forms, as follows:

$$WQ = f(Sq, SCq, Dq)$$

or WQ may take on the ratings of very good, good, fair, bad and very bad.

(7) The fulfilment of energy requirements (ER) to evaluate the energy, non-monetary impacts of the planned equilibrium. It integrates the evaluation of Constraints 5 and 8. It can be expressed, for example, by the energy factor which indicates the ratio of produced (Ep) to consumed (Ec) energy by the system and by considering the acceptable limit energy uncertainties (LEe);

$$ER = f(Se, SCe, De) \approx ff\left(\frac{Ep}{Ec} ; LUe\right) \qquad (10)$$

(8) Cooperation possibility (CP) which measures the capability of WMS to develop harmonized cooperation with its natural (river basin) and socio-economic (regional development) environment, by ratings of very good, good, fair, bad and very bad. It also includes the evaluation of waste disposal.

(9) The utilization of land resources (LU) needed to develop the WMS, which evaluates the social and environmental values of land use. This criterion is expressed by the area occupied, as one of the main natural resources involved.

(10) Flexibility(FL) of each alternative to changes in inputs and errors in planning and development elements to insufficient information, to development possibility, to sensitivity of the system to various uncertainties and to effects of resource-demand systems outside of the planning area (e.g. upstream influences). It is a subjective criterion with five possible ratings very good, good, fair, poor and very poor.

The purpose of the ranking process is to find the alternative which minimizes TC, TL, PS, WC, LU and maximizes RF, WQ, ER, CP, FL. To solve this multiobjective planning problem, an array of alternatives versus criterion should be prepared. With this information in hand, ranking of the alternatives can be undertaken using, for example, one of the following methods: ELECTRE [3], concordance analysis [11] or multiattribute utility theory [12]. Here, the ELECTRE approach is presented under the form of an application example.

EXAMPLE FOR PLANNING OF MULTIPURPOSE INDUSTRIAL WATER MANAGEMENT SYSTEM

FOR ILLUSTRATION of application of the present methodology, the results of a feasibility study are presented. Based on the long-term development alternatives for the Tisza river basin in Hungary [3] four alternative industrial WMSs have been developed to meet the requirements of a large, complex industrial area in the middle-part of the Tisza basin with shortages of natural water supply. Based on the technical and economic characteristics of the alternative systems, the system versus criteria array (Table 1) has been generated. It presents the main characteristics of the WMSs.

System I is mainly oriented to surface runoff regulation, including inter-basin water transfer to the area. System II is also oriented to surface runoff regulation but by the storage of own water resources of the area. System III is oriented to the conjunctive use and development of surface and sub-surface water resources and a high-level water demand regulation. Problems of waste water disposal occur. System IV involves mainly the use of a sub-surface water with high-level demand regulation and difficulties of waste water treatment and disposal.

Based on the information in Table 1, the comparison of alternative systems was done by the ELECTRE method, elimination and (et) choice translating reality [13]. Considering the applied description of this method in Reference 3,

Table 1. System versus criteria array

Number	Criteria	Units	Alternative system (y)			
			I	II	III	IV
1	Total annual costs (TC)	10^6 Ft/yr	130	104	84	70
2	Total annual expected losses (TL)	10^6 Ft/yr	26	32	80	90
3	Probability of fresh water shortage (PS)	%	3	10	15	12
4	Extent of reuse (RF)	%	0.3	0.4	0.7	0.9
5	Extent of water consumption (WC)	%	0.2	0.3	0.4	0.4
6	Water quality requirements (WQ)	—	good	very good	fair	bad
7	Energy factor (ER)	%	0.4	0.3	0.05	0.01
8	Cooperation possibility (CP)		very good	good	bad	very bad
9	Land use (LU)	hectares	800	550	40	60
10	Flexibility (FL)	—	good	very good	very bad	fair

only the used inputs and the outputs are presented here. The weighting data for computing concord and discord indices are shown in Table 2.

The results of ELECTRE analysis state that for the range of $0.5 \leqslant p \leqslant 0.65$ and $0.45 \geqslant q \geqslant 0.15$ comparison levels, System II represents a reasonable compromise among costs, expected losses, shortage, water quality and other criteria. Therefore, this WMS is suggested for further study.

Table 2. Input data for computing concord and discord indices

Number	Criteria	Criterion weight (for concord index)	Maximum scale interval (for discord index)
1	TC	3	12
2	TL	2	12
3	PS	2	15
4	RF	3	8
5	WC	1	8
6	WQ	3	12
7	ER	1	10
8	CP	2	10
9	LU	1	6
10	FL	2	10

CONCLUSIONS

THE FOLLOWING main conclusions may be drawn:

(1) It is a basic requirement for planning of water resource-demand equilibrium that the quantity, quality and energy components of equilibrium and the water supply and waste water disposal activities cannot be separated. They form an integrated system.

(2) The multicriteria methodology leads to a trade-off among the regulation of natural water supply and water demand and the increase of system capacity. For the comparison of alternative WMSs, a system of ten criteria is proposed.

References

1. Dávid, L. (1980) *Multicriteria model for regulation of resources-demand equilibrium in river basins.* Presented to the Second International Conference on State of-the-art of Ecological Modelling. International Society for Ecological Modelling.
2. de Neufville, R. and Marks, D. (1974) *Systems Planning and design: Case Studies in Modelling, Optimization and Evaluation.* Prentice-Hall, New York, NY.
3. Dávid, L. and Duckstein, L. (1976) *Multicriterion ranking of alternative long-range water resource systems.* Water Resources Bulletin, Vol. 12. No. 3. August, 731–754.
4. Dávid, L., Duckstein, L. and Krzysztofowicz, R. (1977) *Multiobjective planning of runoff regulation under uncertain water demands.* Proceedings, International Conference on Applied Numerical Modelling, University of Southampton, Southampton, England.
5. Greenberg, R.M. and Hordon, R.M. (1976) *A test of alternatives for meeting public potable water requirements.* Water Resources Bulletin, Vol. 12. No. 4. August.
6. United Nations (1976) *River basin development policies and planning.* Proceedings, UN Interregional Seminar on river basin and interbasin development. Natural Resources/Water series No. 6, New York-Budapest.
7. Moss, M.E. and Dawdy, R.D. (1977) *Optimization problems with stochastic supply and demand curves, Session on Decision-making Under Risk and Uncertainty in Water Resources.* TIMS/ORSA Joint Spring Meeting, San Francisco, CA.
8. Kuzin, A.K. (1979) *Razvitie szisztemü planirovanie vodoohranü* (Development of water conservation planning system—in Russian). Vodnüe Reszorszü, No. 5, Moscow.
9. Dávid, L. (1978) *System development of water resources and quality control.* Proceedings, Baden Symposium on modelling the water quality of the hydrological cycle. IAHS-AISH Publ. No. 125.
10. Dávid, L. (1980) *Multiattribute analysis of decision problems in regional water management.* Hungarian experiences presented to the Workshop on Criteria, Conflicts, Uncertainty and Institutions in Regional Water Management, IIASA, Laxenburg, Austria.
11. Nijkamp, P. (1976) *Multiobjective programming models: new ways in regional decision-making.* Research Memorandum, No. 43. Dept. of Economics, Free University, Amsterdam.
12. Keeney, R.L., Wood, E.F., Dávid, L. and Csontos, K. (1977) *Evaluating Tisza River Basin Development Plans Using Multiattrabute Utility Theory.* CP-76-3, IIASA, Laxenburg, Austria.
13. Benayoun, R.O., Larichev, J., de Montgolfier and Tergny, J. (1972) *Linear programming with multiple objective functions, the method of constraints.* Automation and Remote Control, January.

Water Quality Management in Industrial Areas

Based on a paper prepared for presentation by

Blair T. Bower
3718-25th Street North, Arlington, Virginia 22207, USA

SYNOPSIS

This paper surveys—and illustrates with specific examples—the multiple interrelated factors that must be considered in attempting to achieve rational water quality management in industrial areas. A framework for discussion is provided by defining an industrial area and those terms used frequently in the succeeding description of industrial water demands and water quality management. Water and the services directly derived from its use are commodities or factor inputs, whose users must respond to a whole set of 'prices.' Many variables—economic, political, technological, and behavioral—affect water demand, all dimensions of which are interrelated and are simultaneously determined as a function of multiple factors. Product characteristics and product mix comprise one important factor affecting all dimensions of industrial water demand.

Because no activity transforms 100 per cent of inputs into desired products or services, residuals—whether material or energy—are generated and must be disposed of. Both water intake for production and consequent residual discharges fluctuate over time, and the assimilative capacity of the environment may also vary, so that a given activity's demand for the use of the resource is not constant. Water resources management takes place in a dynamic context, subject to changes in exogenous factors often not directly related to water (e.g., price of energy), and to changes in technology, factor prices, product characteristics, governmental regulations, and social tastes.

As one component of water resources management, water quality management is a continuous process, linking analysis of activities and their water demands to the effects of these on natural systems and receptors, then formulating and implementing strategies for achieving/maintaining specified levels of ambient water quality. In virtually all areas water resources are experiencing increasing demands, both at intake and effluent ends, resulting in increased interaction among users, increased incidence of conflicts, and increased prices. The primary objective of rational water quality management in industrial areas should be to allocate the finite capacity of the resource effectively and efficiently.

RÉSUMÉ

Cette communication passe en revue—et illustre à l'aide d'exemples choisis—les nombreux facteurs interdépendants qui doivent êtres considérés lorsque l'on cherche une gestion rationnelle de la qualité des eaux dans les zones industrielles. Un cadre pour la discussion est fourni par la définition d'une zone industrielle et par les termes utilisés fréquemment dans la description qui suit des demandes en eaux industrielles et la gestion de la qualité des eaux. L'eau et les services derivant directement de son utilisation sont des avantages ou facteurs d'entrée, les utilisateurs desquels doivent répondre à tout un jeu de 'prix'. De nombreuses variables— économiques, politiques, technologiques, et circonstancielles— affectent la demande en eaux, dont toutes les dimensions sont imbriquées et sont déterminées simultanément comme une fonction de nombreux facteurs. Les caractéristiques du produit et son mélange comprennent un facteur important qui affecte toutes les dimensions de la demande en eaux industrielles.

Parce qu'aucune activité transforme 100 per cent de ses entrées en produits ou services désirés, des résidus—soit matériels soit énergétiques—sont générés et doivent être éliminés. A la fois, eau prélevée pour la production, et les débits résiduels résultants fluctuent avec le temps, et la capacité d'assimilation du milieu peut aussi varier, de telle sorte que la demande, pour une activité donnée, pour l'usage d'une ressource, n'est pas constante. La gestion des ressources en eau se situe dans un contexte dynamique, sujet à des changements en des facteurs exogènes, souvent reliés directement non à l'eau (p. ex. prix de l'énergie), et à des variations dans la technologie, prix, caractéristiques du produit, règlements gouvernementaux, et goûts sociaux.

Comme l'un des composants de la gestion des ressources en eaux, la gestion de la qualité de l'eau est un procédé continu, reliant l'analyse des activités et leurs besoins en eaux aux effets de ceux-ci sur les systèmes naturels et les récepteurs, puis formulant et mettant en place des stratégies pour réaliser et entretenir des niveaux préétablis de la qualité des eaux du milieu. Dans pratiquement toutes les zones, les ressources en eau sont sujettes à une demande accrue aussi bien côté prise, qu'effluent, représentant une interaction accrue parmi les utilisateurs, une incidence accrue de conflits, et des prix accrus. L'objectif primaire d'une gestion rationnelle de la qualité des eaux dans les zones industrielles devrait être de répartir la capacité limitée de la ressource de façon effective et efficace.

RESUMEN

Este documento examina—e illustra con ejemplos específicos—los factores múltiples interrelacionados que deben ser tenídos en cuenta cuando se quiere conseguir un manejo racional de la calidad del agua en áreas industriales. Al definir lo que es un área industrial y los términos frecuentemente usados en la subsiguiente descripción de demanda de agua industrial y de ordenación de la calidad del agua se proporciona un marco adecuado para discusión. El agua y los servicios directamente derivados de su uso son bienes o factores de insumo cuyos usarios deben responder a todo un conjunto de 'precios.' Muchas variables—económicas, políticas, tecnológicas y ambientales—afectan la demanda de agua, y sus dimensiones están interrelacionadas y determinadas simultáneamente como función de múltiples factores. Las caraterísticas del producto, y la mezcla del producto comprenden un importante factor que afecta a todas las dimensiones de la demanda industrial de agua.

Como ninguna actividad transforma el 100 por ciento del insumo en los deseados productos/servicios, se producen residuos—materiales o energéticos—y hay que eliminarlos. Tanto el agua consumida para la fabricación como las descargas residuales consiguientes fluctuan a lo largo del tiempo, y también varía la capacidad de asimilación del medio ambiente, con el resultado de que la demanda del recurso para una actividad dada no es constante. El manejo del agua transcurre en un contexto dinámico, sujeto a cambios en factores exógenos a menudo no relacionados directamente con el agua (p.e., el precio de la energía), y a cambios en tecnología, precios de factores, características del producto, reglamentos gubernamentales y gustos sociales.

En tanto que un componente de la ordenación de los recursos hídricos, la ordenación de la calidad del agua es un proceso contínuo, relacionado con análisis de actividades y la demanda de agua con sus efectos en los receptores y en los sistemas naturales, y formulando y llevando a cabo estrategias para alcanzar/mantener niveles específicos de calidad de agua ambiental. En la práctica en todas las áreas los recursos hidricos experimentan demandas crecientes, tanto en las tomas como en los afluentes, resultando en una creciente interacción entre usuarios, incidencia de conflictos, y precios. El objetivo primero de un manejo racional de la calidad del agua en áreas industriales debería ser una asignación efectiva y eficiente de la limitada capacidad del recurso.

INTRODUCTION

THIS PAPER is based on two assumptions. First, an industrial area is defined as a geographic area in which industrial activities comprise the predominant source of water demands, in terms of water withdrawals, liquid residuals discharges or both withdrawals and discharges. Such an area could be: an industrial park, an industrial section of a metropolitan area or a heavily industrialized section of an estuary, such as the upper Delaware estuary in the United States (U.S.). Although industrial activities may predominate with respect to water withdrawals, they may not predominate with respect to discharges of all liquid residuals of interest having adverse effects on ambient water quality. Other sources—in addition to urban activities other than industrial—for a particular residual which may be more important than industrial activities in an industrial area are: channel erosion with respect to suspended solids (SS) and phosphorus (P); urban storm runoff with respect to SS, biochemical or chemical oxygen demand (BOD_5/COD), metals, oil, grease; and deposition from the atmosphere with respect to SS, P, metals and acid. For example, in the Great Lakes Basin (U.S. and Canada), from 20 to 50 per cent of phosphorus loads into Lakes Superior, Michigan, and Huron were estimated to be a result of of deposition from the atmosphere [1]. In developing a water-quality management strategy for an industrialized area, it is critical that the relative importance of the various sources of the liquid residuals of concern be determined.

Second, an industrial area is defined by boundaries which represent the boundaries of some existing governmental agency—or set of agencies—which has jurisdiction and authority to perform the tasks of water resources management in the industrial area. The governmental agency may be: a department of a government of general jurisdiction, such as in a province in The Netherlands and Canada; a regional water authority such as in the U.K. and Hungary; a multi-

gemeinde or multi-county agency such as some Waterschappens in The Netherlands and multi-county irrigation districts in the U.S. What is essential is that, if
the task of water resources management is to be performed, the authority for
doing so must be clearly specified in relation to political boundaries and geographic areas, and in relation to the authorities of other ministries.

DEFINITIONS

IN ORDER TO provide a common basis for discussion, some terms must be defined. The
definitions presented below may not be acceptable to all. However, they are
operational, have been found to be useful and enable understanding of the subsequent discussion in the paper.

Activity (*Enterprise*): An activity is a decision unit which consists of a set of one
or more unit processes and unit operations. An industrial plant, a farm, a mining
operation, a restaurant, an office building, a household—each is an activity and
each uses water and generates residuals according to some time patterns.

Firm: It is important to clarify the use of the term 'firm'. Traditionally—
particularly in Western economic and business literature—the term 'firm' has
been used to refer to an activity in the classical sense of Adam Smith and the
individual entrepreneur who owned a single plant. This has long since ceased to
be the reality, with the multi-plant firm, company or corporation becoming
common in both production and service sectors. Thus, there are single-plant firms
and multi-plant firms.

Residual: A residual is an non-utilizable output of material or energy from an
activity which has zero value or a value less than the cost of its recovery and
transport for use in the same or another activity. Traditionally, such residuals
have been termed pollutants, with the implicit assumption that their discharge
would have adverse effects on ambient environmental quality and hence on users
of the environment. Because not all discharges of residuals result in adverse
effects — in some cases the effects are actually positive — the neutral term
'residuals' is used.

Materials and/or energy recovery refers to recovery and reuse in the same
production activity.

By-product production refers to non-product materials and energy which are used
as inputs into another production activity, at the same location as, or at a different
location than, the production activity which generated the original non-product
outputs.

Water demand: Operationally, water demand can usefully be considered to be comprised of seven interrelated dimensions, two of which might be termed 'derivative dimensions'. The first six dimensions, shown in Figure 1, are: water intake (abstraction, withdrawal); gross water applied; consumptive use of water; wastewater discharge, including the quantities of material and energy in the wastewater; intake water treatment sludge; and wastewater treatment sludge. The last two listed are the derivatives of the first four. The seventh dimension is time. That is, there is a time pattern related to each dimension, e.g., the time pattern of water withdrawal by a given activity, the time pattern of wastewater treatment sludge generated.

Abstraction (intake, withdrawal): These terms refer to the quantity of water taken in at the intake of the water system of an activity. This intake may be the end of a pipe in a surface water body, a well tapping a ground water aquifer or the beginning of the pipe connection from a communal water distribution system to the individual activity.

Emission (discharge, effluent): These terms refer to the quantities of water and contained materials and heat passing beyond the boundary of an activity and entering a surface or ground water body or a communal sewer system.

Discharge standard: This is a condition imposed on the quantity, quality, time pattern, and/or location of a discharge.

Licence or permit: A licence or permit is an authorization given by a governmental agency to withdraw water or discharge wastewater under specified conditions.

Fee: A fee is the amount of money which must be paid to obtain a permit or a licence.

Abstraction (withdrawal) charge: This is the amount of money paid for withdrawing water from a surface or ground water body, based on each unit of volume or flow rate of water withdrawn.

User charge: A user charge is the amount of money paid for a service rendered, e.g., treating intake water to potable standards, developing a reservoir and piping system to convey water to individual users, treating wastewater.

Effluent charge: Conceptually, an effluent charge is a payment for use of the assimilative capacity of the water environment and is imposed on each unit of residual (material and energy) discharged to a surface or ground water body. Operationally, an effluent charge is conceived of as an economic incentive to induce reduction in discharge. However, only if the charge is high enough will it act as an incentive to reduce discharges. If the charge is less than the marginal cost of reducing discharge for most dischargers, there will be little incentive effect and the charge simply becomes a means of raising revenue.

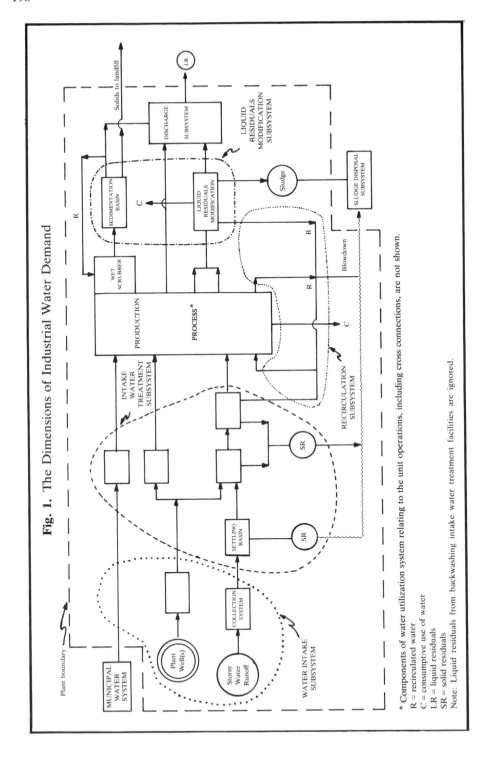

Fig. 1. The Dimensions of Industrial Water Demand

* Components of water utilization system relating to the unit operations, including cross connections, are not shown.

R = recirculated water
C = consumptive use of water
LR = liquid residuals
SR = solid residuals
Note: Liquid residuals from backwashing intake water treatment facilities are ignored.

Pollution charge: As commonly used, the term includes both user charges and effluent charges. It is applied to each unit of a residual discharged.

Tax: A tax is a payment exacted by a governmental body in order to raise revenue, e.g., personal and corporate income taxes, value added tax, sales tax, real estate tax. In the U.S. there is a critical legal distinction between charges and taxes; the terms are not synonymous.

Implementation incentive: An implementation incentive is that which induces an activity to reduce discharges of residuals or to reduce or modify water withdrawals. It may be economic, regulatory, administrative, informal, judicial or combinations of these.

Implementation incentive system: An implementation incentive system consists of one or more implementation incentives plus the related monitoring, sampling, inspection, reporting, sanctions and sanction-imposing procedures.

Strategy: A water quality management strategy for an industrial—or for any area—is comprised of: (1) the physical measures for improving ambient water quality; (2) the implementation of incentive systems to induce activities generating residuals to install and operate the physical measures; and (3) the institutional arrangement by which the responsibilities for executing incentive systems, and for executing other tasks of water quality management, are allocated among governmental agencies. Implicit in a strategy is the set of rules for operating the physical measures on a day-to-day basis under varying hydrologic, meteorologic and demand conditions.

THE NATURE OF WATER DEMAND

BECAUSE UNDERSTANDING industrial water demands is essential to achieving efficient and effective water quality management in industrial areas, some discussion of the nature of those demands is merited. Water and the services directly derived from the use of water—such as intake water and the assimilative capacity of water resources needed for the disposal of liquid residuals—are commodities or factor inputs analogous to other factor inputs to an activity, such as chemicals, energy and iron ore used in the production of steel. Hence, water and water-related services have values and the demands for them should represent what users would be willing to pay to obtain them if in fact they had to be purchased.

Demand, then, is a function of the price of the factor input—water or water-related service—faced by the activity, e.g., as the activity 'sees it'. Two points merit emphasis. First, a water-user faces not one price for water, but several prices simultaneously. For example, if the user purchases water from a municipal water authority and discharges wastewater to a municipal sewage system, he is likely to face a price on each unit (volume) of intake water purchased, a price on each unit (volume) of wastewater discharged, a price on each unit (kilogram) of biochemical oxygen-demanding material and/or suspended solids material discharged, plus prohibitions on the discharge of certain materials, e.g., grease and oil, and constraints relating to other indicators of the quality of his discharge, e.g., pH must be between 5.5 and 9.5. He may also face a charge on the amount of water actually consumed and either a charge or a constraint on peak flow.

Second, in many cases a water-user has additional options in terms of his own: possible sources of supply, such as wells; possible facilities for treating intake water and modifying wastewater before discharge; and possible facilities for recirculating water within his activity. Given the externally established prices, and the internally established costs, for different levels of water supply, intake water treatment, water recirculation, wastewater modification, and sludge disposal, the rational water-user compares the total costs of different combinations of these options and selects that combination which best satisfies his choice criteria. Thus, a water user is responding to a set of prices and costs—either direct or in the form of constraints—not to a single price.

A water-using activity consists of one, a few, or many unit processes and unit operations, in each of which water may be applied, consumed, recirculated, discharged. For each unit process/operation, there is a time pattern of water intake demand and associated water quality 'requirements'. Depending on the process/operation, the water quality requirements may be stringent, as for feedwater for high pressure boilers, or lenient, as for water to wash incoming sugar beets. Because there often are many processes and operations in a given industrial activity, there are multiple opportunities for direct and sequential uses of water. For example, in the integrated steel mill in Fontana, California, each cubic meter of water is used an average of 42 times.

In an industrial activity, it is not always easy to distinguish the water utilization system from the production process. The production of electrical energy requires water for cooling and for boiler feedwater. Water is used for cooling various types of production machinery. Water can serve as a feedstock and become incorporated in the product itself. The beverage industry is an obvious example. But water or steam is also used as feedstock or processing agent in numerous chemical and pharmaceutical processes. Water is sometimes used to convey a product from one stage of production to another In the canning industry, fruits and vegetables are often transported through the production process in a water stream. Water is used for washing and cleaning throughout industrial facilities. It is also used to wash final products, equipment, floors, trucks and other vehicles; in sanitary systems; for drinking water; to water vegetation; for fire protection; and water bodies are used for the disposal of non-product outputs from industrial activities. Steam may be used for space heating. Moreover, an examination of the water utilization system of an industrial plant may show that water is actually a net output of some stages of the production activity. Liquid residuals result from the production of some dry foods.

An increasingly significant use of water in industrial operations is in residuals modification. For example, water is used in the wet scrubbing of stack gases and in the pumping of manure, fly ash and tailings to evaporation ponds or other disposal areas. Solid residuals from industrial operations are often transported by water streams from the area of generation to the place of disposal.

Finally, it has become increasingly recognized that the demand on the assimilative capacity of water courses for disposal of storm runoff from plant sites is often a significant factor in terms of effects on ambient water quality in an industrial area. Thus, both process wastewater and storm water runoff are parts of wastewater discharge demand. Precipitation falling on the site of the activity must be explicitly considered, either because effluent charges are imposed on the discharges of the activity, or because the high cost of intake water induces the activity to use storm water internally, or both.

SOME FACTS OF LIFE

INTEGRAL TO DEVELOPING an efficient and effective water quality management strategy for an industrial area is a recognition of some basic facts of life. Several of these are identified and discussed below.

Interrelationships among Residuals

No activity, whether a manufacturing process, residential activity or agricultural operation, transforms 100 per cent of inputs into desired products and services. There is always something 'left over', i.e., residuals, which must be disposed of in some manner. Most often disposal is to one or more of the environmental media: water, air or land.

Material and energy are the two classes of residuals. The three forms of material residuals are liquid, gaseous and solid; energy residuals include heat, noise, light, vibrations and certain forms of radioactivity. One form of material residual can be transformed into one or more other forms, or different types of the same form. Thus, a liquid residual may be converted into another type of liquid residual plus a gaseous residual plus a separated 'solid' residual, to be disposed of in a water body, in the atmosphere and on land, respectively. A solid residual may be transformed into liquid, gaseous and other solid residuals. The modification of a residual into other forms requires material and energy inputs which themselves become residuals. Modification is undertaken on the assumption that the discharge of the set of residuals resulting from the modification will have fewer adverse effects on ambient environmental quality than the discharge of the original residual.

Thus, modification of sewage in a sewage treatment plant results in the generation of a semi-solid residual (sludge) plus various types of liquid and

gaseous residuals. If the sludge is incinerated, gaseous residuals, such as particulates, are generated. If the sludge is placed in a landfill, there may be seepage of
residuals into ground or surface water bodies. Finally, because virtually all
residuals modification requires energy inputs, additional gaseous, liquid, and solid
residuals are generated in fuel combustion to produce energy for residuals
modification. Thus, conventional waste treatment increases the total quantity of
residuals discharged into the environment. Figure 2 illustrates the interrelationships among the three forms of material residuals.

The residuals originally generated by an activity are termed primary residuals, i.e., they result from a set of one or more unit processes and/or operations to
produce a product, service or utility. Secondary residuals are generated in the
handling and/or modification of primary residuals. Tertiary residuals are
generated in the handling and/or modification of secondary residuals, and so on.

Variability of demand

There is great variability in individual industrial activities from day to day,
and even from hour to hour, in water intake and in the generation and discharge
of liquid (and gaseous, solid) residuals, even under normal operating conditions.
Rarely, if ever, is there an activity in which water intake and/or residuals
generation and discharge (per unit and total) is constant over time, in the short-
run and in the long run. For example, in residences there are diurnal, weekend
and seasonal fluctuations in water intake and residuals discharges, representing different activities that occur at different times of the day, week and season.
These are reflected in the time pattern of discharges from municipal sewage
treatment plants. Similar, short-run fluctuations in residuals generation and discharge occur in industrial, commercial, institutional and transportation activities.

In manufacturing activities, at least six types of conditions occur which result
in short-run variations in water intake and/or in residuals generation and discharge: (1) start-up/shut-down of production processes; (2) clean-up operations;
(3) upsets during production with no halt in production; (4) breakdowns so that
production ceases; (5) accidental spills; and (6) variations during 'normal' production operations. The reasons for the first five types of short-run variations are
obvious.

It is important to emphasize that trade-offs are almost always possible
between increasing production in an industrial activity and water demand. For
example, on a modern Fourdrinier paper machine, the standard procedure
increasingly is to make grade changes without stopping the machine. This means
that for some period of time all of the output is wasted to the broke system—to
be returned subsequently to the paper machine—and all water used provides no
product output. In total, change of grade probably is responsible for more water
use in this context than dry-end breaks. For example, for a product output of 480
tons per day, or 20 tons per hour, a 15-minute grade change would involve in the
order of 5 tons of broke. At 6 per cent moisture off the machine, the amount of
water needed to dilute the paper to 0.25 per cent consistency is about 500,000

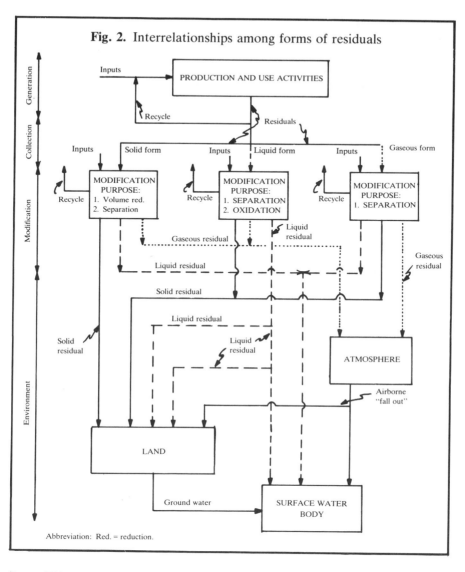

Fig. 2. Interrelationships among forms of residuals

gallons. This represents a significant increase in total daily water demand over a production procedure which would shut down between grade changes. But shutting down is more expensive than the additional water used.

In addition to the within-day and the day-to-day variations in water demand, definite seasonal patterns exist for some industrial operations. These seasonal variations often exhibit some regularity, in that certain activities take place each year during a certain season, although the specific beginning and ending dates, and levels of activity, can vary from year to year. One example consists of the times when the product mix in a petroleum refinery shifts from more fuel oil to more gasoline in the spring and back in the fall, depending on the weather. Where steam is used for space heating in an industrial activity, whenever space heating ceases for the year, the withdrawal of water for steam also ceases. Water demand for cooling obviously varies by season, as a function of ambient temperature.

Of course, in addition to the variability in water intake and residuals generation and discharge, the assimilative capacity of water courses varies by season, as illustrated in Figure 3. The two types of variability compound the problem of achieving desired ambient, water-quality targets in industrial areas.

Exogenous Factors

Decisions about water resources management at the level of the individual activity (the water user) are affected by many decisions and factors exognous to the activity, over which the activity has no control and which are often not related directly to water. That is, the decision with respect to the value, price, magnitude of this type of factor is essentially outside the control of the decision-makers of the activity. Examples include prices of energy, water, fuel and other raw material inputs, i.e., chemicals, ores, secondary materials; tax policies; freight rates; tariffs; import and export restrictions. These factors influence decisions on the degree of internal water recirculation and the levels of materials and energy recovery and by-product production which would take place in the absence of any constraints on water withdrawals and/or residuals discharges to the environment.

It should be emphasised that many of these factors are not under the jurisdiction of water resources management agencies, as well as not being directly related to water. Tax provisions represent one prime example. The objectives of the finance ministry in establishing taxes, tax procedures and incentives are to raise revenues, to stimulate investment, and/or to redistribute income. They are not directed toward water resources management [3]. Further, there may be several links in the 'chain' of effects before arriving at water demand. For example, increases in postal rates for magazines stimulated a demand for lower-weight, publication grade paper. This resulted in changed product output characteristics, leading to changes in raw material production technology combinations and hence, in water demand.

Dynamic context

Water resources management takes place in a dynamic context. There are continual changes in societies in technology, factor prices, product mix, product characteristics, governmental regulations and social tastes. Failure to understand, or at least to recognize the existence of, the impacts of these changing factors can lead to unanticipated impacts on water resources management. For example, technological change is simulated by: (1) changes in factor prices, e.g., raw materials, labour, capital; (2) research and development (R&D) on technological processes/operations; (3) R&D on new products, which can induce changes in

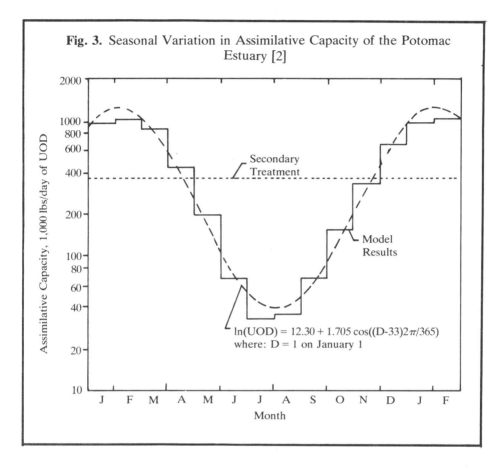

Fig. 3. Seasonal Variation in Assimilative Capacity of the Potomac Estuary [2]

$\ln(\text{UOD}) = 12.30 + 1.705 \cos((D-33)2\pi/365)$
where: $D = 1$ on January 1

production technology and raw materials; (4) R&D on new raw materials; (5) suggestions from sales departments; and (6) exogenously imposed restrictions, regulations, charges on raw materials, product specifications. Thus, technological change takes place as a result of the interaction of multiple factors, including various types of governmental actions.

Even where technology in a given industrial plant remains 'the same' water demand, in terms of water intake and/or wastewater discharge, is likely to change over time as a result of a deterioration of equipment, even with good maintenance. For example, the heat rate of a power plant increases over time, thereby requiring more water for cooling for the same net energy output. The chippers in a pulp/paper mill become dull, increasing water demand and residuals generation per unit of output.

WATER QUALITY MANAGEMENT IN INDUSTRIAL AREAS

WATER RESOURCES MANAGEMENT is comprised of the totality of functions/tasks required to produce water and water-related goods and services. Water resources management can be considered a production function which transforms the quantity, quality, time and location characteristics of surface and ground water resources into the quantity, quality, time and location characteristics of the desired outputs, e.g., irrigation water, hydroelectric energy, water-based recreation opportunities, flood damage reduction, municipal water, industrial water, navigation possibilities and fish biomass. Water quality management is a component of water resources management. As such it involves a set of tasks with the objective of achieving and maintaining whatever levels of ambient water quality are desired, within whatever constraints may exist in any given context. For example, there may be constraints on: total costs; the distribution of costs; the timing of physical measures to be installed; and meeting production levels for other outputs, e.g., hydroelectric energy, the production of which can adversely affect ambient water quality. The ambient water quality standards may be explicit or implicit. In both cases, they usually are established in relation to the uses of the water bodies.

The functions of water quality management include: data collection; research; analysis to generate information for selection of water quality management strategies; planning, i.e., the process of selecting a strategy; design and construction of facilities; operation and maintenance of facilities; forecasting quantity and quality of streamflows; forecasting quality of lakes and ground water bodies; monitoring water withdrawals, wastewater and residuals discharges, and ambient water quality; providing quality control of laboratory analyses; inspecting facilities; setting of regulations, standards, charges, constraints on withdrawals and discharges; imposing implementation incentives on activities; collecting fees/charges; imposing sanctions for non-compliance with standards/regulations/procedures; training operators, laboratory analysts, inspectors; and continual evaluation of performance of facilities and effectiveness of implementation incentives to feed back resulting information into analysis and the process of selecting a strategy. It is the carrying out of this total set of tasks which results in the desired product of ambient water quality.

Because the focus is on management, the geographic context must be for some a real unit for which management activities can be undertaken by duly constituted governmental agencies. Although in most countries all layers of government perform at least one or a few of the activities, the day-to-day activities are performed primarily at the local or regional level. As noted previously, the region can be a county, a soil conservation district, a metropolitan area or a multi-county or multi-gemeinde district, or some combination of local jurisdictions. Often political boundaries will not coincide with water quality problem areas, with river basins or with economic regions. However, experience indicates that it is less important for the boundaries of the water quality management region to include all of the residuals dischargers and all those affected by changes in ambient water quality, than it is for the boundaries to represent some area for which there is an institutional arrangement which is directly responsible for water quality management.

The 'operating function' is particularly critical in water quality management in industrial areas. That is, at any point in time in a given management area, a system of physical facilities exists, such as surface water reservoirs, well fields, intake structures and raw water treatment facilities, waste treatment plants, in-stream aerators and spray irrigation systems for disposal of wastewater. Associated with this system of facilities, and with the ultimate users of water and water-related products services produced by the system, is an 'operating procedure'. An operating procedure is a set of rules for withholding water in, and releasing water from, surface and ground water reservoirs, operating in-stream aerators, closing and opening valves/gates/diversion structures, cleaning debris basins, and prescribing/proscribing behaviour of water-users during other-than-normal conditions. Thus, operating procedures must be specified for four types of conditions: (1) 'normal' water; (2) excess water (flooding); (3) shortage of water; and (4) spills, e.g., spill of toxic material into a stream as a result of faulty valve, incorrect procedure or accident. To be able to develop efficient and effective operating procedures, the water quality management agency must have detailed understanding of the 'water management behaviour' of the major individual activities in its area.

Analysis for water quality management

The analysis task in water quality management is central to the development of water quantity management strategies. Operationally, analysis can be divided into the following segments: (1) estimating levels and spatial pattern of activities in the management area; (2) analyzing water demands of activities; (3) analyzing effects of wastewater and residuals discharges on natural systems and subsequently on receptors; (4) formulating and analyzing water quality management strategies; and (5) developing criteria for, and evaluating, water quality management strategies.

INDUCING RESPONSES

To REITERATE, an implementation incentive is a behaviour-modifying factor which induces an activity to modify water withdrawals and/or discharges of residuals. Implementation incentives are imposed to achieve socially established goals. Figure 4 shows the loci where the implementation incentives can be imposed. However, regardless of the type of implementation incentive—effluent charge,

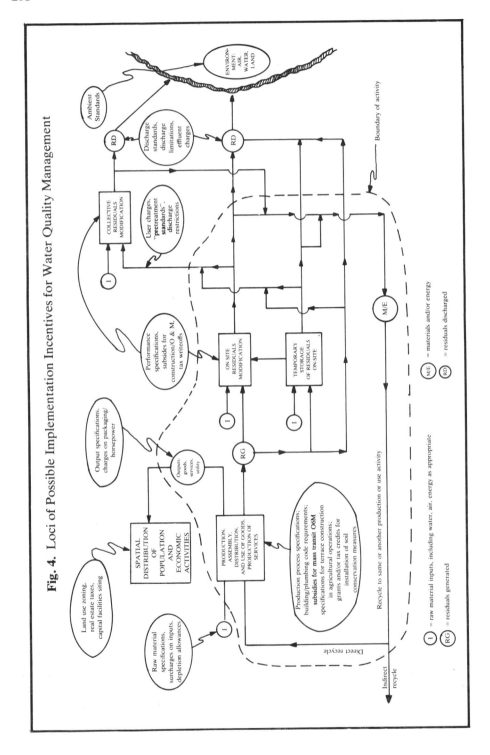

Fig. 4. Loci of Possible Implementation Incentives for Water Quality Management

input material standard, process specification, effluent standard, marketable permit to discharge—the associated monitoring and sanction-imposing activities are essential. Thus, what is involved is an implementation incentive system. This system consists of:

(1) a set of implementation incentives, e.g., rules or procedures that an activity must follow, a set of abstraction and/or discharge limitations which must not be exceeded by some amount some portion of the time, and/or a set of charges related to inputs to the activity, to residuals discharges from the activity or to some measure of performance;

(2) a system of measuring performance, e.g., the quantities of materials discharged, the qualities and/or quantities of material and/or energy inputs, the quantity of residuals removed from the discharge streams, quality of product output;

(3) a system of on-site inspection to determine if, for example, specified equipment is in place and operating, the system for measuring performance is in place and operating, the analyses of the samples taken are accurate; and

(4) a set of sanctions for failure to comply with the rules/procedures/standards or failing to pay charges.

Table 1 shows examples of control variables which could be used to monitor performance in relation to various possible economic incentives applied to hydrocarbon discharges. Table 2 lists the sanctions available in the US which can be applied for non-compliance.

Comments on Implementation Incentive Systems [4]

Empirical experiences in various countries provide the basis for the following comments on implementation incentive systems.

Firstly, despite much verbiage (written and oral) concerning the relative merits of regulatory versus economic incentive systems, no 'pure' implementative incentive system exists for water quality management (or air quality management, or solid residuals management). All existing systems have some mix of regulatory and economic, administrative, judicial, and informational incentives. For example, industrial activities may have imposed on them two or more of the following: input standards; product standards; discharge standards; specifications with respect to technology of production; specifications of residuals modification equipment by type and/or level of performance; grants for some portion of the construction cost of 'pollution-control' facilities; grants for some portion of the operation and maintenance costs of 'pollution-control' facilities; grants to cover some portion of investment in 'less polluting' production technology; low (less than market) interest rate loans to cover some portion of investment in 'pollution-control' facilities and/or 'less polluting' production technology; tax credits for investment in 'less pollution' production technology; low (less than market) interest rate loans to cover some portion of investment in 'pollution-control' facilities and/or 'less polluting' production technology; tax credits for investment;

Table 1. Possible Control Variables for Use in Monitoring Performance in Relation to Selected Economic Incentives

Control Variable	Examples of Economic Incentives
Installation of physical measure	
Air pollution control equipment	Daily fine for not installing double seals on floating roof storage tank
Production process	Annual charge for operation of spray booths that used solvent (rather than water) based paints
Production inputs	Fine for use of prohibited cleaning solvents
Production outputs	Per-pound tax on production of solvent based paint
Performance of physical measure	
Amount of emissions	Constant and non-linear charge on emissions; nonlinear emission charge schedule with unit charge increasing with emission rate
Emission rate	Charge for emissions greater than specified daily rate; Charge based on daily emission rate with charge higher during summer months
Concentration of emissions	Charge formula with higher charges for higher ppm emission concentrations
Emissions per process weight unit	Charge for any emission in excess of specified hydrocarbons/ton of laundry limit
Specified operation	Fine for failure to operate degreasers properly
Operation of activity	
Amount of output	Charge for each gallon of gas sold
Amount of process weight	Charge for each ton of solvent used in printing operations

rapid-depreciation allowances for investment in 'pollution control' facilities; withdrawal of operating permits; fines; and finally, technical assistance. For example, in water quality management in France, in the Ruhr area of the Federal Republic of Germany, and in many U.S. cities, the mix of incentives generally includes: (1) economic subsidies for construction and/or operation and maintenance of discharge reduction facilities; (2) discharge standards in the form of permits which specify standards on inputs, production processes, products, and/or quantities of materials/energy in discharges; and (3) effluent charges or sewer charges. It is the mix of incentives to which the activity responds.

Secondly, an implementation incentive system imposed on a given activity in relation to a given residual usually represents only one of several implementation incentive systems imposed on different liquid residuals, and others on gaseous and solid residuals, to which the activity responds. For some residuals, the same physical measure will reduce the discharge of more than one residual, e.g., BOD_5

Table 2. Administrative and Judicial Sanctions Available in the United States

ADMINISTRATIVE SANCTIONS (imposed by management agencies)
A. Informal administrative sanctions
      phone calls
      site visits
      warning letters
      reminder letters
      directive letters
      summoning letters

B. Formal administrative sanctions
      administrative orders
      consent orders
      emergency orders
      shut-down orders
      sewer bans
      civil administrative penalties, e.g., delayed compliance fees
      revocation/suspension of permits
      permit modification
      referral to attorney

C. Ancillary sanctions
      blacklisting
      adverse publicity
      withholding of governmental benefits, e.g., contracts

JUDICIAL SANCTIONS (imposed by courts)

A. Civil penalties
      monetary penalties (fines)

B. Injunctive relief
      mandate specific behaviour on part of discharger
      prohibit specific behaviour on part of discharger

C. Criminal penalties
      fines (usually higher than civil penalties)
      incarceration of corporate or public officials
      fines and incarceration

and suspended solids, although not to the same extent. Often physical measures designed to reduce the discharge of a given residual may increase the generation of one or more other residuals. It is particularly important to recognize the joint cost and intermedia problems.

Thirdly, some implementation incentives can be imposed at any of the levels of government. Further, the same type of implementation incentive can be imposed simultaneously by more than one level of government; for example, a Federal effluent charge on suspended solids discharges into water courses combined with an additional State effluent charge on such discharges. Also, different types of implementation incentives can be imposed on the same residual discharged by different levels of government; for example, a national effluent charge on suspended solids combined with a provincial permit which specifies a limit on kilograms of suspended solids discharged.

Fourthly, implementation incentive systems can be characterized as being either biased or neutral with respect to inducing the adoption of physical measures (technology). For example, implementation incentives which specify waste treatment technology, or provide favourable tax treatment only for investment in 'end-of-pipe' measures, bias the decision of the activity. In contrast, an investment tax credit which is granted for investment in any type of technology allows the water-user to choose among the various options including production process changes.

Fifthly, many relevant implementation incentives are not under the jurisdiction of water quality management agencies. Probably the clearest examples are tax provisions such as those relating to depletion allowances, capital gains, severance taxes, accelerated depreciation and real estate taxes.

Sixthly, implementation incentive systems are imposed in relation both to original compliance and continuing compliance. The former refers to inducing the original installation of physical measures which are presumed to be able to meet, or do better than, the conditions specified in the discharge permit, whatever the basis for the permit and the means by which it was obtained. Continuing compliance refers to the activity's day-to-day meeting of the conditions specified in the discharge permit. The same implementation incentive or implementation incentive system may not be effective with respect to both original and continuing compliance.

Monitoring

Three types of monitoring are essential in water quality management. These are: (a) compliance monitoring of activities withdrawing water or discharging wastewater; (b) monitoring of ambient water quality to determine the extent to which water quality standards are being met; and (c) biological monitoring of water bodies to determine if achievement of the specified water quality standard does, in fact, result in the desired aquatic life. Compliance monitoring is undertaken to:

(1) determine whether or not a source is in compliance with withdrawal and/or discharge permit conditions;

(2) provide the basis, (i.e., number of units) on which to assess abstraction and/or effluent charges;

(3) monitor a source's progress in correcting violations;

(4) provide additional evidence of a violation for enforcement actions; and
(5) verify that a source is not constructing a new facility without the required construction or operating permits.

Compliance monitoring is essential whether abstraction and discharge are directly from and to a surface or ground water body, or from a communal water purveyor and to a communal sewerage system. If intake charges, effluent charges and/or standards are varied by time of day or time of year, the monitoring system must be designed to obtain the necessary information on time variations in abstractions and/or discharges.

The other problem is that of determining the 'optimal' frequency of monitoring, with respect to both inspections and sampling. Costs to the water quality management agency increase with increasing frequency of inspection; but presumably the degree of compliance by the water-user also increases with increasing frequency of inspection.

Effectiveness of Mixed Implementation Incentive Systems [4]

Although factors other than costs do affect decisions of managers of industrial activities, a good start toward estimating likely responses by individual activities can be made by assuming that decision-makers are cost-minimizers or profit-maximizers. But what are relevant in estimating responses are the costs 'as the activity sees them', not as the water quality management agency or the society sees them. The costs to the activity are not likely to be the same as actual resource costs. This fact results from the wide array of direct and indirect subsidies which exist, and from internal company accounting procedures. Table 3 illustrates only the array of tax provisions which affect costs of water utilization systems to an industrial activity. Additional examples include subsidies relating to certain virgin raw materials, certain forms of energy and the attaining of capital. Thus, unless costs are estimated as the activities in an industrial area see them, the implementation incentive component of water quality management strategies will be ineffective.

Given the above fact with respect to costs, and given the various types of mixed implementation incentive systems in water quality management, what can be said about the responses by individual activities induced by these systems? Ideally, responses are best evaluated by obtaining empirical data on the actual behavior of individual plants. Rarely have such data been compiled. However, in a recent study in the U.S. [5], 101 individual plants in five U.S. cities were visited to determine responses to mixed systems including pretreatment (discharge) standards and sewer charges. Types of plants visited included canning, production of chemicals, dairies and other food processing, meat packing, pulp and paper manufacturing, metal finishing and commercial laundries.

In assessing responses, it is important to recognize that a multiplicity of factors are operating to affect the behaviour of an individual activity. Included are: prices of factor inputs other than water, including energy and labour; capital availability; technical information available; regulations on discharges of gaseous

Table 3. Relevant Factors Used in Calculating Discharge Reduction Costs to Activities in California*

1. Federal rates of tax on corporate profits are as follows:

Profits	Federal Tax Rate
Less than $25,000/yr	17%
$25,000–$50,000/yr	20%
$50,000–$75,000/yr	30%
$75,000–$100,000/yr	40%
More than $100,000/yr	46%

2. The California state rate of tax on corporate profits is 9%.
3. Federal depreciation writeoffs and investment tax credits for pollution control equipment are as follows:
   a. For equipment with useful life less than 10 years
      10% initial tax credit;
      $2,000 first year "additional" depreciation;
      double-declining-balance method for first year depreciation; and
      sum-of-digits method for remaining years' depreciation.
   b. For equipment with useful life of 10 years or more
      5% initial tax credit;
      $2,000 first year "additional" depreciation;
      five-year accelerated amortization allowable for that portion of pollution control equipment which is eligible; and
      depreciation as above in 3a for the ineligible portion of the equipment.
4. Federal depreciation writeoffs and investment tax credit for physical measures which are not eligible for rules relating to pollution control equipment are the same as in 3a above.
5. State depreciation writeoffs for pollution control equipment are taken on a one-year accelerated basis.
6. State depreciation writeoffs for physical measures which are not eligible for special pollution control writeoffs are the same as in 3a above except that there is no investment tax credit.

* Rates and procedures valid as of 1979.

and solid residuals; regulations concerning food safety; and regulations concerning worker safety. Attempting to isolate the effects of the implementation incentives relating to liquid residuals within this milieu is difficult. However, based on the 101 individual plant units, the following conclusions seem warranted.

(1) Despite the fact that the sewer charges were low in all cases in relation both to total production costs of the activity and to the costs of reducing discharges of liquid residuals by the activity, the charges did induce responses. These included better housekeeping, some changes in production processes and some changes in by-product production. In a few cases, significant innovation in production systems was induced.

(2) The sewer charges induced more continuous adherence to the pretreatment (discharge) standards. The cumbersome nature of the regulatory system in imposing sanctions for each time the pretreatment standards are exceeded results

in a relatively ineffective inducement for continuing compliance. Whereas, receiving a bill each month reflecting actual behaviour is a readily observable signal to plant management.

(3) Responses in terms of discharge reduction beyond discharge standards were a function of the level of charges. As charges increase in proportion to total production costs, responses are induced which yield greater reductions in discharges.

(4) Physical measures to reduce water intake, wastewater discharge and energy use often reinforced one another.

(5) Stringent regulations imposed on the discharge of toxics generally also resulted in reductions in discharges of BOD_5 and total suspended solids.

(6) Regulations directed toward air quality management, solid residuals management, food safety and worker safety, often led to increased water withdrawals and increased discharges of liquid residuals, i.e., they exacerbated the problems of water quality management.

(7) The availability of information is an important factor affecting responses. For plants producing the same product or products, some significant differences in responses were found between single-plant firms and multi-plant firms. In general, a plant which was one unit of a multi-plant firm had more relevant information available than did single-plant firms.

Although some evidence is available, and is indicative of the effectiveness of implementation incentive systems, further experimentation is necessary. The fundamental question in water quality management remains: namely, what set of economic incentives, combined with other types of incentives and all the components of implementation incentive systems (i.e., monitoring, inspection, sanctions), will be most effective in inducing private and public entities to adopt preventive rather than curative measures to reduce their demands on the finite capacity of the water environment?

CONCLUDING COMMENT

UNTIL RELATIVELY RECENTLY, use of the environment for the disposal of residuals was free. Similarly, there was no charge for withdrawing water from water bodies. Consequently, a rational plant manager, individual farmer or householder used as much of those inexpensive factor inputs as possible in producing his goods or services.

However, this condition no longer exists. In essentially all countries, there is increasing pressure on the water resource, on both intake and effluent ends. As demands grow in relation to supply—as appears likely with increasing population and/or production of goods and services and without a major change in life style—the increased demand will result in increased patterns of interaction among users and in increased incidence of conflicts. Because the assimilative capacity of the environment is essentially fixed, ignoring long-run climatic changes, and hence will only become more scarce in the future relative to the demands on it, the price on the use of that resource will inevitably increase, just as for any increasingly scarce resource. This is true no matter how the price is reflected, e.g., in withdrawal changes, effluent standards, input constraints, product restrictions or effluent charges.

The primary objective of rational water quality management in industrial areas should be to allocate that capacity effectively and efficiently.

References

1. International Joint Commission (1978) *Environmental Strategy for the Great Lakes System*. Final Report to the International Joint Commission from the International Reference Group on Great Lakes Pollution from Land Use Activities (PLUARG), IJC, Windsor, Ontario.
2. Flaherty, T. (1980) *The Environmental Defense Fund's Potomac Estuary Project*. Paper presented at Annual Meeting, Interstate Commission on the Potomac River Basin.
3. Bower, B.T. et al. (1981) *Incentives in Water Quality Management: France and the Ruhr Area*. Research Paper R-24, Part II, Washington, D.C., Resources for the Future.
4. Bower, B.T. (1981) *Mixed implementation systems for water quality management in France, the Ruhr and the U.S.*, in Downing and Hanf, Editors, *Implementing Pollution Laws: International Comparisons*. Policy Science Program, Florida State University, Tallahasse, FL.
5. Hudson, J.F. et al. (1981) *Pollution-pricing, Industrial Response to Wastewater Charges*. Lexington Books, D.C. Heath & Co., Lexington, Mass., USA.

Industrial Water Pollution Control in Developing Countries

Enzo Fano and Marcia R. Brewster
Department of Technical Co-operation for
Development, United Nations, New York

SYNOPSIS

This paper provides a general description of the differences in water-use patterns and sources of pollution between developing and developed countries. Some of the international trade and investment trends which have resulted from generally stricter enforcement of pollution control measures in developed countries are considered. Specific instruments available to governments for dealing with industrial water pollution are discussed, including effluent charges, standards, permits and the requirement of environmental impact statements. Monitoring methods are also considered as essential elements of any pollution control method. It is considered important for developing countries, which have not already done so, to develop strategies to improve water quality in rivers and lakes and to preserve the environment for future generations.

RÉSUMÉ

Cet article donne une description génerale des differences, en ce qui concerne les formes d'utilisation de l'eau et les sources de con-

217

tamination entre pays en développement et les pays développés. On considère certaines tendances du commerce international et de l'investissement, qui ont résulté d'une application généralement plus stricte dans les pays développés, des mesures de contrôle de la contamination. Des moyens spécifiques, à la disposition des gouvernements pour traiter du problème de la contamination de l'eau par l'industrie sont discutés, y compris les charges en effluents, les normes, les permis et l'obligation de préparer une estimation de l'impact de tout nouveau projet sur l'environnement. Des methodes de vérification sont aussi considérées comme des éléments fondamentaux de toute méthode de contrôle de la contamination. On considère qu'il est important, pour les pays en développement qui ne l'ont pas encore fait, de développer des stratégies pour améliorer la qualité des eaux dans les rivières et dans les lacs, et de protéger l'environnement pour les générations à venir.

RESUMEN

Este informe da una descripción general de las diferencias entre los distintos esquemas del uso del agua y las fuentes de polución entre países desarrollados y los países en desarrollo. Se consideran algunas de las tendencias del comercio internacional y de inversión que han resultado de la aplicación generalmente más estricta de medidas de control de polución en países desarrollados. Se discuten los medios específicos disponibles a los gobiernos para tratar sobre la polución industrial del agua, incluso la descarga de efluentes, normas, permisos y la necesidad de proveer una declaración del impacto de los proyectos al medio ambiente. También son considerados medios de monitoreo como elementos esenciales de cualquier medio de control de polución. Se considera importante para los países en desarrollo que no lo hayan hecho todavía, el desarrollar estrategias para mejorar la calidad del agua en ríos y lagos y conservar el medio ambiente para generaciones futuras.

INTRODUCTION

INDUSTRIAL WATER POLLUTION, until recently considered a lesser problem in numerous developing countries, has now been recognized as a serious one and a major health hazard. Developing countries have generally considered economic growth and industrialization as key development priorities and preservation of the environment has not been given the same weight. However, it has become clear that urgent pollution-control measures are necessary to avoid a major ecological upset, even though this may mean slower economic growth in certain industries. The objectives of this paper are to describe some of the aspects of industrial water pollution peculiar to developing countries, to suggest some alternative policy instruments for dealing with them and, hopefully, to provoke some discussion on existing and potential pollution-control measures in developing countries.

Firstly, a general description is given of the differences in water-use patterns and sources of pollution between developing and developed countries. Some of the international trade and investment trends resulting from stricter enforcement of pollution-control measures in developed countries are then considered. Secondly, some policy instruments are discussed which are available to governments for dealing with industrial water pollution within the framework of a national strategy or a regional water plan. These instruments include effluent charges, standards, permits and the requirement of environmental impact statements. Monitoring methods are also considered as essential elements of any pollution-control programme. Some of the measures and methods may provide opportunities for discussion or technical co-operation among developing countries.

It has now become urgent for developing countries to recognize the rapid deterioration of the environment that can occur, particularly in the quality of water flowing through rivers and streams, and therefore in the quality of life in rural and urban areas. It will not be possible to sustain long-term growth, development and an improvement in the standard of living if the water courses carry toxic chemicals, phenols and other pollutants which endanger human and animal life. Action should be initiated immediately to prevent further deterioration and to preserve the environment for future generations.

GENERAL PERSPECTIVE

WATER-USE PATTERNS differ markedly between industrialized and developing countries. In developed countries, industrial water use generally accounts for at least 40 per cent of the total water use, and in some eastern European countries may reach more than 80 per cent [1]. In developing countries, on the other hand, by far the main consumptive use is for irrigation, while industry seldom accounts for even 10 per cent of total use. Therefore, water use in industry, waste-water treatment and recycling are much more important issues in the developed than in the developing countries.

Since industrial water demand is generally relatively small in developing countries, most of them have not been too concerned with increases in industrial water demand. Industrial development has been encouraged and infrastructure, in the form of water supply, has often been provided by the government of the developing country as an incentive to business. If supplies are not made available by the government, industries are often allowed to develop their own (from surface or ground water), without much interference from the host government.

However, it is estimated that the demand for water from industrial and other non-agricultural uses will increase rapidly over the next two decades in the developing countries, causing basic water-use conflicts over the allocation of water among agricultural, industrial and domestic uses. For example, it has been estimated that in India, irrigation will claim only 84 per cent of consumptive use in the year 2000 as compared to 92 per cent in 1975 [2]. It is likely that water-use patterns in other developing countries will reflect those of India. While, in the future, irrigation will still represent the major use of water, the demands of industry are becoming increasingly important. Rising demands from all sectors, in terms of both quantity and quality, will make it necessary for all countries to consider conservation and pollution-control measures in anticipation of future shortages.

Sources of Industrial Water Pollution

Despite the relatively small demand for water from industry in developing countries, pollution from industry has had a significant effect on the water supplies of those countries. Industrial water pollution can be found in both modern and traditional sectors in developing countries: in the traditional factories processing primary products and in the factories of the major cities, which often use technologies imported from developed countries. Although pollution has often been assumed to be a minor problem in developing countries, it is in fact fouling rivers and streams in Asia, Africa and Latin America. Untreated waste from agro-industrial processes and effluent from new factories have destroyed fisheries, reduced available water supplies and impaired agricultural productivity [3]. Water bodies in almost all major urban areas are polluted by untreated organic discharges from human and industrial activities.

Primary Product Processing. The major industries in the traditional sector which are causing widespread water pollution are those which process primary products (often for export), such as sugar and oilseed mills, mineral extraction and processing facilities, coffee factories and tanneries. Agro-industries can become a major source of pollution when an increasing proportion of the population becomes involved in production of cash crops and industries begin concentrating in growing areas.

In Africa, agro-industrial activities present some of the most serious environmental problems in terms of industrial pollution. For example, in Nigeria, the brewing, slaughtering and sugar-refining industries have few or no facilities for either air or water pollution control. Waste water is discharged directly into rivers, other receiving waters or open drains. In Kenya, there is a wide range of organic effluents containing soluble substances, of which coffee wastes are the most widespread and the most serious [3]. The problems of organic loads from hair and fats, as well as chromium and sulphide pollution from the tanning industry in Kenya, are documented in Mr. Mwelesa's paper for this Meeting (not included in this publication). Although Kenya now has a Pollution Control Division, it has not been able to reduce pollution effectively from long-established plants.

In Asia, localized pollution from agro-industrial operations, such as sugar and palm-oil processing mills, adversely affects water supplies and fisheries and has become a major problem in some areas [3]. The disastrous effects of the concentration of agro-industry were evident in the increase from 6 to 17 sugar mills along a 20 km stretch of the Maw Klong River in western Thailand. When there were only six mills, the aquatic ecosystem continued to be very productive. By the mid-1970s, however, the increasing price for sugar had resulted in a more than doubling of Thailand's productive capacity. The result was that several sections of the river became so heavily polluted that the fisheries were nearly destroyed [3]. The Government invoked the seldom-used water pollution control provision in its Factories Act and forced several of the plants to construct sedimentation ponds. Since that time fishery resources have been largely restored.

One of Malaysia's most successful economic developments has been the establishment of palm-oil plantations and processing mills, which have made Malaysia the world's major exporter of the oil. However, the effluent from the processing plants has a high organic concentration and is rarely treated, thus polluting water supplies, damaging fisheries and adversely affecting the health of people in the countryside. The total organic waste loading from palm-oil wastes in 1975 was equivalent to the total wastes from a community with a population slightly larger than the population of West Malaysia [3].

Pollution resulting from the concentration of traditional industries in local areas must be recognized, especially its damaging effect on the health of the people in rural areas.

Concentration in Urban Areas. During the last two decades, concentration of modern industry, population and government in larger metropolitan areas in the developing countries has led to disequilibrium in the ecological balance and widespread deterioration in the quality of air and water. In Latin America, rapid industrial development, based on petroleum refineries and large petrochemical and steel complexes in urban areas of Venezuela and Mexico, and on metallurgical industries in Peru and Chile, has resulted in high levels of suspended particulate matter in water courses in those countries. In Mexico City, foundries, metal processing, ceramic and paint manufacturing, cement production, smelting and other industrial operations contribute to the total pollution burden in the enclosed valley of the city [3]. Latin America will have many of the largest urban complexes in the world within the next decade, which, combined with large-scale industrialization, can be expected to result in increased environmental degradation.

In the Middle East, the main industries are oil and gas processing facilities. Industrialization is progressing rapidly in Algeria, Egypt, Iraq, Saudi Arabia and Turkey, where pollution is mainly confined to large cities, ports and resource-processing areas such as oil fields and mines. Although most countries recognize the need to combat pollution, controls are generally inadequate.

In the rapidly industrializing, developing countries of Asia, the same phenomenon is evident. Toxic substances are found in concentrations exceeding natural levels in the Republic of Korea. The presence of cadmium, mercury, copper and lead in the rivers and coastal waters of Korea exceeds water-quality standards of Japan, the United States and those suggested by the World Health Organization [3]. In India, heavy industries such as steel processing and petrochemical complexes have brought about a serious deterioration of water supplies in Bombay, Calcutta and Madras [4]. In China, with the rapid expansion of the energy, chemicals and metallurgical industries and the growth of cities, there is widespread water pollution. All major rivers have been seriously contaminated in the stretches of, and downstream from, large cities that discharge great quantities of untreated industrial and urban wastes [5].

Most studies that have been conducted in the more industrialized, developing countries to measure toxic pollutants have found them to exist at levels which exceed accepted health standards. It is likely that industrial pollution in developing countries is more of a problem than has been documented. More monitoring and control of water pollution are urgently needed [3].

Trade and Investment Effects of Pollution Controls

Despite the rising level of pollution in many developing countries, they have historically put lighter burdens on their environmental resources than have the industrialized countries. As a result of differences in the environmental assimilative capacity between developing and developed countries, and the relatively lower priority generally given to the environment in the former, certain trends in international trade and investment have emerged.

Comparative advantage of developing countries. First, the relatively less-stringent, environmental standards so far imposed by numerous developing countries have given them a comparative advantage in the production and export of certain commodities, subject to stricter environmental controls in developed countries. An industry which is allowed to discharge effluents directly into the water course saves on the costs of treatment and can, therefore, in principle produce more cheaply than the same industry subject to stricter controls. Industries which can take advantage of the lower costs of production may, therefore, be attracted by this circumstance which could in turn benefit the recipient country, through industrialization, increased exports and a higher standard of living. This kind of consideration may be particularly attractive to light industries, such as textiles, food processing and plastics fabrication.

Secondly, extraction and export of minerals and other primary products may also have a comparative advantage when environmental controls are not too strict. Primary processing is increasingly being carried out within the developing countries. Exporters of minerals are smelting their ores and exporting refined metal; similarly, they are exporting vegetable oil rather than seeds. This increases the value of exports and may have generated more favourable development linkages than those arising from the export of raw materials. At the same time, the pollution content of such materials is likely to be high. It should, nevertheless, be possible for developing countries which have not yet done so to apply at least basic environmental safeguards without significantly narrowing their competitive advantage [6].

A third trade effect which works to the advantage of the developing countries is a shift away from 'pollution-intensive' products, which have become increasingly expensive, to 'natural' products, which are less damaging to the environment. During the post-war period, there has been a significant displacement of natural fibres (cotton, jute and wool) by synthetic ones, rubber and lumber by plastics, soap by detergents, steel by aluminium and concrete, and returnable by non-returnable bottles [7]. The synthetics, plastics and detergents have been responsible for a large proportion of the non-biodegradable and toxic substances which are polluting the water courses of the world. More recently, there has been a shift in demand back to the natural products. To the extent that the developing countries are major exporters of natural products which compete with synthetics, they should stand to benefit in terms of both price and quantity.

The view that they should take advantage of their competitive position in environmental terms had been voiced by many of the developing countries at the United Nations Conference on the Human Environment held at Stockholm in 1972 (recommendation 106b). Such an advantage had arisen from the greater capacity of their natural environments, as yet unsaturated, to assimilate and dilute wastes [8]. However, as discussed below, this view has now shifted in most developing countries, where the environment has already been strained beyond its assimilative capacity.

Establishment of polluting industries in developing countries. The comparative advantage of developing countries discussed above has led in some cases to the establishment of polluting industries in those countries. In particular, the processes of newly established basic industries, such as steel, chemicals and metals smelting, were not necessarily modified or treatment plants constructed to conform with environmental controls introduced elsewhere in the late 1960s and 1970s. This created industrial pockets in many large cities and reinforced the dualistic structure of economies with distinct modern and traditional sectors. Such investments were often supported because they promised new employment opportunities, development and higher standards of living. It was felt that there was still sufficient time to take care of environmental improvement at a later date and top priority was given to industrialization programmes.

However, it was soon revealed that the pollution-absorbing capacity of the developing countries was not large enough to prevent dangerous environmental disruption in emerging industrial complexes and overcrowded areas. Widespread water pollution in capital cities had caused disease, a decline in fishery resources and a reduction in the supply of water of suitable quality. Most governments of developing countries have recognized deteriorating environmental conditions and in some cases have forced polluting factories to alter their production processes or construct treatment facilities, which has proved to be very expensive. Although the inclusion of treatment facilities at the time of construction of a plant is also expensive it is less so than altering processes to repair damages once they have occurred.

It has become clear that the unplanned promotion of industrialization cannot be sustained on a long-term basis because of environmental damage, and that some controls included at the planning stage are necessary. It appears desirable that developing countries introduce and enforce general controls on water and air pollution before new industries are established, in order to prevent the introduction of processes which may have a detrimental effect on the environment. Such controls may lessen the comparative and locational advantage of the developing country but they are essential to the attainment of long-term development goals.

POLICY INSTRUMENTS

Legal and Institutional Framework

As recommended at the United Nations Water conference, the first step towards effective water management is the formulation of a national water policy. Policy is here considered to be a set of strategies or a plan of action drawn up by the government to guide water resources development, within which laws and policy instruments can be formulated to deal with specific problems such as water pollution. The water policy must allocate water among various competing economic sectors and should be linked to use, conservation and development of water resources in the different sectors. Although the overall policy should be drawn up at the national level, it will have to take into consideration differences in geographical regions and water basins, always recognizing the environmental dimension.

While a comprehensive water policy must be defined with the co-operation of all entities concerned with water, the responsibility for implementation of that policy should ideally be entrusted to a single authority which co-ordinates the activities of those entities in the water field at all levels [9]. Such an authority should be capable of gathering and assimilating data and of basing long- and short-range planning on the resulting body of empirical information. In the water field, as in other areas of administration, the government must have the ability to implement programmes effectively. This calls for rational budgeting, inter-agency co-ordination, efficient delivery of services to the field, continuous monitoring and evaluation, enforcement mechanisms and the establishment of a meaningful dialogue with the public.

Environmental law. Unless the efforts of environmental and water-resources management rest on a solid legal foundation, they are almost certain to fall short of achieving their objectives. While virtually all developing countries have basic legislation empowering government agencies to control some forms of water pollution, the laws may be of questionable suitability to prevailing political, economic and cultural realities. For this reason, they may not be as effective as would be desirable. Close co-ordination with carefully designed social and economic programmes, especially those related to water and environment, is thus essential to an equitable legal framework.

In most African countries, environmental laws dealing directly with water pollution are in the early stages of development, although many of the colonial governments had left general public health codes which prohibited 'nuisances', such as water pollution, and authorized their regulation. In Asia, laws on water pollution vary widely. In some cases, water pollution is covered by general statutes (Bangladesh, Pakistan and Thailand); in others, there is specific water-quality legislation (India, Indonesia, Malaysia, and Philippines and Singapore). However, legislation that does exist generally relates to drinking water quality, rather than industrial pollution. Regulations on the latter are more often found in industrial legislation [3].

In Latin America, three countries—Colombia, Mexico and Venezuela—have comprehensive laws and dominant institutions for environmental management, including water-pollution control. Most of the other countries have at least established environmental units with a primary co-ordinating function; so far, few of the Caribbean island nations have paid attention to environmental management.

All regulations governing water resources development can be drawn up to include an environmental dimension as part of the planning process if the relevant information is made available. Thus, for example, laws governing coastal developments, dam construction, factory licensing and fisheries might all incorporate provisions calling for the routine evaluations of environmental impact as part of the normal approval procedure. Such provisions are essential to the development of a genuine awareness on the part of government and yet, they are absent from the laws of many developing countries. New legislation might include a provision calling for a mandatory examination of the feasibility of waste-water treatment facilities with the construction of any new factory, perhaps in co-operation with the government [3].

Policy Instruments. Within the unique institutional framework developed by the government, each country will have several policy instruments available to it for dealing with water pollution, among which are the following:

(a) Direct charges on industrial effluents as an incentive to polluting industries to reduce waste loads;

(b) Subsidies to promote pollution control using tax rebates or payments to industry to offset costs of pollution control;

(c) Government standards on effluents from production processes, limiting discharge levels of certain substances into water courses;

(d) Government licences under which permits will only be issued to industries using 'clean' processes;

(e) Requirements of environmental impact statements from potential investors or new projects.

These instruments will be discussed below. Each government must choose for itself the appropriate combination of measures which will maximize the effectiveness of anti-pollution expenditures. The necessary responses of governments and industries to environmental requirements will not be inexpensive. Industries will have to pay significant amounts for anti-pollution measures, while governments will contribute the substantial costs of administration, monitoring and research.

Economic Incentives

The first group of policy instruments available to developing countries is based on economic incentives, which should induce industries to reduce discharges of pollutants simply because it is in their own best interest. In a market economy, prices perform the key function of allocating all types of resources to their most efficient use. However, many environmental resources are still unpriced and remain outside the market. Such environmental assets are 'used up' but their use is not accurately reflected in the price system. Economists describe the harm caused by such use as 'externalities' because the burden of resources consumed falls on society at large, not just on the consumer who uses them [10].

Externalities frequently lead to a breakdown in the performance of the market mechanism. The producer does not factor their cost into his profit-maximizing computations. Economic theory states that if the producer had to pay for the costs of pollution, he would discharge less. An effluent charge levied by government on the quantity of pollutants in the discharge of an industrial firm should have the same effect as the market price on the firm's decision to consume environmental resources. Externalized costs should be internalized by the firm to some degree. The concept of effluent charges levied against polluters has come to be known as the 'polluter pays principle'. The introduction of such a policy presupposes the existence of a system and facilities for measuring and assessing the quantity of water used and of effluents discharged by each user.

Effluent charges. Effluent charges have been introduced with varying degrees of success in several European countries and are generally considered by economists to be the most effective means to reduce water pollution. Ideally, the government should set the charge at the level at which the cost of increasing pollution by an additional unit is slightly greater than the cost of treating the additional unit. The objective of effluent charges is to induce individual firms to take pollution-control steps, the overall result of which will be attainment of prescribed water-quality goals. Studies have shown that with the imposition of such a charge, much of the pollution is eliminated immediately. After the initial reduction, however, it is more difficult to reach higher levels of water quality.

Czechoslovakia provides a good example of a working system of effluent charges. The country has been using such a system to maintain water quality at predetermined levels since 1967 [10]. A basic charge is placed on biochemical oxygen demand (BOD) and suspended solids (SS). A surtax of from 10 to 100 per cent of the basic change is added, depending on the extent to which the discharge increases the concentration of BOD or SS in the receiving waters.

The incentive effect of the scheme seems to be directed at inducing proper operation of existing treatment facilities. Charge amounts are based on the operating costs of available treatment systems and do not reflect capital costs of pollution-control treatment. Thus, they are too low to induce investments in treatment systems or process changes. However, the Czech system does allocate revenue from effluent charges to subsidies for such investments.

Self-monitoring, regulated through random checks by government inspectors and penalties for false reporting, provides information on discharge levels. The charge for each source is calculated on the basis of total yearly discharges but is paid in equal monthly installments. A penalty of 0.1 per cent of the charge is levied for every day the payment is late.

The Federal Republic of Germany, Hungary, France and The Netherlands have also developed versions of effluent charges with some degree of success. Furthermore, the 'polluter pays principle' has been accepted by the Organization for Economic Co-operation and Development (OECD) as the most appropriate implementation framework for dealing with pollution [6].

Various programmes of effluent charges geared to the achievement of water-quality goals have been advocated in the United States since the 1960s. Under the programme developed by Allen Kneese and Blair Bower, charges would be set on one or a few pollution indicators, such as BOD. The rates would be set separately for each river basin to achieve the desired level of water quality for that basin. Initial charge rates would be calculated using marginal control cost data on classes of sources in the basin and approximate hydrological models so as to come as close as possible to the 'correct' charge. The charge scheme would be supplemented by regulatory controls where discharge prohibitions were more appropriate, as with toxic substances [11].

Under Malaysia's Environmental Quality Act, the Division of Environment in 1978 introduced licence fees and pollution fees. For palm-oil mills, licence fees are to be calculated on the basis of the quantity of crude oil processed, while effluent fees are based on predicted levels of BOD discharged. These are innovative measures which are to be used in conjunction with standards, and their initial results are not yet known. However, other developing countries may benefit from the Malaysian experiment [12].

For developing countries, one of the most important advantages of an effluent-charge system is that it brings in revenue which can be used for regional or local pollution-abatement programmes. As in Czechoslovakia, revenues earned can be allocated as subsidies to industries for construction of waste-water treatment facilities.

Finally, a system of charges has the advantage of requiring less information than other approaches and therefore, lower costs associated with water-quality management. This should be particularly appealing to developing countries which generally lack funds and comprehensive information networks. The major administrative costs are for monitoring, rather than for legal and enforcement measures.

The disadvantages of the charge system arise mainly because of difficulties in defining the 'polluter' who is to pay. In some cases, pollution is 'old' or a factory discharges from many outlets, some of which cannot be located. In other cases, the sources of pollution are so numerous that it is difficult to determine the appropriate level of effluent which should be allowed to each. Some minimal amount of pollution may be unavoidable, although it seems to be only a small fraction of the amount many industries would discharge without regulation. It should be possible to determine that amount and allow firms to discharge it when river flow is great enough to assimilate it. Finally, assessment of effluent charges has been attacked as a 'licence to pollute at a fee'. Where marginal charges are less than the marginal cost of treating effluents, the industry will prefer to discharge pollutants rather than treat the wastes.

For developing countries considering the introduction of effluent charges, some of the following suggestions [13] regarding favourable ingredients of such a system might be useful:

(a) When an effluent-charge system is introduced, initially low rates can be established, with dates for specified rate increases indicated;

(b) The charges can be related to a few pollutants which are comparatively easy to measure by techniques which yield consistent results;

(c) The administration of an effluent-charge system is greatly simplified by a table of pollution coefficients, establishing levels of pollution per unit of output or per employee. Provisions must be made for sampling and for basing payments on actual discharge of pollutants;

(d) An effluent-charge system should emphasize regional differences, including the assimilative capacity of the water course.

Tax incentives. Other economic incentives which have been introduced in some developing countries are tax concessions or low-interest loans for the construction of treatment facilities. In the Philippines, for example, one half of the tariff duties and compensating tax on imported pollution-control equipment is to be waived for five years from the effective date of the Environment Code (June 1977). Similar rebates are available for domestically produced equipment. Moreover, tax deductions are available for research aimed at improving pollution-control technology [12]. In other countries, industrial promotion boards offer tax incentives to new industries to locate away from urban concentrations or permit industries to amortize or write off investment in treatment facilities in the short-term (accelerated depreciation).

Although such measures may be beneficial for developing countries, many economists consider them subsidies which should be avoided. They argue that such 'subsidies' are mainly for treatment equipment and do not encourage alterations in production processes, recovery of materials, utilization of by-products or changes in raw materials. In developing countries, however, promotional measures could be applied to new industries utilizing 'clean' production processes and recovery methods. The developing countries have an advantage in that many of the industries have not yet been established, whereas in developed countries, old industries using obsolete processes must be induced to change. Subsidies may be an important means to bring about pollution abatement in countries which have only recently become serious about water-quality improvement.

Pollution Control Standards

The method that many countries, particularly the United States, have used to carry out their programmes in water-pollution control is direct regulation. Under the direct regulatory approach, the appropriate level of government sets maximum allowable limits on discharges for particular pollutants or industries, and establishes the administrative and judicial means used to enforce these standards. In the United States and the United Kingdom, this approach has yielded important gains in the struggle against environmental harm. The growth of environmental pollution and environmentally harmful activities has slowed down and in some cases has been reversed [10].

Stream and effluent standards. Two types of standards are typically involved in water-pollution control regulations. First, ambient or stream standards are the legal specifications of the minimum conditions which must be met for a given indicator of water quality at a specified location along the stream. For example, a stream standard may require that dissolved oxygen, averaged over a 24-hour period at a selected river mile point, must not fall below 4 parts per million (ppm) more than one day per year. Secondly, effluent standards are those which specify the mean or maximum permissible discharge of a pollutant, such as SS or BOD, from one particular source. Effluent standards are requirements (either by weight of materials or concentrations) set on the quality characteristics of actual discharges, while stream standards refer to the quality requirements for the receiving watercourse [10].

Stream and effluent standards coexist in control programmes today and must be viewed as potential complements in a rational programme of management. In a situation where there are numerous waste dischargers, achieving a stream standard through several independent decisions will be impossible. Therefore, a central agency must provide information and incentives which will produce co-ordinated behaviour. Effluent standards will be meaningful only in the context of water-quality goals or standards in the water course [14].

Sometimes a combined approach of stream and effluent standards may be used by setting individual effluent standards which reflect the size and location of the discharge relative to the waste-assimilative capacity of the stretch of river.

When setting water-quality standards in developing countries, factors such as technological feasibility and cost must be considered, as well as the possible effects of pollutants on human health or aquatic organisms. Such standards should minimize all the known environmental and health hazards and should be regularly reviewed in the light of new knowledge. Since water quality must be considered in relation to the intended use of water, there is no unique set of standards for streams, lakes or ground water, and the problem cannot be solved in a general way [15]. Standards on water intended for drinking will generally be higher than those for most industrial uses.

Water quality standards are usually issued on the national level, based on the water quality goals of the country. International stream and effluent standards are only applicable where a common water resource is shared by two or more countries, such as the Great Lakes or large river systems. The Lake Chad Basin Committee has drafted a regional convention on uniform water-quality standards which is to be legally binding on member states. A very detailed description of water-quality parameters and sampling techniques for different types of water bodies, which is extremely useful for developing countries, can be found in the UNESCO/WHO manual, entitled Water Quality Surveys, 1978 [15].

The major disadvantage to a system of regulatory standards alone is that it does not provide an incentive to the sources of pollution to treat their wastes or alter their production processes. Enforcement is generally carried out by random checks on factory effluents by government agencies, followed by fines or warnings to those industries not complying with regulations. The delinquent industry may prefer to delay compliance with standards and to engage the government in long legal battles. The charge on effluents, on the other hand, provides an immediate incentive for the industry to reduce its waste discharges. Furthermore, the administrative and enforcement expenses needed to make the system function effectively are enormous. In practice the political and economic costs of a fully effective programme of direct regulation are simply too high for most governments to bear [10].

Mixed systems: charges and standards. Effluent charges may be used in conjunction with effluent standards in mixed systems, which demonstrate that the two instruments are not mutually exclusive. These systems may be viewed as either regulatory programmes, in which charges play an enforcement role, or as *bona fide* charge systems, in which specified discharge levels have been exempted from the charge.

The German Democratic Republic and Hungary have enacted water-pollution control programmes which combine charges and standards. Both levy charges on all discharges in excess of fixed effluent standards. Charges in Hungary are based on costs of attaining the discharge standards, taking into account the condition of the receiving water and other factors. Revenue from the German Democratic Republic's charge is directed at abatement, environmental improvement measures and compensation to some pollution victims. The Hungarian system seems to rely solely on discharge-sampling by the government for its monitoring data. The charges in Hungary initially had little effect but, after they were raised, there was an upsurge in the installation of treatment systems [10].

Starting in 1978, Malaysia attached broad standards for palm-oil effluents onto licences which were to be issued to all existing and proposed palm-oil mills. The guidelines were to serve as interim effluent standards to be met by all mills until more specific standards were developed for each one. Effluent fees are to be charged on BOD concentrations above a certain level. Standards for rubber, tapioca and other industrial effluents have also been proposed, based on temperature of effluent, pH and metal concentrations [12].

Other forms of government control. Licences or permits are other important forms of direct government control which may be used in conjunction with effluent standards or charges. Licences are an essential tool for prevention of environmental damages; in Malaysia, guidelines on effluent standards are annexed to the licence. In other countries, a permit may be given only to a plant using a process which is relatively safe to the environment or which discharges less than a set amount of harmful substances.

Effluent permits may be preferable to charges in certain situations, such as when waste dischargers have historically had a right to discharge material into a river and there is no desire to take this right away from them. The permit would allow an industry to discharge a specified amount. If the main goal is to improve the quality of a stream quickly, then it might be wiser to begin by granting effluent permits rather than imposing charges. Effluent permits could be granted to industries for a given period, say five years, after that, charges could gradually be introduced [13].

Finally, where adverse external effects are too large, neither standards nor permits would be sufficient to restrain polluters. Prohibitions would then be the only instrument available to the government to eliminate the hazardous waste.

Environmental Impact Assessment

Many developing countries have already become aware of the necessity for predicting the impact a new development or industry will have on the environment before it is implemented. Such a prediction is called an 'environmental impact assessment' and is often required by governments from investors in the form of an environmental impact statement. The concept of environmental impact assessment has been adopted by several Asian countries. The Philippines has a strongly worded statute, modelled on the United States National Environmental Policy Act, requiring the submission of environmental impact statements in connexion with all major project proposals. Recent legislative provisions in Malaysia and Thailand furnish an ample legislative basis for requiring similar information. Several other nations, including India, Indonesia, Pakistan, Singapore and Sri Lanka, state that even in the absence of statutory legislation, they conduct such an analysis as a policy matter [3].

The legislation in the Philippines empowers the National Environmental Protection Council (NEPC) to require environmental impact statements from all projects likely to have an effect on the ecological and environmental balance. Guidelines for the implementation of environmental impact statements were formulated by the NEPC, and provision was made for Philippine officials to receive training in environmental impact assessment techniques.

Environmental impact assessments have not yet been widely introduced in Latin America and Africa. The importance of such analyses will become more apparent as national and international funding agencies require consideration of environmental impact as a condition to loans or grants for development projects.

One international forum [16] suggested that the pattern for evaluation of the environmental impact of a foreign investment project in a developing country could be adopted as follows: (1) natural resource linkage; (2) processes in the plant; (3) site assimilative capacity; (4) waste management; (5) operation and control; (6) health aspects; (7) social aspects; (8) ultimate disposal of wastes. The examination of potential foreign investment must be intensified by recipient countries, international financing institutions, multinational corporations and donor countries, to make sure obsolete and dirty processes are not being introduced to developing countries. The moré a firm is required to make an advance disclosure of its project and environmental control plans, the more likely it will consider in advance the potential environmental impact objections that might be raised later.

Many developing countries have gained good experience in preparing environmental impact statements through submitting project proposals to development assistance agencies. Although environmental considerations may increase the total cost of a project, developing countries are increasingly required to prepare impact statements in support of projects for which external financing is sought. Such statements greatly reduce the environmental uncertainty and minimize unforeseen consequences.

Environmental impact statements are required by the World Bank as part of any project appraisal [6]. As early as 1971, leading officials of the World Bank were alerted to the environmental repercussions of projects financed by that institution. The appropriate organizational changes were instituted with a view to helping the developing countries avoid some of the adverse environmental consequences of industrial development. The general feeling was that the costs of prevention were far smaller than the costs of environmental reparation later on—if then it would be possible at all [6]. Other international development assistance agencies in 1980 declared their intention of requiring appropriate environmental measures in the design and implementation of economic development activities [17].

International development assistance agencies have thus provided a framework within which developing countries can learn to prepare, and require of others, environmental impact statements prior to the implementation of projects. The international agencies, including the United Nations, should be able to provide training in the preparation of such statements. Developing countries would benefit in the long-run if new industries were required to reveal their potential impact. Such a requirement should encourage them to begin with cleaner processes.

Monitoring

Any system of charges, standards or impact-assessment presupposes the existence of a system for monitoring changes in effluent or stream conditions periodically or continuously. Monitoring and information-gathering are essential elements in any pollution-control system and should be given priority by governments of developing countries.

Obviously, there is no single measure of water pollution. Whether a substance discharged into a waterway 'pollutes' it depends on a number of factors, including the way in which the waterway is used, the location of the discharge and the time of day or year. Keeping those factors in mind, parameters must be selected to measure pollution, based on harmfulness to human health, among others. Under an effluent-charge system, it is also necessary to identify the party responsible for payment of the charge. Finally, an acceptably accurate and reliable means of measuring the selected parameters over time must be chosen [10].

In developing countries, although many government agencies may have some experience with monitoring of limited scope, few have developed comprehensive monitoring systems. Many African countries do not have a clearly defined water-quality control programme, and have not yet established monitoring systems. A few, like Zambia, do have a systematic monitoring programme to control effluents from factories, mining, textiles and canning industries. Zambian factories are required to pre-treat their wastes. Despite the monitoring system, however, Zambia does not have sufficient resources to maintain the required levels of pollution control [18].

Many other developing countries monitor pollution only in their major rivers, without regard to actual discharges of individual factories. Even in the most scientifically advanced Latin American states, comprehensive water-quality monitoring systems have not yet been established. The methods and equipment required to identify the presence and level of certain pollutants are considered too expensive and sophisticated. Only a few research centres, often limited to one in each country, have the capability to perform the complicated analyses needed to identify the level and presence of specific residuals. In most cases, residuals are first noted when an effect has already been produced, such as the death of fish or vegetation [3].

Efficient management of wastes and water quality requires adequate systems of data acquisition and a scientific understanding of the assimilative capacity of receiving waters. The development of such an information base is one of the first steps to be taken in the effort to control water pollution by developing countries.

United Nations Activities

The United Nations has developed several programmes designed to improve water supply and health conditions in developing countries. Under the United Nations Technical Co-operation among Developing Countries (TCDC) programme, those developing countries which have emphasized water-pollution control and preservation of the environment in their legislation can assist others which have not yet introduced comprehensive legislation. Countries such as Malaysia, the Philippines and Venezuela may be able to offer suggestions to policy-makers from other countries. The United Nations is willing to assist countries in such co-operative efforts.

Furthermore, the Department of Technical Co-operation for Development (DTCD) has technical and interregional advisers who execute UNDP projects designed to assist developing countries prepare master plans for integrated river basin development. These master plans generally include a water-pollution control component. For example, the water management master plan for the Vistula River Basin took into account the dilution required to improve the river's water quality, which has been seriously affected by industrial pollution. Under the master plans for some river basins now being prepared by the National Water Resources Council of the Philippines, a United Nations consultant has prepared pollution-control guidelines.

Finally, under such United Nations projects, there are provisions for training of technical staff. In the field of water pollution control, technical staff are needed to define quality standards, establish laboratories and monitor water pollution. Training programmes may be developed with United Nations assistance.

CONCLUSION

MANY OF THE DEVELOPING countries still retain an advantage over developed countries in environmental terms since their use of highly pollutive and non-biodegradable substances has not yet reached unmanageable proportions. With the new treatment technology available, they may be able to avoid the worst pollution and move into cleaner processing methods. As the developing countries become more aware of the dangers posed to their environments by the discharge into rivers and streams of dangerous industrial wastes, they can incorporate preventive measures into their planning processes. Such measures include requiring environmental impact statements for any new projects and the setting of water quality and effluent standards to which existing factories should comply. The planning of water supplies for urban and industrial purposes must be accompanied by consideration of requirements for disposal of liquid wastes from human, industrial and other sources. Monitoring of effluents discharged by factories and fines for polluting industries will be essential for enforcement.

If the developing countries were to meet the targets of industrial growth envisaged in the Lima Declaration and Plan of Action on Industrial Development and Co-operation, first formulated in 1975, their share of global manufacturing output would reach 25 per cent by the year 2000. That would mean a substantial increase in industrial water requirements for developing countries over the next two decades. Their ability to meet the challenge will depend on planning for efficient use of water by industry, anticipating adverse effects on the environment before they occur and taking immediate steps to establish standards and monitoring systems to ensure water quality.

References

1. United Nations. Economic and Social Commission for Asia and the Pacific (ESCAP). *Industrial Water Use in relation to the Overall Management of Water Resources.* Bangkok, 19 June 1980 (E/ESCAP/NR. 7/4).
2. Varma, C.V.J. *Efficiency in the Use and Re-use of Water in India.* Water International 3:2:21–30, June 1978.
3. United States Agency for International Development. *Environmental and Natural Resource Management in Developing Countries: A Report to Congress,* Volume I. Washington, D.C., USAID, February 1979.
4. Anand, R.P. *Development and Environment: The Case of the Developing Countries.* The Indian Journal of International Law, 20:1:1–19, January–March 1980.
5. Smil, Vaclav. *Environmental Degradation in China.* Asian Survey, XX:8:777–778, August 1980.
6. Walter, Ingo, *International Economics of Pollution.* London, The Macmillan Press Ltd., 1975.
7. Commoner, Barry. *The Environmental Costs of Economic Growth,* in Dorfman, Robert and Dorfman, Nancy, S., Eds., *Economics of the Environment.* New York, W.W. Norton and Co. Inc., 1972.
8. MacLeod, Scott. *One Earth and the Third World: A Stockholm Review.* International Development Review, XIV::4:3–8, 1972.
9. Cunha, Luis V. *et al. Management and Law for Water Resources.* Fort Collins, CO, Water Resources Publications, 1977.
10. Anderson, Frederick R. *et al. Environmental Improvement through Economic Incentives.* Baltimore, Johns Hopkins Press for Resources for the Future 1977.
11. Kneese, Allen V. and Bower, Blair T. *Managing Water Quality: Economics, Technology and Institutions.* Baltimore, Johns Hopkins Press for Resources for the Future, 1968.
12. United Nations. *Task Force on the Human Environment. Project Findings and Recommendations.* New York, United Nations, 1978 (DP/UN/RAS-73-012/1).
13. United Nations. *Efficiency and Distributional Equity in the Use and Treatment of Water: Guidelines for Pricing and Regulations.* Natural Resources/Water Series No. 8. New York, United Nations, 1980 (E.80.II.A.11).
14. Kneese, Allen V. and Bower, Blair T. *Standards, Charges and Equity,* in Dorfman, Robert and Dorfman, Nancy, S., Eds., *Economics of the Environment.* New York, Norton and Co., 1972.
15. United Nations. Educational, Scientific and Cultural Organization (UNESCO) and the World Health Organization (WHO). *Water Quality Surveys.* Dorset, Sydenhams Printers, 1978.
16. Bielenstein, Deiter, Ed. *One World Only: Industrialization and Environment.* International Forum held at Tokyo, 25 November–1 December 1973 under the auspices of the Freidrich-Ebert-Stiftung. Tokyo, Toppan Printing Co., 1974.
17. United Nations. *Declaration of Environmental Policies and Procedures Relating to Economic Development.* Environmental Policy and Law, 6:1980:104.
18. Burke, Eric. *Laws to Look After the Environment.* Environment Africa (Nairobi), 1:1:19–20, December 1980.

Considerations in setting Industrial Effluent Standards

K.R. Ranganathan
*Environmental Engineer, Central Board for the
Prevention and Control of Water Pollution,
New Delhi, India*

SYNOPSIS

The various considerations which will have to be taken into account in setting effluent standards for industrial waste water discharges are detailed and discussed. The major considerations are characteristics of the recipient system, characteristics of the waste water, technological character of the industry, economics of treatment and variability in the performance of waste water treatment systems. A model for evolving effluent standards, based on the considerations of characteristics of the recipient system and economics of treatment where the recipient system is a water body, is presented. The model envisages a minimum level of treatment irrespective of the quality requirements of the recipient water body. The quality requirements are dictated by the best use of the particular stretch of the recipient water body. The model is based on the mixed approach of stream standards and uniform effluent standards.

RÉSUMÉ

Nous avons énuméré et discuté les divers aspects qu'il faudrait prendre en considération afin de fixer les titres de l'effluent pour

237

déterminer la qualité du débit des eaux usées industrielles. Les lignes de force principales sont, à savoir: les particularités du système récepteur et celles des eaux usées; le caractère technologique de l'industrie, les aspects financiers de traitement et la variabilité dans la performance des système de traitement des eaux usées. Nous avons également proposé un modèle dans le but de développer des titres d'effluent fondés sur, au cas où une rivière fonctionne en tant que système recepteur, des considérations relatives aux particularités du système. Le modèle envisage un niveau minimal de traitement sans tenir compte des besoins en qualité de la rivière réceptrice. Ces besoins en qualité sont prescrits par la meilleure exploitation possible de l'étendue particulière de la rivière réceptrice. Ce modèle découle d'une approche mixte des qualités des fleuves et des titres uniformes de l'effluent.

RESUMEN

Se trata en detalle de las varias consideraciones que se deben tener en cuenta en formular las normas de efluentes para las descargas del desagü industrial. Las principales consideraciones son las características de desagüe, carácter tecnologico de la industrial, las economias de tratamiento y la variabilidad en el funcionamiento del sistema del tratamiento de desagüe. Se presenta un modelo para sentar las normas de effluente basadas en las consideraciones de las características del sistema recipiente y las economías del tratamiento donde el sistema recipiente es un rio. El modelo prevee un nivel minimo de tratamiento sin considerar los requisitos de calidad recomendados para el major uso de la parte particular del rio recipiente. Se basa el modelo en el enfoque mixto de las normas de corriente y las normas uniformes de efluente.

INTRODUCTION

THE PAST TWO DECADES have witnessed the deep concern of all countries over the pollution of water resources. Worldwide, the concern has manifested itself in legislation on water pollution control. The legislations differ in their scope and contents [1]. However, the objectives by and large are the same. Generally, the administrative and legal mechanisms are covered in the statutes, leaving the technical aspects to be dealt with by the regulations issued under the main statute or to be decided upon by the administrative body. The statutes provide for a consent system to control water pollution resulting from discharges emanating from industries, human settlements or any other human activity. The consent is not a permit to pollute but an instrument to cut down the discharge of pollutions. The question immediately following is "cut down to what level?" This level, in terms of concentration or mass per unit of production or mass per unit time, is termed as the discharge standards. The considerations that should precede the setting of the standards for discharges are discussed in this paper. The considerations are many and for some of them a strong data base is a prerequisite. Such a data base may not exist in the developing countries but the lack of it should not preclude setting the effluent standards based on other considerations and enforcing the standards through the consent system. The implication is that the standards may have to be changed if required by the considerations for which data have since become available. The reaction of the industries to such shifting standards may be unfavourable but then it may not be advisable, even temporarily, to halt pollution control until complete data are collected to enable framing of standards based on all the considerations.

CONSIDERATIONS IN SETTING STANDARDS

Characteristics of the recipient system

The primary consideration in framing the standards is the nature of the recipient system. The industrial effluent may be disposed of into municipal sewers or combined industrial waste water sewers, inland surface sweet waters, estuaries, coastal waters or lakes or on land. It is not only these types of recipient systems that have bearing on the stipulation of standards but also, in some cases, the characteristics of the particular system, such as inland surface sweet waters.

Municipal Sewers: Treatment of industrial waste water with domestic waste water has the following inherent advantages: due to economy of scale, national cost on pollution control is reduced; treatability of the industrial waste water is enhanced; the problem of non-availability of space for constructing treatment units in industries located in cities is solved; and the difficulties experienced by small industries in installing and successfully operating waste-water treatment plants are sorted out. However, industrial waste waters cannot be accepted indiscriminately into the municipal sewers. The sewers have to be protected, as well as the men who work there. The biological treatment process given to the combined waste waters must also be protected. Table 1 presents the concentration of heavy metals that would affect the aerobic treatment process [2].

Table 1. Threshold toxic level of heavy metals to aerobic treatment process

Metal	Concentration in mg/l
Chromium (IV)	10
Copper	1
Nickel	1.25
Zinc	5–10

Therefore, limits on heavy metals will have to be imposed on industrial discharges into the sewers in order to protect the biological treatment process. Similarly, limits on pH and sulphate will have to be incorporated to protect the material of the sewer. The limits on biochemical oxygen demand (BOD) and suspended solids are governed by the treatment capacity available at the terminal point and how much of it the municipality can allocate to industrial load.

It is seen from the above that industries, if need be, may have to provide some preliminary treatment. In the developing countries, if India is a typical example, industries, especially the small- and medium-sized, are attracted to well-established human settlement areas. Perhaps the solution to water-pollution control in such situations lies only in the collection and treatment of domestic and industrial waste waters through a combined system. Industries will have to comply with the standards as applicable to the sewer and recipient system. In Table 2, suggested standards for the discharge of industrial effluent into sewers are presented. The suggested limits for BOD and suspended solids can be varied by the authority owning the sewer and the terminal treatment facility. Another common situation is the case of industrial estates, where a large number of small- and medium-sized industries (at times as many as 400 in number) are located in an area of a few hundred hectares. Owing to the size of the individual industries, from the points of view of overall pollution-control cost, operation and performance of treatment units and the objective of improving the quality of the receiving water body, the best solution will be to provide a combined collection system and a terminal treatment facility. The individual industrial unit would have to treat its effluent only to the extent of protecting the sewers and the terminal treatment. If the combined waste water after treatment is utilized for irrigation purposes, special parameters, such as Boron, total dissolved solids and chloride, may have to be included in the list of parameters furnished in Table 2. However, stipulation of these parameters to a relevent industrial unit will depend on relative flows.

Rivers: The rivers transport materials in dissolved and suspended forms to the ultimate sink—the oceans. The transport imparts certain quality characteristics to the water, depending upon the nature of the materials. Such quality acquisition may result from natural causes or human interference. These acquired quality characteristics may render the water unfit for a particular use. It is not necessary,

Table 2. Tolerance limits for industrial effluent discharged into sewers

Serial Number	Characteristics	Limits
1	pH	5.5–9
2	Temperature, °C	45
3	Suspended solids mg/l	600
4	Biochemical oxygen Demand for 5 days at 20°C, mg/l	500
5	Oil and Grease, mg/l	100
6	Phenolic compounds (as C_6H_5OH), mg/l	5.0
7	Ammonia coal Nitrogen (as N), mg/l	50 2.0
8	Cyanides (as N), mg/l	2.0
9	Sulphates (as SO4), mg/l	1000
10	Chromium (hexavalent) (as Cr), mg/l	2.0
11	Copper (as Cu), mg/l	3.0
12	Lead (as Pb), mg/l	1.0
13	Nickel (as Nc), mg/l	2.0
14	Zinc (as Zn), mg/l	15

Source: Indian Standards Institution IS: 3306-1974

and may be impossible, to keep riverine systems in pristine condition or even at an uniform quality throughout their length. However, it is necessary that the various stretches of a river are maintained at the characteristic quality level which will sustain the best use of the stretches. Thus, water-quality criteria for all uses have to be evolved. In the development of criteria, the target for protection has to be identified. The targets could be human health and aquatic fauna and flora. The inter-relationship of the targets is realised but the extent to which it should affect the immediate water-quality objectives of a country is governed by the compulsions and priorities in the goals of the society and so also is the extent to which protection has to be given. Once the best uses of the various stretches of the river are determined, based on present and future uses, the water quality to be maintained at each stretch to sustain these uses, in then known. The effluent standards to be set for an industry, or a group of industries, discharging into any stretch is governed by the required water quality of that stretch. The allocated pollution load for a stretch may be equitably distributed among the polluting sources, so that the total cost of pollution control remains optimal. It should not be construed, however, that industries could be given the advantage of dilution so that they do not need to provide any pollution-control devices. Because under the pretext of presently available dilution, industries, discharging into that stretch of river, may get a blanket clearance for using the stretch as a sewer and would be reluctant to install pollution-control devices when a future situation demands it. At this point, it should be noted that a sound water-quality management programme should take cognizance of dilution and dispersion available with the recipient water body, providing, of course, that certain basic minimal pollution-control devices are installed by the industries. Toxic, biomagnifiable and bioac-cumulative chemicals are to be considered on a different footing.

In the preceding paragraph, the evolution of effluent standards based on water-quality criteria of the receiving water, is explained. This is a logical blending of the two methods developed to control pollution of water at the sources. In one method, effluent standards are specified, regardless of location and type of industry, but some specify industry-specific standards, regardless of location. In the second method, the water-quality standards of the receiving water are only specified, leaving the industry to control the quality of its discharge so that the water-quality standards are maintained. The latter-method is abandoned by most countries because of the difficulty in administering the system. In locations where more than one industry discharge effluents, it is difficult to identify the violator in the event of failure to maintain the standard of the receiving water. The method of uniform effluent standards, regardless of type of industry and location, although easy to administer, suffers from many limitations. The limitations are: the method is inequitable from both the view points of dischargers and maintenance of receiving-water standards; the method becomes insensitive to the quantum of pollutant cast in the receiving water if effluent standards are only in terms of concentration; the method gives hardship to industries whose waste waters are difficult to treat; and finally, the method in few cases may induce the industry to dilute its waste water in order to conform to the effluent standards, thus jeopardizing the very concept of water resources conservation. In order to overcome the limitations of the two methods, the logical step is to evolve effluent standards related to water-quality requirement of the receiving water. The model presented later in this paper attempts to lay out the procedure for evolving such an effluent standard.

The variation in the flow of a river should reflect in the effluent standards if optimum utilization of the resource is our prime objective. It is safer to evolve the effluent standards to maintain the required water quality of the river at its minimum flow. But it would be ideal if seasonal effluent standards could be set, especially in respect of rivers whose flow variation is considerable. There are some inherent difficulties in doing this but attempts may be made to use the very large dilution available at times, as in the case of monsoon-fed rivers, in respect to certain pollutants such as oxygen-consuming substances.

Estuaries and Coastal waters: Rivers being unidirectional in flow, the rate of flow is the only hydraulic parameter of concern. In the case of estuaries, dispersion of pollutants is of importance. In the scheme for setting effluent standards, presented later in the paper, the water quality at which the estuarine portion of the river is to be maintained is considered. That water quality is dependent upon the criteria of the identified best use of the estuary. Predictive capacity should form part of the water-quality management programme, to estimate the permissible additional pollutional load into the estuarine and river systems and the water quality consequent to a discharge. The biological sensitivity of the estuaries will be reflected in the development of water-quality requirement.

The two important criteria for coastal waters are coliform organisms and floatables. The effluent standard to be set for a discharge into coastal waters may be based on the required water quality on the beach where bathing or other activities occur. The place and manner of disposal are of considerable importance in the case of marine discharges. They may be considered as equally important components of the consent, or permit, system as the effluent quality standards is in other cases. Water quality criteria for coastal waters for different beneficial uses are presented in Table 3.

Land: Perhaps the best recipient system for industrial waste waters is the land. By land application is meant the utilization of waste water for agricultural purposes. The soil mantle has considerable capacity to adsorb various components of industrial waste waters and, moreover, the ground water gets recharged. Direct pollution of surface waters is prevented. However, the required area of land is not always available. The main considerations in setting effluent standards for discharge on land are the concentration of total dissolved solids, chlorides, sulphates, boron and percent sodium.

Characteristics of waste water

The second consideration in setting effluent standards is the characteristics of the waste water.

Composition of waste water: The choice of pollution parameters on which limits will be stipulated in the effluent standard for an industrial discharge, naturally, will depend on the composition of the waste water. The industrial waste waters may contain oxygen-consuming organic substances, heavy metals, toxic chemicals, mineral oils and others. The substances may also be grouped as biodegradable, non-biodegradable, bioaccumulative and biomagnifiable. The consideration in setting limits in respect of biodegradable matter would be the demand on the oxygen resources of the receiving water body. The requirement of 4 to 5 mg/l of minimum dissolved oxygen in the ambient water, to protect fish life, is well documented. The criteria for fresh water uses include the parameters of BOD and dissolved oxygen since they speak of the pollutional state with respect to biodegradable matter. Limits on the parameter of chemical oxygen demand (COD) are laid down to regulate discharge of organics not measured by BOD. Some of the substances contributing to COD which cannot be biologically degraded in the aquatic environment may have effects, individually or in combination, on human health or on aquatic fauna. In case the effluent is suspected to be toxic, a tolerance limit, in terms of survival of fifty percent of a specified test organism over a specified period of time, may be stipulated.

In the case of substances such as pesticides and mercury, the standards may have to be based on their bioaccumulative/biomagnifiable characteristics.

Table 3. Water quality criteria for marine waters

Sl. No.	Characteristic	Criteria for	
		Bathing, Recreation, Shell Fish and Commercial Fish Culture and Salt Manufacture	Harbour Water
1	2	3	4
1)	Colour and Odour	No noticeable colour or offensive odour	No noticeable colour or offensive odour
2)	Floating material	No visible floating matter of sewage or industrial waste origin	No visible floating matter
3)	Suspended Solids	No visible suspended solids of sewage or industrial waste origin	—
4)	pH value	6.5 to 8.5	6.5 to 9.0
5)	Free ammonia (as N), mg/l, Max.	1.2	—
6)	Phenolic compounds (as C_6H_5OH), mg/l Max.	0.1	—
7)	Dissolved oxygen, Min.	40 per cent saturation value or 3 mg/l, whichever is higher	3 mg/l
8)	Pesticides (chlorinated hydrocarbons) (as Cl), mg/l, Max.	0.002	—
9)	Arsenic (as As), mg/l, Max.	0.2	—
10)	Mercury (as Hg),	0.0003	—
11)	Oil & grease substances (sampled in 30 cm surface layer) mg/l, Max.	0.1	10
12)	Biochemical Oxygen demand (5 days at 20°C), mg/l, Max.	5	5
13)	Confirm bacteria, MPN index per 100 ml, Max.	1000	2500
14)	Bio-assay test	Not less than 90 per cent of test animals shall survive in 96 hr. test.	—

Source: Indian Standards Institution, IS: 7967-1976.

Other factors: The following factors resulting from the composition of the waste water have bearing on the standards and they are grouped together since they are interdependent:

—treatability of the waste water;

—technological availability for treatment;

—cost of treatment.

Before setting a limit on any of the constituents, it is necessary for the regulatory agency to consider whether the limit could be achieved in practice within a reasonable cost. Standards may be set based solely on availability of practicable technology, without considering the factors of cost and the capacity to take up pollution by the recipient system. However, setting standards is conditioned by what the society wants and can afford. By the same token, it is also the responsibility of the regulatory agencies to set objectives and design the pollution-control efforts accordingly, taking into account the overall needs of the society. The cost of treatment is not directly proportional to the levels of treatment and at high levels become very high. Certain waste waters cannot be treated within reasonable cost to levels which could be achieved easily for other waste waters. An example would be the spentwash from molasses distilleries. The concentration of the biodegradable organics is high at about 40,000 to 50,000 mg/l in terms of BOD, rendering it economically impossible to reduce it to the normal standards of 30 mg/l or so. The availability of technology in the country has also to be considered. The cost of pollution control is, after all, borne by the society. The effluent standards are to be set so that the expenditure on this front is consistent with the benefits derived by the society. The model presented for evolving effluent standards for discharge into water bodies attempts to take into consideration the factors discussed thus far:

(1) the water quality requirement of receiving water;

(2) the treatability and cost of waste water treatment;

(3) economic viability of the treatment.

Technological Character of the Industry

The technological character of the industry should be taken into account while setting the effluent standards for it. There is bound to be conflict while considering so many factors but some compromise will have to be arrived at. The built-in systems for recovery and reuse of chemicals, the nature of catalysts used and the nature of raw materials used are some of the factors which characterise the technological age of an industry. The quantum of pollutions discharged from an industry is dependent on the technological age. Generally, older technologies result in higher discharge of pollutants. Since the cost of treatment is not directly proportional to levels of treatment, industries based on older technology would find it comparatively too costly to achieve the same standard as the industries based on newer technology.

An example of how raw materials used could affect the standards, from

Indian experience, would be laying down standards for mercury loss in caustic soda plants. The common salt available to the industry contains considerable impurities. The salt has to be purified and considerable mercury is lost with the brine mud. Therefore, setting a standard in this case may not be right, compared to situations where pure brine is available.

Variability in Performance of Waste Water Treatment Systems

The performance of physico-chemical and especially biological treatment units are subject to variation. Therefore, in setting effluent standards, variability in performance should be taken into account. As an example, the effluent limitations developed for organic pesticide chemicals manufacturing industries in the United States of America is presented in Table 4.

Expression of Effluent Standards

The effluent standards may be expressed in the following ways:
   —concentration;
   —mass per unit time;
   —mass per unit of product.
The shift in emphasis from a mere concentration standard to that of quantum of pollutant is reflected in the modification of units of expression. The units of expression also indirectly indicate how the compliance will be ensured. The mass per unit time or mass per unit of product will not be based on a single grab sample and thus, variations in the performance of the treatment plant are taken care of.

Table 4. Effluent Limitations for Organic Pesticide Manufacturing Industries

Effluent characteristics	Effluent limitations (Average of daily values for 30 consecutive days)
BOD (5 days)	1.6 kg/K Kg
Chemical Oxygen Demand	9.0 kg/K Kg
Total Suspended Solids	1.8 kg/K Kg
Pesticide Chemicals	0.0018 kg/K Kg
pH	6 to 8 kg /K Kg

Source: Effluent limitation guidelines for the pesticides chemicals manufacturing point source category—PB 285 480 April 1978, U.S. Environmental Protection Agency Development Document.

A MODEL FOR EVOLVING EFFLUENT STANDARDS

THE CONCEPT of evolving effluent standards based on the following factors has been discussed:
—the water-quality requirement of receiving water
—the treatability and cost of treatment
—the economic viability of treatment

The model, illustrated in Figure 1, is designed to evolve industry-specific and location-specific effluent standards [3]. At the national level, it is possible to evolve industry-specific effluent standards and not beyond that. The industry-specific effluent standards are to be examined at the local level by the concerned authority, giving due regard to the water-quality requirement of the receiving water into which the discharge is to be made. Such an examination would result in the modification of the industry-specific standards into location-specific also. The industry-specific effluent standards, which will be evolved at the national level, are termed the Minimal National Standards (MINAS). The model envisages a minimum treatment to the waste waters consistent with the annual burden of expenditure which a particular industry can bear. The annual burden is reckoned as a percentage of the annual turnover of the industry. Before the percentage is arrived at, dialogues are held with the industrial units belonging to the industrial group under consideration, based on the comprehensive document prepared on the industry. The comprehensive document is a status report on the industry in the country and would deal with, among other aspects, waste-water treatment, providing the following details:
—identification of different unit processes specific for the waste water;
—identification of different treatment schemes comprising individual unit processes:
—estimating capital and operation and maintenance cost expressed as annual burdens for each of those schemes in respect of typical capacity of production;
—estimating the quality of treated effluent corresponding to each of the schemes:
—expressing each of the annual burdens as a percentage of annual turnover of the industrial unit.

At the dialogues, the critical percentage of annual turn-over is finalised. The treatment scheme corresponding to the critical percentage being known, the effluent quality achievable by the treatment scheme is the MINAS. In the case of certain industries, even the best stage of treatment would not result in an annual burden which is higher than the critical percentage or it may be just equal. Such industries are termed soft industries. There may be medium hard industry for whom the annual burden of the minimal stage of treatment is above the critical percentage of annual turnover, but below the super-critical percentage. The

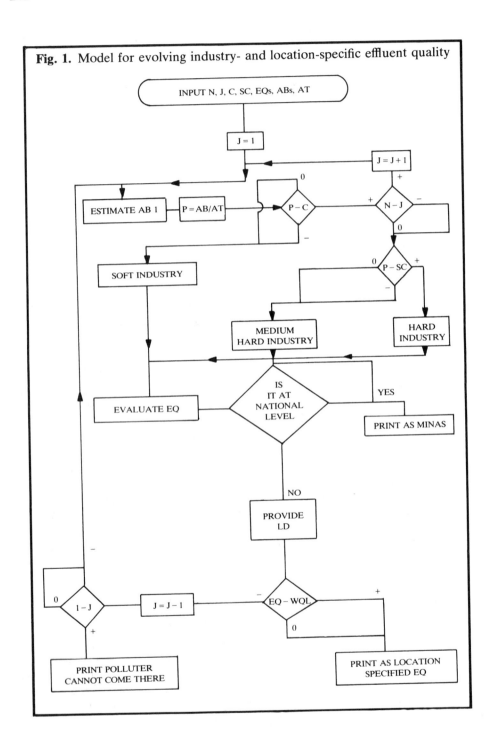

Fig. 1. Model for evolving industry- and location-specific effluent quality

Explanation for notation used in Figure 1

N = Total number of pollution control stages, the annual burden of each stage of treatment is required to be evaluated.

J = Stage of pollution control under consideration; when $J = 1$, it indicates the best stage of treatment which obviously uses the best available technology of treatment.

C = Critical percentage of Annual Turnover of the Industry

SC = Super-critical percentage of Annual Turnover of the industry.

EQ = Quality of treated effluent corresponding to any stage of treatment.

AB = Annual Burden of any stage of treatment.

AT = Annual Turnover of the Industry.

P = AB/AT, expressed as percentage.

LD = Location Details of disposal of treated effluent; inland surface water, estuaries, coastal waters.

WQL = Water Quality requirement for the location.

super-critical percentage is also finalised at the dialogues with the industry. The industries for whom the annual burden for minimal stage of treatment remains above the super-critical percentage of annual turnover are called hard industries.

The determination of location-specific effluent quality requires the input of details of the location of disposal. Previously, reference has been made to the best-use and water-quality criteria for different uses of recipient water bodies. From these two considerations, the permissible quality of effluent from the industry is determined. When the quality achievable by a particular stage of treatment matches the permissible effluent quality, then it becomes the effluent standard for the industry. In certain cases, even the highest stage of treatment may not match the permissible quality, in which case the industry, if it is a proposed one, cannot be established at the location.

Classification of Waters

It is seen that in order to evolve the permissible effluent quality in a particular situation, the primary requirement is to determine the best use of the recipient system and the water quality required to sustain that use. The following uses are identified for fresh and sea waters.

Fresh Water

—Drinking water source without conventional treatment but after disinfection;

—Outdoor bathing (organised);

—Drinking water source with conventional treatment followed by disinfection;

—Propagation of wildlife;

—Fisheries;

—Irrigation;
—Industrial cooling;
—Controlled waste disposal.

Sea Water (including estuaries and coastal waters)
—Salt pans;
—Shell fishing;
—Contact water sport;
—Commercial fishing;
—Recreation (non-contact);
—Industrial cooling;
—Harbour;
—Navigation;
—Controlled waste disposal.

The listing of the uses is in the order of the degree of water-quality requirement. It is obvious that any stretch of flowing (lotic) water will be subjected to more than one of the above listed uses. The scheme of classification, to deal with such multiple uses, is evolved based on that use which demands the highest degree of water quality. The use identified is referred to as the designated best use. The designated best uses are grouped into a class system as follows:

Fresh Water

Designated best use	Nomenclature (class of water)
Drinking water source without conventional treatment but after disinfection	A
Outdoor bathing	B
Drinking water source with conventional treatment followed by disinfection	C
Propagation of wildlife, fisheries	D
Irrigation, industrial cooling and controlled waste disposal	E

Sea Water (including estuaries and coastal waters)

Salt pans, shell fishing, contact water sport	SWI
Commercial fishing, recreation (non-contact)	SWII
Industrial cooling	SWIII
Harbour	SWIV
Navigation, controlled waste disposal	SWV

The variously zoned stretches of the country's water bodies are classified according to the scheme, after identifying the uses and determining the designated best use of the stretches. With the knowledge of the water-quality criteria for the various uses, criteria for each class are developed. It is this water quality of the recipient system that has to be taken into account in determining the location-specific effluent standard for an industry. While developing the water-quality requirement for each class, it may not be necessary to include all the parameters relevant to a use.

References

1. Ozolins, G., Fluss, S.S. and Helmer, R. (1977) *Global Trends in Water Pollution Control Legislation.* Report on a Government of India/WHO Seminar on the Implementation and Adminstration of the Water (Prevention and Control of Pollution) Act, 1974. World Health Organisation, New Delhi, India.
2. Jones, R.H., Frank, W.R. and Harding, C.I. (1970) *Waste water treatment methods in the wood-preserving industry.* Proceedings of the 25th Industrial Waste Conference, Purdue University, Lafayette, IN, USA, May 1970.
3. Chaudhuri, N. and Ranganathan, K.R. (1980) *Classification and Zoning—A tool for Water Quality Management.* Proceedings of the Symposium, Hydrology in Water Resources Development, Central Board for Irrigation, April 1980.

Relations between Industrial Area Programming and Waste Management

Wanda J. Mołoniewicz

Expert for Polish Association of Sanitary Engineers and Technicians, Warsaw, Poland

SYNOPSIS

Industrial waste-water management has not yet been given a sufficiently high rank in the programming and planning of industrial and urban regions. Premises for the development of technical infrastructure are, as a rule, treated as a problem of secondary importance and are formulated after decisions regarding location and programming of industrial projects in a given region have already been made. It is still common practice to design and develop individual parts of the infrastructure treating them as separate problems. Also, their effects on particular elements of the natural environment are investigated in isolation, not in a comprehensive way. Thus, there is a lack of complementariness in the approach to both waste generation, particularly in industry, and elements of the natural environment taken as a whole.

Figure 1 in the paper illustrates the basic relationships affecting the choice of a strategy for industrial wastes management in a region with particular emphasis on the role and influence, needs and pressures from social groups.

A considerable part of the discussion in the paper is devoted to industrial sludge management, a problem whose importance is still underestimated.

RÉSUMÉ

Dans la planification urbaine le problème de l'évacuation des égouts n'a pas encore un rang trop important. Des programmes et des plans du développement de l'infrastructure technique sont établis en principe indépendemment, comme des annexes qui suivent des programmes ainsi que des décisions de localisation de l'industrie dans la région.

Les differentes branches de l'infrastructure sont étudiées séparement. Les differents types de pollution et leurs influence sur l'environnement sont également considéres comme systèmes independantes. Par consequent il manque de complexité dans les modalités d'action en ce qui concerne des problèmes des sources du pollution.

Le schema annexe No 1 explique des relations les plus importantes qui influencent le choix des règles de l'evacuation des égouts industrielles. Dans ce schema on souligne le role et l'influence des facteurs sociaux dans ce choix.

Dans le document présente on traite souligné aussi le problème d'utilisation du boues provenant des égouts industrielles qui est encore sous-estimé—le schema annex No 2.

RESUMEN

La economia de los desagües industriales no a adquirido todavía su rango correspondiente en la programación y planificación de los terrenos industrializados y urbanizados. Los principios del desarrollo de los sistemas de infraestructura técnica suelen ser elaborados como secundarios, frente a las decisiones concernientes a la ubicación y al programa de la industria en la región. Las particulares ramas de la infraestructura siguen siendo elaboradas separadamente; tampoco hay simultaneidad en determinar su influencia sobre los distintos elementos del medio ambiente. Lo que falta, pues, es la examinación complementaria de las fuentes de los residuos y varios elementos del medio ambiente considerados como un sistema.

El dibujo no 1 adjuntado al informe presenta las dependencias básicas que determinan la estrategia de la economía de los desagües industriales en la región. Se subraya particularmente la importancia e influencia de las necesidades y presiones sociales.

El informe destaca uno de los problemas minusvalorizados hasta ahora, o sea, la economía de los sedimentos de los residuos industriales, dibujo no 2.

CONCEPTS FOR WASTE MANAGEMENT IN REGIONAL PLANNING

INSUFFICIENT KNOWLEDGE of the relationships between the programming, planning and designing of industrial projects on the one hand and waste-water management on the other is one of the main causes of difficulties encountered in maintaining the required quality of the natural environment.

Systems for waste-water disposal and treatment are not only designed after programming and spatial decisions concerning industry have already been taken, but also any subsequent changes in these decisions are frequently made without any regard to the problem of waste-water and sludge management.

This approach restricts to a considerable degree the probability of selecting the optimum solution from the viewpoint of waste disposal and environmental protection and prevents the efficient operation of existing systems. Moreover, it disregards the interdependencies linking the development of all the different systems operating in the industrial area and in the whole region.

The concept of waste management described above has undergone a thorough change in recent years. The notion that "air and water are free" and therefore can be drawn upon without any restrictions is being replaced by the opinion that the assimilative capacity of the environment is finite and that the need to maintain an ecological balance requires a change in the approach to development problems, that is, that the town and industry development-to-environment approach must be replaced by the environment-to-town and country planning and industry programming concept.

The system of waste materials management presented in Figure 1 is proposed as the first stage in the subsequent choice of a policy for managing different types of waste in industrial and urban regions. The elements of the system have been treated in a highly integrated manner and therefore require further development, which is the object of this investigation. The instrumental criteria of system development are determined in each case by the current and future possibilities, namely: (1) the required degree of detail of the model, (2) the time available for preparing the model and obtaining results, (3) the type of available input data, and (4) the organizational structure of the administrative units responsible for the decision or for future operation of the system.

In relation to the industrial area programming and waste management strategy, the following problems should be considered in the greatest detail: (1) determination of the assimilative capacity of the receiver, (2) inventory of the sources of wastes generation (existing and foreseen), (3) social needs and behaviours that are of decisive importance in the formulation of the preferred line of action, and (4) choice of the methods of treatment and disposal. Up to now the importance of the last problem has been underestimated in water and waste-water management strategy.

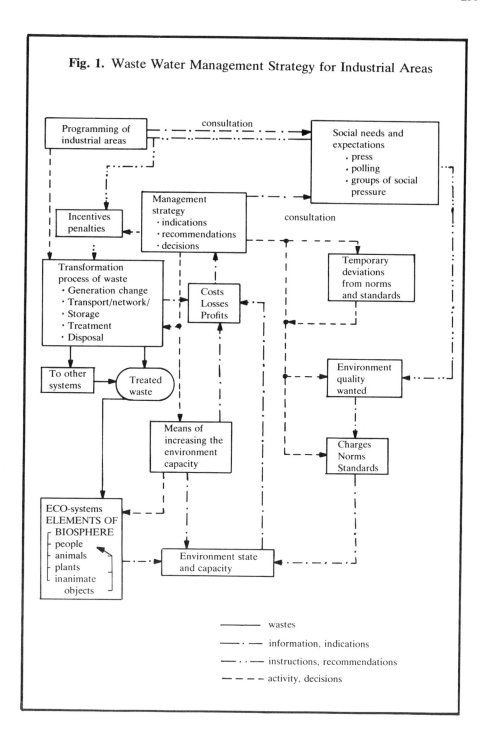

Fig. 1. Waste Water Management Strategy for Industrial Areas

The Assimilative Capacity of a Receiver

The assimilative capacity should be determined on the assumption that there must be no degradation of the ambient environment. By degradation of the environment we mean: a relative permanent reduction of biological activity, deterioration of the quality parameters of ecosystem and plant products, and reduction of the climate-forming, sanitary and landscape-forming qualities of the vegetation. Biological activity of the environment is determined by all the biological processes taking place in the water, soil and atmosphere [1].

The assimilative capacity of receiving waters can be increased by: (1) technical means, (2) increasing the range of distribution of discharges, (3) reducing the existing degree of degradation of the elements of the environment taken into account, and (4) regulating the time pattern of discharges.

Technical means include a variety of procedures like augmentation of streamflow, aeration of surface waters, addition of nitrates, and so on.

The range of distribution of waste discharges consists in selecting the location and distribution pattern of discharges, i.e. point or non-point discharge. As regards distribution patterns, there are two extreme possibilities: (1) minimizing the range of waste discharge by increasing the waste-load to the technically and technologically motivated limits, (2) maximizing the discharge range by setting a maximum discharge area that is practical from the technical and operational points of view. The actual choice of preferred variant is determined by economic and ecological considerations.

The existing degree of degradation of receiving waters can be decreased primarily by eliminating sources of pollution, removing accumulated untreated wastes or resorting to various technological measures aimed at improving the quality of the environment. Identification of factors degrading the environment and assessment of the damage caused by them are of decisive importance in selecting suitable means of immunizing ecosystems and increasing their biological activity.

Regulating the time pattern of waste discharges can compensate for the irregularities in the generation of waste-waters and sludges. In particular, shock loads have an adverse impact on sewerage networks, treatment plants and receivers. This is especially true for industrial establishments where waste generation is determined by the type of product, production technology, shift work, and so on. For each plant, the generation of wastes must be carefully analysed and a timetable of discharges prepared in coordination with all other users of the same receiver. In many cases it is necessary to alter the time pattern of waste discharges and disposal by the use of various storage tanks and other facilities for holding waste and sludge until they can be utilized.

Inventory of the Sources of Wastes Generation

Insufficient progress is noted in identifying sources of pollution and ways of its dispersal. Attention is primarily focussed on some point sources while non-point ones and some particular wastes are more or less neglected. One of them is sludge, that in various forms and at various phases of treatment is precipitated out of waste water, either on purpose or unintentionally. For example, unintended precipitation of sludge occurs in sewerage systems and various devices employed in such systems, storage reservoirs and, finally, in receiving waters where sludge forms bottom deposits. Intentional precipitation of different forms of sludge takes place in various devices used in waste-water treatment plants.

The quantity, type and composition of precipitated sludge depends specifically on the characteristics of the waste water, and the applied sewage-purification and sludge treatment techniques. However, a comprehensive evaluation of the properties and parameters of waste and sludge in a given region should be based on an inventory of all sources of waste and sludge, as indicated by the regional development plan and industrial area programme.

By making a preliminary inventory of existing sources of pollution and those envisaged in the plan, it is very difficult to evaluate their future effect on the environment, propose changes in individual development programmes and indicate locations for industrial areas. One of the most difficult problems that must be solved when programming and designing a waste-water treatment plant is the problem of determining the quantity, composition and discharge irregularity of waste generated in industrial establishments. The reason is that the quality indicators for waste and sludge generated by different industries and future technologies rapidly become obsolete.

Ways of influencing the quality and type of generated wastes can be also found in the sphere of social activity. Therefore in regional planning, consideration is given to the relationships between social structures and the way of life, needs and behaviour of social groups which result in a variety of pressures on the market followed by changes in the structure and location of industry. This makes forecasting of the volume and type of generated waste and sludge a very difficult task because of the uncertainty in determining the future development of social needs. The development of a region is characterized by many spontaneous processes. Forecasts concerning such processes often prove to be either totally erroneous or only partly true. The degree of uncertainty in forecasting the volume and composition of sludge that will be generated in the future is today greater than ever because of rapid technological progress and the appearance of new fields of production. Also, we are not able to anticipate the direction of many social reactions and needs. It is very difficult indeed to forecast the conditions for a future balance in the system-technology-environment. This is particularly true of perspective planning and long-range planning (after the year 2010). However, the durable character of the technical infrastructure makes it necessary to adopt such a farsighted approach to the problem.

Choice of an Optimal Solution of Waste Treatment and Disposal

The choice should be related to the technology of treatment of all the different kinds of wastes contributing to the total waste load discharged to the environment. This is particularly true of highly industrialized areas with a high concentration of emission of all kinds of wastes and a limited assimilative capacity of the environment. Sludges with different characteristics are generated at different points of the sewage systems and are affected by a variety of factors. The most important factors affecting the quality and quantity of sludge are the following: (1) type and technical design of the sewerage network (combined, separate, industrial, storm water), (2) type of devices used in the network (rainfall overflow, storage reservoir, waste-water and sludge pump stations etc.), (3) type of waste treatment plant, technology and degree of treatment of waste (mechanical, biological, chemical, etc.), and (4) applied method of sludge treatment (aerobic and anaerobic digestion, dewatering, coagulation, etc. and combination of them).

Less advanced are studies of the losses and damages caused by excessive loading of the environment and of the benefits resulting from the use of various technical procedures in the transformation and utilization of sludge. High transport costs make it necessary to locate waste treatment facilities as close as possible to the site of their generation. However, if sludge is to be discharged to the soil, then a variety of factors should be considered, such as terrain features and ways of land utilization, soil quality class, groundwater level, possible occurrence of insulating layers in the soil, and many other factors, mostly quite independent of industrial area programme. Choice of the method of sludge utilization is one of the main factors affecting waste-water treatment management and has a decisive impact on location of industrial areas.

This is especially true when, out of the many methods of sludge utilization (composting, landfill, land application and reclamation, sale as soil conditioner, ocean disposal, combustion and, if needed, pasteurization, etc.) the utilization of sludge on land is planned.

In recent years much research work has been done in Poland on utilization of sludge in land reclamation in areas where the soil has been degraded as a result of industrial activity (mainly lignite strip mines, construction of large sea-ports, etc.). From the results of such studies, it has been possible to determine the optimum amounts of liquid sludge and the correct time of discharge onto the land being reclaimed. (Variants were used in these studies, involving the application of 250 to 500 tons of dry matter per hectare.)

LOCATION OF INDUSTRIAL AREAS

As FAR AS WATER SUPPLIES and waste-water disposal are concerned, three basic types of industrial locations may be distinguished: (1) industrial plants located within the range of municipal sewage and/or water supply systems, (2) plants located beyond the range of municipal systems but discharging waste waters (pre-treated or not) to a regional waste-water treatment plant, and (3) plants located beyond the range of municipal sewage and water systems and operating their own sewage facilities. It is fairly frequent practice to build combined waste treatment plants serving both municipal and industrial needs.

The combined treatment is generally considered to be for many reasons the most economical solution. Advantages also lie in the simplicity of administration, operation and control. Particularly in the case of smaller industrial establishments located within or close to a municipal sewage system, mixed waste can generally be treated in one plant more efficiently, economically and with a greater degree of reliability than in individual plants. When the establishment is located beyond the range of a municipal system, each case must at all times be carefully analyzed depending on the distance of location, the characteristics (quality and quantity) of the industrial waste, the indispensable degree of pretreatment, and other local conditions, that is to say the investment, operational and environmental costs must be taken into account [2].

Although the regulations in force usually specify the standards that must be met by the waste water discharged into municipal sewers (in Poland 38 indicators are required) and the industrial establishments must only pay the rates and take care not to exceed standards specified by the municipal sewage authorities, these regulations are often violated and the authorities are not able to detect such violations. For example, an engineering or automobile factory might discharge an excessive amount of oil as a result of an unexpected failure of its pretreatment plant.

In a large industrial town in Poland the local sewage treatment plant is now and again put out of operation because of periodic failures of the waste-water neutralization facility in a large viscose rayon factory. The same factory has caused, during the forty years of its operation, considerable damage to the municipal sewage system as a result of the powerful corrosive action of the soluble part of calcium sulphate, even in waste water that has been subjected to proper neutralization [3].

The weakest point in the existing waste-management system is undoubtedly the problem of treatment and disposal of sludge. Estimates from various sources put the total volume of sewage-sludge in Poland at approximately 20 to 30 m^3 a year. Of this, approximately 55 per cent is generated in municipal waste treatment plants.

Up to now the control of industrial waste discharges into municipal sewage systems has concentrated mainly on the protection of sewers and prevention of disturbances in the sewage treatment process. A total elimination of industrial waste discharges into municipal sewers is neither possible nor necessary. The same can be said of the use of sophisticated pre-treatment methods prior to discharging industrial waste into sewers.

However, potentially useful domestic sludge must not be permitted to became a burden because of pollution with toxic or other harmful substances from industrial discharges. More stringent control of the content of unwanted substances discharged into municipal sewers will unavoidably increase the volume of concentrated liquid wastes, the disposal of which will have to be handled by the producer. Obviously this requires that adequate provisions be made when programming, planning and designing an industrial project for a sufficiently large site on which to build facilities for pre-treatment of waste waters and treatment of sludge. Also, further expansion of an industrial plant or modification of production technology might be limited as a result of problems with waste water and sludge treatment and disposal.

Considerable problems are encountered in the disposal of sludge generated in industrial waste treatment plants if the sludge contains harmful or toxic substances in high concentrations. These include not only compounds of heavy metals, but also sulphide and cyanide anions, oxidising and reducing agents, detergents, etc. Such sludge increases the total volume of solid wastes generated in the production processes, which are also toxic. Among the latter are wastes generated in chemical plants. An example of this is furnished by the problems encountered in the storage of phosphogypsum, a waste generated in the phosphoric fertilizer industry. In one of the phosphoric fertilizer factories in Poland, a special plant had to be built to treat the strongly acidic waste water from the phosphogypsum.

It is clear from the above that, irrespective of whether an industrial project is to be located within the range of a municipal sewage network, or will discharge waste water into a regional sewage treatment plant, or will have an on-site sewage system and discharge treated waste into receiving waters, the problem of industrial sludge management is an important factor in selecting the location and size of the site and protective zones. In many cases the problem of sludge disposal determines the choice of the sewage management system to be employed in the region and in industrial areas.

With reference to Figure 2, the proposed sequence of steps to be taken in the sludge-management planning procedure is based on an estimation of the assimilative capacity of the elements of the environment. By determining the general balance for consecutive time horizons, it is possible to formulate proposals for regional development plans. It is stipulated that the question of sludge treatment and disposal be given more prominence than is the case today in the planning of sewage systems in industrial areas.

In an attempt to determine the degree of importance that should be given to the problem of sludge management in the general conception of industrial and regional development programmes, the elements and relationships affecting the choice of an optimum system solution have been identified. A solution is considered optimal when the system is capable of protecting particular elements of the environment, treated as a whole, at minimum cost, with the use of the available technical means in accordance with the accepted social and economic policy.

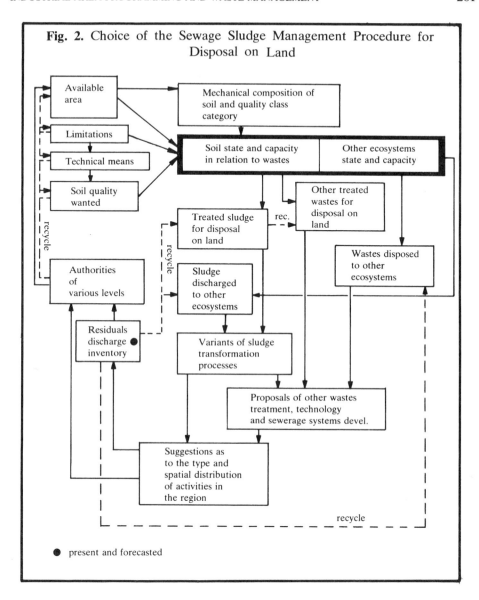

Fig. 2. Choice of the Sewage Sludge Management Procedure for Disposal on Land

CONCLUSION

WAYS OF IMPROVING economic and ecological indicators of investment projects are to be found not only in the choice of technologies for waste treatment and disposal, but also in programming and planning industrial areas in relation to other waste sources in the region. Close collaboration of industry, town and country planners, technical infrastructure specialists, ecologists and sociologists representing the social needs and wishes, administrative and legislative authorities and economists, including step-by-step consultations, should produce considerable economic results and a faster improvement of the quality of life, so expected and wanted everywhere. It is clear from the above that improvement of environmental conditions in industrial areas calls for a more holistic approach to the problem.

References

1. Siuta, J. *The mechanism of soil degradation and development in the industrial areas.* Eksploatacja Maszyn. In Polish only. Warszawa 1980.
2. Roman, M. *Principles of combined waste-waste treatment plants use.* Arkady, Warszawa 1970.
3. Koziorowski, B., Kucharski, J. *Industrial Waste Disposal.* Pergamon Press, second edn, modified, in Polish only, 1980, Warszawa.

Economic and Institutional Implications of Alternative Effluent-Control Strategies

Robin Bidwell

*Deputy Managing Director, Environmental Resources Limited,
London, UK*

SYNOPSIS

*The paper examines different strategies for the control of water
pollution and their implications for both the dischargers and the
administrative authorities. Alternative types of system are reviewed
under the headings of: (1) permits: variable and fixed standards, etc;
(2) charging systems: taxes, distributive charges and incentive
charges. The implications of alternative strategies are examined and
the conditions under which the different strategies may be most
appropriate are noted.*

RÉSUMÉ

*Cet article éxamine des différentes stratégies pour le contrôle de la
pollution des eaux et ses implications tant pour les agents polluants
comme pour les autorités administratives. On discute des systèmes
altérnatifs sous les titres: (1) Permis: standards variables et fixes, etc.
(2) Systémes de taxes: taxes, charges distributives et charges d'incitation. On éxamine les implications des stratégies alternatives et on*

fait noter les conditions dans lesquelles les différentes stratégies peuvent être les plus appropriées.

RESUMEN

El estudio examina estrategias distintas para el control de polución del água y su implicancia tanto para los descargadores como para las autoridades administrativas. Se discuten diferentes tipos alternativos de sistemas bajo los títulos de: (1) Permisos: padrónes variables y fijos, etc. (2) Sistemas de débitos: tasas, despesas de distribución y despesas de incentivo. Se examinan las implicancias de estrátegias alternativas y se toma nota de las condiciones en que las diferentes estrategias podrán ser mas apropriadas.

INTRODUCTION

THIS PAPER EXAMINES the relationship between the type of the water-pollution control adopted for a particular area and the implications for the dischargers, the control authority and the local community. Any water-pollution control strategy will have considerable economic, institutional and environmental impacts; but only recently has there been an awareness that these impacts need to be examined and that selection of an appropriate strategy can considerably increase the cost-effectiveness of a water-pollution control programme.

It should be stressed that the paper focusses solely on the administrative aspects of water-pollution control and the resulting costs. Administrative costs are, of course, only a very small part of the total water-pollution control costs borne by the community. The effectiveness of the controls and the overall costs (including treatment cost borne by dischargers as well as the authority) must be taken into account when examining the full impact of the type of administrative measures to be employed. But the following analysis does provide an indication of the way in which different approaches may be expected to affect an administration's costs. In particular it indicates the implications of one administrative strategy compared with another.

The key elements in a system to control water pollution are:

—controls to limit potentially polluting discharges from entering natural waters (rivers, lakes, estuaries or the sea);

—controls to limit discharges to sewers:
—enforcement of these controls;
—meeting the costs of the water pollution control programme.

These four elements need to be considered as an integral part of the system. As will be shown, the type of control influences the enforcement requirements and both influence the cost to the authority as well as to the dischargers and the rest of the community.

TYPES OF CONTROL

PERMITS ARE THE MAIN METHOD used to control discharges; charges are also used but only in conjunction with permits. The principal types of permit and charging systems will be reviewed and the implications of each noted.

Permit Systems

Use of Permits. Discharges may be controlled through a system of permits. Permits set out the conditions (referred to as 'consent conditions' in the U.K.) under which the discharger is permitted to discharge. These conditions may include:

—the quantity that may be discharged. This may be expressed as maximum permissible concentration, average concentration which may be exceeded for a proportion of days, etc; it may specify load (weight of contaminants) as well as concentration or it may specify volume and concentration;
—other restrictions such as colouring, temperature, etc.

Permits may be used to control:

—discharges to sewers, principally for the purpose of protecting the sewer fabric and the health of the sewer workers. But they will also be required where the effluent is treated at a communal treatment plant in order to protect the plant from hazardous material or overloading;
—direct discharges, where it is necessary to protect the quality of the receiving waters.

It will be appreciated that since discharges to sewers will eventually enter the environment, controls over discharges to sewers (e.g. over toxic metals) can play an important part in pollution control by preventing certain substances entering the environment.

Variations in Permit Systems. There are two distinct approaches that may be used to set permit conditions.

Variable emission standards (favoured in the U.K.): In this case, the conditions may be established according to local environmental factors, such as the assimilative capability of the river, its intended use, etc. This approach enables control authorities to set conditions which are no more stringent than are required and which can take account of other factors such as the ability of different dischargers to install and pay for the necessary treatment.

Uniform emission standards: Alternatively, the conditions may be fixed for all dischargers; that is, a single emission standard for all dischargers of a particular contaminant, irrespective of the existing quality or intended use of the receiving waters. The level is then set only once by the authority and it is likely to take account of such factors as best technical means, impact on the economy etc.

The advantage of the first alternative (variable emission standards) is that it is, in principle, a least-cost method since the controls are adjusted to take account of the water quality needs; the disadvantages include additional work required to establish the conditions and the greater opportunities for corruption. The system of uniform standards has the advantage of equity (fairness) between dischargers, since one factory will not be required to put in more treatment plant to control a particular substance than another. It is also administratively more simple. The disadvantage, of course, is that it may either impose unnecessary costs on dischargers or, where the environment is particularly sensitive, may result in inadequate controls.

In practice permit systems often incorporate both approaches: with fixed standards established for hazardous substances at as low a level as is technically feasible, and with variable standards for degradable substances. Where there are fixed standards, these are often adjusted according to the type and/or use of the receiving waters.

Other variations in the form and use of permit systems include:
—the nature of the conditions laid down (number of parameters, whether conditions refer to average or peak flows, etc);
—the type and size of discharge requiring a permit, in other words, whether all categories of discharge are required to have a permit or only significant dischargers;
—the period of the permit; whether it is for a fixed period, or alternatively, the circumstances under which the permit conditions can be adjusted;
—the extent and method of enforcement.

While the overall approach used to fix the consent condition will considerably influence the impact on industry and other dischargers, the influence of the other variables (type of permit, enforcement, etc.) will be mainly on the control authority.

Administrative Implications of Permits. Throughout this paper we examine the administrative implications by reference to a 'model' region. This is derived from a model designed by ERL for the purposes of examining the administrative implications of different approaches to water-pollution control. A more detailed review is included in Reference 1. Figure 1 indicates the principal features of the region, which are:

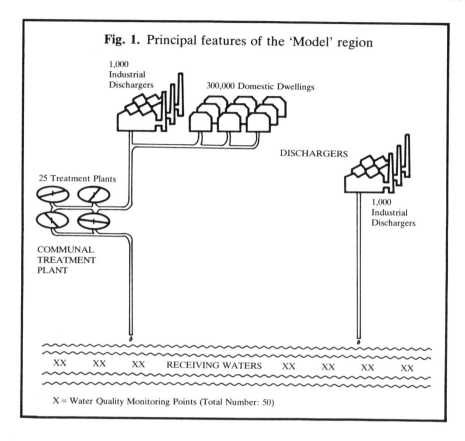

Fig. 1. Principal features of the 'Model' region

—2,000 large industrial dischargers of which 1,000 discharge to sewer and 1,000 to rivers direct;

—300,000 dwellings most of which discharge to sewer but some to septic tanks;

—25 public-sector treatment plants;

—50 water-quality monitoring points (ten samples per year, fifteen parameters analysed).

Elements in the costs. It will be obvious that the administrative costs will be strongly influenced by the nature of the area and local factors such as man-power costs, etc. However, using costs derived from European information, an analysis of the principal cost elements shows:

—17 per cent of the cost is employed on administering the permit system: that is, principally establishing new permits with the associated paper work;

—78 per cent on enforcing the system. This assumes that 90 per cent of the dischargers are inspected with samples being taken 8 times each year and analyses carried out for 7 parameters on each sample;

—5 per cent for monitoring water quality to ensure that the objectives are being achieved. This assumes that ten samples are taken at each location per year and fifteen parameters are analysed.

In Europe, the total administrative cost of such a system would be of the order of US $3M for an area such as that described above. These figures indicate the importance of enforcement in total costs to the authority.

Enforcement costs are influenced by:

—the percentage of dischargers that are inspected each year;
—the number of times they are inspected;
—the number of parameters (e.g. BOD, COD, pH, etc.) that are examined per sample.

Figure 2 indicates that reducing the number of inspections to 3 times a year would more than halve the cost of enforcement. As a result, it would cut the costs of administering permits to about half of the US $3M per annum indicated above.

The enforcement requirements will vary considerably from area to area, and even between types of discharger, depending on:

—whether it is essential for water-quality management purposes that the conditions are complied with;
—and on how law-abiding the dischargers are.

Because of the high cost of enforcement as a proportion of total cost, it is worthwhile examining ways of reducing the need for frequent inspections; for example:

—heavy penalties for infringement of consent conditions may help build up respect for the law;
—self-monitoring: large dischargers in particular may be required to regularly sample their own discharges (preferably using a continuous sampling device) and supply the results to the control authority. This of course does not obviate the need for the regulatory authority to check the dischargers' own results but it can help the regulatory authority to reduce the frequency of its own inspections.

CHARGING SYSTEMS

Use of Charges

Charges may be levied on dischargers. There are the following types of charges:

—effluent treatment charges which are levied on discharges that are treated at a communal sewage-treatment plant and are designed to recover the costs of treating that discharge;
—pollution charges which may be levied on discharges to sewer or direct discharges for purposes other than recovering the costs of sewage treatment.

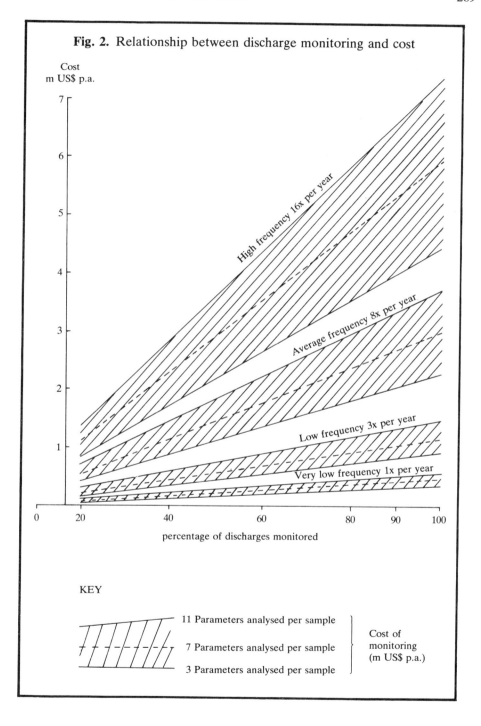

Fig. 2. Relationship between discharge monitoring and cost

The second type of charges is known as pollution charges: this may be divided into two categories:

    —distributive charges: those that are set so as to recover some aspects of the control authority's costs, such as the costs of a pollution-control programme or other water-quality related services, administration, etc;

    —incentive charges: those that have been set so as to 'make the dischargers pay for polluting' with the specific intention of encouraging the dischargers to improve the quality of their effluents.

It should be stressed that while both effluent treatment charges and distributive pollution charges are methods of ensuring that dischargers pay for the services they receive in accordance with the burden they impose on the system, incentive pollution charges are a means of control. The levels of the charges are set so as to make it more economical for the discharger to improve the quality of his discharge through treatment, etc; whereas the levels of distributive charges will be set so as to provide enough money to pay for a particular aspect of the service. For a more detailed discussion on charging systems, see Reference 2.

The main difference between distributive and incentive charges is one of principle: in the former case, the charge is being used primarily as a fund-raising mechanism and in the latter case as a control. In practice, this is likely to mean that the level of charge will be very much higher when it is used as a control. However, it will be appreciated that for some dischargers any level of charge will have the effect of acting as an incentive mechanism; but, paradoxically, where this is the case a true distributive charge will, all things being equal, increase in level as the individual users reduce their load, leaving the authority to cover their costs from a smaller charging base.

In some cases a single charge is levied to recover costs of communal treatment and the other costs of the administration: this is known as a 'combined charge'. In addition to these 'discharge-related' charges, administrative and other communal control costs may also be recovered through general or local taxes. These four types of charge are shown diagrammatically in Figure 3.

The Impact on Dischargers of Charging Systems

Where the charge is not discharge-related (i.e. the costs of water pollution control are paid out of fixed taxation or are related to property taxes), then the costs will be paid by all members of the community in a manner similar to other general public services. However, if a discharge-related charge is employed, the impact on the discharger will depend on the type of charge employed. In particular, it would depend on:

    —whether the charge was primarily distributive or established as an incentive;

    —if distributive, what types of costs it would be designed to recover;

    —whether it would be a combined charge and so do away with existing trade-effluent charges;

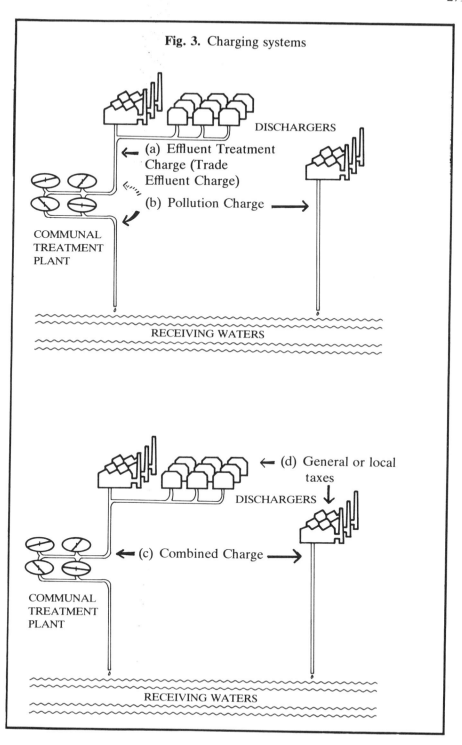

Fig. 3. Charging systems

—whether the charge should be levied on all discharges (including domestic discharges);

—the basis of the charge: the number and type of the parameters in the formula and the way the formula was constructed.

Implications of a distributive charge: By definition, a distributive charge would not increase the overall costs of water pollution control. There would, however, be a likely shift in the burden between different groups of dischargers if the previous system had been to pay the costs out of general taxes. However, the type of formula used as a basis for the charge would strongly influence the distribution of costs between dischargers. In particular, the number of parameters in the formula will strongly influence the amount paid by the different categories of industry. In the Netherlands, for example, the formula on which charges for discharges to state waters are based takes account of only COD (or BOD for treated discharges) and nitrogen; whereas in Germany, the charge will be based on solids, BOD, COD, fish toxicity, mercury, cadmium and a bacterial parameter, but in many cases, charges are based solely on quantity.

Implications of an incentive scheme: A scheme of incentive charges would probably only be levied on direct dischargers. The implications would depend on:

—whether the incentive charge would be levied only on industrial discharges or also on municipal discharges (inland, municipal discharges are principally those from treatment plants);

—whether there would be a uniform level of charge or alternatively, whether this would be varied according to the nature and the intended use of the receiving waters;

—how the money would be used: whether it would be used for providing grants and, if so, whether industry would be able to benefit and under what conditions.

Administrative Implications of Charging Systems

Provided that the results from the permit inspections can be used for the purposes of calculating the charges, then the additional administrative costs for introducing a charging system should be small: principally calculating charges and sending out bills. These operations can be undertaken by, for example, the water or electricity authority once the system has been set up and the basis to be used for calculating the charges has been agreed.

However, if the charges are administered and enforced separately from the permit system, and information on the quality of the discharge has to be collected specifically for calculating the charge, then not only will the additional costs of the charging system be considerably higher but also, the type of charging system will influence these costs.

Once again using the same assumptions for the model region, and assuming a permit system such as those described above is in force, the additional costs would be:

— a further 20 per cent if the formula was based on 3 parameters and the charge was calculated from a 'table of charges' (as in France, Germany and the Netherlands) rather than actually measured;

— or almost double the cost if 7 parameters were used to calculate the formula and the charge was based on regular measurement (90 per cent of dischargers 8 times a year).

CONTROL STRATEGIES AND THEIR IMPACTS

THE IMPLICATIONS of the separate elements in a control system have so far been examined. From this a number of general points about alternative control strategies and their impacts can be concluded. These are again considered under the headings of permits and charges. Figure 4 indicates possible combinations of the elements that may be used when devising a control strategy.

Permit Systems

For industrial discharges, fixed emission standards may result in the controls being more stringent than is necessary to achieve the waste-quality objectives and the economic impact consequently greater. Variable standards offer greater flexibility, with the possibility that the control authority can consider the effect of a number of different discharges on a particular stretch of water and devise a strategy that minimises the cost to all dischargers. However, while variable standards may in this way favour industrial dischargers, industry often states a preference for fixed standards on two grounds: that the alternative may make some of their members less competitive and that they are unhappy if the control authority is allowed too much discretion.

Administratively, fixed standards are easier and less costly to establish; variable standards require that a considerable amount of monitoring and modelling of the receiving waters be carried out before the correct level can be determined. But of course, this does allow the control authority to upgrade the receiving waters in the most cost-effective way. One of the main dangers of variable standards is the opportunity provided for corruption; remedial action is likely to place a heavy financial burden on the discharger and there is always a danger of a 'deal' being struck between the discharger and the authority (or one of its inspectors) that is not in the public interest.

There is no evidence of differences in the enforcement requirements associated with the two systems. This is more likely to be determined by the sensitivity

Fig. 4. Alternative control strategies

PERMITS

+

Uniform standards for
all parameters and for
all areas

Variable standards
for all parameters
and all areas

Uniform standards
for all parameters
but fixed according
to intended use of
receiving waters

Uniform standards
for some parameters
(toxics) with
variable standards
for other (bio-
degradables, etc.)

either

and/or

and

CHARGING SYSTEMS

Taxes

property tax
general tax

Distributive Charges

For cost of treatment

For some or all of
control authorities,
costs

Incentive Charges

Uniform charge
Variable charge
Some combination

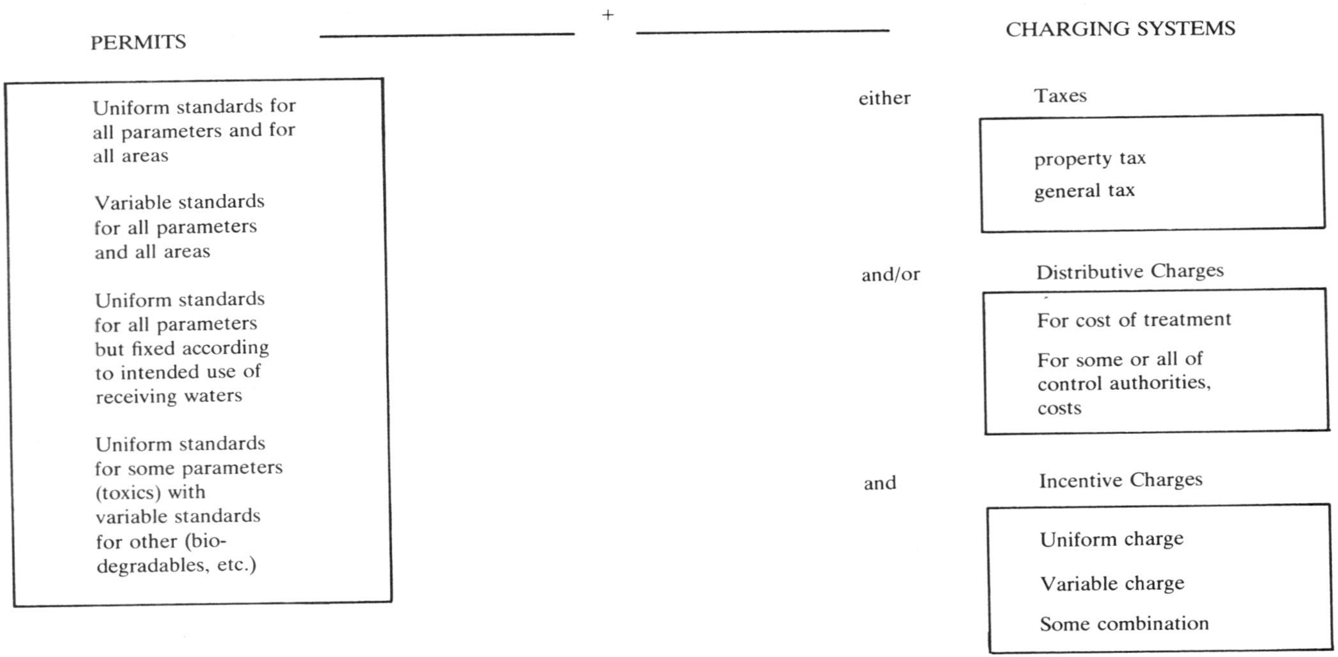

Note: Figure shows elements from which alternative control strategies may be
developed. All require some form of permit and charging system; alternative charging systems are taxes and/or distributive charges and incentive
charges. Variations on each element is shown in boxes.

of the receiving waters (where the receiving waters are already polluted, the impact of dischargers exceeding the standards may be less serious); it may also be determined by the attitude of the dischargers.

Environmentally and economically the variable standards are in principle preferable. They allow the authority the discretion to protect and upgrade certain areas and not others; they therefore ensure that resources are used effectively. In reality, few areas organise the use of their resources in such a rational fashion; and variable standards may mean that less is achieved than would be if the standards had to be complied with, whatever the economic climate.

Charging systems

From an economic standpoint, it is essential to recognise that there is always some form of charging system in operation; someone somewhere is paying for the control system. If, as is usual, payment for water-pollution control services is through local or general taxes, then there will inevitably be a degree of subsidisation of the major polluters; that is, the major polluter will not be paying his fair share of the costs he imposes on the water authority and, if treatment is undertaken, on the treatment authority. Distributive charges that are based on the effluent load and quantity are preferable, because each discharger bears his fair share.

Incentive charges provide an added spur for the discharger to reduce his discharge to a certain level. Used in conjunction with a permit system, they have the advantage that the discharger may, within certain limits, take his own decision about whether or not he will treat his effluent. Where the aim is to upgrade a certain stretch of river over a period of time, this can provide a flexible and equitable mechanism. It is less attractive where it is necessary to protect a river ensuring a consistent high quality. Incentive charges raise money that can be used for upgrading water quality (e.g. providing grants for treatment works) but care needs to be taken not to use the money for subsidising polluters.

For industrial dischargers, distributive charges are preferable to general taxes for those industries where the nature of the discharge is weaker than average; assuming of course that the element allocated to water pollution control is then removed from general taxes. Incentive charges, as already noted, can provide added flexibility but where there is an existing system of control, it is likely to be seen as an additional financial burden. Administratively, and assuming there is already a permit system in operation, charging systems should add little if anything to existing costs once the transition has been made. But, as discussed in the section on the administrative implications of charging, this depends crucially on the type of system implemented.

CONCLUDING COMMENTS

FROM THE ABOVE, it will have been seen that there is a wide range of possible control systems. The strategy selected will depend on local circumstances. However the following general points can be made:
  —where a new system is being implemented, controls based on variable standards may not be satisfactory. It is preferable to identify those areas that are to be upgraded and set fixed standards that are reasonably liberal for existing dischargers but stringent for all new dischargers.
  —Incentive charges may prove useful where, as in France and Germany, there is a programme to upgrade the quality of the rivers. It provides a useful mechanism for raising money from the main polluters. But once the objectives have been achieved, incentive charges may not be of continuing value.
  —Distributive charges are in general preferable to general taxation as a way of paying for the control system (or for communal treatment). But such charges should be based, at least initially, on a 'table of charges' to reduce the administrative cost associated with regular inspection.
  —In general, care should be taken when setting up a system to select an approach that minimises the administrative cost. Most importantly, the authority should keep monitoring and analysis to the lowest level consistent with reasonable compliance.

References

1. Bidwell, R. and Mason, S. (November 1980) *Effluent charging systems and their administrative implications.* IAWPR (UK Committee) Specialised Conference on the Environmental Impact of Man's Use of Water, Brighton, U.K.
2. Bidwell, R. (February 1981) *The implications of a directive on effluent charges.* Water and Effluent Treatment Journal.

The Relevance of Cost Information to the Choice of Effluent-Control Policy

D.J. Elliott

*Lecturer in Civil and Environmental Control Engineering,
Department of Civil Engineering, University of
Newcastle-upon-Tyne, UK*

SYNOPSIS

Efficient effluent control policies for direct discharges to water courses enable specified water quality levels to be achieved at minimum cost. Advocates of effluent-taxing schemes argue that efficiency is implicit in the tax control mechanism. Analysis of abatement cost data for the Tees Estuary shows that considerable savings can be made if efficient control schemes are adopted. However, with an effluent-tax scheme the least cost solution can only be achieved if comprehensive cost data and water quality data are available. With this information control may be obtained using efficient consents. Efficiency is, therefore, no longer a discriminating factor in the pricing/regulation debate and the choice of appropriate control mechanism must be based on other criteria.

RÉSUMÉ

Des niveaux spécifiés de la qualité d'eau peuvent être atteints aux frais minima par des polices efficaces qui ont à contrôler l'effluent dans le cas de décharges directes dans les cours d'eau. Ceux qui défendent l'idée des plans d'impôts d'effluent maintiennent que le mécanisme du contrôle par les impôts garantit de l'efficacité. Une analyse des renseignements sur la rèduction des frais pour l'estuaire

de la rivière Tees montre qu'on peut faire des économies considé-
rables si on adopte des plans de contrôle efficaces. Cependant, avec
un plan d'impôt d'effluent, la solution des moindres frais ne peut
être atteinte que si on peut se servir des renseignements et sur les
frais comprèhensifs et sur la qualité d'eau. Avec ces détails on peut
obtenir du contrôle en utilisant efficient consents. L'efficacitè, dès
lors, n'est plus un facteur de discrimination dans le débat sur la
méthode de fixer les prix ou de régulariser l'eau et le choix d'un
mècanisme de contrôle qui convient doit être basé sur d'autres
critères.

RESUMEN

La eficacia de las políticas de control de residuos para las descargas
directas en las corrientes de agua permiten la realización de niveles
específicos en la calidad de agua con un coste mínimo. Los que
abogan por los esquemas de tasación de residuos argumentan que la
eficacia es implicita en el mecanismo de control de tasación. Un
análisis de los datos de disminución de coste para el estuario del Tees
muestra considerables ahorros por medio de la adopción de esquemas
eficaces de control. No obstante, en un esquema de tasación de
residuos la solución de coste mínimo sólo puede lograrse si se dispone
de datos comprensivos de coste y de calidad de agua. Con esta
información puede obtenerse el control usando consentimientos
eficaces. La eficacia ya no es, por tanto, un factor discriminatorio en el
debate entre precio y regulación y la elección de un mecanismo de
control apropiado debe basarse en otros criterios.

INTRODUCTION

THE RECENT DEBATE on control policies for direct discharges of effluent to receiving waters has centred on the comparison between the traditional empirical method of control by consent and the theoretical arguments supporting the introduction of taxes for each unit of effluent discharged. Economic efficiency (the achievement of a prescribed receiving water quality at minimum cost) or lack of it, in the case of traditional regulation by consent, has been the main criterion against which various proposed control policies have been judged. This paper attempts to consider some aspects of efficiency using data obtained from a case study of effluent discharges to the Tees Estuary on the north-east coast of England.

THE 'POLLUTER PAYS' PRINCIPLE

THE 'POLLUTER PAYS' principle provides the basic framework for policy information. Kinnersley [1] argues that the principle itself is not novel and cites the case in which a property owner adjacent to a water course under the consent system agrees to accept a regular annual payment from the polluter as compensation for damage. The payment can be regarded as a rent for part-use of his property, or his foregoing of some enjoyment in the use of his property. Kinnersley argues that the increases in the numbers of landowners, together with the increase in number of dischargers, has distorted the traditional relationship between the polluter and those suffering damage. The cause-effect relationship is difficult to identify and the transaction costs incurred by those seeking compensation for damage are so great that the polluter has been able to continue to discharge with impunity. Kinnersley suggests the introduction of a permit system controlling the total amount discharged together with an annual charge on the discharger. The annual charge is not a penalty for breach of permit but a payment for the right to discharge within the limits set, and the polluter referred to in the 'principle' is the discharger complying with his authorization.

In the simple case of the discharger paying the local landowner for reduced enjoyment of amenity, the valuation of damage is that perceived by the two parties to the transaction. It may not reflect the ecological damage or the damage incurred by the rest of society. Obtaining a value for the societal loss from pollution is a major problem since perception and valuation of damage varies between individuals. The community may accept spatial and temporal differences in receiving water quality standards depending on the interrelationship between the uses required for the receiving water. For any given receiving water, once the community has decided on a particular quality level, taking into account the costs of implementation, that level may be assumed to be optional from the community's point of view. Hence a discharger or combination of dischargers, as long as their combined effluents do not violate the given water-quality levels, are not polluters in the sense described by Kinnersley.

This paper assumes that a policy conforms to the 'polluter pays' principle if the costs of meeting receiving water quality standards are borne directly by the discharger. The market price of goods will incorporate costs of achieving societal environmental quality levels. It is also assumed that the policies discussed are applicable to an equilibrium situation in which the policy is known and understood by both manufacturer and controlling agency and has been operating for some time. It is recognised that the transition period from an existing situation to a new control policy may require transient controls which do not strictly comply with the 'polluter pays' principle.

TEES STUDY DESCRIPTION

THE TEES STUDY [2] team was established to investigate the feasibility of a charging scheme for controlling direct discharges of effluent to the Tees estuary. The estuary is grossly polluted from both industrial and domestic sources and has been the subject of intensive investigation by industry and local government authorities in the area. Water-quality models developed during these investigations were available to the team. The approach taken was to collect information on abatement costs from all industrial dischargers and to use this information together with the water-quality model to estimate the costs of achieving a range of specified water-quality levels assuming various policy control methods. Co-operation from industrialists was virtually complete since the confidentiality of the information supplied was guaranteed.

Cost Information

Detailed cost information was collected from both industrial dischargers and the Regional Water Authority in the following form:

(1) A time profile of planned rates of effluent discharge through the period 1976–1985 (assuming no change in the existing policy of control);

(2) An estimate was made of the reduction in effluent discharges from each firm which would achieve the maximum possible cutback in load by 1985. Each discharger was asked to specify the procedures he could implement and for each procedure

(a) the capital and average annual running costs,

(b) the expected life.

(3) Factors related to the feasibility of the procedure (e.g. research and development requirements, planning restrictions, mutually exclusive procedures, conditional procedures, time constraints regarding implementation, etc.).

Cost Model

The cost information was used as input data to an empirical cost of abatement model based on a modified version of a dynamic process analysis model formulated by Ortolano [3]. The Tees model used a mixed integer programming approach to minimize the aggregate costs of abatement for the estuary, assuming that a predetermined water-quality level is not violated. Various water-quality levels were defined and used to investigate the sensitivity of abatement cost to environmental quality. Output from the water-quality model is incorporated in the form of constraints to the cost function. The cost model is multi-period with a time horizon restricted to 9 years, a period within which industrialists felt able to predict conditions with reasonable accuracy. Costs of each abatement procedure are expressed in present value terms, each procedure being assumed to operate at its design capacity for its expected life. A mathematical description of the cost abatement model is given in Reference 2.

Water Quality Objectives

The study did not assess the benefits of improved quality in monetary terms. Instead, four objectives were selected and examined for the extent to which costs of achievement varied according to the policies for implementation. The four water-quality objectives chosen were:
   (1) The maintenance of existing water quality with minimum treatment to remove aesthetic nuisance;
   (2) Improvement in water quality to maintain the existence of coarse fish in the estuary;
   (3) Improvement to allow the passage of migratory fish;
   (4) Improvement to the level achieved by treating all discharges to the best technical means available.

For each objective, concentration levels were chosen for appropriate categories of effluent. Parameters of interest were dissolved oxygen, ammonia, copper and cyanide. The complex nature of estuarine ecological systems is such that precise levels of pollutant concentrations cannot be related to the damage effect on flora and fauna. The levels chosen were not considered to be definitive in the sense that they should be used as estuary water-quality standards for the Tees; rather, they have been used in a qualitative sense so that abatement costs can be related to readily identifiable improvements in water quality. Parameter levels chosen were, therefore, selected purely to enable the economic model to be tested.

Two methods of assessing toxicity were assumed. Firstly, the fractional toxicity approach as used in the Trent Study and, secondly, the magnitude analysis approach described by Carter [4]. These two approaches produced significantly different aggregate-abatement costs.

Use of the Cost Abatement Model (least cost solutions)

The main purpose of the model was to provide least cost criteria for achieving each water-quality objective at three different future dates. These minimum cost solutions may be used for comparison with costs of achieving the same water-quality levels using different effluent control policies. It is a characteristic of abatement procedures that they are cheaper to implement when introducing new items of capital expenditure than by the modification of equipment which is already installed. Costs of abatement are, therefore, time-dependent (irrespective of discounting factors) where treatment equipment may be 'designed into' a new plant which is coming on-stream five years hence. To achieve the same level of reduction in two years time would be considerably more expensive. Time-dependency was included to investigate the problems which may occur during the transition period from one method of control to another. As shown in Table 1, increasing the time available to dischargers for installation of abatement pro-cedures significantly reduces the aggregate-abatement costs for the estuary.

Table 1. Costs of Achieving Objective 1 (January 1976 prices)

	Jan 1979	Jan 1982	Jan 1985
Discounted Aggregate Cost £10⁶	28.4	6.8	1.8
Annualised Cost £10⁶	10.3	4.7	4.7

Costs of achieving objectives 2 and 3, evaluated assuming toxic levels conforming to Carter's criteria, are shown in Table 2 for various levels of dissolved oxygen.

Table 2 shows that aggregate-abatement costs are sensitive to dissolved oxygen level and time. The sensitivity to time deadline was mainly due to the maintenance of improved water quality over a longer period of time rather than the introduction of high cost, end-of-pipe, abatement procedures to meet earlier deadlines. It is interesting to note that if all feasible abatement procedures were introduced by 1985, equivalent to treatment by best technical means, the maxi-mum dissolved oxygen level achieved would be 6.5 p.p.m., the aggregate dis-counted cost £11.6 million and the annualised cost £30.1 million. In addition, the toxicity criteria would be significantly over-achieved.

Table 2. Costs of Achieving Given Quality Levels (January 1976 prices)

Dissolved Oxygen Level p.p.m.		Discounted Aggregate Cost £10⁶		Annualised Cost £10⁶	
		1982	1985	1982	1985
2)		14.1	3.8	9.8	9.8
3) } Objective 2		17.3	4.4	11.4	11.4
4)		18.3	4.6	11.9	11.9
5) } Objective 3		21.0	5.5	14.3	14.3
6)		27.5	7.3	18.9	18.9

ALTERNATIVE CONTROL SCHEMES

Having established minimum cost solutions for various water-quality objectives, it is possible to compare these to the cost of achieving those objectives by alternative control policies. To do this it is proposed to use a subset of the water-quality levels for 1985.

(1) 3 p.p.m. D.O. + Carter toxic levels
(2) 4 p.p.m. D.O. + Carter toxic levels
(3) 5 p.p.m. D.O. + Carter toxic levels

The Tees study made a comprehensive cost analysis of alternative water-quality objectives, including using a fractional toxicity approach. However, for the purposes of this paper, the above subset of levels will suffice.

EFFICIENT CONTROL SCHEMES

SUCH SCHEMES are those that ensure least cost solutions by ensuring that spatially weighted, marginal abatement costs are equal for all discharges of specific pollutants into specific stretches of estuary.

Efficient Consents

If the information derived from the Tees study were available to the controlling Water Authority, it would be possible for consents to be issued restricting discharges in such a way that given water-quality levels would be met at minimum aggregate cost to the community. These costs are shown in Table 3 on an annualised basis for the three separate water-quality levels shown above.

Table 3. Costs of Achieving given Water-Quality Levels

Water-Quality Level	Annualised Costs (£mill. 1976 prices)
1	11.4
2	11.9
3	14.3

Efficient Effluent Charges

There are major differences in the impact which a discharge of 1 tonne of BOD has upon dissolved oxygen depending on where that discharge is made in the estuary. It is not possible to use a single effluent tax to produce a least cost solution that satisfies the water-quality constraints in all stretches of the estuary. A level of tax which just satisfies the water-quality constraints in the upper reaches would vastly over-achieve the standard elsewhere. To overcome this problem, the water-quality model was used to predict concentrations of pollutant in each stretch of the river resulting from a particular discharge.

Concentration predictions can be made in the form:

$$c = Ax \tag{1}$$

where c is the vector of predicted concentrations;
$\quad x$ is a vector of discharge rates; and
$\quad A$ is a matrix of transfer coefficients in which a_{ij} represents concentration increases in stretch i caused by a unit of effluent discharged in stretch j.
In the minimum cost solution, the vector c must satisfy the imposed water-quality constraints and so derives for each 'critical' stretch of the estuary a positive shadow price which reflects the marginal cost of changing the constraint level. Stretches designated as critical are those in which the water-quality constraint is exactly met.

The tax per unit of effluent which, if imposed, would achieve the given water quality standard is derived in the following way.

Let the jth stretch be critical in the above sense and the shadow price be £Z per p.p.m. of pollutant.

The implied tax on the discharger would then be £Za_{ij} per tonne, where a_{ij} reflects the impact of 1 tonne discharged into stretch i upon j. If more than one stretch proves to be critical, the tax on discharger i would be the sum of the shadow prices weighted by a vector of transfer coefficients

e.g.
$$t_i = \sum_{j=1}^{n} a_{ij}Z_j \tag{2}$$

where t_i is the tax per tonne on firm i;
$\quad a_{ij}$ is a matrix of transfer coefficients;
$\quad Z_j$ is the shadow price of stretch j; and
$\quad n$ is the number of critical stretches.

Shadow prices were calculated for each water-quality criterion. All pollutants have a separate vector of shadow prices which reflect the cost of specific abatement procedures. It is worth noting here two problems with effluent taxes. First, central domestic treatment facilities are not amenable to taxing because they exhibit significant scale economies. For example, where the marginal cost of introducing secondary treatment is below that of primary treatment, a taxation policy could never induce an Authority to install primary alone, even though it may be all that is required for a least cost achievement of a given water-quality level. Secondly, large abatement procedures may be introduced by industrialists in response to taxes, making it unlikely to exactly achieve the water-quality constraints set, although in this respect taxing and consent systems have the same problem.

The optimal taxation results assume all dischargers are cost minimizers and equate their marginal costs to the tax rate. It was found that the tax rates obtained from equation (2) offered a close approximation to the minimum cost solution. Costs for quality levels 1 and 2 were 27 percent and 22 percent respectively above the least cost solution, whilst level 3 was obtained within 5 percent of the least cost solution. Spatially weighted taxes did not achieve a least cost solution because they induced investment in large abatement procedures which resulted in an over-achievement of the given water-quality level. Thus a large, low marginal abatement cost procedure might be induced when, to achieve a given quality level, only a small total, but high marginal cost procedure is all that is required.

It is possible, with suitable modification of taxes both relatively and absolutely, to reduce the extra resource costs for objectives 1 and 2, to 7 percent and 2 percent above the least cost solution. The actual tax levels per tonne of biochemical oxygen demand to achieve the above results are shown in Table 4.

Water Quality Level	Stretch of River	Taxes payable per annum for discharging 1 tonne/day BOD ($£10^6$)
1	15	0.23
	40	0.003
2	15	0.25
	40	0.003
3	15	0.47
	40	0.01

Table 4. Taxes per Tonne of BOD Discharged

In Table 4, stretch 15 is the worst polluted stretch and stretch 40 is at the mouth of the estuary. To achieve 5 p.p.m. of dissolved oxygen in the Tees estuary, a sliding scale of charges upon direct dischargers would have to be employed. For those discharging into the 'worst' stretch, an annual payment of £230,000 per tonne of BOD discharged per day would be required. For those at the mouth of the estuary a payment of £3,000 would be required. If each firm were a cost minimizer such a configuration of taxes would induce them to install sufficient abatement equipment to achieve the 5 p.p.m. objective.

The actual annual payments by dischargers in taxes to achieve each of the three water-quality levels are shown in Table 5. The taxes required to abate toxic discharges are seen to contribute significantly to the tax bill of the dischargers, with the total cost to the dischargers (taxes and abatement) amounting to £24.8 million, £25.1 million and £29.7 million for water qualities 1, 2 and 3 respectively.

Table 5. Total Tax Revenue Generated £10^6

Water Quality Level	BOD Taxes	Total Taxes (BOD + Toxic)
1	4.5	12.6
2	5.7	12.8
3	7.2	13.4

INEFFICIENT CONTROL SCHEMES

SEVERAL CONTROL schemes are available which may be described as inefficient. Such schemes, at present used extensively in the United Kingdom, are in the form of control by consent. However, taxing schemes may be included in the inefficient category if the rate of tax levied does not exactly achieve the required level of water quality. (It is recognised that subject to behavioural vagaries, taxing will always be efficient in the sense that the required level may not be achieved but the level which is achieved is done so in an efficient manner.)

The costs of a number of inefficient control schemes were evaluated in the Tees Study for comparison with least cost solutions. Seven alternative schemes were considered, namely:

(a) *Uniform Cutback of Discharges.* All discharge cutback by the same proportion regardless of position of discharge or category of effluent. For water-quality level 3 achieved in 1985, the increase in cost above the minimum cost solution was 103 per cent and for lower objectives the increase could be as high as 155 per cent.

(b) *Weighted Cutback of Effluents.* The controlling authority may differentiate between pollutant categories but still require all dischargers to cut back the same proportion for the parameter of concern. Costs determined with reference to water-quality level 3 were of the order of 101 per cent greater than the minimum cost, which is not significantly different from the Uniform Cutback approach.

(c) *Uniform Taxes.* A single tax is imposed regardless of position of discharge or effluent category. This is the tax counterpart of the method of Uniform Cutback. Costs were 69 per cent greater than the least cost solution for category 3, but significantly less than for uniform cutbacks.

(d) *Weighted Uniform Taxes.* This is the tax counterpart to the Weighted Cutback method. No saving in costs is obtained by comparison with Uniform Taxes.

(e) *Spatial Uniform Cutback Effluents.* If a water-quality model is available, the controlling authority can spatially weight the uniform percentages in (b) according to location of the discharge. A significant reduction in cost can be achieved by this method. For water-quality 3, the cost is 39 per cent greater than the least cost solution, but with lower water quality levels the difference rises to 73 per cent.

(f) *Spatial Weighted Uniform Cutback.* No improvement in cost saving is achieved over the Spatial Uniform Cutback method of control indicating that spatial considerations, rather than differential weights on particular effluents, are of real significance.

(g) *Spatial Weighted Taxes.* This approach modifies the Uniform Tax system to allow for spatial variation in taxes and also includes a weighting factor for each effluent category. The increase in cost above the least cost solution is of the order of 10 per cent for achievement of water-quality level 3 by 1985. For lower quality levels this solution gives increased costs of the order of 30 per cent above the minimum.

DISCUSSION OF RESULTS

ALTHOUGH MANY CONTROLLING water authorities might like to include the concept of efficiency into their control programme, it is unlikely that comprehensive cost and water-quality information, equivalent to that collected for the Tees Study, would be available to them. In these circumstances, Baumol and Oates [5] suggested an iterative pricing scheme, whereby an effluent charge would be imposed on all dischargers. If the charge failed to achieve the given water quality, it would be successively raised until achievement was complete. In practice, there are several problems with this approach. Firstly, Baumol and Oates' solution (based initially on assumptions of a single-stretch single-pollutant situation) becomes very complex where there are several categories of effluent. Joint-cost problems arise where an abatement procedure removes more than one pollutant. It is, therefore, impossible to iterate one pollutant at a time, even if the water-quality level is met for one pollutant, the least cost solution is not achieved unless all other constraints are met. Problems also occur with the requirement for differing tax rates based on the varying assimilative capacity of the estuary. Determination of the critical reaches of the estuary is not always possible by a prior analysis.

Further difficulties for iterative procedures are the time-lag for the estuary to adjust to the new level of discharge, possible change in relative prices causing taxes to change, and the 'lock-in' effect of the introduction of capital equipment in response to one tax rate restricting the ability of the discharger to respond to further changes in tax rate. These arguments suggest a requirement for the collection of both cost and water-quality data. These are reinforced by the extra costs of the inefficient solutions shown in the previous section. Assuming a water quality model is available but cost information is not, most water authorities in the United Kingdom would adopt a Spatial Uniform Cutback of effluents. This scheme conforms with existing consent controls and performs better in terms of cost than Uniform Cutback or Uniform Taxes, but is still significantly higher than the least cost solution.

Spatial Weighted Taxes achieve a cost difference of the order of 10 per cent (at the 5 p.p.m. DO level) greater than the least cost and thus, considerably outperform the Spatial Uniform Cutback solution. This comparison was used in the Tees Study to argue that a tax solution based on some knowledge of spatial water quality considerations may be considerably less costly than the best of the inefficient consent solutions. However, further consideration of the tax solution casts doubt on the validity of the above argument.

It is necessary to discuss the way in which the levels of tax are obtained for the Spatial Weighted Tax solution. Consider the case of a single discharge into stretch i. An estimate of the damage to the critical stretch j can be obtained using the transfer coefficient a_{ij} derived from the water-quality model. The tax t_i per unit of effluent discharged is:

$$t_i = a_{ij}Z_j \qquad \text{(see Equation 2)}$$

Although the water-quality model defines a_{ij}, giving the relative tax level in a spatial sense, without detailed costs it is not possible to place an initial value on Z_j, the shadow price of stretch j and hence impossible to calculate t_i.

In the Tees Study, an iterative solution was used to evaluate t_i. Initially a very low value for Z_j was chosen based on the critical stretch. The value of t_i was then calculated for all discharge stretches. Knowing t_i and assuming that cost-minimising firms equate their marginal abatement costs to the tax rate, it was possible to assess which abatement procedures would be implemented at that tax rate. The water-quality constraints were then checked assuming for the particular combination of procedures. If the quality constraints were not met, the value of λ was increased and the calculation repeated. The calculation was complete when the water-quality constraints were satisfied.

Clearly, the tax rates for each stretch can only be evaluated with the prior knowledge of marginal abatement costs. Thus, comparison of Spatial Uniform Cutback and Spatial Weighted Tax schemes is not valid because the absolute level of tax cannot be defined without abatement-cost data.

CONCLUSION

COST DATA obtained in the Tees Study show that inefficient effluent control schemes may cost up to 150 per cent more than the least cost solution for obtaining a predetermined water quality. OECD estimate that 5 per cent of total industrial capital expenditure is on waste disposal, indicating that if the Tees is in any way representative of other estuaries, there may be opportunities for saving resources while implementing an environmental programme.

The Tees Study shows that the introduction of a tax scheme is feasible in principle and could approximate closely to the minimum cost solution, but only if extensive abatement cost and water-quality data are available. The same information may, however, be used to set efficiency consents. Thus, in the pricing-regulation debate, efficiency is not a discriminating factor as both systems require the same information for implementation.

The choice of control methods must therefore be made using criteria other than short-term economic efficiency. For example:

(a) Pricing provides, through technological change, a continuing incentive to abate:

(b) More effective control may be achieved by the diligent collection of taxes than by an inconsistent judicial system;

(c) The degree of flexibility given to the controlling bureaucracy by alternative policies is important;

(d) There is a reluctance to damage existing goodwill and co-operation between controlling authorities and dischargers;

(e) The concept of equity and the individual firm's reaction to the distribution of abatement costs are important.

References

1. Kinnersley, D.J. (1980) *The application of charges for discharges to rivers*, in *River Pollution Control*, ed. M.J. Stiff, WRC, Ellis Horwood Ltd.

2. Rowley, C.K. *et al.* (1979) *A study of Effluent Discharges to the River Tees*. Department of Environmental Transport, Research Report 31.

3. Ortolano, L. (1972) *Artificial Aeration as a substitute for waste water Treatment*, in Dorfman, R. *et al.* (Eds), *Models for Managing Regional Water Quality*, Harvard Univ. Press, Cambridge, MA.

4. Carter, L. (1976) *Marine Pollution and Sea Disposals of Wastes*. Chemistry and Industry.

5. Baumol, W.J. and Oates, W.F. (1971) *The Use of Standards and Prices for the Protection of the Environment*. Swedish Journal of Economics, March.

Water Quality Management in Coastal Industrial Regions

Neil S. Grigg

*Assistant Secretary for Natural Resources, State of
North Carolina, and Director, University of North Carolina
Water Resources Research Institute, Raleigh,
North Carolina, USA*

SYNOPSIS

*Water quality problems in coastal industrial regions can be more
severe than in other areas. Much of the world's population lives in
such regions, and these problems need a great deal of scientific
attention if balanced solutions are to be found. Conclusions from a
case study are described and eight principles for water management
are suggested.*

RÉSUMÉ

*Les problèmes concernant la qualitè des eaux dans les regions
industrielles sur les côtes peuvent être plus sévères que dans d'autres
regions. Une grande partie de la population mondiale se trouve
dans de telles regions, de sorte que ces problèmes ont grand besoin
d'attention scientifique. Nous decrivons ici les conclusions tirées
d'une étude de cas et nous proposons huit principes pour la gestion
des eaux.*

RESUMEN

Los problemas referentes a la calidad de las aguas pueden ser más severos en las regiones industriales costeras que en otras partes. Gran parte de la población del mundo vive en tales regiones, por lo cual tales problemas necesitan una intensa atención científica. Aquí describimos las conclusiones de un caso estudiado y sugerimos ocho principios de política hidráulica.

INTRODUCTION

IN DEVELOPED COUNTRIES, pollution control regulations have become more stringent in recent years. The United States has, in particular, made significant changes since the passage of the Clean Water Act of 1972. Stringent enforcement of regulations was instituted, and several billions of dollars have been spent on the construction of wastewater treatment plants. However, significant problems remain which will require attention beyond the original concepts of the 1972 legislation.

Water quality problems in coastal industrial regions are particularly acute. It is in these regions that much of the world's population lives and, although water often appears to be abundant, water quality problems can persist for years. Population growth and development in coastal regions are particularly rapid in the developing countries, but the same problems appear in the developed countries. For example, in the United States the greatest population densities are on the east and west coasts, and some of the most rapid new growth is occurring on the east coast, in the southern states. One such state, North Carolina, has experienced significant water quality problems related to industrial and agricultural development in its coastal regions. In this paper I will describe one of the most significant of these problems, explain why the problem is serious, why it may be expected in other places in future times, discuss management arrangements we are following to seek a solution, and outline several principles of water quality management that are suggested by this experience.

THE CHOWAN RIVER AND ALBEMARLE SOUND PROBLEM

ALBEMARLE SOUND in North Carolina is a body of water located immediately south of Norfolk, Virginia, and the mouth of Chesapeake Bay (Figure 1). It is a major

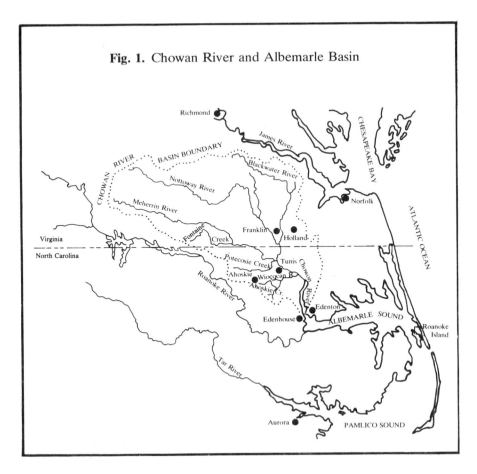

Fig. 1. Chowan River and Albemarle Basin

recreational and sports fishery as well as an important source of commercial fishing revenues. The historical region is also the centre of an important tourist industry. In recent years there have been significant water quality problems in the Sound with the worst on a major tributary, the Chowan River.

Due to public demand, the State of North Carolina initiated a comprehensive project to restore the Chowan River. Named the Chowan River Restoration Project (CHORE), this project has been underway since 1979 and has resulted in a great deal of attention given to the problem at regional and national level [1].

Seasonal algal blooms occur naturally in the Chowan River. Blooms of short duration occur in the late spring and at the end of summer, but usually they do not last long enough to cause nuisance conditions. In 1972, the seasonal blooms lasted from May until October, however, with disastrous results. Fishing and recreation were ruined. Public outcry reached very intense levels. Due to this problem, a series of research investigations was undertaken sponsored by several State and university agencies with support from the U.S. Office of Water Research and Technology, the U.S. Geological Survey and the U.S. Environmental Protection Agency. Studies undertaken included primary productivity, nitrogen recycling, phytoplankton response to changes in water quality, and flow and water quality management modelling of the river system. Data was collected to verify research results by the State's Division of Environmental Management [2].

There were no further serious algal blooms through 1977. As in many cases, this created a false atmosphere of security that the problem was transitory. However, a devastating algal bloom hit the river again in 1978. These new blooms and their impact rapidly gained the personal attention of the Governor of the State and his cabinet members. The Chowan River was elevated to first priority in the Governor's environmental programme. He directed that an action plan to clean up the river be developed by July 15 1979, and the Chowan River Restoration Project was the response of the State Department of Natural Resources.

The project has long-term and short-term components. The long-term components are intended to result in a permanent water quality management plan for the basin. The short-term plan intends to take the clean-up effort as far as it can be taken given current economic conditions and knowledge about the problem. The short-term plan includes the following five basic components:

(1) Reduction of industrial nutrient discharges;
(2) Reduction of municipal nutrient discharges;
(3) Control of farm and forest runoff;
(4) Control of dry-weather raw water withdrawals by industries and municipalities;
(5) Consideration of innovative management approaches.

One stumbling block to a rapid solution of the river's problems was lack of agreement among the two states, the local governments and industries about the solutions needed. The scientific aspects of the pollution problem have been very challenging. Because of the disagreements, Governor Hunt of North Carolina requested the U.S. Environmental Protection Agency (EPA) to assign a top level scientific team to audit the restoration project. The EPA responded by organizing a team which undertook its work during the summer of 1980. Its brief included the following: (1) To determine the technical adequacy of the existing data base and study results relative to the best approach for solving the algal bloom problem in the tidal portion of the Chowan River; (2) To review the existing bi-state institutional arrangements and develop recommendations for modifications that encourage closer coordination; and (3) To make specific recommendations for any additional scientific evaluation deemed necessary to support regulatory controls.

The report of the EPA panel was delivered in August 1980 [3]. It generally concurred with the approach North Carolina had been taking to clean up the river. It made a number of conclusions, recommendations and suggestions for further study. In effect, the EPA report concurred with the feelings of State officials that the restoration of the river represented a major challenge to political and environmental officials and will require a long period of time for solution.

Implementation plans for the EPA report have gone slowly. The States of North Carolina and Virginia and the U.S. Environmental Protection Agency continue to meet to seek ways of resolving outstanding issues and to find cost-effective and politically feasible solutions for the Chowan River problem.

Now it is realised in North Carolina that the Chowan River difficulty is part of a larger water quality problem in the Albemarle region. This is caused by: a general shortage of surface waters for supplying a developing municipal-industrial complex in the Norfolk, Virginia region; ground water problems related to overpumping for industrial and municipal sources in the region; and general water quality problems in Albemarle Sound and its other tributaries caused by industrial, municipal and agricultural activities. To approach the larger problems, the State of North Carolina is seeking to expand the Chowan River Restoration Project to an overall water management programme for the Albemarle region.

Meanwhile, the State of North Carolina continues to pursue the Chowan River Restoration Project. Several conclusions are evident at this time:

(1) There is a definite trend toward worse water problems in the Albemarle-Chowan Region;

(2) A comprehensive regional water management programme is needed involving both State governments and the federal government;

(3) Current tendencies in the U.S. for the federal government to withdraw from water management will require state governments to develop and finance solution to problems such as the Chowan;

(4) There are, and will remain, many unanswered technical questions about the causes of the algal blooms and associated problems, but solutions need to move ahead now;

(5) The scientific-management basis for a successful project is still being evolved;

(6) Since water is of such fundamental importance, solutions must be found and the local populations will demand them;

(7) To successfully resolve these water issues, local-regional-state leadership is urgently needed;

(8) The resolution of these top priority water issues will require new innovative and enlightened public policies, programmes and attitudes [4].

CONCLUSIONS

THE CHOWAN-ALBEMARLE water management problems are symptomatic of problems which can occur in other locations. To conclude, I would like to put forward eight principles which may be helpful for application to water management problems of this kind.

(1) The Chowan-Albemarle problem is typical of those that can happen in rural areas of developed countries and in industrializing regions in the developing countries;

(2) Although some feel that most of the water pollution control problems have been solved in developed countries, there are delicate and subtle pollution control issues still remaining;

(3) In complex area-wide pollution control problems such as those described, laws and regulations alone are not sufficient to find complete solutions;

(4) Local concern, action and persistent followup is necessary to supplement laws and regulations for ultimate cleanup of problems of this kind;

(5) Problems such as those described go beyond academic arguments about approaches to pollution control such as the merits of regulatory versus economic-based systems;

(6) The scientific input to solve problems of this kind is absolutely essential and the expenditures required for research and investigations are usually underestimated;

(7) Agricultural and forestry problems must be considered along with industrial and municipal sources to find balanced solutions to these problems;

(8) To find permanent solutions to such problems, long-term resource management approaches must be taken rather than pollution control measures alone.

The Chowan-Albemarle problems are of great importance to the local area and to the State of North Carolina. These problems have worsened since 1972 when the U.S. Water Pollution Act was passed. In spite of billions of dollars expended nationally, problems such as these persist. The ideas contained in this paper attempt to explain why, and to offer potential solutions for other areas with similar problems.

References

1. Grigg, N.S. *et al. Action Plan for the Chowan River Restoration Project*, North Carolina Department of Natural Resources and Community Development, 1979.
2. Bond, S. Cook, G. and Howells, D.H., *Summary Report: The Chowan River Project*, Water Resources Research Institute, The University of North Carolina, 1977.
3. Chowan River Review Committee (U.S. Environmental Protection Agency), *An Assessment of Algal Bloom and Related Problems of the Chowan and Recommendations Toward Its Recovery*, August 1980.
4. Grigg, N.S., *The Chowan River Restoration Project*, 1981 National Conference on Environmental Engineering, ASCE, Atlanta, GA, July 1981.

EEC Legislation controlling Aquatic Pollution from Dangerous Substances: Legal and Economic Implications with special reference to Mercury

L.D. Guruswamy
Department of Law, University of Durham, UK

I. Papps
Department of Economics, University of Durham, UK

and

D.J. Storey
Centre for Urban and Regional Studies, University of Newcastle-upon-Tyne, and Department of Economics, University of Durham, UK

SYNOPSIS

This paper is concerned with a study of the implications for water management policy of Britain's entry into the European Economic Community. The analysis will concentrate upon the legal and economic effects of the proposed directive on mercury discharges by the chlor-alkali industry. The paper examines the problems of harmonizing national with international and EEC laws and of their enforcement. An economic model is developed which could be used to predict the impact upon prices, profits and output of the industry in each of the member states.

RÉSUMÉ

Cet exposé étudie les conséquences qu'aura sur la gestion des eaux l'entrée de la Grande Bretagne dans la Communauté Economique Européene. L'analyse portera principalement sur les effets économiques et légaux de la proposition de loi sur les déchets de mercure provenant des industries produisant le chlore par électrolyse. Sont examinés les problèmes que pose l'harmonisation des lois nationales avec les lois internationales et communautaires, ainsi que leur application. Un modèle économique est élaboré, modèle qui pourrait servir pour prédire les effets d'une telle loi sur les prix, les bénéfices, et le rendement de l'industrie dans chacun des états membres.

RESUMEN

Este trabajo es un estudio de las consecuencias sobre las medidas reguladoras de la administración del agua derivadas de la entrada de Gran Bretaña en la Comunidad Económica Europea. El análisis se concentra en los efectos legales y económicos de las directrices propuestas sobre los vertidos de mercurio por la industria chloro-alkalina. El trabajo examina los problemas presentados por la armonización de leyes nacionalese internacionales y de la Comunidad Económica Europea, así como los de su puesta en práctica. Se desarrolla un modelo económico que podría usarse para predecir el impacto sobre precios, beneficios y rendimiento de la industria en cada uno de los países miembros.

INTRODUCTION

THE EEC DIRECTIVE on dangerous substances and the proposal for a Directive on mercury illustrates some of the implications for the UK of membership of the EEC and the wider international community. This paper examines the challenge made to the UK's philosophy and law of pollution control, based on a pragmatic case-by-case approach, and the EEC approach, based on more easily applied, uniform standards. To what extent, therefore, is it likely that the price of membership will be paid through a modification of Britain's traditional environmental policy and what would be the effect upon British industry? Alternatively, if the Community is able to accommodate the British approach, what are the likely implications for the industry?

THE CURRENT LEGAL FRAMEWORK

THREE SYSTEMS OF LAW govern the discharge of mercury into the aquatic environment of the UK, namely national (UK) law, EEC law and international law. In this section we attempt a brief description of the relevant laws. There are a variety of complex jural issues arising out of the operation and interaction of these systems but we do not intend to explore these issues in any depth.

EEC Law

The law relevant to this discussion derives from instruments (called regulations, directives and decisions) which are made under the treaties. The general implementation of the Community treaties was effected in the UK by section 2(1) of the European Communities Act 1972. The effect of this provision was to incorporate into English law, present and future Community law which, under the treaties, is to be given legal effect without further enactment. The instrument of Community law employed to execute its environment programme has been the directive, which usually, but not invariably, requires implementation by specific enactment within the member states.

The Directive of 4 May 1976 [1], on Pollution caused by certain dangerous substances discharged into the aquatic environment, represented a compromise among the member states. It directs them to "eliminate pollution . . . caused by dangerous substances" and this parent Directive was to be implemented by means of offspring Directives dealing with specific substances. The Commission was to make Proposals to the Council which would then need to adopt them by a unanimous vote. These offspring Directives would lay down (a) limit values for the uniform emission standard (UES) method; and (b) quality objectives together with monitoring procedures for the environmental quality objective (EQO) method. The Commission has made a Proposal [2], dated 20 June 1979, for a Council Directive on mercury based both on UES and EQOs which provides for a full review at a later stage.

International Law

The UK has signed and ratified the Convention on the Prevention of Land-Based Pollution, Paris, 1974. It has thereby undertaken "to eliminate if necessary by stages" pollution caused *inter alia* by mercury. The terms of this convention also oblige the UK to set up a "permanent monitoring system". In compliance with this obligation, the UK has in fact begun monitoring the waters of some estuaries.

UK Law

UK legislation is centred upon a licencing or 'consent' system operated by Regional Water Authorities. (This description is to be confined to law and policy in England and Wales. The laws dealing with Scotland, though similar, are different in some respects.) These bodies were created under the 1973 Water Act to provide an integrated management of the hydrological cycle on a catchment basis. All discharges of effluent to UK waterways (except for pre-1960 discharges into estuaries and tidal waters) have required the prior consent of the relevant Authority who may impose conditions upon the discharger. The power to grant 'consents' is governed by a series of Acts from 1876 onward. The Control of Pollution Act of 1974, when brought into force, will replace most of the provisions of these Acts. The 1974 Act will also provide for information on discharges of effluent to be publicly available and it charges the Regional Water Authorities with this responsibility.

THE RATIONALE BEHIND THE LAWS

UK Law

Pragmatism: Although concern about problems of pollution and human health did lead to legislative intervention and were not left to be solved by the common law (i.e. the judge-made customary law of England), the philosophy underpinning such legislation was and is a pragmatic one. Pragmatism and empiricism are reflected as much in English legislation as in the common law.

A striking feature of the common law is that it proceeds on a case-by-case basis. Unlike the European civil law tradition, which is rooted in rationalism, it does not work with broad general principles from which the right conclusion in a particular case is theoretically deducible by the application of strict logic. English dislike of theory is not based on a reluctance to understand and accept the reasons for acting in a particular way, but rather on an instinctive distrust of broad generalisations which may inhibit any learning by experience. A belief in the importance of learning in this way, by trial and error, has become the basis of the UK's pragmatic philosophy. The British feel that their experience has vindicated the case-by-case approach and believe that such an approach should be followed until it is found wanting. By its very nature, they argue, pragmatism is particularly responsive to change, generates self-renewal, as and when required, and thus prevents stagnation of policy and law.

Decentralised Control: The pragmatism of the common law which was preserved in legislation dealing with pollution was paired with a cognate principle, namely 'legislative commitment to decentralised control'. Because the effects of pollution are first experienced locally, the second principle underlying such legislation was that the primary responsibility for dealing with pollution problems should rest, as far as was practicable, with authorities operating at a local or regional level.

The Evolution of Environmental Quality Objectives (EQOs): A distinguishing feature of the consents (the legal instrument by which the licencing system is operated) is that the statutes do not specify particular emission standards or environmental quality objectives (EQOs). In keeping with the rationale of the relevant legislation, Regional Water Authorities (RWAs) were given a wide discretion as to how they set their own standards. They laid down standards that were 'practicable', "having regard among other things to local conditions and circumstances, to the current state of scientific and technical knowledge and to the financial implications..." [3]. The authorities have traditionally discussed and negotiated with major dischargers on appropriate levels of discharge, taking into account the location of the discharge, the cost of abatement and the character of the receiving waters.

In the years 1976–1979, a number of EEC proposals on environmental protection (draft Directives) were criticised in the UK because they did not take account of the use to which the receiving waters were put, or of the UK principle of placing variable limits according to the nature, situation and condition of the receiving waters.

It might justifiably be contended, however, that prior to 1978, the UK did not possess a coherent set of standards explicitly related to pre-determined and formulated objectives (EQOs), but only a form of institutional 'ad hocery' passing off as water management. This is no longer the case with regard to its rivers. Regional Water Authorities have drawn up a comprehensive, but non-mandatory, scheme of designation use for rivers under their control, defined what their short-term and long-term (target) objectives are for the different lengths of river for which they are responsible and tailored their consents in accordance with these objectives. In anticipation of the implementation of the Control of Pollution Act, 1974, some RWAs have opened their registers to the public and are publishing their consents.

EEC Law

Much of the rationale behind pollution control is common to all countries in the EEC. There is one area in which EEC thinking is at some variance with UK philosophy and this relates to the setting up of uniform emission standards (UES) for dangerous (blacklisted) substances. It would be true to say that the Commission and the rest of the UK's Common Market partners feel that the way forward for them with regard to these substances is by way of UES, while the UK favours an EQO approach. This is not to suggest that the EEC rejects EQOs. On the contrary it has employed EQOs as instruments of environmental protection and the Council has adopted four Directives establishing EQOs governing surface waters intended for drinking, bathing waters, fresh waters supporting fish and shellfish waters. These Directives adopt an approach similar to that of the UK. With regard to dangerous (black-listed) substances, however, the view taken is that these substances are causing such serious hazards and eroding the quality of existing water so fast, that it is necessary to take practical and quick initial action to arrest this deterioration of water quality. While EQOs may be the ultimate aim, they are very difficult to set up in the absence of the necessary administrative infrastructure, are very complicated to operate and monitor, and could create almost insuperable problems where transfrontier rivers are concerned. Rather than waiting for the ideal system, UES constitute a practical *pro tem* measure which will secure speedy initial improvement of the aquatic environment and one that is well suited to the conditions of continental Europe.

THE LEGAL IMPLICATIONS OF THE DANGEROUS SUBSTANCES DIRECTIVE AND THE PARIS CONVENTION FOR UK LAW AND POLICY

The Dangerous Substances Directive

In pursuance of the environmental programme, in 1974, the Commission submitted to the Council a Proposal for a Council Directive on the reduction of pollution caused by certain dangerous substances discharged into the aquatic environment of the Community. Within those waters, member states were asked to eliminate the pollution resulting from the discharge of 'blacklist' substances. The blacklist proposed by the Commission included mercury and cadmium, organohalogen, organophosphorous and organostannic compounds, carcinogenic substances and persistent oils.

The Commission proposed to fulfill this obligation by: (1) the definition on a Community basis of certain maximum 'limit values' which are to be fixed in the light of the toxicity, permanence and bioaccumulative character of the substances under consideration, taking into account the best technical means available for the elimination of such substances from a discharge; and (2) the obligation of the competent authorities in member states not to exceed these Community 'limit values' whenever they give 'consent' to a discharge. This proposal was strenuously opposed by the UK which favoured an approach to environmental protection based on EQOs and would not accept a system which sought to regulate dangerous substances only by UES.

The 'parent' Directive of 1976 represented a compromise between the EQO philosophy of the UK and the UES favoured by the rest of Europe. While the Directive permitted EQOs to be adopted in exceptional circumstances, it qualified this with the condition that EQOs, unlike UES, should be used only in accordance with a monitoring procedure to be set up by the Council.

With regard to Quality Objectives themselves, the UK is directed to "eliminate pollution . . . by the dangerous substances . . ." in the entire aquatic environment, including estuaries, with pollution being defined as:

> "the discharge by man, directly or indirectly, of substances or energy into the aquatic environment, the results of which are such as to cause hazards to human health, harm to living resources and to aquatic systems, damage to amenities or interference with other legitimate uses of water". (Art. 1, C).

This creates problems for the UK since discharges into UK estuaries are by and large still uncontrolled and the classification of inland waters in terms of use and EQOs does not extend to estuaries. The Royal Commission on Environmental Pollution has pointed out that many industries have been placed at or near estuaries in order to avoid the controls operating upstream. The Control of Pollution Act, 1974, which will control all discharges into estuaries has still not been brought into force. The UK, it has been pointed out, had no written EQO dealing comprehensively with mercury until one was produced by way of reaction to the objectives set out in the Proposal. Secondly, UK EQOs have hitherto been directed towards controlling hazards to human health. The definition of pollution extends this to living resources, aquatic systems and amenities, qualities which have not hitherto been considered in the setting up of EQOs. Thirdly, this has implications for the monitoring system. The UK has taken up the position that water quality could be monitored by fish alone and that there is no need for additional biological or chemical monitoring. But, even if fish could satisfactorily monitor hazards to human health, the other attributes of harm to ecosystems and interference with amenities require that monitoring is not confined to fish alone. Secondly, Art 6(2) refers to both living organisms and sediment. These obligations, created in such specific terms, are difficult to reconcile with the UK position.

The Paris Convention

The definition of pollution in this Convention is very similar to that contained in the Directive and, together with the obligation to set up a "permanent monitoring system", seem to impose obligations almost identical to the Directive. While, therefore, the UK has evolved and is evolving environmental laws and policies that are geared to its own conditions, it is subject to two other systems of law and is under an obligation to harmonize its laws with these European and international laws.

ECONOMIC ISSUES

THE DEBATE over the alternative approaches to environmental protection set out in the 1976 'parent' Directive will continue since it is proposed to keep these two systems under review. Central to this review will be an assessment of the economic impact of the Directive upon the chlor-alkali industry with a view to incorporating this into an assessment of the relative merits of EQO and UES within each of the member states. For the rest of this paper, we examine those factors relevant to an economic study.

Uniform Emission Standards and Environmental Quality Objectives

It has been well-documented in studies in both Europe and in the United States that a given water quality obtained by requiring all dischargers to reduce their effluent loads by a given proportion is more expensive (i.e. less efficient) than taking into account differences in the abatement cost and location differences of each discharger. For example, in a study of the River Tees in north-east England, it was estimated that the UES method was the most costly way of enabling migratory fish to pass through this river. Indeed, the cost was twice that which would have been incurred if pollution were reduced by taking into account the differences in abatement costs faced by different dischargers [4]. We have already seen that the British have argued that requiring all dischargers in the same industry to meet identical effluent requirements is as inefficient as uniform reductions are for a specific river.

The Chlor-alkali Industry

The chlor-alkali industry is a major discharger of mercury to waterways, although some discharges (primarily into the atmosphere) are made by the mercury-battery industry. The industry is present in virtually all major European countries and is dominated by larger international firms operating large plants. In most cases, the chlorine and the caustic soda produced are used as inputs to other chemical processes on the same or an adjacent site. Capital requirements are high and entry into the industry on a small scale is virtually excluded.

It has been estimated that total European chlorine capacity is approximately $8\frac{1}{2}$ m tonnes annually, of which three-quarters is currently produced in mercury-cell plants and the remainder in mercury-free diaphragm cell plants. Of the mercury-cell plants, none could be considered wholly typical. Some use a spent-brine process, whereas others use a re-circulatory technique. Works also vary markedly in terms of size, age, operating efficiency, location and according to the quality and scale of inputs used. All these factors are likely to influence the reaction of the company to the imposition of effluent controls.

An Economic Model of Abatement Costs

A mercury-cell plant with a given technology is assumed to discharge mercury in proportion to its output of chlorine/caustic soda. In the very short-run therefore, the marginal abatement cost curve (MAC^1) facing the plant is equal to the negative of the first derivative of the total profit function, with respect to output. In Figure 1, M_1 is the level of discharge which maximizes profits in the absence of controls. In the longer run, the firm may install abatement processes, depending upon the level of discharge reduction which it expects to have to meet. MAC^{11} is an abatement process which the firm would introduce if it expected to have to reach the discharge level M_2. There is, however, no reason to necessarily expect MAC^{11} to be below MAC^1 at all discharge-reduction levels, and there are likely to be a set of MAC curves such as MAC^{11} and MAC^{111} which represent the firm's preferred way of reaching given levels of cut-back. Since, however, effluent is assumed to be related to output, a firm which has installed procedure MAC^{111}, with the intention of operating at point C and discharging M_3 units, has some flexibility in terms of the actual quantity which it can discharge. For example, it may temporarily reduce its discharge beyond M_3 by reducing output but, from Figure 1, it is clear that the costs of this are high and that if abatement substantially beyond M_3 is required for a lengthy period, then the installation of MAC^{11} is to be preferred. The long-run cost curve for a mercury-cell plant is therefore the envelope of these curves and is shown as MAC^*. In practice, of course, it is unlikely to be of the smooth shape shown in Figure 1.

One option facing the firm, however, is to scrap the mercury-cell plant and install a diaphragm plant. If OA represents the present value of the additional costs of the diaphragm plants, and the firm knows that a standard beyond $\bar{M}$ will be imposed upon it, then it will choose to switch rather than modify. The long-run MAC curve is therefore point A and the section BM_1, so the firm will only plan to operate a mercury-cell plant if it is allowed to discharge more than $\bar{M}$.

The total abatement costs of installing a given abatement process are the present value of profits compared with those achievable with a level of discharge equal to M_1. Both capital and operating costs and revenues can be, in theory,

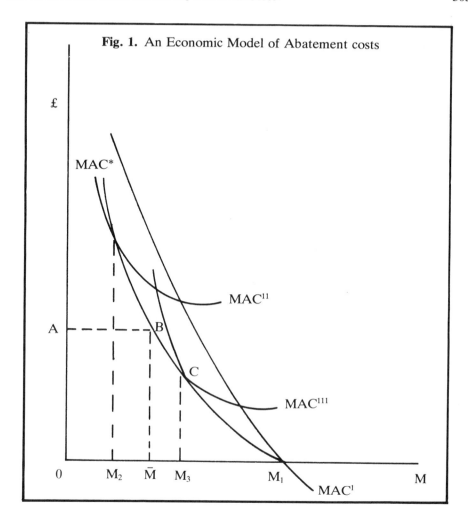

Fig. 1. An Economic Model of Abatement costs

expressed in present value terms and a marginal abatement cost schedule be derived. The firm, again in theory, has the option of choosing that combination of abatement packages which minimise its costs of reducing discharges to the desired level.

In practice matters are more complicated. Observing the firm's reactions to having stricter emission controls imposed upon it presents problems in determining the factors which influenced the firm's choice. For example, if a firm chooses to construct a diaphragm plant this could be because it anticipates a change in demand for the final output, or because it expects emission standards to become stricter in the future, or because its internal accounting procedures, at that time, favoured major items of capital expenditure, or because the price of inputs, such as energy, are expected to rise.

Uncertainty over the emission standards imposed upon the firm, the prices of inputs and the final product, and the price of mercury—all create considerable problems. If the firm expects the standard to become increasingly strict, then it may switch to a diaphragm plant. If solid-disposal costs are expected to rise, then it may improve the quality of the salt inputs. If it feels that high quality caustic soda is likely to be priced at a premium, then it may choose to modify its existing mercury-cell plant. The net effect of this uncertainty may be that firms choose an abatement technology which offers the opportunity to react flexibly to changes in effluent standards imposed upon it. Such flexibility is, of course, not without cost.

The Economic Implications

Since plants of different ages, on different sites, in different countries, face different cost structures, their choice of abatement technologies will differ. The effect on the European chlor-alkali industry of the Directives has not been thoroughly investigated. The Economist Intelligence Unit produced a report [5] which purported to describe the effect upon the industry of the Directives but contained no hard data on the costs of abatement.

What is needed is a financial examination of each of the approximately 60 mercury plants in the European Community, to determine their current expenditure on pollution control, their expected future plans in terms of output and pollution control measures, the costs of reaching specified discharge reductions together with an estimate of the impact of those reductions upon mercury concentrations in the receiving waters. From such data, it would then be possible to determine:

(1) The total costs of reducing all discharge to a given UES together with an estimate of the associated water quality;
(2) The total costs of reaching a given EQO in all European waters.
(3) The impact which these cost increases will have on the price of chlorine and hence,
  (i) its substitution by other materials
  (ii) general contraction in demand.
(4) The substitution of membrane and diaphragm-cell plants for mercury-cell plants.
(5) The extent to which this would happen for reasons unconnected with pollution control.

The real interest would be to examine the impact of EQO/UES policy upon the countries involved. Would, for example, certain countries (or regions) suffer disproportionately from following a UES policy? Would an EQO policy give a competitive advantage to one country (or one firm)? In essence, the responsiveness of the industry to environmental controls (its elasticity) has to be estimated and it can only be undertaken through the collection of cost data at the level of the individual plant. Some of this information has already been collected by BNF Metals [6] but it now has to be undertaken on a more formal basis so that a comprehensive economic evaluation may be undertaken.

CONCLUSIONS

THIS PAPER has briefly described the evolution of laws applicable to environmental pollution from mercury. We have demonstrated the conflict between a pragmatic, though complicated, British approach which currently favours EQOs and the simpler UES approach favoured by her EEC partners.

The compromise achieved by the 1976 parent directive will be tested by its application in relation to mercury discharge from the Chlor-alkali industry. The economic analysis will provide a significant input into the proposed review and could determine whether amendments to the law are necessary.

ACKNOWLEDGEMENTS

The research for this paper was financed by a Special Research Grant from the University of Durham. We are grateful to Professor J.L. Brooks of the Department of Spanish and to Dr. A.C. Pugh of the Department of French for their help in translating the synopsis and to Mrs. P. Wears for her speedy and accurate typing of the final draft. We, alone, are responsible for any errors.

References

1. European Communities Commission. *Council Directive of 4 May 1976.* (76/464). Of L 129 of 18 May 1976.
2. European Communities Commission. *Proposal for a Council Directive of 20 June 1979.* (7735/79). Of C 169 of 6 July 1979.
3. Great Britain. Department of the Environment. *Environmental Standards, A Description of the Practice.* Pollution Paper No. 11, 1977.
4. Great Britain. Department of the Environment and Transport. *A Study of Effluent Discharges to the River Tees.* Research Report No. 31, 1979.
5. Economist Intelligence Unit. *The Economic Effects of Pollution Control Measures on Defined Industrial Sectors: Mercury Discharging Industries.* Report prepared for the Environment and Consumer Protection Service, Commission of the European Communities, Brussels, December 1977.
6. B.N.F. Metals Technology Centre. *Abatement Techniques in the Control of Mercury Pollution.* Wantage, Oxon: Grove Laboratories.

A Methodology for Pollutant Discharge Data for the Tejo Estuary Project

J.P. O'Kane

Dept. of Civil Engineering, University College, Dublin,
Ireland and UNESCO Chief Technical Adviser Project
POR/77/016

Filipa G. Ribeiro

Chemical Engineer, General-Directorate for Quality,
Lisbon, Portugal,

and

Jorge M.S. Castanheiro

Civil Engineer, National Commission for Environment,
Tejo Project, Lisbon, Portugal

SYNOPSIS

In the aim of the Project "Environmental Study of the Tejo Estuary", a closed mass-balance or budget of several pollutants in the estuary is being made. Among the several balance components, there is the item referring to industrial loads. The evaluation of this component is done according to two methods: direct evaluation through effluent analyses and indirect evaluation based on data of production or consumption of raw materials for each industry. The indirect evaluations are done according to the method used by UNIDO for the Mediterranean Action Plan. Examples of the application of this method are presented for some industries, whose effluents are directly discharged into the estuary; the results obtained are compared with the evaluations of the polluting loads, based on analytical data and effluent flows produced by the industries.

RÉSUMÉ

Dans le cadre du Projet "Etude de l'Environnement dans l'Estuaire du Tage", on prétend de faire un bilan ou budget de masse fermé concernant plusieurs polluants dans l'estuaire. Parmi les différentes composantes de ce bilan, on mentionne la partie concernant les décharges industrielles. On estime cette composante selon deux méthodes: évaluation directe à travers des analyses des effluents et évaluation indirecte qui se base sur des données de production ou consommation de matières premières pour chaque industrie. Les évaluations indirectes sont effectuées selon la méthode utilisée par l'UNIDO pour le Plan d'Action pour la Méditerranée. On présente des exemples d'application de cette méthode relativement à quelques industries dont les effluents sont directement déversés dans l'estuaire; on fait la comparaison des résultats obtenus avec l'évaluation des charges polluantes estimées sur des données analytiques et flux des effluents causés par les industries.

RESUMEN

En el cuadro del proyecto "Estudio del Medio Ambiente en el Estuario del rio Tajo", se procura hacer un balance cerrado de masa involucrando distintos contaminantes en el estuario. De los contaminantes cubiertos por este balance, se considera la parte que respecta a los desechos liquidos industriales. Se calcula este componente de acuerdo a dos métodos: evaluación directa por análisis de los desechos liquidos y evaluación indirecta en base a datos sobre la producción o consumo de materias primas en cada industria. Las evaluaciones indirectas son hechas según el método utilizado por la ONUDI en el Plan de Acción para el Mediterráneo. Se apresentan ejemplos de la aplicación de este método a ciertas industrias que vierten directamente sus desechos en el estu-

ario; se hace la comparación de los resultados obtenidos con la evaluación de los vertidos contaminantes estimados en base a datos de análisis y flujo de vertidos de las industrias.

ENVIRONMENTAL STUDY OF THE TAGUS ESTUARY

IN 1975, the Portuguese National Commission for the Environment organized an interministerial working-group to study the estuary and to provide guidelines for its management—to develop a methodology for assessing water-quality problems, to identify management problems, to determine appropriate courses of action to restore the quality of the water and to correct water-quality degradation within the constraints of the community. With the assistance of UNDP, and with UNESCO as executing agency, a project agreement on the Environmental Study of the Tagus Estuary was signed by the Portuguese Government in 1978.

Since the National Commission for the Environment is principally a co-ordinating agency, the work was carried out mainly by participating agencies, i.e. the Port Authorities of Lisbon, Hydraulic Services, Health Services, Hydrographic Institute, Nuclear Physical Laboratory, National Civil Engineering Laboratory, Secretariat of State for Fishing and the Environmental Study Services. An advisory technical panel, consisting of experts in biochemistry, biology, fluid dynamics, oceanography and coastal engineering, was also established to provide general technical guidance.

A steering committee was formed, consisting of United Nations Agency specialists and senior staff from the national agencies collaborating in the project. Its role is to review all projects in the estuary, to facilitate communication and co-operation and to eliminate duplication of work whenever possible [1].

Project Objectives

The ultimate objective of the project as described in the Project Document is "the achievement of the rational management of the Tagus estuary water-resource, harmonizing the existing multiplicity of water use with the socio-economic development of the region and the safeguard of the public health". The immediate objective of the project is "to understand the basic physical, chemical and biological processes occurring in the estuary as a basis for conservation of water quality".

The essential elements in environmental quality management are:
(1) An inventory of environmental quality objectives (EQOs);
(2) Environmental quality criteria;
(3) Licencing;
(4) Monitoring.

The essential activity of management is feedback control. Licences are issued so as to maintain the measured (monitoring) quality of the environment at that criterion which achieves a chosen quality objective. Deviations from the criterion are corrected by changes in the licences. The associate files of information, which enable the controller to 'manage', constitute the environmental management plan. The choice of environmental quality objectives, and the consequent balancing of gains and losses to various groups, is a policy decision at a higher level.

Some of the environmental quality objectives which are important in the Tagus estuary are:

—Assurance of the suitability of fish, shellfish and crustacea for human consumption;

—Creation of acceptable aesthetic conditions and assurance that waters are safe for bathing;

—Maintenance of fisheries and their ecological support-systems;

—Restoration of the oyster fishery and its maintenance;

—Assurance that the tidal fresh waters of the estuary are suitable for industrial, agricultural and other uses;

—Maintenance of the "Natural Reserve" (Reserva Natural do Estuário do Tejo) and its migratory birds;

—Maintenance of the Tagus estuary as an important port with all its ancillary industries;

—Maintenance or expansion of the industrial complex of the Tagus.

A wide-ranging research programme is currently under way in order to provide the scientific understanding of the estuary which is a pre-requisite for achieving these objectives and for harmonizing them when there is conflict with the last two industrial objectives. The rest of this paper describes one part of this work.

Environmental quality management requires routine monitoring in order to determine: (a) whether various criteria are being satisfied or not and (b) whether licenced waste flow rates are being exceeded. Hence, an important output of the project is an initial file of all waste discharges to the estuary. Since there are many other flows across the boundaries of the estuary, the relative importance of the waste discharges must also be assessed. The best way to start is to make closed mass-balances or budgets for the estuary as a whole.

ESTUARINE MASS-BALANCES

A MASS-BALANCE on the estuary is 'closed' by calculating the error term in the expression:

$$M_1(s) + M_2(s) + M_3(s) + \cdots + M_n(s) = \varepsilon$$

where the $M_i(s)$ are all the mass flow rates of substances s across the boundaries of the estuary during an average year. Inward flows are positive. The flows being considered are:

M_1 River Tagus
M_2 River Sorraia and other tributaries
M_3 Industrial discharges
M_4 Domestic discharges
M_5 Atmospheric inputs
M_6 Non-point inputs from land
M_7 Sedimentation losses and resuspension
M_8 Exchange with the sea
M_9 Ground-water inflow

Salt marshes are considered initially as part of the superficial sediments. Two independent methods of estimation are being used for each M_i, except for M_6 and M_9. Budgets for Hg, As, Cd, Pb, Zn, and C, N, P, are being attempted. In each case, an examination of ε will show the success of the attempt and may point to systematic errors in assuming for example, negligible input in the dissolved phase, $M_9 = 0$, or no change in storage at the year's end. The rest of this paper deals with the industrial discharges M_3 and illustrates the two methods of estimation.

Industrial Discharge Rate

(a) *Direct estimates of industrial discharges*:
    Measurements of chemical quality and flow rate were made at 52 locations around the estuary by the Directorate General for Hydraulic Services and Water Resources [2]. Samples were taken on two days during each of four seasons. Each sample was analysed for temperature, turbidity, conductivity, pH, settleable-suspended-dissolved solids and their fixed and volatile fractions, alkalinity, Cl, PO_4, SO_4, SO_3, S_{tot}, NO_2, NO_3, ammoniacal N, Kjeldahl N, P_{tot}, oxidability, phenolic compounds, anionic detergents, oils and grease, Hg, Cu, Pb, Fe, Mn, Cr_{tot}, Cd, Zn, Ni, cyanides, total coliforms, faecal coliforms, E. coli, faecal streptococus, pesticides—lindane, aldrin, dieldrin, endrin, DDT, DDE, TDE. Since the frequency of sampling was low, it was also thought necessary to estimate the mass-inputs rates using an indirect method based on production data for each major factory. However, direct measurements are being continued on six industries.

(b) *Indirect estimates of industrial discharges*:
    There are several thousand businesses in the greater Lisbon area. However, an examination of industrial statistics indicated that only 500 were likely to have significant waste discharges. Of these, 50 were thought to be the most important and 6 were singled out for special attention. We may summarise this as follows:

Group	Number of businesses	Importance
A	500	+
B	50	+ +
C	6	+ + +

With the assistance of UNIDO, two questionnaires were designed. Short forms were sent to all companies in group A, while the complete form was sent to companies in groups B and C. Discharge measurements were continued only for group C. The following information was requested on the complete form of 20 pages in Portuguese. It follows very closely a similar form designed by UNIDO for surveys of waste discharges.

1. Industry-name, address, type of location, place of waste disposal.
2. Classification according to a supplied list of categories.
3. Production of goods:
    3.1 Type of product, max/min. and average rate of production during each of the past 6 years stating the units of production as tonnes/year, cases/year, m²/year etc. The industries in group C were asked to extend this as far back as possible.
    3.2 The same information as in 3.1 was requested for all raw materials used.
    3.3 The max/min. and average number of workers at the plant during each year over the past 6 years.
    3.4 The number of daily shifts.
    3.5 Percentage of the local community employed at the plant.
4. Industrial uses of water:
    4.1 Water source—own well or river intake, public source.
    4.2 Water use—process, cooling, boiler, sanitation, as average flows per day.
    4.3 Brief description of the main water-using processes.
5. Industrial waste-water collection:
    5.1 Combined or separate sewer system for process water, sewage and rain run-off.
    5.2 One or many outfalls. Type and rate of discharge from each outfall.
6. Industrial waste-water treatment:
    6.1 Total industrial waste-water flow and fractions which are re-used or recirculated, discharged to municipal sewer systems, or to receiving waters. Breakdown of flows into treated and untreated parts.
    6.2 Further details on the type and degree of treatment applied to each waste water: process, cooling, boiler, sewage, etc., as in section 6.1.
    6.3 Type and stage efficiency of final treatment before discharge.
    6.4 Estimated operation and maintenance costs per annum and per cubic meter of waste.
    6.5 Capital cost of treatment plant (and year of construction).
7. Waste water:
    7.1 Availability or feasibility of data on waste discharges.

7.2 Max/min. and average composition of samples taken from each outfall and the method of analysis. Flow rate, physical characteristics, solids, organic matter, heavy metals, specific organic pollutants, nutrients and bacteria. Sample number and frequency.

7.3 For each pollutant calculate the mass-input rate as kg/day and as tonnes/year by multiplying flow rate and concentration, and assess the accuracy of the results.

8. Location of discharges: Discharge to land, lake, river, estuary, sea, municipal sewer, other.

9. Uses of the receiving waters: Use of drinking, irrigation, fishing, swimming, other—and general observations on the quality of the receiving water.

10. Name of the water-pollution control authority having jurisdiction at the point of discharge.

11. Distance to the nearest municipal sewer system and type of treatment available, if any.

12. Solid wastes:

12.1 Annual rate of generation. Quantity disposed of to a municipal or centralised system and by the industry's own means.

12.2 Own disposal method. Fraction disposed of to the sea, lake, river, estuary, on land or by other means.

12.3 Organic and inorganic fractions of the waste.

12.4 Treatment—storage, compression, recovery, incineration or other method.

13. Gaseous wastes:

13.1 Major contaminants produced.

13.2 Treatment used—filter, electrostatic precipitation, scrubbers, other.

13.3 Discharges rates of each contaminant by year.

13.4 Stack height above ground level.

The short form consisted of two pages and requested the production and consumption data in section 3. All other sections were suitably condensed. Gaseous wastes are the object of a parallel study of air-pollution in the greater Lisbon area and the results of these were made available to the Tagus project. In addition, the air-pollution project has been requested to provide estimates of M_5—atmospheric inputs to the estuary—by two methods, direct measurements and indirect estimation.

The forms were distributed by the Directorate General for Quality. The initial response was better than expected for this type of survey. Follow-up enquiries are being continued in order to ensure as complete a response as possible.

Processing the Data

The approach being followed was that used by UNIDO for the estimation of waste discharges for the Mediterranean Action Plan. The method consists of a set of multipliers which, when multiplied by production/consumption data, yields the mass-discharge rate of the important pollutants from a given industry. Whether production or consumption data are used in this multiplication depends on the particular industry and the available multipliers. The UNIDO multipliers are mainly based on the 1977 EPA Effluent Guidelines as collated by Nemerow [3]. The EPA guidelines are used as follows:

The discharge rate d_p of each pollutant p can be determined from the expression:

$$d_p = fg_pX$$

where g_p is the 'level for contaminant' p in the EPA guidelines per unit of production (or consumption) of X; f is a factor which converts the guideline for treated effluent to what it would be, if there were no treatment. Since the guidelines are based on the application of Best Practicable Treatment Technology—BPTT—we may presume 85 per cent removal efficiency for most pollutants. Hence the EPA guidelines must be increased by a factor $F = 1/0.15$ in order to convert them to multipliers for untreated discharges. When there is a doubt about the removal efficiency, from which f is calculated, or any entry in Nemerow's tables, reference is made to the original EPA document for that industry. As an example, let us take the problem of estimating the BOD discharge rate from a factory which cans and preserves citrus fruit. The guidelines state that the discharge rate, as a 30 day average, should not exceed 0.4 kg per 1000 kg of raw material. If we know from the questionnaire survey that the rate of consumption of raw material by the factory is 100 tonnes of citrus fruit per day during the canning season, then the permitted discharge rate is 40 kg per day. If no treatment is provided, then the discharge of BOD_5 is (40)/0.15 or 267 kg per day. This in turn can be converted into an ultimate oxygen demand by multiplying by 1.45 to yield $267 \times 1.45 = 387$ g O, on the assumption that only the carbon compounds are bio-oxidised during the first 5 days of the standard BOD test [4]. From the stoichiometry of reaction $C + O_2 = CO_2$, 1 g of oxygen combines with (12/32) g of carbon. Hence an oxygen demand of 387 g O implies an initial carbon content of (387) (12/32) = 145 g C. If we further assume values for the ratios N/C and P/C, which are typical for plant tissue or fruit, we can also estimate the input rates for N and P.

Besides the BOD_5, total suspended solids and nutrients, the EPA effluent guidelines also have multipliers to make the estimates of the input rates of pollutants, such as heavy metals and specific organic pollutants. It has been found necessary to expand the UNIDO/EPA/Nemerow set of multipliers to cover the full variety of industry which occurs around the Tagus estuary, for comparison and/or complementation for some specific industries which were not included in the guidelines mentioned above.

An example where it is necessary to use another source of information is the estimation of the mercury-loading from a chloroalkali industry, using the mercury-cell process with the spent-brine technique, because in the EPA effluent guidelines there are only multipliers for the recirculatory brine technique. There are also more appropriate multipliers available for the Portuguese tomato industry in a study carried out by the General Directorate for Hydraulic Services.

RESULTS AND DISCUSSION

FOUR EXAMPLES based on the information given in the answers to the questionnaires are presented in Table 1. Two of these show acceptable agreement.

Concerning these and other initial results, a further comparison of multipliers with those from France, Germany and the Economic Commission for Europe was also made. There is a broad agreement among the European multipliers but they differ sometimes from the UNIDO/EPA/Nemerow set. An example of this is shown in Table 2. The UNIDO values are too low in this case.

Table 1

Industry	Pollutant	Indirect Estimated Load		Direct Estimated load Kg/day
		Multiplier	Load Kg/day	
Urea	Ammonia—N	0.375 Kg/ton product [3]	96	17
Ammonia		0.0625 Kg/ton product [3]		
Phosphoric Acid	Total—P	0.40 Kg/ton product [3]	242	368
Petroleum Refining	Total Suspended Solids	0.279 Kg/ton of feedstock [3]	1 322	9 100
	Chemical oxygen Demand	0.564 Kg/ton of feedstock [3]	2 673	12 400
	Phenols	0.0012 Kg/ton of feedstock [3]	6	116
Chloroalkali Industry	Mercury	40 g/ton Cl$_2$ [5]	2.6	4.1

Table 2. Slaughterhouse

	BOD$_5$		TSS		P$_{total}$		N$_{total}$		Oils and Grease	
	Multiplier	Load (kg/year)	Multiplier	Load (kg/year)	Multiplier	Load (kg/year)	Multiplier	Load (kg/year)	Multiplier	Load (kg/year)
UNIDO [6, 7] France [8]	0.80 kg/t	1 634 kg	1.33 kg/t 20.0 kg/t (pigs and cattle) 10.0 kg/t (sheep) 5.0 kg/t (horses)	2 724 kg 25 854 kg					0.4 kg/t	817 kg
Germany [9]	3.402 kg head of cattle	69 503 kg								
ECE [10]	864 kg/ employee and year	51 840 kg	605 kg/ employee and year	36 300 kg	1.73 kg/ employee and year	1 038 kg	63.1 kg/ employee and year	3 804 kg		
Direct Estimate		51 636 kg		31 070 kg		2 440 kg		2 418 kg		4 654 kg

References

1. Palmer, M. and Espírito Santo, T. *Environmental Study of the Tagus Estuary.* Natural Resources, Vol. XVI, No. 3, July–September 1980, pp. 14–20.
2. Janeiro, A.F.F. *Avaliação da carga poluidora afluente.* Relatório I. Direcção dos Serviços de Controle da Poluição. Lisboa, Janeiro 1981.
3. Nemerow, N.L. *Industrial Water Pollution: Origin, Characteristics and Treatment.* Addison–Wesley, New York, NY. 2nd Edition. 1979.
4. O'Kane, J.P. *Estuarine Water Quality Management—with Moving Element Models and Optimization Techniques.* Pitman. London. 1980.
5. Commission of the European Communities. *Survey of Mercury Consumptions and Emissions in Selected Industries within the EEC.* ENV/128/78.
6. *Survey of Marine Pollutants from industrial sources in the West African Region,* prepared by UNIDO, Division of Industrial Studies.
7. *EPA Code of Regulations.* U.S. Environmental Protection Agency, Washington, D.C. 1977.
8. Arrete du 28 Octobre 1975, Anexe 1—*Tableau des coefficients spècifiques de pollution pour l'estimation forfaitaire*—Paris 1975.
9. Stecher, E. and Rupprecht, G. *Die Münchener Schlachthofawässer und ihr. Einfluss auf die städtischen.* Abwässer, Ges-Ing, 63/1949, 151–155, from F. Meinsk, H. Stooff, H. Kohlschütter, *Les Eaux Résiduaires Industrielles Masson 1977*, 2ᵉ-édition.
10. Economic Commission for Europe—*Industrial Wastes discharged from Coastal Areas of EEC countries,* 1977.

Some Fundamental Aspects of Water Pollution Control

T.H.Y. Tebbutt

*Senior Lecturer and Supervisor, Postgraduate School of
Water Resources Technology, Department of Civil
Engineering, University of Birmingham, UK*

SYNOPSIS

*Because of the complex nature of water pollution and its effects on
the uses of water, it is important that control measures take into
account the various factors affecting the system. The differences in
behaviour of conservative and nonconservative pollutants should be
appreciated and water-pollution standards should be based on
rational analysis of each individual situation. Fixed emission
standards for water-pollution control are unlikely to give the best
return on investment.*

RÉSUMÉ

*A cause de la nature complexe de la pollution des eaux et de ses
effets sur l'utilisation de l'eau, il est important que les mesures de
contrôle tiennent compte des différents facteurs influent sur le
système. Les différences de comportement entre pollutants con-*

319

*servatifs et non-conservatifs devraient être évalués et les normes de
pollution des eaux devraient être basées sur une analyse rationale
de chaque situation. Les normes d'émission fixées pour la contrôle
de la pollution sont peu probable de donner le meilleure compensation sur invertissement.*

RESUMEN

*A causa de la complejidad de la polución del agua y de sus efectos
sobre los usos del agua es importante que las medidas de control
tengan en cuenta los distintos factores que afectan el sistema. Hay
que apreciar las diferencias en el comportamiento de los contaminantes conservadores y no conservadores, y hay que basar las
normas de la polución del agua en un análisis racional de cada
situación individual. Es poco probable que las normas fijas de
emisión para el control de la polución del agua den el mejor
beneficio relativo a la inversión.*

INTRODUCTION

WATER HAS ALWAYS been a vital factor in the development of communities since
without a reliable supply, little can be achieved in the way of growth and improved
living standards. In a sparsely populated rural area, it may be possible for the
population to obtain its water requirements from a nearby stream or pond and
dispose of its wastes so that significant contamination of the water supply does not
occur. As populations grow in size, the natural self-purification processes are
unlikely to be able to cope with the additional pollution load so that water quality
deteriorates. Urbanization and industrialization of a community bring increasing
problems of environmental pollution with serious consequences in terms of public
health. The International Drinking Water Supply and Sanitation Decade has
highlighted the problems in developing countries, many of which are directly
related to the hazards of faecally contaminated water supplies. Similar problems
were apparent in Western Europe and the USA during the Industrial Revolution,
when dense urban populations without safe water supplies and adequate sanitation were subjected to the ravages of water-borne diseases such as cholera and
typhoid. In the latter half of the 19th century, public concern resulted in the
construction of water supply and sewerage schemes for urban communities, but in
densely populated areas it is not sufficient to transport waste water to a con-

venient discharge point without treatment since serious water pollution will still be likely to occur. At the turn of the century, water pollution in the industrial areas of the UK was so widespread that a major study of water pollution was instigated and control measures, which are still the basis of present-day thinking in the field of water-pollution control, were recommended.

EFFECTS OF WATER POLLUTION

IT MIGHT BE ARGUED that it would be desirable for all natural waters to exist in an unpolluted state but it must be appreciated that pollution does occur due to natural processes. When rainwater reaches the ground it contains a small amount of contamination, mainly in the form of inorganic salts washed from the atmosphere. As water flows over the ground surface, it inevitably picks up further contamination in the form of inorganic and organic matter from soil, plants and animals. Thus, the further water travels from the original site of precipitation the less pure it becomes. To this natural contamination is added pollution resulting from human activities: domestic sewage discharges, industrial effluents and agricultural operations. The significance of water pollution depends upon the nature of the pollutants, the dilution available and the use or potential use of the water downstream. The main effects of pollution may be:

(1) Contamination of water sources leading to possible disease hazards and increased load on water-treatment facilities;
(2) Polluted irrigation water may pose a health hazard or may inhibit the growth of crops;
(3) Effects on fish life;
(4) Recreational and amenity aspects of water can be harmed by pollution;
(5) Excessive pollution can create odour nuisances;
(6) Discharges of suspended matter can hinder navigation.

The relative importance of these points will be a function of the use to which a particular body of water is put which may include one or more of the following:

(1) Domestic water supply;
(2) Industrial water supply;
(3) Irrigation;
(4) Commercial fishing;
(5) Recreation and amenity;
(6) Transportation;
(7) Power generation;
(8) Waste disposal.

Each use will have specific quality requirements so that a particular form of pollution might be unacceptable in water used for potable supply but acceptable if that water were only used for industrial-cooling purposes. Since water is often a scarce resource, it is desirable where possible to practice the concept of multi-purpose use but, as can be appreciated, the requirements and effects of various uses will not always be compatible.

NATURE OF POLLUTANTS

SERIOUS WATER POLLUTION produces an obvious deterioration in the quality of the environment and should be prevented if at all possible, although practical and economic factors may make some improvements in water quality slow to achieve at the present time. The activities of environmental pressure groups should not be looked upon as an unqualified asset because they have sometimes encouraged legislation and controls which are difficult or impossible to enforce and which bring little tangible benefit in return for considerable expenditure. It is, therefore, desirable that water-quality control measures be based on rational assessments of their feasibility, costs and potential benefits [1].

Conservative and Non-conservative Pollutants

It is important to appreciate that contaminants behave in different ways when added to water. Certain materials, such as organics, some inorganics and many micro-organisms, are degraded by natural self-purification processes so that their concentration reduces with time. The rate of decay of these non-conservative pollutants is a function of the particular pollutant, receiving-water quality, temperature and other environmental factors. Many inorganic compounds are not affected by natural processes so that the concentration of these conservative pollutants can only be reduced by dilution. Conservative pollutants are often unaffected by normal water and waste-water treatment processes so that their presence in a water source may limit the use of that source.

Toxic Pollutants

Two aspects of toxicity are of importance in water-quality considerations. Since natural waters normally support a balanced ecological community, the presence of contaminants which have a toxic effect on even one species in the system would be detrimental. Fish are usually the most sensitive organisms as far as toxicity problems in water are concerned. The whole question of fish toxicity is highly complex because of the effect of other environmental factors such as dissolved oxygen concentration, temperature and other constituents in the water. The species, age and sex of the fish can also have a considerable influence on toxicity.

When considering raw waters for potable supply, the presence of toxic substances must always be seen as a potential hazard. The accidental discharge of toxic materials into a watercourse will hopefully be reported so that appropriate remedial measures can be undertaken. Bankside storage of raw water is advisable for waters at risk from this type of event. A more insidious form of toxic pollution is that due to long-term ingestion of trace concentrations of certain materials such as heavy metals, complex organics etc., some of which may pose carcinogenic risks. In the latter type of toxic contamination, monitoring and control can be very difficult particularly if allowable levels are set close to the limits of detection as is sometimes the case.

Overall Effects of Pollution

In addition to well-established effects, such as depletion of dissolved oxygen and fish kills, pollution is likely to cause significant increases in dissolved solids, organic content, nutrients, colour and turbidity, all of which may give rise to undesirable changes in downstream quality. Nutrient build-up can be a serious problem in lakes since the ensuing increase in productivity can cause prolific algal growths with rapid eutrophication, which may eventually render the water unsuitable for most purposes.

POLLUTION CONTROL POLICIES

WHEN ESTABLISHING methods for the control of water pollution, standards can be based either on the quality required in the receiving water or they can be applied directly to the discharge. The former approach appears logical but causes problems when a new discharge is made to the system since, either all existing discharge levels must be revised downward or the new discharge may be faced with an impossibly high standard. There could also be inequalities in effluent standards between similar discharges into the same river—a downstream discharge would require a higher standard because the dilution water would be of poorer quality as a result of the upstream discharge. The adoption of effluent standards based on the use of the receiving water has the merit of often being easier to enforce than the stipulation of receiving-water quality standards but does not in itself ensure the maintenance of river quality under changing effluent discharge conditions.

UK Practice

In its Eighth Report, the Royal Commission on Sewage Disposal [2] proposed the adoption of effluent standards related to the dilution and quality of the receiving water based on the classification shown in Table 1.

Table 1. Royal Commission river quality classification (1912)

Classification	Average quality mg/l						
	BOD	PV	Amm.N	NO$_3$N	SS	Cl	DO
Very clean	1	2	0.04	0.5	4	10	11
Clean	2	2.5	0.24	2	15	25	9.3
Fairly clean	3	3	0.67	2.2	15	30	8.6
Doubtful	5	5	2.5	5	21	50	6.6
Bad	10	7	6.7	4	35	>50	low

From their studies the Commission suggested that a biochemical oxygen demand (BOD) of 4 mg/l in a watercourse was a limit which if exceeded would indicate a significant degree of pollution. Their recommendations on effluent standards with a norm of 30 mg/l suspended solids (SS) and 20 mg/l BOD were based on the need to provide sufficient dilution to prevent the downstream BOD exceeding 4 mg/l. Unfortunately, in many cases where the recommendations were implemented, insufficient dilution was available so the BOD limit was exceeded. However, with a non-conservative parameter like BOD, the self-purification characteristics of the receiving water have a major effect on the results of a discharge and later work has shown that many rivers can tolerate BOD levels greater than 4 mg/l without serious effects. In the case of conservative pollutants, the available dilution and the acceptable level of the pollutant relative to the particular uses envisaged are the only factors which can be taken into account. Relatively little change has taken place in the philosophy of water-pollution control in the UK and current water-quality classification [3] is shown in Table 2.

The application of classification schemes linked to water quality and use have been discussed in the UK context by Lester [4]. In England and Wales, all aspects of the water cycle come under the control of Regional Water Authorities whose water-quality objectives include:

(i) The provision of a sufficient quantity of water of suitable quality for domestic and industrial abstractions. (ii) The safeguarding of public health. (iii) The maintenance and improvement of fisheries. (iv) Maintenance and restoration of water quality and conservation of flora and fauna associated with water. To fulfill these objectives the Water Authorities have in general adopted the following aims: (i) There should be no deterioration in river quality. (ii) Class-4 rivers should be eliminated. (iii) Class-3 rivers should normally be upgraded to class 2.

Although the normal effluent standard of 30 mg/l SS and 20 mg/l BOD is still often used in the UK as a basis of control, each case is assessed in the light of the particular conditions. With industrial waste-water discharges, a similar concept is adopted with local effluent standards being set on the basis of the predicted effect of the particular contaminants on the receiving water. For many industrial discharges, treatment in admixture with domestic sewage is an attractive pro-position and the cost of the industrial waste treatment is recovered by means of a charge based partly on the cost of conveyance in the sewers and partly on the cost of treatment. The formula used to establish the appropriate charge is of the form:

$$C = R + V + \frac{O_i}{O_s} B + \frac{S_i}{S_s} S$$

where C = total charge per m^3 of industrial effluent
R = reception and conveyance charge per m^3
V = volumetric and primary treatment cost per m^3
O_i = COD (mg/l) of the industrial effluent after 1 hour quiescent settlement at pH7
O_s = COD (mg/l) of settled sewage
B = biological oxidation cost per m^3 of settled sewage
S_i = total SS (mg/l) of industrial effluent
S_s = total SS (mg/l) of crude sewage
S = treatment and disposal costs of primary sludge per m^3

This type of charging scheme encourages the industrial discharger to take steps to reduce the volume and strength of the waste water by careful process control and, possibly, modification of processes. A good example of this is the replacement of batch-rinsing of electro-plated products by a counter-current flow system. A side effect of such process modifications is often that reagent or by-product recovery becomes attractive. If industrial discharges are taken into the municipal sewerage system, it is important to ensure that the constituents of the waste water are not harmful to the sewers themselves, to sewer workers or to the sewage-treatment processes. In some cases therefore, it may be necessary for pretreatment to be undertaken before the waste is acceptable in the sewer. The 'polluter must pay' policy, sometimes recommended for dealing with industrial waste waters, may not be altogether satisfactory unless the charges made are rationally based. In some cases an industrial concern might prefer to pay the cost of pollution as an operating expense rather than having capital invested in a treatment plant. Such an approach could be detrimental to water quality and UK experience suggests that it would have little to commend it [5].

River Quality Objectives or Fixed Emission Standards

As outlined above, pollution-control practice in the UK is based on river quality objectives related to use criteria, local emission standards for effluents being set with the objectives in mind. In some parts of the world, fixed emission standards

Table 2. National Water Council river quality classification (1977)

River class	Quality criteria	Remarks	Current potential uses
	(i) DO saturation greater than 80%. (ii) BOD not greater than 3 mg/l. (iii) Ammonia not greater than 0.4 mg/l. (iv) Where the water is abstracted for drinking water, it complies with requirements for A2* water. (v) Non-toxic to fish in EIFAC terms (or best estimates if EIFAC figures not available).	(i) Average BOD probably not greater than 1.5 mg/l. (ii) Visible evidence of pollution should be absent.	(i) Water of high quality suitable for potable supply abstractions and for all other abstractions. (ii) Game or other high class fisheries. (iii) High amenity value.
1B	(i) DO greater than 60% saturation. (ii) BOD not greater than 5 mg/l. (iii) Ammonia not greater than 0.9 mg/l. (iv) Where water is abstracted for drinking water, it complies with the requirements for A2* water. (v) Non-toxic to fish in EIFAC terms (or best estimates if EIFAC figures not available).	(i) Average BOD probably not greater than 2 mg/l. (ii) Average ammonia probably not greater than 0.5 mg/l. (iii) Visible evidence of pollution should be absent. (iv) Waters of high quality which cannot be placed in Class 1A because of high proportion of high quality effluent present or because of the effect of physical factors such as canalization, low gradient or eutrophication.	Water of less high quality than Class 1A but usable for substantially the same purposes.
2	(i) DO greater than 40% saturation. (ii) BOD not greater than 9 mg/l. (iii) Where water is abstracted for drinking water, it complies with the requirements for A3* water. (iv) Non-toxic to fish in EIFAC terms (or best estimates if EIFAC figures not available).	(i) Average BOD probably not greater than 5 mg/l. (ii) Water not showing physical signs of pollution other than humic coloration and a little foaming below weirs.	(i) Waters suitable for potable supply after advanced treatment. (ii) Supporting reasonably good coarse fisheries. (iii) Moderate amenity value.

continued

continuation

River class	Quality criteria	Remarks	Current potential uses
3	(i) DO greater than 10% saturation. (ii) Not likely to be anaerobic. (iii) BOD not greater than 17 mg/l.†		Waters which are polluted to an extent that fish are absent or only sporadically present. May be used for low grade industrial abstraction purposes. Considerable potential for further use if cleaned up.
4	(i) DO less than 10% saturation. (ii) Likely to be anaerobic at times.		Waters which are grossly polluted and are likely to cause nuisance.
X	DO greater than 10% saturation.		Insignificant watercourses and ditches not usable, where objective is simply to prevent nuisance developing.

Notes: (a) Under extreme weather conditions (e.g. flood, drought, freeze-up), or when dominated by plant growth, or by aquatic plant decay, rivers usually in Classes 1, 2 and 3 may have BODs and dissolved oxygen levels, or ammonia content outside the stated levels for those Classes. When this occurs the cause should be stated along with analytical results.

(b) The BOD determinations refer to 5-day carbonaceous BOD (ATU). Ammonia figures are expressed as NH_4.

(c) In most instances the chemical classification given above will be suitable. However, the basis of the classification is restricted to a finite number of chemical determinants and there may be a few cases where the presence of a chemical substance other than those used in the classification markedly reduces the quality of the water. In such cases, the quality classification of the water should be downgraded on the basis of the biota actually present, and the reasons stated.

(d) EIFAC (European Inland Fisheries Advisory Commission) limits should be expressed as 95% percentile limits.

* EEC category A2 and A3 requirements are those specified in the EEC Council Directive of 16 June 1975 concerning the Quality of Surface Water intended for Abstraction of Drinking Water in the Member States.

† This may not apply if there is a high degree of reaeration.

for effluent discharges have become popular and these certainly have the bureaucratic advantage of easy application. There is also the analogy of such standards to be found in air-pollution control. However, the nature and use of the receiving water has such an influence on the effect of a particular contaminant that it is impossible to set a fixed standard which, if based on the worst case, does not penalize less critical situations or, if based on average conditions, does not fail to provide protection in more extreme circumstances. The use of best available technology or even zero discharge requirements could well lead to an unnecessary diversion of funds to water-pollution control measures with little or no tangible benefits. Expenditure to improve environmental quality should be initially examined on a factual, cost-benefit basis with subjective factors being added to the equation at a later stage if appropriate.

In the case of conservative pollutants, the concentration of the pollutant in the receiving water is a function of the available dilution. It may be possible to justify the removal of chlorides to say 50 mg/l from discharges where there is little dilution but patently absurd to make a similar requirement where there is a large dilution available. With non-conservative pollutants, the self-purification capacity of the receiving water as well as the dilution factor will influence downstream conditions. Self-purification is probably most commonly expressed in terms of the stabilization of organic matter and its effect on the oxygen balance but the same principles can also be applied to the oxidation of ammonia and to the die-off of bacteria. The concept of fixed emission standards is seen to be quite unrealistic if the effect of different reaeration characteristics on DO levels is considered. In stagnant or slowly flowing water, oxygen transfer takes place mainly by diffusion but, as the velocity of flow increases, turbulent mixing greatly accelerates oxygen transfer. The channel cross-section also affects the reaeration capacity of the watercourse. Figure 1 shows the effect of different velocities to flow on the reaeration characteristics of a receiving water. It is clear that a given amount of BOD can have vastly different effects on a volume of water depending upon its oxygen transfer characteristics. An effluent discharged to a canal with a velocity of 0.05 m/s would produce a serious oxygen depletion, whereas the same discharge to a channel with a velocity of 0.5 m/s would produce little oxygen depletion. Indeed, in many cases, the initial oxygen concentration of the effluent may be more relevant to the oxygen balance than the BOD uptake [6]. In such circumstances, some form of effluent aeration may be more beneficial to downstream conditions than further BOD removal [7]. Whilst the reaeration characteristics can have a major effect on the oxygen balance, it is important to appreciate that the downstream concentration of BOD is a function of the BOD rate constant which does not vary to the same extent as the reaeration constant. Thus, if the limiting-pollution criterion is dissolved oxygen, reaeration will be of primary importance. If, however, the concentration of the pollutant itself is limiting, control must be based on the predicted reduction of the pollutant by dilution and self-purification and here the differences between various types of receiving water are not so great. Some authorities believe that no account should be taken of natural self-purification capacity, so that pollutants could only be discharged at a level which immediately gave the desired concentration in the receiving water. This may be justifiable where the direct effect of the pollutant on particular water uses is the major concern but is difficult to justify if the major effect is an indirect one, such as oxygen depletion which is a function of time and stream characteristics.

Fig. 1. Predicted dissolved oxygen concentrations for constant BOD load, 2 m deep channel with various velocities of flow

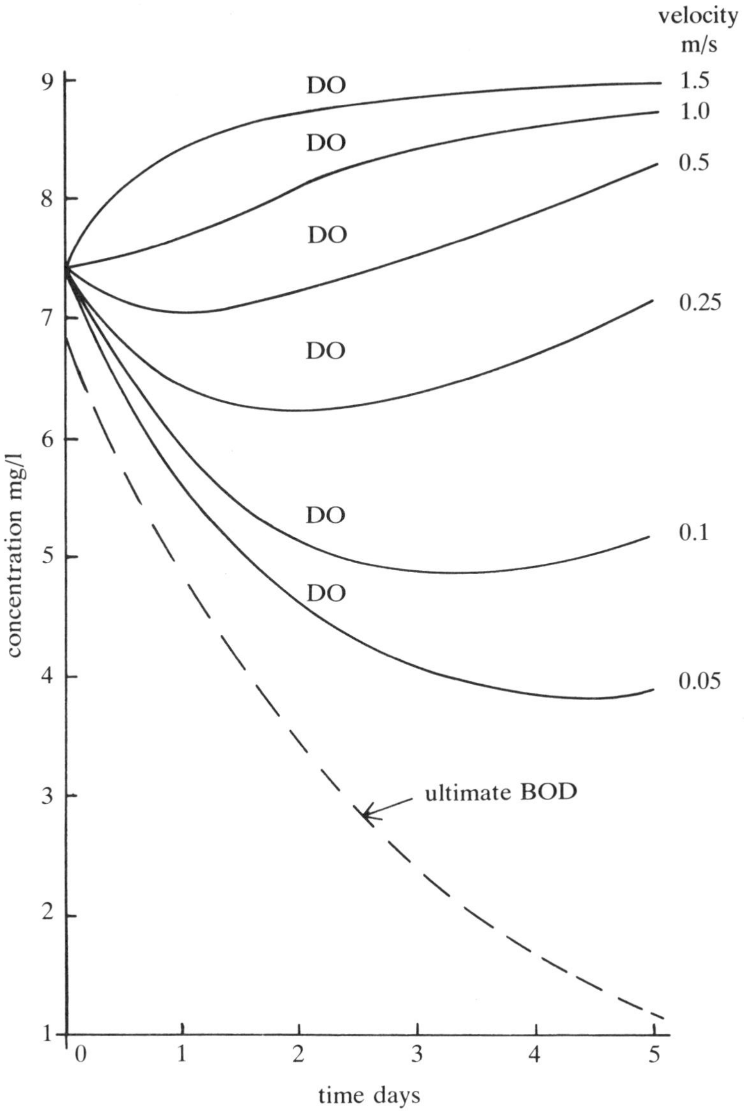

stream flow 4   DO 8   BOD 2   DOS 9.16
effluent flow 1   DO 5   BOD 20 k_1 0.15

CONCLUSION

THE CONTROL OF water pollution in industrialized catchments involves study of a complex system in which many factors can influence the behaviour and importance of particular pollutants. To avoid unnecessary expenditure it is important that control of pollution is undertaken on a sound logical basis and that standards can be clearly justified. If this approach is not adopted, there is danger of inappropriate standards being used and the expenditure not producing the maximum benefits to the community at large.

References

1. Tebbutt, T.H.Y. (1979) *A rational approach to water quality control.* Wat. Supply Management, **3**, 41.
2. Royal Commission on Sewage Disposal (1912) *Eighth Report*, HMSO, London.
3. National Water Council (1977) *Review of discharge consent conditions: consultation paper.* NWC, London.
4. Lester, W.F. (1980) *Implementation of the Control of Pollutation Act*, 1974. Wat. Pollut. Control, **79**, 165.
5. McIntosh, P.T. and Wilcox, J. (1979) *Water Pollution charging systems in the EEC.* Wat. Pollut. Control, **78**, 183.
6. Tebbutt, T.H.Y. (1971) *Dissolved oxygen—its significance in effluents.* Effl. Wat. Treat. Journal, **13**, 39.
7. Tebbutt, T.H.Y., Essery, I.T.S. and Rasaratnam, S.K. (1977) *Reaeration performance of stepped cascades.* J. Inst. Wat. Engrs Scits, **31**, 285.

Water Quality Assessment in Bursa Organized Industrial District

Semra Siber
Department of Environmental Engineering,
Middle East Technical University,
Ankara, Turkey

and

Gülseren Ergüden
Engineer, BMB Engineering Company, Ankara, Turkey

SYNOPSIS

A short-term investigation on Bursa Organized Industrial District waste-water quality in the period of May to September 1975 is presented. To be able to determine the response of waste water to biological treatment, a treatability study was carried out in the laboratory. Possible waste-water disposal alternatives have been proposed by considering the self-purification capacity of the receiving water course, Nilüfer Creek, with respect to the water-quality requirements in Turkey.

RÉSUMÉ

Les résultats d'une recherche à courte dureé couvrant la période Mai-Septembre 1975 sur la qualité des eaux résiduaires de la zone

*industrielle organisée de Bursa ont été presentés. En vue de deter-
miner le comportement de l'eau résiduaire vis à vis de traitement
biologique, une étude éxperimentale sur la possibilité de traitement
a été effectuée. Les alternatives possibles pour la décharge des eaux
résiduaires ont été proposés, en considerant la capacité d'auto-
épuration de la rivière Nilüfer, et les standards conventionels adoptés en Turquie pour les qualités des eaux.*

RESUMEN

*Se presenta aquí una investigación a corto plazo llevada a cabo
durante el período de mayo a septiembre de 1975 sobre las características de las aguas sucias del Distrito Industrial Organizado de
Bursa (Turquía). Para poder determinar la reacción del agua a un
tratamiento biológico, un estudio sobre la "tratabilidad" fue lle-
vado a cabo en el laboratorio. Se proponen varias alternativas para
redimir las aguas sucias, teniendo en cuenta la capacidad de
autopurificación del arroyo Nilüfer donde desembocan estas aguas,
con respecto a la calidad de agua exigida en Turquía.*

INTRODUCTION

Bursa organized Industrial District (BOID) has been located on the Bursa-
Mudanya road, approximately 20 km away from Bursa, on flat terrain. The water
for the District is supplied from Nilüfer Creek and it is consumed after natural
filtration. The waste water of the BOID is given to the same creek downstream of
the water intake without any treatment. Nilüfer Creek collects the waste water of
Bursa and some industries located upstream of the District. BOID has been
planned for 58 factories and, up to 1975, 51 factories have been installed. The
major industries involved can be classified into five groups, namely:

Name of the industry	Number of factories
(1) Textile and dye	21
(2) Synthetic fibre	5
(3) Plastics fibre	5
(4) Metal plating	8
(5) Motor and motor vehicle	10
Miscellaneous	5

The water-consumption characteristics have been determined by the District Authorities for the period of January 1974 to February 1975. A summary is given as:

monthly maximum = 324,572 m³/month
daily average   = 13524 m²/day (24 working days per month)
                  = 0.16 m³/sec
daily maximum   = 0.6 × 2.5 = 0.4 m³/sec.

It has been assumed that 90 percent of the water supply is captured by the sewerage system of the BOID and the waste-water flows have been calculated as:

$Q_{monthly\ max.}$ = 324572 × 0.9 = 292115 m³/day
$Q_{daily\ aver.}$ = 13524 × 0.9 = 12172 m³/day.

A simple water balance can be schematized as follows (Figure 1).

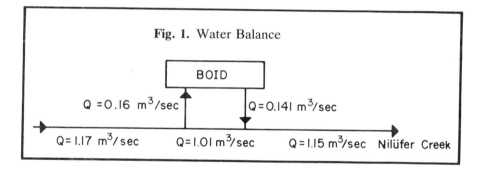

Fig. 1. Water Balance

EXPERIMENTAL STUDY

THE SAMPLING PROGRAMME has been carried out during the period of May to September 1975. The District waste-water samples have been taken from the main discharge channel. Twelve-hour composite sampling has been done by collecting 1 litre of sample at every half-hour period. Table 1 shows the results of the analyses performed on the composite-sampled BOID wastewater.

Table 1. The characteristics of BOID waste water. All values (except temperature, pH and EC) are in mg/l

Parameter	Minimum*	Average*	Maximum*
Temperature, °C	20.00	23.1	25.0
pH	7.8	8.2	8.6
Total Solids	1100	1620	1960
Volatile Solids	620	730	980
Suspended Solids	120	180	260
BOD_5	140	200	240
COD	300	400	484
NH_3	4.8	10.0	16.0
NO_3^-	0.00	0.06	0.32
NO_2^-	0.00	0.01	0.06
TKN	10.65	18.00	29.00
Cr^{6+}	0.00	0.038	0.10
CN^-	0.00	0.04	0.10
Dissolved oxygen	0.0	1.2	2.0
$EC \times 10^6$ (Micromhos/cm)	1100	1645	1945
PO_4^{3-}	3.7	6.2	9.00
Boron	0.00	0.01	0.04

* The minimum, average and maximum values have been obtained out of 6 samples.

Physical parameters of the reactors:

Reactor	Aeration volume (l)	Feed volume (l/day)	Hydraulic detention time (day)	Solids retention time, t, (day)
1	3	3	1	10
2	3	6	1/2	5
3	3	1 1/2	2	20

Treatability determination:

To be able to determine the biochemical treatability response of BOID waste water, continous flow model reactors have been employed (Figure 2).

The kinetic coefficients are calculated by Eckenfelder's model [1], with the BOD_5 data given in Table 2 as follows:

k (reaction rate coefficient) = 0.02 $(mg/l\ d)^{-1}$
a (sludge synthesis coefficient) = 0.67
b (endogeneous respiration coefficient) = 0.064 $(day)^{-1}$
a' (0_2 utilization coeff. for synthesis) = 0.41
b' (0_2 utilization coeff. for respiration) = 0.056 $(day)^{-1}$

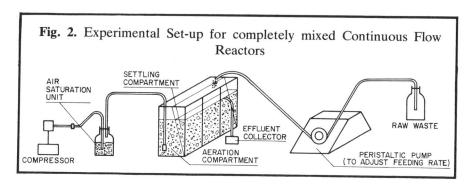

Fig. 2. Experimental Set-up for completely mixed Continuous Flow Reactors

Table 2. Summary of reactor-experiment results

	Influent		Effluent					MLVSS in Reactor	Removal Efficiency %	
	BOD$_5^*$	COD*	BOD$_5$		COD		Volatile			
	(S$_0$)		(S)*	Total	*	Total	Solids	(X)	BOD$_5$	COD
Reactor I	−200	334.8	13.2	26.4	37.6	65.7	34	746	93.6	89
Reactor II	−220	376.2	21.3	25.2	59.9	90.0	12	1074	90.3	84
Reactor III	−200	330.2	12.5	20.0	32.5	56.6	11	562	93.7	90

All values are in mg/l.   *Dissolved

The reaction rate coefficient $k = 0.02$ (mg/l day)$^{-1}$ is in the range of domestic waste waters and closer to the lower limit. As comparison, the k value is within the range for chemical and petroleum industries, being closer to the upper limit, a small fraction higher than the k value of pharmaceutical waste waters. According to the above comparisons, the reaction rate coefficient, k, of BOID waste water may be assumed to have treatability characteristics similar to that of domestic waste water but with a relatively lower response.

The sludge yield coefficient, a, is within the range of domestic waste water and the endogeneous respiration rate constant, b, is out of the domestic waste water range, being close to the lower limit (Table 3).

DISPOSAL ALTERNATIVES

THE METHOD and the efficiency of treatment depends on the final disposal alternatives for the BOID waste water, which in this case may be either disposal into Nilüfer Creek, reuse in irrigation or discharge into the municipal sewerage system.

To be able to analyse the discharge possibility of BOID waste water into Nilüfer Creek, the self-purification capacity of the Nilüfer Creek water has to be

Table 3. Some values of removal rate constant k, sludge synthesis coefficient a, and respiration rate coefficient b [2]

Type of Waste water	$k(mg/l, d)^{-1}$	a	$b(day)^{-1}$
Domestic	0.017–0.038	0.5–0.73	0.075–0.125
Brewery	–	0.56	0.10
Refinery	0.074	0.49–0.62	0.10–0.16
Pharmaceutical	0.018	0.72–0.77	–
Chemical and Petroleum	0.0029–0.018	0.31–0.72	0.05–0.18
Milk production	0.017	0.667	0.073

investigated. The treatment of this waste water should be adjusted considering the purification capacity of the Creek to avoid overloading. Water quality of Nilüfer Creek is shown in Table 4.

The design flow of 50 per cent occurrence is taken instead of the common 10 per cent practice in Nilüfer Creek, with economic considerations for the discharge of organic load. The reaeration coefficient $k_2 = 1.06$ $(day)^{-1}$ is approximated with O'Conner's formula [3]. By Streeter-Phelps equation [3], the deoxygenation coefficient, k_1, is calculated as 0.53 $(day)^{-1}$; k_1 and k_2 have been assumed to be

Table 4. The characteristics of Nilüfer Creek Water before BOID waste-water discharge. All values (except temperature and pH) are in mg/l

Parameter	Minimum*	Average*	Maximum*
Temperature, T °C	17.6	19.8	21.0
pH	7.7	7.9	8.2
Total solids	470.0	510.0	630.0
Volatile solids	132.0	210.0	380.0
Suspended solids	26.0	–	–
Dissolved oxygen	4.6	5.8	6.2
BOD	30.0	49.0	80.0
COD	116.0	125.0	133.0
NH_3	0.0	0.12	0.38
$N\bar{O}_3$	1.6	3.8	5.2
$N\bar{O}_2$	0.0	0.03	0.07
Cr^{6+}	0.0	0.0	0.0
CN^-	0.0	0.0	0.0

*The minimum, average and maximum values have been obtained out of 6 samples.

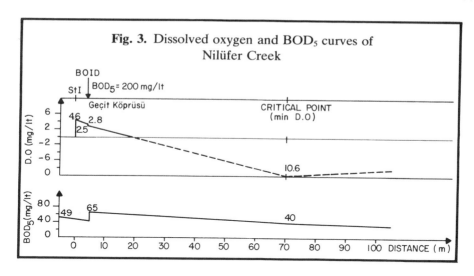

Fig. 3. Dissolved oxygen and BOD₅ curves of Nilüfer Creek

constant in the study area. Dissolved oxygen and BOD₅ variations of Nilüfer Creek are shown in Figure 3.

Considering the minimum DO concentration at the critical point of the Creek, downstream of BOID waste-water discharge, should not be less than 4 mg/l to satisfy the receiving-water standards as specified by *Aquatic Products Law in Turkey No. 1380*—"in a receiving water, minimum dissolved oxygen concentration should not be less than 4 mg/l and the maximum allowable BOD₅ is 50 mg/l both at 20°C."

Therefore, the required treatment efficiency for BOID waste water should be:

$$\frac{200 - 50}{200} \times 100 = 75\%$$

The deficit at the critical point,

$$D_c = 9.2 - 4.0 = 5.2 \text{ mg/l}$$

$$\frac{D_0}{D_c} = \frac{4.6}{5.2} = 0.88, \quad \frac{k_2}{k_1} = \frac{1.06}{0.53} = 2$$

From Fair's Graph [4],

$$\frac{L_0}{D_c} = 2.1$$

where $L_0 = 2.1 \ (5.2) = 11$ mg/l

BOD₅ $= 11(1 - e^{-5(0.53)}) = 10$ mg/l

BOD₅ load at station $= 1.01(49)(86\ 400) \times 10^{-6} = 4.3$ t/day.

Allowable BOD₅ at downstream of industrial district waste-water discharge $= 10(1.15) \ (86\ 400) \times 10^{-6} = 0.99$ t/day.

$$\begin{array}{cc} \text{Allowable BOD}_5 & \text{Actual BOD}_5 \\ 0.99 \text{ t/day} & 4.3 \text{ t/day} \end{array} \quad <$$

It may be concluded that the self-purification capacity of Nilüfer Creek has been utilized before BOID waste-water discharge. Thus the treatment of BOID and the individual industries located upstream, as well the sewage of Bursa, is essential. Unintentional reuse of the mixture of Nilüfer Creek and BOID waste water without treatment of industrial waste water within the natural cycle, or sequential use of water by communities located one below another in the direction of flow, is continuous practice. The assessment of the potential hazard of this usage and evaluation of the second disposal alternative (the irrigational reuse of BOID) are achieved by the following steps employing the available data:

(1) Slope of the ground in the agricultural land around the BOID has a value of less than 6 per cent [2] which is acceptable.

(2) Exchangeable sodium percentage (ESP) and sodium adsorption ratio (SAR) of BOID soil are calculated as follows [5]:

$$SAR = \frac{Na^+}{\left(\dfrac{Ca^{++} + Mg^{++}}{2}\right)^{1/2}}$$

$$= \frac{8.87}{\left(\dfrac{3.18 + 2.50}{2}\right)^{1/2}}$$

$$SAR = 5.26 < 10$$

$$ESP = \frac{100(-0.0126 + 0.01475\, SAR)}{1 + (-0.0126 + 0.01475\, SAR)}$$

$$ESP = 6.1\% < 10 - 12\%.$$

Per cent sodium is an index of the alkali hazard of water and its value is determined as 60%.

Residual Na_2CO_3 = 1.61 meq/l < 2.5 meq/l.

Boron = trace amounts < 1 ppm.

$EC \times 10^6$ = 1645 micromhos/cm (acceptable range 500–3000 $EC \times 10^6$ micromhos/cm).

Sar and ESP values and the other parameters satisfy the irrigational water-quality requirements [5].

(3) Organic matter of the waste water should also be considered to prevent the potential anaerobiosis if the application of waste water to the soil is continuous. In general, odours can be controlled by liquid chlorine (or sodium hypochlorite) concentration of 10–20 mg/l [6]. However, chlorine dosage will be adjusted after critical season microbiological quality and heavy metal determinations of waste water.

It may be said that industrial waste waters can be used for irrigation after proper pre-treatment during the dry season, which corresponds to high water demand. As the final alternative, the discharge of BOID waste water into the municipal sewerage system will be considered. The first attempt is to study the feasibility and the practicability of transportation of the waste water to the sewerage network or directly to the municipal treatment plant. Since the sewerage and treatment plant project of Bursa City is not completed yet, it is impossible to evaluate this alternative until the project is constructed and actual data available.

CONCLUSIONS

THE TREATABILITY COEFFICIENT k has been found to be 0.02 (mg/l d)$^{-1}$ and the other coefficients on BOD basis related to biochemical treatment were $a = 0.67$, $b = 0.064$ (day)$^{-1}$, $a' = 0.41$ and $b' = 0.056$ (day)$^{-1}$. Therefore, the proposed biochemical treatment processes which can be employed for the treatment of BOID waste water are [7]:

(1) extended aeration, oxidation ditch;
(2) Carrousel-type oxidation ditch;
(3) aerobic flow through aerated lagoon followed by facultative aerated lagoon; or
(4) aerobic flow through aerated lagoon followed by stabilization pond.

The selection of a suitable treatment method should be achieved after a minimum of a one-year, follow-up monitor period of Nilüfer Creek and BOID waste water. Also, the final decision on a proper disposal alternative will follow this qualitative/quantitative investigation of waste water. However, it is already definite that at least a pretreatment, combined with biochemical treatment, is required for the first alternative because the stream analysis performed on Nilüfer Creek has shown that the self-purification capacity of the Creek is fully utilized and is not capable of receiving any more pollution loads.

The waste-water quality and quantity has changed since 1975. For further research, the analyses and the design works should be based on one year, up-to-date data. Since most of the factories had not performed recycling, the waste-water pollution load may be diluted with discharge of cooling water. After proper recycling, the pollution concentration is expected to increase. Therefore, in the next study, the factories should be examined individually and in-plant recovery/recycling, combined with in-plant improvement programmes, will be put into effect. After monitoring the waste water and Creek water quality and quantity for a minimum of one year, the final treatment plant will be designed and constructed using these data to be able to satisfy receiving-water and effluent-quality standards, to obtain the best usage of water resources.

References

1. Eckenfelder and Adams (1974) *Process Design Techniques for Industrial Waste Treatment*. Enviro Press.
2. Arceivala (1973) *Simple Waste Treatment Methods*. Middle East Technical University, Ankara, Turkey.
3. Nemerow (1974) *Scientific Stream Pollution Analysis*. McGraw Hill.
4. Fair *et al.* (1968) *Water and Wastewater Engineering*. John Wiley and Sons.
5. McKee and Wolf (1963) *Water Quality Criteria*. California State Water Resources Control Board.
6. Rabbitt and Baumann (1958) *Sewerage and Sewage Treatment*. 8th edn, John Wiley.
7. Ergüden (1978) *Waste Water Problems of Bursa Organized Industrial District*. Middle East Technical University, Ankara, Turkey.

Impact of Effluent Discharge into Receiving Water: Some Case Studies by the DGRAH — DSCP

António F. Fonseca Janeiro
Chief of the Water Quality and Studies Division of the
Pollution Control Services, DGRAH, Lisbon, Portugal

SYNOPSIS

In this report we try to reveal the procedure and techniques used in Portugal by the Directorate of Pollution Control Services and by the General Direction of the Resources and Hydraulic Improvements, with respect to the evaluation of the pollution loads caused by industrial activities and the pollution effects caused by the discharge of the effluents in the receiving media. We refer, generally, to some works that have been done and to the methodology usually followed and hereby schematically indicated. A report is presented of a concrete sample of this type of work, the case of an industry of cellulose paste Kraft (sulphite), discharging effluents on a site of the Tejo River retained by a dam. In this case, we refer to the characteristics of the receiving media, the selection of the sampling stations, techniques of sampling used, determined parameters, interpretation of the results and the conclusions drawn from these.

RÉSUMÉ

Dans cette communication on se propose de présenter la procedure et les techniques utilisées dans ce pays pour la Direcção des Serviços de Controle de Poluição, de la Direcção-General des Recursos e Aproveitamentos Hidráulicos, dans l'évaluation des charges polluantes produites pour les activités industrielles, et des effets polluants produits pour la décharge de leurs effluents dans le milieu récepteur. On se réfère en general à quelques études qui ont déjà été realisées et on présente schématiquement la mèthodologie normalement suivie. On présente le rapport d'un cas concret de ce type d'étude—cas d'une industrie de cellulose Kraft (au sulfhate) qui décharge ses effluents dans le Tejo, dans une partie de la rivière où les eaux sont retenues par un barrage (avec faible circulation d'eau). Dans ce rapport on se refère aux charactéristiques de l'effluent industrial, aux charactéristiques du milieu récépteur, à la selection des stations d'echantillonage, aux techniques' d'echantillonage utilisées, aux parametres qui ont été determinés, et à l'interpretation des résultats et les conclusions qui eu ont découlé.

RESUMEN

En esta comunicación se pretende divulgar el procedimiento y tecnicas utilizadas en el país—"Direcção de Serviços de Controle de Poluição de Direcção-Geral dos Recursos e Aproveitamentos Hidráulicos"— en la evaluación de las cargas contaminantes producidas por actividades industriales y de los efectos contaminantes provocados por las descargas de los respectivos efluentes en los medios receptores. Se hace referencia en general a algunos trabajos que han sido realizados y se indica esquematicamente la metodologia seguida usualmente. Se presenta el relato de un ejemplo concreto de este tipo de trabajo para el caso de una industria de pasta celulosa Kraft (sulfato) al descargar los vertidos en un embalse del rio Tajo. En este se hace referencia à las características del vertido industrial, características del médio receptor, selección de las estaciones de muestreo, técnicas de muestreo utilizadas, parametros determinados, interpretación de los resultados y conclusiones extraidas de estos.

INTRODUCTION

THE DIRECÇÃO dos Recursos e Aproveitamentos Hidráulicos (DGRAH), through the Pollution Control Services (DSCP), has been working on the appraisal of pollution load transmitted by liquid effluents of various industrial units, and also conducting analytical studies in the receiving waters to appraise the implications to water quality by the introduction of these loads.

Studies of this type have been done in diverse industrial sectors, for example chemical industries, food products, thermal-power generating plants, tanneries, distilleries, fieldlots, mining, pulp, etc. These studies include chemical, physical, biological and bacteriological determinations of the water and sediments and they refer to rivers, natural and artificial lagoons and estuaries.

We are presenting in some detail a recent work concerning a pulp factory by the Kraft method, in which the waste water is discharged into a caudal river and in a damming area. This work follows in some ways the methodology used in other cases.

DESCRIPTION OF THE METHODOLOGY USED

THE METHODOLOGY used in this type of work follows a classic orientation, consisting of the following:

—An analysis of the specific characteristiçs of the polluting agent based on elements collected directly from the industry. The set of elements to be obtained include data regarding the manufacturing process involved, the utilized raw materials, medium production, labouring regime, number of shifts, personnel on duty, sewerage system and type of waste water used by each one of them, quantitative and qualitative variability of the waste water discharged, location of the discharges, treatment existence and its efficiency, etc.

—Sampling programming, both in the waste-water pollutant source and in the receiving waters. In the first case, the type of sampling will accord with the data obtained in the pollutant source. In the second case, those same elements will be accounted for, as well as data regarding the hydro-dynamic conditions of the receiving water. This includes: the definition of the chemical, physical, biological and bacteriological parameters to be determined according to the specific locations; the selection of sampling sites, keeping in mind the information required as essential for the objectives in view, with the minimum expense; the frequency and time of sampling; definition of the type of measures to be done on site and the respective equipment, as well as the methods used in the sampling and its preservation.

—Realization of a trial pre-campaign, including sampling in the sampling stations, whose objective will be to permit contact with local reality which can lead to a readjustment of the sampling programme previously established. This readjustment can lead to a better knowledge of the access conditions at various places and of the representativeness and validity of each sampling, that will help to eliminate some sampling stations previously considered or to increase them if necessary.

—Execution of the working programme definitively established.

GENERIC CHARACTERISTICS OF THE PULPWOOD FACTORY'S WASTE WATER

Generality

The waste water of this type of industry normally has various types of suspended matter (formed essentially by fibre, ashes and clay residuals) and dissolved matter, mainly of organic nature such as carbon hydrate, organic acids and alcohol. Besides these substances, the waste waters also have different quantities of the chemical products used in the various manufacturing processes. The cleaning water forms a residual dark liquid, made of lignine and sodium salts. The residual water, resulting from the vapour condensation proceeding from evaporation of the dark liquid, has an unpleasant smell as a result of the presence of volatile compounds like mercaptan. In addition, we have the waste water originating from the various treatments of the paste and its cleaning, where chemical products are used, such as $NaOH$, Cl_2, ClO_2, SO_2, $NaHClO$. This type of industry discharges great quantities of residual waters containing organic and inorganic substances and presents, therefore, great values of biochemical oxygen demand.

Data on the Industry

This example refers to an important pulp industry located on the right-bank of the Tejo River, near Vila Velha de Rodão, and around 14 kilometers from the beginning of the river in Portuguese territory. The manufacturing process used is the Kraft (sulphide or sodium) process and the medium production expected is 225 tons of pulp per day. Eucalyptus, especially, and pine wood are used. It is a continuous production system of three shifts, each of 8 hours. The quantity of water consumed for the production of 1 ton of pulp is estimated at 139 m^3. The estimated value for the load indicated as BOD_5 (20°C) is 26.6 Kg of O_2 per ton of produced pulp.

The waste-water collection system is separate but the effluents are combined in one outfall to the river. The industry refers to four groups of effluent characterized as follows:

(1) Industrial effluent without fibre, which represents 54 to 55 per cent of the total volume of the effluent, and around 9 percent of the total load indicated as BOD_5.

(2) Industrial effluent with fibre, which represents 42 to 42.5 per cent of the total volume of the effluent, and around 54 per cent of the total load indicated as BOD_5.

(3) Chemical effluent, which represents around 3.5 per cent of the total volume of the effluent and around 37 per cent of the total load indicated as BOD_5.

(4) Sanitary effluent, without great meaning in the total volume of the effluent (less than 0.1 per cent) and in the total load indicated as BOD_5 (less than 0.15 per cent).

The factory has equipment for the primary treatment of some of its effluents, even though it does not correspond with the necessary efficiency. Thus, the 'industrial effluent with fibres' is conducted through a screen to a settling tank with a retention time of 2 hours. The settled fibres from the settling tank are conducted to drying beds and, after being dried, are incinerated. The so-called 'chemical effluent' is conducted to a homogenation tank and then submitted to correction of the pH in a second neutralization tank.

GENERIC CHARACTERISTICS OF THE RECEIVING WATERS

THE LOCATION in the Tejo River where the effluents of the pulp factor are discharged is 18 km upstream of the storage dam of Fratel. We are dealing with a section of the river with weak-water circulation. The area of the dam is $10^7 \, m^2$, with a total capacity of $93 \times 10^6 \, m^3$ and a useful capacity of $20.5 \times 10^6 \, m^3$.

The section of river near the site of the industrial effluent discharge point is shown in Figures 2 and 3. Its average depth at the time of study was around 5 to 6 meters. This section of the river shows a slim narrowing near the bridge, where the bottom is rocky and deeper. Some hundreds of meters downstream, there is a greater narrowing of the river, between a high and steep rock which forms a geomorphologic feature designated as Portas de Rodão, and this is the deepest area. The water level of the dam has great daily variations which are subject to the discharges of the dam and the discharges upstream of the Spanish dam of Cedilho.

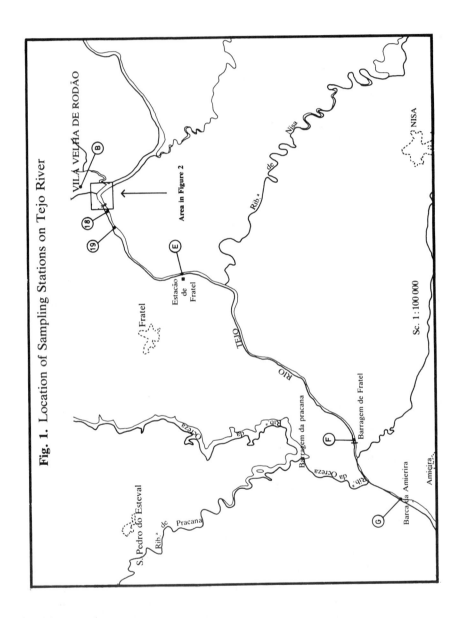

Fig. 1. Location of Sampling Stations on Tejo River

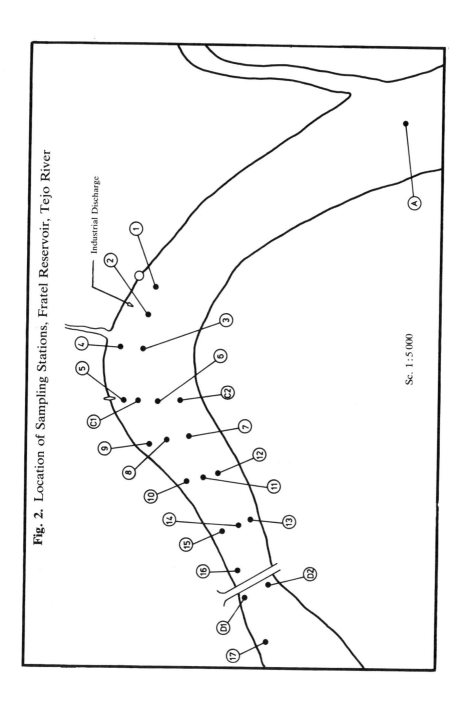

Fig. 2. Location of Sampling Stations, Fratel Reservoir, Tejo River

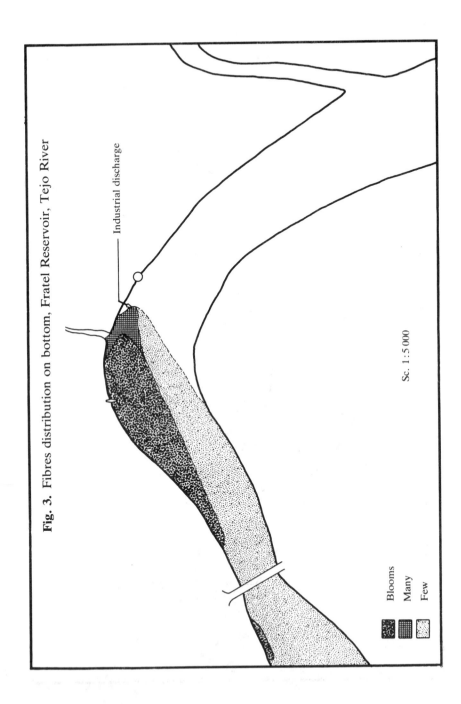

Fig. 3. Fibres distribution on bottom, Fratel Reservoir, Tejo River

SAMPLING

Location of the Sampling Sites

Figures 1 and 2 represent the location of the sampling sites selected for this study. The sampling sites shown by letters A through G are the ones initially chosen. Later on, after a first sampling campaign test, the necessity of increasing the number of sampling sites was recognized, essentially for a better appraisal of the settled fibres on the bottom and their distribution. The sampling sites selected afterwards for this purpose are shown by numbers 1 to 19. All in all, 28 sampling stations were considered. The sampling station identified by the letter B corresponds to the factory's total effluent.

Types of Samples. Methods for Sample Collections and their Preservation

The sampling campaigns were held during the drought period (September and October) for two consecutive years, 1979 and 1980. In choosing this period, we intended to obtain the characterization of the receiving media under the most unfavourable conditions. Each sampling campaign took place weekly. For sampling station B, industrial effluent samples were taken in almost all the sampling campaigns. We took samples from two depths in most of the sampling stations for the characterization of the waters of the receiving media.

For the collections of water samples, Van Dorn samplers were used. We determined on the site the values of the temperature and dissolved oxygen, by means of sounding-leads YSI Model 57—Oxygen Meter, and the value of the pH by means of the sounding-lead Methrohm pH-Meter E 488. Simultaneously, the fixation of the dissolved oxygen was also determined on a sample kept in a glass container. For its determination, we used the Winkler method. Apart from this parameter, the phenol, sulphide and sulphite samples were treated on the site. For the sediment collections, the bottom sampler, Model 404 TSK USE Marukawa was used.

ANALYSED PARAMETERS

Physical-Chemical

The analysis of the samples of the industrial effluent and of the river waters included the following physical-chemical parameters: temperatures; pH; electrical conductivity; settled solids; suspended solids, both fixed and volatile; dissolved solids, both fixed and volatile; alkalinity total; chloride; sulphate; sulphite; sulphide; nitrate; dissolved oxygen; biochemical oxygen demand; chemical oxygen demand; permanganate value; phenols; sodium; magnesium; and calcium.

Biological

The biological method used was the 'saprophite system' which uses the Pantle and Buck formula indicated below:

$$S = \frac{\Sigma h.s}{\Sigma h}$$

in which S = the station's 'sapprobity index', h = the 'abundance class' or 'frequency index' of each species found in the sample and s = the sapprobic 'valency' for each 'indicator' species existing in the sampling station. This system determines four levels of organic contamination, the so-called sapprobian zones, each of which correspond to a degree of organic pollution. Thus we have:

Value of S from 1 to 1.5 — Aligosaprobic Zone — weak organic pollution.
Value of S from 1.5 to 2.5 — β — Mesosaprobic Zone — moderate organic pollution.
Value of S from 2.5 to 3.5 — α — Mesosaprobic Zone — strong organic pollution.
Value of S from 3.5 to 4 — Polisaprobic Zone — very strong organic pollution.

Bottom Sediments

Local observation was made of the appearance and dimension of the elements composing the sediment, abundance, quantity of the fibrous matter, colouring, odour and their respective consistency.
Laboratory observation was made under a magnifying-glass, and to observe weight losses by heating, and resistance of thermic decomposition.

INTERPRETATION OF THE RESULTS OBTAINED

Physical and Chemical Analysis

Temperature: No change in temperature of the river waters was verified downstream of the discharge of the effluent. The temperatures at the various sampling stations did not present any sensitive variations.

pH: The pH value of the factory's effluent presents a minimum of 8.1 and maximum of 9.3. In the sampling stations on the river, sensitive variations of the pH value were not detected.

Electrical conductivity: The values found for the effluent are slightly higher than the values found in the river sampling stations where there was no sensitive variation.

Settled Solids, Suspended Solids and Dissolved Solids: The near absence of decantable solids was verified for the samples of the river water, which was predictable due to the weak circulation of water in the dam, where, as a natural result, settlement takes place. Also, on the effluent samples, the value of the decantable solids was low, with the exception of one of the samples where a higher value was found (20 ml/l). The values of the total dissolved solids found for the samples of river water are not significantly different from the measured values for the samples of the factory's effluent. The values of the total suspended solids of the effluent samples are high (minimum 75 and maximum 1127 mg/l). However, sensitive alteration in the values of the total suspended solids in the water river samples was not verified, owing to the existing great dilution and to a rapid decantment of materials.

Alkalinity: The values measured in the effluent samples are high. There is no variation in the alkalinity of the river water, being constant in all sampling stations.

Chloride, Sulphate, Sulphite, Sulphide: As for the values of chloride and sulphate, no change was noticed in their concentration along the river in each period of sampling. The concentration values of the sulphites, found in the samples of the factory's effluent, oscillated between the maximum value of 14 mg/l and the minimum value of 3 mg/l and the total sulphides, between the maximum value of 5.3 mg/l and the minimum value of 0.5 mg/l. No change was revealed in the concentrations of sulphites and sulphides in the samples from the river water; upstream and downstream, the discharge in the case of the sulphites presented a very low concentration and in the case of the sulphides, nil values; that is to say, a concentration inferior to the sensitivity of the method used.

Dissolved Oxygen, Biochemical Oxygen Demand, Chemical Oxygen Demand and Permanganate Value: The total absence of dissolved oxygen in the industrial effluent and high values for the BOD_5 (minimum 80 and maximum 125 mg/l of O_2), and for the COD (296 mg/l of O_2), were registered. The introduction of the factory's effluent to the river water clearly leads to a reduction in the concentration of dissolved oxygen in the sampling stations immediately downstream of the discharge. An increase of the BOD_5 and of the permanganate value is also noticed in the sampling stations immediately downstream of the discharge, although this increase is not very remarkable, which can be justified by the difficult biodegrability of the effluent.

Phenols: The concentrations of phenols in the factory's effluent are high (maximum value found 810 μg/l). However, the characteristic of instability and of change in the phenolic components, and the great power of the river dilution, make it noticeable only in the sampling stations immediately downstream of the effluent's discharge. This phenolic influence is felt for about 500 meters downstream of the discharge, disappearing afterwards.

Sodium, Magnesium and Calcium: The concentrations of sodium are obviously superior in the effluent but due to the existing great dilution, this value is almost immediately absorbed by the river waters. As for the magnesium and calcium, there was no change with the introduction of the effluent in the river water.

Biological Analysis

Through this type of observation, it is verified that there is an increase of organic pollution in the river zone immediately downstream of the discharge of the factory's effluent. In the sampling stations upstream, the river is in the β-mesosaprobic zone (moderate organic pollution); in the stations downstream near the discharge, the river is essentially in the α-mesosaprobic zone (strong organic pollution). This situation is practically recovered about 500 m downstream of the discharging point, where the river recovers its previous characteristics.

Bottom Sediments

The consistency and abundance of the sediments, as well as the quantity of the existing fibrous materials were variable, depending on the sampling station: abundant sediments composed of mud and black slime exuding a bad odour and with great quantity of fibres; fine sands with an abundance of dark, fibrous materials; bulky sands with small stones and some fibrous materials; fine or bulky sands, with or without stones without fibrous matter.

From the investigations made, the existence of a vast zone of deposition of fibrous matter, originating in the factory's effluent, can be concluded. This zone stretches from near the discharge point to the geomorphological feature of the Portas de Rodão. Most of the fibrous matter deposited was found towards the right bank, between this and the median line of the river. This distribution can be justified by the localization on the right bank of the factory's effluent discharge and by the point configuration of the drainage. We had hoped for a more even distribution of the fibres from the section of the river about 300 meters from this discharge point but this was not the case. This aspect should also be related to the difference in the characteristics of the ground of the river bed between the two banks. Thus, it was verified, and it was foreseen, that in the zones with ground composed of muds and fine sands, there was a greater retention and penetration of fibrous matter; in the zones with ground composed of bulkier sands and stones, the retention of fibres was smaller; and in the rocky and irregular ground, the fibres were hardly retained at all.

The interpretation of these observations should take into account these two aspects (configuration of the drainage and ground characteristics) which can, up to a certain point, justify the existence of few fibres and even their absence in some of the studied zones.

In Figure 3, a symbolic representation of the distribution of fibrous materials in the sediments of the receiving media is presented.

CONCLUSION

THE VALUE of the organic load expressed in BOD_5 of the factory's effluent (4,488 Kg of O_2/day), represents 75 per cent of the value of the organic load estimated from predicted data on the characterization of the effluent. Assuming that these elements are precise, one can conclude that the efficiency of the measures for depuration used by industry is 25 per cent.

From the analytical characterization of the waters in the dam, obtained through the values of the physical and chemical parameters and biological measures, it is verified that the influence of the introduction of the industry's effluents means an increase in the state of pollution of the waters, mainly in the section of the river up to about 500 meters from the discharge. These characteristic alterations, resulting from the introduction of the factory's effluent, are, however, neither constant nor very marked and were not detected in the sampling station E, situated 6 km from the discharge. This is probably due to the fact that there is a great dilution in the receiving medium and also to its regeneration power.

With reference to the bottom sediments, a remarkable influence of the discharge of the factory's effluent was verified, expressed by the formation of sediments of fibrous matter to a considerable extent. This situation is typical of a discharge of this type of effluent in river sites subject to backwater influence by dams, or with a weak-water circulation; the deposition and accumulation of fibres and pieces of biological film, torn out from developing surfaces, is made easy in such a situation. These substances, mixed with the mud, build up a putrescible mud whose decomposition products provoke a secondary pollution of the water.

The fibrous matter accumulated is not easily biodegraded, especially if it contains ligneous material. In the areas where most of it was found, a black decomposing slime was formed, with the inevitable result of anaerobiosis zones, releasing gas with a bad odour, and all the other baneful consequences inherent in such situations. One of the results of this situation, already proved, is that the fish in this dam, where sports fishing and even small-scale commercial fishing is practised, become unpalatable.

Effects on Agricultural Crops of Water Pollution by the Tanning Industry

Margarida C. Barros

Chem. Eng. Head Contamination Division, Direcção Geral de Protecção da Produção Agrícola, Lisbon, Portugal

and

Fátima Rocha

Agron. Eng. Contamination Division, Direcção Geral de Protecção da Produção Agrícola, Lisbon, Portugal

SYNOPSIS

In this paper, an overview of the pollutants discharged by the tanning industry is presented. Considering the impact on agricultural crops resulting from the use of polluted water for irrigation, the most important pollutants are identified and their potential effect reviewed. In Portugal, 401 tanning plants are licensed, 231 of which are located in the district of Santarém, very few if any having any type of treatment. Farmers complained very often on productivity impairment or total losses when using polluted water for irrigation and a study was conducted to determine the extent of damage and the dilution factor for the waste water that could be advised. It is concluded that any irrigation water containing 10 per cent or more of the tanning industry's non-treated effluent will be damaging to horticultural crops.

RÉSUMÉ

Cette communication présente une étude bibliographique des pollutants émis para l'industrie du tannage et l'identification de ceux qui sont les plus nocifs pour l'agriculture, quand l'eau polluée par des rejects est utilisé pour l'arrosage. Au Portugal il y a 401 usines de tannage licenciés, dont 231 sont établies dans le district de Santarém. Les agriculteurs se plaignent des effects produits dans des cultures irriguées et une étude a été conduite pour determiner l'extension des dégâts et, aussi, si un facteur de dilution pouvait être reccomandé. On conclut que des concentrations de 10 per cent ou plus de l'effluent non-traitée dans l'eau d'arrosage sont nocifs pour les cultures.

RESUMEN

Esta comunicación presenta uno estudio bibliográfico de los poluentes emitidos por la industria de curtimienta, y la identificación de aquellos que son más nocivos para la agricultura, cuando el agua contaminada por los vertimientos es utilizada para el riego. En Portugal de 401 fábricas de curtimienta licenciadas y 231 se situam en el districto de Santarém. Los agricultores se quejan de los efectos producidos en los cultivos regados, y uno estudio fué conducido para determinar la extensión de los daños y también si un factor de dilución podria ser recomendado. Se concluyó que concentraciones del 10 por ciento ó mas del efluente no tratado en el agua de irrigación son nocivas para los cultivos.

INTRODUCTION

IN PORTUGAL the tanning industry has been operating for many years, the plants usually being installed in rural areas where agriculture and animal husbandry coexist. While in most developed countries, this highly polluting industry is subject to strict effluent control, in Portugal most, if not all, of the usually small existing plants still discharge liquid wastes directly into rivers, polluting the water needed for irrigation. This fact has been mentioned by all those concerned with agricultural development and, in particular, was frequently referred to in the answers to a questionnaire on pollution problems affecting agricultural productivity, launched in 1980 by the Direcção Geral de Protecção da Produção Agrícola. It was then considered that factual data on the effects of waste water discharged by the tanning industry were necessary as background information for actions to be taken in order to prevent or control irrigation-water pollution. In this paper, we present the studies conducted to assess the impact on several crops of water polluted by the tanning industry, as well as an overview on the polluting characteristics and distribution of this industry in Portugal.

CHARACTERISTICS OF WASTE WATER AND EFFECTS ON AGRICULTURAL CROPS

THE LIQUID EFFLUENTS discharged by the tanning industry have a highly variable composition which depends on the technology employed and the phases of the process performed during the working day [1]. The waste waters are characterized, in particular, by high levels of chromium, sodium chloride, ammonia nitrogen, oil and grease, and detergents, presenting very low dissolved oxygen. Basic information on the environmental characteristics and flow of waste water from the leather-tanning industry has been compiled by the U.S. Environmental Protection Agency on a production basis [2] and is presented in Table 1.

A few examples of analysis of raw effluents from this industry may be found in the open literature, reflecting the above mentioned variability. The biochemical oxygen demand ranges between 400 and 900 mg/l, ammonia nitrogen is reported between 8 and 17 mg/l, chloride between 375 and 977 mg/l, while dissolved oxygen is nil. After Wims [3] the composition of sludge after waste-water treatment contains 7 to 10 per cent of chromium, 4.5–6 per cent of NaCl, as well as calcium (16–18 per cent $CaCO_3$) and iron (2–4 per cent Fe_2O_3). These levels reflect the high concentration of these pollutants in the waste water.

When the potential for deleterious effects from such waste water on agricultural crops is considered, the pollutants of concern are mainly chloride, sodium and chromium which are toxic to plants when certain concentration levels in soil or irrigation water are reached. The presence of oil and grease and the high content of organic matter and suspended solids may also have a negative effect but the toxicities of the former have a greater impact on crops.

Plants are usually more resistant to pollutants in water irrigation than aquatic organisms or other animals and the existence of large farmlands adjacent to polluted rivers is still frequent. In most cases, depressive effects on productivity exist but, being difficult to quantify or to prove definitively, are seldom taken into consideration. The salinity and sodicity soil conditions are most important for horticulture. Ions that contribute to soil salinity include Cl^-, SO_4^{2-}, HCO_3^-, NA^+,

Table 1. Characteristics of raw waste water from leather-tanning industry

Parameter (kg/kkg)	Pulp-Chrome Finish	Save-Chrome Finish	Unhairing Veg-Finish	Finish	Veg or Chrome	Unhairing Chrome Tan
Flow Range (l/kkg)	7M/156M	1M/189M	7M/106M	3M/33M	6M/205M	14M/56M
Flow Type	B	B	B	B	B	B
BOD	5/270	20/140	8/130	7/70	10/140	30/160
TSS	7/600	30/350	20/450	7/130	3/870	40/190
Oil & Grease	0.1/70	0.7/110	0.1/160	2.2/19	0.6/46	1/19
COD	10/600	90/220	25/700	5.5/65	11/270	50/160
Total Nitrogen	3/44	3.5/25	1/25	1/7	0.6/30	14/18
Sulphide	0.1/46	0.1/3	0.1/4	2	4/5	2/6.5
Chromium	0.1/19	0.3/12	0.2/0.6	0.4/5	0.1/2.1	3.8/6
Alkalinity	0.5/300	60/90	4/140	40	6.5/180	35/55

Note: M—thousand

B—batch process

kg/kkg—kilogram pollutant/1000 kilograms of product produced (lower limit/upper limit)

l/kkg—liters of waste water/1000 kilograms of product.

Source: EPA 430/9-76-017c.

Ca^{2+}, Mg^{2+} and rarely NO_3^- or K^+. The salts of these ions will occur in highly variable concentrations most frequently being brought to the soil by irrigation water. Wehrman [4] has suggested critical values for water salinity above which yield depressions may be expected to occur. The more sensitive crops will be affected by 50 mg/l of either Cl^- or Na^+, or 300 mg/l of Cl^-. The simultaneous presence of other ions, such as SO_4^{2-} or other elements like boron or iron, may significantly alter these critical values. The effect of salinity differs with the stages of growth and classifications have been developed for salt tolerance of various horticultural species [5]; the range of sensitivity to salt is from beets, kale, spinach and asparagus, which are the least affected, to beans, celery and radish which are sensitive to very low concentrations. Tomato, cruciferous crops, lettuce, potato and onion are medium-sensitive. Low concentration of salt will impair growth but high levels in irrigation water may cause necrosis, bronzing, premature yellowing, abscission of leaves and other visual symptoms that will strongly reduce the commercial value of the commodity [6]. The most consistent of the general symptoms of excess chloride is reduced leaf size and slower growth rate.

. Plants can absorb Cr from the soil but this element is not considered of nutritional value. High levels of both Cr(III) or Cr(VI) cause toxicity; the soil type having a marked effect on the intensity of the effects. While in solution both oxidation forms are available to plants, in soils only Cr(VI) remains mobile and available. Chromium absorbed by plants remains primarily in the roots, being poorly translocated to the leaves [7]. Accumulated in the roots, Cr(VI) will interfere with the uptake and translocation of essential elements, this being the most important toxic action. Levels of 8 and 16 ppm of chromium as chromic ion or chromate ion respectively, produced ion chlorosis on sugar beets [8]. The same author also reported growth reduction of 50 to 90 per cent on tomatoes, potatoes, oats and kale when the concentration of chromate ion was 16 ppm. Several other studies report the same range of concentrations for a toxic effect. Another aspect needs to be considered: chromium is toxic to many important solid micro-organisms, thus interfering with the essential soil process. Again the oxidation form, the type of soil and other elements will determine the severity of the effect [9]. An example of such interference has been studied by Liang and Tabatabay [10] who determined the inhibition of mineral nitrogen production by Cr(III) in acid soils at the levels tested.

NOTE ON THE TANNING INDUSTRY IN PORTUGAL

A TOTAL OF 401 tanning industries are licensed in Portugal, 231 of them being located in the district of Santarém. The number of plants per district is included in Figure 1. The highest density of these plants is found near the River Alviela, which receives discharges from several of them. Analysis of this river water has been done several times always showing the high level of pollution [11]. The agricul-

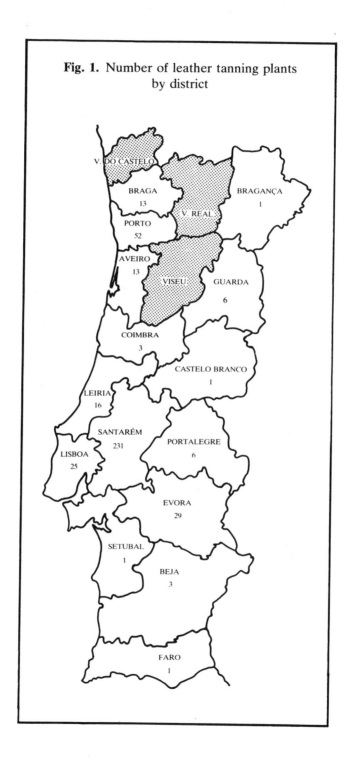

Fig. 1. Number of leather tanning plants by district

tural crops prevailing in the most important area of Santarém are horticultural, in particular, tomato, cabbage and melon. To these crops are often associated small orchards, vineyards and grassland. The situation at present is such that the fields have either been abandoned or well-water is used for irrigation. Complaints from farmers are received from other areas of the country and water pollution by the tanning industry was referred to as one of the most important pollution problems affecting agricultural productivity in the answers to a nation-wide survey [12].

RESULTS OF CONTROLLED TRIALS FOR EFFECTS ON HORTICULTURAL CROPS

THE EFFECTS of the actual load of pollutants in waste water for each of the six modalities chosen: pure waste water, dilutions of 75, 50, 25 and 10 per cent, and non-polluted water. Effects on germination and development were to be studied. The waste water was collected once a week from one of the larger plants in the region of Santarém and results of the analysis of the 5 samples are presented in Table 2.

The crops chosen were cabbage, tomato and melon. For all the species, 10 seeds were sown in 'jiffy-pots', containing a standard soil, and were watered daily with the several dilutions of the effluent and with clean water. The number of seeds germinated was counted every day for two weeks. The results were statistically compared. In those pots where germination occurred, two plants were left and watering continued with the same dilution of the effluent. The study was terminated one month later.

Germination of all crops was inhibited by effluent concentrations of 100 or 75 per cent. With the 50 per cent dilution, only 2 out of 10 seeds of cabbage germinated and none of the tomato or melon. At the level of 25% of the effluent, 5 of the cabbage seeds germinated but only 2 of melon and none of tomato. The 10% level had no effect on the melon seeds which developed as well as the

Table 2. Results of the analysis of waste water

Parameter	Sample				
	1	2	3	4	5
Chromium (Cr mg/l)	2.3	8.0	10.7	15.0	10.0
Sodium (Na mg/l)	11000	770	4000	940	3200
Chloride (Cl⁻ mg/l)	12135	1349	4615	2059	4083
Salinity (‰)	46.55	2.79	10.52	3.16	8.52

controls, but for cabbage a lower number still was counted and tomato germination was very low. In all cases where at least two plants were growing the observations continued for one month more, using the same dilutions of the waste water for irrigation. In fact, this only happened for the 10 per cent dilution. At this level of dilution the plants developed but never attained the same growth rate as the control.

CONCLUSION

THE HIGHLY DAMAGING effect of water containing effluents from the tanning industry is well demonstrated and the most important pollutant is probably the high salt content. In fact, the mean sodium and chlorine concentration were respectively 3982 mg/l and 5048 mg/l which, even at a 10% dilution are well above any critical value reported in the literature. Chromium was at a mean concentration of 9.2 which is slightly lower than the threshold value for toxicity. Since the dilution of 10 per cent still produced a lower germination rate, the dilution factor for the tanning waste water will have to be higher than 10 per cent if productivity of crops is to be maintained at normal values.

The long-term effect on growth and development of the plants could not be assessed in view of the low germination rate but it is expected that further investigations will be conducted.

ACKNOWLEDGEMENTS

The authors wish to express their thanks to Ms. M. Valente, from Direcção de Serviços de Controle de Poluição for the analysis of pollutants in the waste water and to Mr. J. Biscaia from the Instituto Hidrográfico for the determination of the salinity.

References

1. Meinck, F., Stooff, H. and Kohlshutter, H. (1977) *Les eaux residuaires industrielles.* (Transl. by A. Gasser) Masson, Paris.
2. Anderson, F.W., Anderson, P.W., Dunstan, W.M., Falk, L.L., Kerrigan, J.E., Rose, C.D. and Tollefson, R. (1979). In E. Goldberg, ed. *Proceedings of a Workshop on Assimilative Capacity of U.S. Coastal Waters for Pollutions.* December 1979, CO, U.S.A.
3. Wims, F.J. (1965) *Treatment of chrome-tanning wastes for acceptance by an activated sludge plant.* Proc. 18th Industr. Waste Conf., Purdue Univ. Engng. Ext. Series no. 115, 534–549.
4. Wehrman, J. (1974) *Polluted water problems in horticulture.* Proc. XIX Int. Hort. Congr.: 73–82.
5. Hayward, H.E. and Bernstein, L. (1958) *Plant-growth relationships on salt affected soils.* Bot. Rev. 24: 584–635.
6. Bernstein, L. (1975) *Effects of salinity and sodicity on plant growth.* Annu. Rev. Phytopathology 13: 295–312.
7. Huffman, E.W.D., and Allaway, W.H. (1953) *Chromium in plants: distribution tissues, organelles, and extracts, and availability of bean leaf Cr to animals.* J. Agric. Food Chem. 21: 982–986.
8. Hewitt, E.J. (1953) *Metal interrelationships in plant nutrition I. Effects of some metal toxicities in sugar beet, tomato, oat, potato and marrowstem kale grown in sand culture.* J. Exp. Bot. 4: 59–64.
9. Fujihara, M.P., Garland, T.R., Wildung, R.E. and Drucker, H. (1973) *Response of heavy metals in soil.* Ann. Meeting Am. Soc. Microbiol. 73: 32.
10. Liang, C.N. and Tabatabay, M.A. (1973) *Effects of trace elements on nitrogen mineralization in soils.* Environ. Pollut. 12: 141–147.
11. Valente, M. (1981) Private communication.
12. Barros, M.C. and Rocha, F. (1981) *A survey on pollution problems affecting agriculture in Portugal*—to be published.

Means of Improving Environmental Standards in the Tanning Industry with Guidelines for Developing Countries

Jack B. Carmichael
Industrial Development Officer, Division for Industrial Studies, United Nations Industrial Development Organization, Vienna, Austria

SYNOPSIS

This paper presents an overview of environmental problems in the tanning industry and alternative means for their effective management. The effluent characteristics of waste waters from the tanning industry are described. This paper also explains means of reducing water pollution through recycling, effluent treatment and proper disposal of sludge and other solid wastes. Effective primary treatment can reduce effluent BOD (Biochemical oxygen demand) from 1,000–1,500 mg/l to 600–900 mg/l. Subsequent treatment by means of a two-stage, lagoon system can produce a satisfactory final effluent with a BOD in the range of 20–30 mg/l. In urban areas, a municipal treatment plant can be designed to treat mixed tannery and municipal effluents. A Japanese example is discussed of an oxygen-activated sludge plant which treats equal volumes of tannery and municipal effluents and achieves a final BOD of less than 20 mg/l. Effective effluent treatment costs about two to three per cent of the finished leather-selling price. However, this is partly offset by cost savings greater than one per cent of the finished leather price achieved through recycling of solutions. Pollution regulations in developed countries are discussed and the Austrian regulations are presented in detail. Guidelines are proposed for regulating effluent discharges in developing countries. Based upon UNIDO experience, one case study is presented for a developing country in Africa and another on a developed country in eastern Europe.

RÉSUMÉ

Cette contribution présente une vue générale des problèmes de l'environnement tels qu'ils se posent dans l'industrie de la tannerie et propose diverses mesures visant à maitriser ces problèmes. On y décrit les caractéristiques des eaux usées par l'industrie de la tannerie et l'on explique les moyens de réduire la pollution de l'eau par recyclage, traitement des effluents et évacuation des boues et autres déchets solides. Un traitement efficace peut réduire l'effluent DOB (demande d'oxygène biochimique) de 1000–1500 mg./l. à 600–900 mg./l. Un traitement subséquent par le moyen du système lagon à deux étapes peut donner lieu au résultat considéré comme satisfaisant d'un effluent terminal dont le DOB est d'environ 20–30 mg./l. Dans les zones urbaines les usines municipales de traitement peuvent être conçues pour traiter les effluents provenant à la fois de la tannerie et de la voirie municipale. On discute un exemple japonais d'une unité de traitement des boues activée à l'oxygène qui traite des volumes égaux d'effluents de tannerie et de voirie et qui atteint une DOB de moins de 20 mg./l. Un traitement efficace des effluents coûte de 2 à 3 pourcent du prix de vente du cuir fini. Ce coût est cependant couvert en partie par des économies, s'élevant à plus d'un pourcent du prix du cuir fini, obtenues par le recyclage des solutions. Les règlements concernant la pollution dans les pays développés sont discutés et les règlements autrichiens sont présentés en détail. Des lignes de conduite pour réglementer l'émission d'effluents dans les pays en développement sont proposées. Des études de cas, basées sur l'expérience de l'Onudi, sont présentées pour un pays en développement d'Afrique et pour un pays développé de l'Europe de l'Est.

RESUMEN

Este documento presenta una revisión general sobre los problemas del medio ambiente en la industria del cuero y medios efectivos para combatirlos. Se describen las características de los efluentes líquidos de la industria del cuero. Este documento también explica cómo reducir la contaminación del agua por medio del reciclado, de tratamiento de efluentes y la manera adecuada para deshacerse de fango y otros deshechos sólidos. Un tratamiento primario eficaz puede reducir la demanda bioquímica de oxígeno (DBO) del efluente desde 1000–1500 mg/l hasta 600–900 mg/l. Un tratamiento posterior por medio de un sistema laguna a dos etapas puede producir un efluente final satisfactorio con un DBO entre 20 y 30 mg/l. Un tratamiento efectivo de deshechos cuesta alrededor del 2 al 3 por ciento del precio de venta del cuero. Se demuestra que ahorros en el costo por medio del reciclado pueden llegar a mas del uno por ciento del precio de venta del cuero. Se discute la legislación en países en vías de desarrollo sobre polución y se describe en detalle la legislación austríaca. Se proponen pautas para la regulación de la descarga de deshechos en países en vías de desarrollo. Se presentan estudios de casos preparados por la ONUDI en un país en desarrollo del Africa y en un país desarrollado de Europa Oriental.

ENVIRONMENTAL ASSESSMENT

Environmental problems resulting from the leather industry: General Considerations

Pollution problems from the leather industry arise from tanned and untanned solid waste, waste waters (as well as the sludge separated therefrom), and some air pollutants. This paper will concentrate on means of reducing water pollution through recycling effluent treatment and proper sludge disposal.

Waste waters: The composition of the liquid effluent from leather factories is very complex and depends upon the manufacturing procedure used in the particular factory concerned and on the starting materials. The particular characteristics of effluent from leather factories which start with the green, or fresh, hides are sulfides (from the liming), high alkalinity, a high concentration of dissolved organic compounds (mainly partially decomposed protein from the liming and bating processes, but also unbound tanning materials, dyestuffs and fat-liquoring oils); in the case of chrome-leather factories, chromium (III) compounds.

The effluent also contains certain amounts of organic and inorganic suspended solids. These form as a result of co-precipitation when the effluents from the various processing stages are mixed.

In Europe, official regulations, which vary from country to country, generally require that before any effluent is discharged into public waters (rivers, lakes, the sea), it must be purified sufficiently to ensure that there is no risk of major disturbances to the biological equilibrium or damage to the public health. Where effluents are to be treated in public waste-water treatment plants, any constituents which might impair the functioning of these plants must first be removed prior to discharge of the effluents into the public sewers. Often a charge is levied by the public authority. This charge is typically assessed according to both the strength and volume of the waste water discharged.

Solid waste: Solid wastes from the leather industry include cuttings of untanned hides with hair, cuttings of limed untanned hides without hair and leather shavings, as well as splits and cuttings, both chrome-tanned and vegetable-tanned. Within Europe the practice is to send some of the untanned waste to hide, glue and gelatine factories for further processing and also to carcass-disposal plants. Sometimes it is disposed in special dumps, in which each day's wastes are covered with a layer of earth (sanitary land fill). Chrome-tanned and vegetable-tanned wastes can be used for making leather-board or disposed in sanitary land fills.

A more detailed description of wastes which arise in different processing operations [1]

Beam-house wastes: The beam-house processes are designed to prepare green, or fresh, hides for tanning. Operations are designed to remove undesirable impurities and leave the collagen receptive to absorb vegetable tannins or chrome.

(a) Washing and soaking: Hides arrive as green, dry, wet-salted or dry-salted (dried after salting). First they are washed to remove dirt, dung and blood. Next these hides are soaked in cold water to remove salt and soften. Dirt, hair, dung, blood and salt are the pollutants.

(b) Green fleshing: Muscle and fatty tissue are cut away with revolving knives during this process. Suspended particles are the main pollutants.

(c) Liming: Hides are placed in vats containing approximately 10 per cent lime based on hide weight. Liming swells the skin and loosens the hair. Some accelerators are added, such as sodium sulphide. A high alkalinity (lime) waste is produced in small volumes; sulphides are present in the waste.

(d) Unhairing: Hair is cut away via rollers with knives. Hair is collected on screens. Hair, suspended particles from the epidermal layer and lime are the main pollutants.

(e) Lime fleshing: This is a mechanical process to remove any flesh and fatty tissue which remains after liming.

(f) Splitting: The hide is split through the middle of its thickness to produce grain and flesh side layers.

(g) Bating: An enzyme, ammonium sulphate, solution is used to remove excess lime from the hides. Small amounts of organic matter and lime are the pollutants.

Tan-yard wastes:

(a) Vegetable-tanning: Tannins from certain tree barks, woods and leaves are used. A small volume of waste is generated but this is highly coloured and heavily concentrated in organic matter.

(b) Chrome-tanning: Hides are first pickled in a solution of sulphuric acid and salt. Tanning is carried out in vats with solutions containing chrome-tanning materials, to which usually alkaline basifying agents are added. The resultant leather is termed 'wet blue' after its characteristic blue colour at this stage. Waste water contains chromium ions and salts.

New chrome-tanning processes have been developed at the Bayer AG firm in Germany [2] which allow much more efficient utilization of the chrome-tanning material. Hence, there is less chrome which reaches the effluent. In these processes, the addition of chrome oxide is kept low. The tannage begins with conventional chrome-tanning materials with 33 per cent basicity and is completed with self-basifying tanning material together with dicarboxylic acids or their salts. In the ordinary process there remains 8–10 g Cr/l; in the new process only 1 g/l is present.

(c) (i) Retanning: With chrome salts, synthetic tanning chemicals or vegetable tanning. Low percentages of chemicals. Mainly taken up by leather.

(ii) Dyeing: Carried out in drums with synthetic and natural dyes. Unbound dyestuffs are the pollutants from this process.

(iii) Fat liquoring: Skins are tumbled in drums containing emulsions of oils (linseed, castor, etc.)—emulsified oils are the main pollutants. Following this step, the leather is dried and the product is termed 'crust leather'.

Composition of mixed effluent from the tannery

The effluents resulting from the manufacture of side leather in central European tanneries, with a water consumption of 40–50 liters/kg raw hide, has the average composition [3], shown in Table 1.

Table 1. Average Effluent Composition

Chrome (III)	100 mg Cr/l*
Chrome (VI)	0 mg Cr/l
SO_4^-	1,500 mg/l
NaCl	4,000 mg/l
Sulphide(S^{--})	150–200 mg/l
BOD[a]	1,000–1,500 mg/l
COD[b]	3,000–4,500 mg/l
Suspended solids	2,000–3,000 mg/l

Following catalytic oxidation of the sulphide in the hair-burn effluent and separation of the primary sludge of the mixed effluent by sedimentation, the composition of the effluent is approximately as follows [3]:

BOD	600–900 mg/l
COD	2,000–2,700 mg/l
Suspended solids	400–600 mg/l
Chrome (III)	10–20 mg/l

*Without previous Cr separation; with previous Cr separation approximately 40 mg Cr/l.

[a]BOD represents the biochemical oxygen demand of the waste measured at 20°C after 5 days.

[b]COD represents the chemical oxygen demand of the waste as measured by amount of material oxidizable by a strong oxidizing agent.

ENVIRONMENTAL MANAGEMENT

Effluent problems

Recycling operations in a tannery may be carried out (a) to utilize excess chemicals from a process, which would otherwise have to be discharged to effluent, and (b) to specifically reduce the pollution load of the effluent. Another benefit of recycling operations will be to save water. The processes of soaking, unhairing, pickling and tanning lend themselves to recycling [4].

Sulphide from the liming process: The best approach is to eliminate the sulphide from the alkaline liming liquors before these liquors are mixed with the rest of the effluent. The most common and technologically simplest method is oxidation with air, utilizing 200 g/m³ manganese(II) sulphate [3].

Hair-burn effluent: The effluent from the unhairing can be collected in a storage tank and then pumped through an Idronova vertical settling tower. The sludge is removed daily for disposal and the supernatant liquor is collected for reuse. Only the necessary chemicals required to bring the waste up to strength are added [5].

Suspended solids can also be removed from commercial unhairing effluents by a continuous flow apparatus when appropriate fluocculents are used (synthetic organic polyelectrolytes of high molecular weight). Addition of concentrations as low as 3 mg/l of flocculent resulted in a reduction in suspended solids of 86.5 per cent [6].

Chromium tannery waste: All waste waters from the chromium-tanning process, including wringer pressings, can be pumped through a hydrosieve to remove suspended particles. These waste waters can then be re-used as pre-tanning liquors in the pickling process. This requires the use of dry salt, rather than brine, in order to reduce the volumes.

Alternatively, the concentration of chromium(III) ions can be considerably reduced by precipitating the chromium through addition of alkalis. The precipitated chromium hydroxide can be filtered out, redissolved in acid and used again in the next tanning batch. The process requires careful analytical supervision [5].

Incineration of chrome-bearing sludge can be carried out with concurrent recovery of the waste heat and recovery of the chromium. The incineration of the sludge under alkaline conditions will produce a chrome-bearing ash. The chrome can then be recovered as a bichromate solution which is subsequently processed to produce a one-bath chrome-tanning agent for reuse in the tanning process [7].

Treatment of the mixed effluent: If the practices of sulphide oxidation and chromium precipitation have been followed, the resultant effluents can be mixed with those from the tanning, dyeing and fat-liquoring processes to form an overall plant mixed effluent. After this effluent is allowed to undergo primary sedimentation and the sludge is separated for separate disposal, the resultant effluent is generally suitable for secondary treatment, utilizing biological purification plants. In the case of a tannery operating in an urban area with little available space, the treatment may be via an activated sludge plant or the effluent may be discharged to a municipal treatment plant. For the case of a tannery in an area with much land available, for example a rural area of a developing country, the preferred method of treatment may be ponds or an oxidation ditch [3].

The economics of pollution control through recycling

The savings which can be obtained by recycling the liming and chrome liquors can reach US$18 (1974 dollars) per ton of hides, according to Centre Technique du Cuir. This represents approximately one per cent of the price of the finished leather. In the case of the application of these recycling measures in a French tannery, an additional US$4.5 credit would be obtained from the reduced amount of pollution taxes required to be paid by the firm for effluent discharges [12].

Effluent treatment in rural areas

A three-lagoon system is suggested. Waste water first enters lagoon A which serves as a primary stage. This lagoon will tend to operate under anaerobic conditions because of the high oxygen demand of the waste. Sastry [8] has reported that reductions in effluent BOD from 1,600 mg/l to 250 mg/l can be achieved in India with a 10-day retention time. The effluent from the primary lagoon then enters a secondary lagoon, or an oxidation ditch, for further biological treatment under aerobic conditions. In either case, another lagoon should be available to receive waste waters when lagoon A must be closed down in order to remove accumulated sludge. In the case of an oxidation ditch, residence time is usually two to three days, and the effluent is circulated and aerated by means of rotating steel brushes [8].

A study in Holland showed treatment of an incoming effluent of BOD from 500–1,500 mg/l resulted in removals of 98 per cent of BOD and 88 per cent of COD [9].

Effluent treatment in urban areas

In Japan a treatment plant, which will treat 28,000 m³/d of tannery waste water from over 300 small tanneries and 28,000 m³/d of municipal waste water, will be established using an oxygen-activated sludge process [10]. The tannery waste waters receive pretreatment prior to entering the joint waste-water treatment plants (range of s.s. following pretreatment: 200–550 mg/l; of BOD: 200–500 mg/l). The oxygen-activated sludge process was chosen because: (i) not enough area is available for trickling filters or aerated lagoons, (ii) a large-scale source of oxygen will be available near by, (iii) odour control is easiest with compact facilities. This was considered necessary because of expected residential development near the plant. Pilot plant data were obtained which allowed establishment of design criteria and operational conditions for the plant to yield an effluent of BOD ≤ 20 mg/l.

Costs of effluent treatment

Detailed cost analysis of alternative effluent treatment procedures have been presented in a recent publication covering environmental practices in the EEC countries [9]. Effluent treatment, incorporating sulphide removal, primary sedimentation and pH adjustment, was reported to cost $0.016/sq. ft. in 1977 or 2.1 per cent of the leather selling price. Effluent treatment, incorporating primary sedimentation, chromium recovery and biological oxidation, is reported to cost $0.025 sq. ft. or 3.2 per cent of the leather-selling price. Calculation of effluent-treatment costs for both of the above processes includes a straight line, 20 per cent annual capital depreciation charge.

Pollution regulations for discharges into public waterways

Each country must decide, in the context of its own development planning, the nature of the pollution-control regulations best suited to allow continued industrial development, while at the same time to provide safeguards for the health of its citizens and to protect the natural environment. It is recommended therefore that the ministries concerned, such as those of industry, health or development, should draw up the relevant regulations, referring as necessary to the experience of other countries [11]. A twelve-country summary of permissible upper limits for discharges of tannery effluents into public sewers (with subsequent municipal treatment) or surface waters, can be found in Tables 30 and 31 of *Tannerie et Pollution* [12] — see also Appendix A of this paper.

Guidelines for effluent discharges from new tanneries in developing countries [13]

Summary: New tanneries should pretreat effluents to remove a portion of suspended solids and BOD, as well as remove specific pollutants, particularly chromium and sulphide ions. If there is a possibility of treating effluents in a municipal treatment plant, then the tannery may carry out primary treatment only and subsequent treatment can be carried out by the municipal treatment plant. This will allow, in general, less expensive overall treatment because of economies of scale.

Proposed design of new tanneries: All new tanneries in developing countries should be designed with segregated flows in order to allow: (a) Removal of chrome from effluent and sludge. Chrome-recycling can then be practised; (b) Removal of sulphides from effluent and sludge. The sulphide content of composite plant effluents should be below 20 ppm.

All new tanneries should have sludge-drying beds and well-designed means of sludge disposal in order to avoid pollution of ground water and air pollution.

Additional guidelines for new tanneries which intend to discharge effluents directly to surface waterways: Tanneries intending to discharge to surface waterways should carry out additional treatment of effluents over that required for discharge of effluents to municipal treatment plants. The minimum standard for a tannery discharging to a larger river should be 75 per cent reduction of suspended solids and 50 per cent reduction of BOD. The efficiency of effluent treatment should be increased whenever the river flow is small. When a tannery is discharging to a small stream, complete effluent treatment may be required to yield effluent with BOD less than 20 ppm and suspended solids less than 30 ppm. Firms wishing to establish tanneries on small streams should recognize that this practice is inherently unsound unless stringent environmental standards are maintained. Under these conditions, the firms must be prepared to bear the additional financial burden of complete effluent treatment in order to ensure that the community does not suffer from completely degraded water resources.

Guidelines for existing tanneries

In general, existing tanneries without effluent treatment (a) should be given three years to install primary sedimentation to reduce BOD and suspended solids, and (b) should be given six years to remove chrome and sulphide from the effluent and to further reduce the load of suspended solids and BOD if the tannery is discharging to a surface water without adequate dilution.

CASE STUDY: COUNTRY X

PRESENTLY, one million hides are produced annually in Country X, a developing country in Africa. The indigenous tannery industry processes only 30 per cent of these. The remaining hides are exported raw. In addition, 5 million each of goatskins and sheepskins are produced. About 40% of these are processed by the indigenous tanning industry.

Serious environmental problems are already present along certain rivers which receive tannery wastes. If Country X establishes facilities to process all hides produced within the country, a serious increase in environmental damage could result unless sound, waste-management practices (in-plant waste reductions, recycling practices, plus effluent treatment) are adopted.

Tannery A is located just outside the capital city of Country X. Untreated liquid effluents are discharged into the River E adjacent to the tannery. A portion of the solid wastes generated by the tannery is buried. The remainder is also disposed into the river.

Tannery B is also located near the capital along the River E. This tannery, however, disposes of no solid waste to the river and only treated liquid effluent. All solid wastes are buried on the company grounds. Liquid effluents are treated by means of screening, settling for 24 hours, coagulation followed by further settling, pH adjustment, final filtration through a clinker bed and chlorination.

River E is badly polluted for 2 to 3 kilometres downstream from Tannery A due to that firm's poor environmental practice. The river waters are used by the inhabitants for laundry and as a source of drinking water for cattle. If all tanneries in Country X followed the practice of Tannery B, the pollution load on the nation's rivers would be substantially reduced at relatively little cost. Planning ahead to reduce pollution from existing and future tanneries is recommended for Country X as the government moves to implement the overall goal of industrial expansion recommended in the Lima Declaration. If this practice is not followed, the social costs concomitant with an order of magnitude increase in river pollution could offset many of the economic benefits of industrial expansion in the leather industry as Country X strives to improve the quality of life for its citizens.

CASE STUDY: COUNTRY Y

A LARGE INDUSTRIAL complex in Country Y, a developed country in eastern Europe, presently consumes 150 tons of raw hides per day and produces 460 million dm^2 per year of upper shoe-leather and some sole-leather. From this upper shoe-leather, approximately 45 million pairs of shoes per year are manufactured. Another factory in the complex produces various leather-treatment chemicals.

In the case of the shoe-leather production portion of the complex, 13 per cent of the capital costs are invested in environmental pollution control. The 13 per cent is divided among 8 per cent for effluent treatment and 5 per cent for air-pollution control. The air-pollution control costs represent both in-plant control for workers' health and safety and external air-pollution control. The 8 per cent expended for effluent treatment represents mostly costs expended for a mechanical, or primary, effluent treatment plant. Included in the 8 per cent were costs of installation of an entirely new sewer system. This was required because the old sewer system dated before World War II. The present mechanical plant removes nearly all suspended solids and about 40 per cent of the BOD from the tannery effluent.

Over the next five to ten years, a biological treatment plant will be added to the treatment process. Therefore, the percentage capital cost for effluent treatment will be higher. Costs will include the installation of an activated sludge plant and the rechannelling of industrial water piping. Experience for the full-scale, activated-sludge, effluent treatment plant is already being obtained through a pilot plant activated-sludge unit presently operating at the site of the mechanical plant.

The sludge from the present mechanical treatment plant is dried in sludge beds near the plant. The odour of the sludge bed in summer is eliminated by treating the surface of the sludge field with either $Ca(OH)_2$ or fly ash. The fly ash is obtained from the air-pollution control cyclones of the coal-burning electricity plant.

Insofar as possible, solid wastes generated in the leather-producing process are utilized. About 50 per cent of the proteins from the raw hides end up as solid waste. Solid wastes are also produced from cutting and the splitting operations, as well as from the tanning operations. This industrial complex manages to utilize about 80 per cent of all solid wastes. The experience in this complex in dealing with solid wastes is summarized below:

    (i) Solids from the liming process are processed for glue and gelatine (an export item), glutin hydrolyzate (a fodder for animal feed) and recovery of fat (further processed for making soap and other items);

(ii) The split leather is used for making sausage skins which are then exported to western Europe;

(iii) Scrapings after chrome-tanning are either used with cuttings for preparing a leather board or combined with solids from the liming process to make the glutin hydrolyzate;

(iv) In the case of pig skins, dehairing is carried out utilizing special enzymes. The hair is then collected and processed for use in brushes. This also represents a good export item.

The tannery sludge is dried and utilized for soil-conditioning on agricultural land. The sludge contains 1.5–3.0% chromium. Of particular interest is the study carried out on uptake of chromium in the sludge by agricultural plants. The conditions are as follows: fertilizing is carried out once every four years, using 30 to 50 tons of dried sludge per hectare. The resultant chromium content in the soil is increased from 10 ppm (background) to 150 ppm as a result of sludge addition. The generally accepted upper limit of chromium content for soils in Europe is 400 to 1,000 ppm. An analysis has been carried out of chromium content in different plants. The reader should note that the chromium concentration in plants depends on when the sample was taken and on the type of the plant. Furthermore, the chromium concentration will not be identical in all parts of the plant. Based upon chromium analysis in crops grown on sludge-fertilized soils, the lower chromium contents were found in potato bulbs (1.7–2.3 ppm), turnip roots (1.0–1.4 ppm) and tomato fruits (0.1–1.0 ppm). Higher chromium contents were determined to occur in the leaves (2.5–13 ppm).

In a Canadian study, varying amounts of chrome-leather shavings, tannery sludge and/or chrome from tanning liquors were added to soils in which geranium and rhubarb were grown. Large amounts of chromium(III) in the soil did not accumulate in the plant nor did they cause permanently retarded growth. Addition of 2,000 kg of chromium(III)/hectare (nine times that permitted on agriculture lands in Ontario Canada) did not increase the chromium content of geraniums after 6 months of growth. Growth was initially retarded but returned to normal rates [15].

Appendix A

Recent Austrian legislation governing discharges from tanneries into sewers and rivers is summarized in the following table [14]:

Parameter	Allowable concentration, discharge into	
	River	Sewer
Settleable solids	0.3 mg/l	10.0 mg/l
pH	6.5–9	6.5–10
COD	≥ 80% removal	—
BOD	{ ≥ 90% removal; 60.0 mg/l	—
Al	10.0 mg/l	—
As	0.1 mg/l	0.1 mg/l
Fe	2.0 mg/l	—
Cr(III)	4.0 mg/l	40.0 mg/l
Cr(VI)	0.5 mg/l	0.5 mg/l
Sulphide	1.0 mg/l	5.0 mg/l
Fats + oils	20.0 mg/l	100.0 mg/l
Formaldehyde	0.5 mg/l	0.1 mg/l

References

1. Bhaskaran, Dr. T.R. Guidelines for the control of industrial wastes, 7. Tannery Wastes. Publication WHO/WD/73.14 of the World Health Organization, Geneva, Switzerland, 1973.
2. Luck, W. J. Amer. Leather Chem. Assoc. 75, pp. 378–388 (1980).
3. Bayer AG. Tanning, dyeing, finishing. Publication GK 765e, April 1977.
4. Slabbert, N.P. J. Soc. Leather Techn. Chem. 64, pp. 89–92 (1980).
5. Agoos, J.E. An approach to tannery effluent control in The Leather Manufacturer, pp. 38–39, September 1977.
6. Bitcover, E.H., J.E. Cooper and D.G. Bailey. Journal American Leather Chem. Association 75, pp. 108–118 (1980).
7. Cartier, J.E. Journal Am. Leather Chem. Association 75, pp. 322–330 (1980).
8. UNIDO. Environmental Considerations in the Leather Producing Industry Vol. II, Ref. 96, Nr. UNIDO/ITD/337/Rev. 1, 1977.
9. EEC Environmental Impacts and Policies for the EEC Tanning Industry. Prepared by Urwick Technology Management Ltd., 1977.
10. Kashiwaya, M. and K. Yoshimoto. J. Water Poll. Control. Fed. 52, pp. 999–1007 (1980).
11. World Bank. Environmental, Health and Human Ecologic Considerations in Economic Development Projects May 1974.
12. Aloy, M., Folachier A. and Vulliermet, B. Tannerie et Pollution. Centre Technique du Cuir, Lyon, France, 1976.
13. Winters, D. (1981) Private communication.
14. Gauglhofer et al. Journal Soc. Leather Techn. Chem. 64, pp. 109–120 (1980).
15. Shivas, S.A. J. Am. Leather Chem. Assoc. 75, pp. 288–298 (1980).

The Discharge of Industrial Effluents to the Public Sewer

John M. Sidwick
Associate, Watson Hawksley High Wycombe, UK and
Director, Environmental Resources Ltd., London, UK

SYNOPSIS

The paper summarises the British legislative background to the control of industrial effluent discharges to the public sewer and gives guidelines for industrial effluent control and general conditions for discharge. The basis of charging for the reception and treatment of industrial effluents is discussed and an example is given of a method of calculating charges. The possible need for industrial effluent pretreatment and the importance of minimising effluent loads are also discussed. The paper concludes with the application of control measures, emphasising the author's belief that each problem should be considered in context and that the controlling authority should exercise flexibility and pragmatism.

RÉSUMÉ

Cet article résume la legislation britannique apliquée aux décharges d'effluents industriels pour les réseaux d'eaux usées doméstiques, et donne le procedé general pour le control des effluents industriels et des conditions des décharges. Les taxes pour la réception et traite-

ment des effluents industriels ont discutées et on examplifie une méthode pour le calcul des taxes. La possibilité de pré-traitements pour les effluents industriels et l'importance de minimiser les charges des effluents sont aussi discutées. Cet article conclue avec l'application des mesures de contrôle en relevant l'opinion de l'auteur que chaque probléme doit être étudié dans son ensemble et que le contrôle des autorités doit être flexible et pragmatique.

RESUMEN

El estudio resume el fondo legislativo britanico del control de descargas de aguas residuales industriales por el alcantarillado público y ofrece líneas para el control de residuos industriales y condiciones generales de descarga. Se discute la base de aplicación de tasas para la recepción y tratamiento de residuos industriales y se da un ejemplo del método de cálculo de las tasas. Se discute también la posible necesidad de prétratamiento y la importancia de minimizar cargas de residuos. El estudio concluye con la aplicación de medidas de control, subrayando la opinión del autor de que cada problema debe ser considerado en su contexto y de que el control de la autoridad deberá ser flexibile y pragmatico.

INTRODUCTION

THE BEST WAY of disposing of industrial effluents is usually to discharge them to the public sewer for ultimate treatment in admixture with other municipal, industrial and domestic effluents. This places treatment in the hands of professionals and takes advantage of the economy of scale of treatment that should attach to municipal sewage treatment works. This concept was recognised in Britain early in this century; it was supported by the Second Report of the Advisory Committee on River Pollution [1] in 1930; incorporated in the Public Health (Drainage of Trade Premises) Act, 1937; and endorsed by the Armer Committee [2] in 1960. Because of this, the control of industrial effluents discharged to the public sewer, and the recovery of the costs of their reception and treatment, is well-established practice in Britain. Under the Water Act of 1973 the water industry was reorganized with the creation, in 1974, of ten Regional Water Authorities in England and Wales based on the major river basins and with responsibility for the entire hydrological cycle. (Scotland and Northern Ireland have somewhat different systems.) This led to a more coordinated approach to industrial effluent control and a more rational and equitable attitude to charging than had necessarily been the case previously. Now, under legislation culminating in the Control of Pollution Act of 1974, the Regional Water Authorities are empowered to practise reasonable control upon each and every industrial effluent discharge and to charge each discharger the actual cost of the reception and treatment of his industrial effluent. This charge is calculated according to the volume of effluent and its polluting characteristics. Domestic sewage generated in the industrial premises is not classified as industrial effluent and the cost of its reception and treatment is included in the general rating charge.

INDUSTRIAL EFFLUENT CONTROL

SINCE THE 1973 ACT, virtually every industrial effluent discharged to the public sewer is controlled. The Regional Water Authorities impose control on the basis of Recommended Guidelines produced by a Confederation of British Industries (CBI) and Regional Water Authorities Working Party [3]. In this document, objectives for industrial effluent control are set out; these have been summarised by Dart [4]:

(1) To prevent industrial effluent discharges to sewers causing;
    (a) damage to sewerage systems and personnel;
    (b) interference with sewage treatment processes;
    (c) the treated effluent from sewage works affecting water resources or the environment;
    (d) unacceptable storm water discharges.
(2) To provide data for future design of sewers and sewage treatment works.
(3) To ensure that the trader pays a fair charge for the services rendered for the reception, conveyance, treatment and disposal of his effluent.

In order to meet these objectives it is necessary to attach standards to the discharge. It was common in the past for standards to form part of a legal agreement between the industrialist and the receiving authority. Under the Public Health (Drainage of Trade Premises) Act of 1937, the receiving authorities were empowered to issue Consents to discharge to the public sewer in many cases. Regional Water Authorities retain the power to enter into an agreement with the discharger but they tend only to use agreements where the discharger is making a capital contribution towards sewerage or sewage treatment facilities. The situation today is that Regional Water Authorities have the power, still subject to appeal, to issue Consents to all dischargers of industrial effluent. Consents impose conditions upon the discharge that are unilaterally set by the Authority but the industrialist has a right of appeal.

Historically in Britain, and elsewhere, standards have been almost infinitely diverse. Today, the trend is towards the use of a limited number of sets of standards or guidelines. In some countries, standards are imposed inflexibly but in others, including Britain, guidelines are used and are applied with flexibility. An example of a typical set of generalised standards from Britain is given in Appendix A. It is fully accepted that both guidelines and standards are useful but flexibility is of paramount importance. In every case, the local situation must be judged on its own merits. To take an extreme example, it cannot be right that the same standards should be applied to a potentially toxic chemical waste making up half of the flow to a small sewage works as to the small electroplating factory discharging to a city sewer. Similarly, some sewage treatment processes are more sensitive to trade effluents than others. For example, toxic metals are of much greater concern when anaerobic sludge digestion is practised, and particularly when the digested sludge is used for agricultural purposes, than when sludge is incinerated. Another important factor is the use to which the waters receiving the sewage works effluent are put. In this context, the abstraction of river water downstream of the point of effluent discharge clearly imposes greater constraints not only upon the sewage works operator, but also indirectly upon the discharger of trade effluent.

Once standards for discharge have been set, the receiving authority should have the right to ensure by sampling and analysis that those standards are adhered to. In practical terms, the degree of control should be related to the potentially hazardous nature of the particular trade effluent and to the record of the trade effluent discharger. Common practice is for an inspector to visit the industrial site without prior notice, but to take a sample of the effluent in the presence of a representative of the company who then has the opportunity to take a duplicate sample for independent analysis. If it is suspected that the effluent is exceeding standards, it is likely that a special sample will be taken which may be used as evidence in any legal action.

CHARGING

IN BRITAIN, the Regional Water Authority responsible for the sewerage system and the sewage treatment works ultimately receiving the trade effluent has a right to charge for the conveyance and treatment of the trade effluent. In doing so it must have regard to the actual cost of performing its services and providing its facilities; it cannot profit from the service. Historically, many receiving authorities calculated trade effluent charges using charging formulae of many types; others based their charges on simple calculations bearing little relationship to reality; still others took the deliberate stand that industry should be subsidised and that charges should therefore be reduced for political reasons. Today, the Regional

Water Authorities all use a formula approach whereby the various principal elements of cost (conveyance, sludge treatment and biological treatment) are related to specific trade effluents, their volume and characteristics. These formulae are essentially of the 'Modgen' type in which the cost of sewage treatment is directly related to the greater or lesser cost of treating the particular trade effluent relative to the total sewage treatment costs.

Formulae vary, but a generalised form is given below:

$$C = V + B \frac{OD_t}{OD_s} + S \frac{SS_t}{SS_s}$$

where C = total cost of treatment, per m^3 of trade effluent,
V = costs related to the volume of flow, per m^3 of mixed crude sewage,
B = costs related to aerobic biological treatment, per m^3 of sewage,
OD_t = oxygen demand (strength) of trade effluent, in mg/l,
OD_s = oxygen demand (strength) of settled sewage, in mg/l,
S = costs related to sludge treatment, per m^3 of sewage,
SS_t = suspended (or settleable) solids in trade effluent, in mg/l,
SS_s = suspended (or settleable) solids in crude sewage, mg/l.

Conveyancing costs and other costs directly related to flow are generally expressed in terms of average metered flow of sewage received at the treatment works and the flow of trade effluent discharged as metered or estimated. Costs related to sludge treatment may be calculated using suspended or settleable solids in the crude sewage and trade effluent, or greater sophistication may be introduced by allowing for secondary sludge production (i.e. that proportion of the BOD converted into solids). Biological treatment costs are often based on the relative strength of the crude sewage and trade effluents as measured by the BOD or COD tests. It is, perhaps, in the calculation of cost apportionment for biological treatment that the greatest flexibility should be allowed; there is much to commend the use of the BOD of settled samples as the basic method of calculation but COD is more commonly used.

Actual cost of trade effluent treatment may be influenced by factors that do not necessarily appear in the generalised formula. For example, the use of COD alone is unlikely to give any indication of any inhibitory effects and benefits will not be given to industry that discharges wastes of high treatability. These and many other factors demand that each trade effluent be considered individually and that consideration should always be given to the possibility of modifying charging formulae in order that trade effluent charges should be fair. However, the greater the flexibility of approach and the greater the accuracy of the system by increased sampling and analysis, the greater the administrative cost. There is very real danger that the law of diminishing returns will apply to the extent that increasing attention to equity will introduce unacceptable costs, costs that must be borne both by the ratepayer and by the industrialist. A balance must be struck that permits just enough flexibility and control to ensure a reasonable degree of fairness but at an acceptable cost.

PRETREATMENT AND MINIMISATION OF EFFLUENT LOADS

WHERE STANDARDS for discharge are set, it may be necessary to pretreat the industrial effluent prior to discharge in order to meet these standards. Common pretreatment techniques include screening, pH control, grease/oil removal, chemical precipitation and balancing. It is impossible to discuss pretreatment in detail here; suffice it to say that almost every technique used for full effluent treatment may also be used for pretreatment and that the selection of a pretreatment plant for a specific situation should rest upon detailed in-factory investigations and an expert evaluation of possible alternative techniques.

Whether or not pretreatment is practised, it is essential that effluent flow and pollutional load should be reduced to a minimum; this reduces both the cost of any pretreatment plant and the reception charges. The importance of this cannot be overstated because experience has shown that very considerable cost savings can often result from a properly designed waste conservation programme. The following possibilities are among the most important that can be considered;
    —elimination of unnecessary use of process water,
    —reduction of contaminants at source,
    —changes to manufacturing processes,
    —recycle of internal effluents,
    —segregation of clean effluents,
    —segregation of effluents requiring pretreatment,
    —recovery of contaminants for re-use, separate disposal or sale.

CONCLUSIONS

EMPHASIS has been placed on the discharge of industrial effluents to sewers in Britain and more specifically in England and Wales. Similar systems do, of course, exist in many countries and others are moving towards environmental legislation and control. The British system may or may not be the best but it does work. Both the control measures and the charges are largely accepted by industry. Where they are not, industry has a right of appeal. Conversely, where industry fails to meet reasonable requirements, prosecution can result but this is something that is rarely resorted to. One of the most important factors is that the system is essentially flexible and its application is pragmatic. However, it must be remembered that industrial effluent control has existed in Britain for very many years and industry expects to have to pay to discharge its effluents to the public sewer. Where countries do not have a legacy of effluent control and charging, there is a case for less flexibility and for a more rigid application of the law; this is particularly important where there is a risk of corruption. However, there is no valid argument in favour of total inflexibility; the specific problem should always be considered in context. In countries where the rigid approach has been introduced, it has soon become evident that standards have to be imposed on the assumption that every case is a 'worst case', resulting in unduly harsh controls and an excessive financial burden on industry and on the national economy. The important point is to introduce a system that is practical in terms of the local situation, that allows for the protection of the environment, that is economically acceptable and that is seen by industry to be equitable. Providing that this is the case, and returning to the opening sentence of this paper, the best way of disposing of industrial effluents is usually to discharge them to the public sewer. Discharge to sewer, after the minimum amount of pretreatment needed to achieve standards, offers many benefits: dilution, nutrients, professional, treatment-plant operators, economy of scale; and the industrialist can concentrate his mind on that which he understands best—manufacturing.

APPENDIX A:
TYPICAL GENERAL REQUIREMENTS FOR DISCHARGES OF INDUSTRIAL EFFLUENTS INTO SEWERS

1. The temperature of the effluent to be discharged shall not exceed 40°C at the point of entry into the public sewer.
2. The pH value of the effluent to be discharged shall not be less than 6, nor more than 10, at the point of entry into the public sewer.
3. The effluent shall not at any time include calcium carbide, chloroform, degreasing solvents of the mono-di-trichlorethylene type, products which in their pure state produce under the conditions appertaining in the sewers an inflammable vapour, including petroleum spirit, all other volatile petroleum products and all inflammable solvents, including carbon disulphide and amyl acetate.
4. The effluent shall not include the substances listed below in proportions greater than those stated:
   (a) Solids in suspension (measured at normal pH of sewage at receiving works) shall not exceed 500 mg/l.
   (b) Hydrocyanic acid and all compounds which produce hydrocyanic acid on acidification shall not exceed 10 mg/l.

(c) Sulphur compounds (e.g. hydrosulphides, sulphides, and polysulphide) which on acidification liberate H_2S (expressed as S) shall not exceed 10 mg/l.

(d) Tar and tar oils not dissolved in the aqueous liquid shall not exceed 50 mg/l.

(e) Grease and oil shall not exceed 200 mg/l.

(f) Carbohydrates in solution (expressed as glucose) shall not exceed 500 mg/l.

(g) Total sulphates (expressed as SO_4) shall not exceed 1000 mg/l.

(h) Free chlorine shall not exceed 100 mg/l.

(i) Total mercury (expressed as Hg) shall not exceed 0.01 mg/l.

(j) Total cadmium (expressed as Cd) shall not exceed 5 mg/l.

(k) Total chromium (expressed as Cr) shall not exceed 5 mg/l.

(l) Total lead (expressed as Pb) shall not exceed 5 mg/l.

(m) Total silver (expressed as Ag) shall not exceed 5 mg/l.

(n) Total zinc (expressed as Zn) shall not exceed 10 mg/l.

(o) Total copper (expressed as Cu) shall not exceed 5 mg/l.

(p) Total nickel (expressed as Ni) shall not exceed 5 mg/l.

(q) The zinc equivalent (defined as the sum of the concentration of the zinc, the concentration of the cadmium, twice the copper concentration and eight times the nickel concentration in mg/l) shall not exceed 35 mg/l.

(r) Total non-ferrous metals shall not exceed 30 mg/l.

(s) Total soluble, non-ferrous metals shall not exceed 10 mg/l.

(t) Limiting concentration of detergents will be calculated to ensure that the sewage received for treatment does not contain, at minimum flows, detergents in excess of 30 mg/l.

(u) Any substance identified as toxic or inhibiting to sewage treatment processes will be limited in concentration following calculations to ensure that at minimum flows, such substances are present in the sewage received for treatment at concentrations significantly below the level of toxicity or inhibition.

(v) Other parameters (such as permanganate value, BOD_5, phenols, colour) may in certain cases be limited; the circumstances will dictate the limits permitted and no general indication can be given.

5. Apart from the substances listed in Condition 4, the effluent shall not include any substance of a nature and quantity likely to injure the sewers into which it is discharged; or to interfere with the free flow of their contents; or cause injury to any persons engaged in such sewers; or to have injurious effects on sewage purification works at which it is treated or any machinery or equipment installed thereat; or to interfere with any processes of purification; or where the sewer connects directly or indirectly with any harbour or tidal water cause, or tend to cause, injury or obstruction to the navigation on, or the use of, the said harbour or tidal water.

6. Sampling or testing points shall be provided through which all effluent shall pass, the point to be agreed with the trader. It should be noted that where the effluent at the sampling point may contain other effluents, such as domestic

sewage or surface water runoff, the concentration of constituents will be set to allow for the dilution afforded by those other effluents.

References

1. HMSO, London (1920) *The reception of trade effluents into the sewers of the local sanitary authorities.* Second report of the Joint Advisory Committee on river pollution.
2. HMSO, London (1960) The trade effluents sub-committee of the Central Advisory Water Committee, Final Report.
3. CBI, London (1976) *Trade effluent discharged to the sewer. Recommended guidelines for control and charging.*
4. Dart, M.C. (1977) *Industrial effluent control and charges.* Wat. Pollut. Cont. 76, (2), 192.

Recycling Plan for Leather Tannery Waste Water Effluent

Herbert C. Preul

Professor of Civil & Environmental Engineering,
University of Cincinnati, Cincinnati, Ohio 45221, USA

SYNOPSIS

This paper presents a feasibility analysis and plan to improve the existing treatment for tannery waste-water discharges from the George Moser Leather Company at New Albany, Indiana, U.S.A. The three most viable alternatives for waste-water treatment have been analyzed on a cost-feasibility basis for compliance with the best available technology standards proposed by the U.S. Environmental Protection Agency for implementation in the year 1984. These alternatives include the following: (1) Improve an existing lagoon-treatment system with provisions for recycling the effluent for process water reuse; (2) Construct a new activated sludge treatment plant with effluent discharge to the Ohio River; or (3) Construct a new activated sludge treatment plant with effluent discharge to a publicly owned collection and treatment system. Alternative (1) was selected on the basis of having the lowest total annual cost, using a 20-year, amortization period, plus the advantages of recycling the effluent for process water purposes and thereby avoiding an effluent to a receiving stream. A flow diagram and description of this proposed system are given. The final cost results for the three treatment alternatives are given in terms of total annual cost and the incremental unit production costs.

385

RÉSUMÉ

Cet écrit présente une analyse de practicabilité et un projet pour améliorer le traitement existant des eaux résiduaires évacuées de la compagnie de cuir George Moser à New Albany en Indiana, Etats-Unis d'Amérique. Les trois alternatives qui seraient le plus appropriées pour le traitement des eaux résiduaires ont été analysées sur la base d'une possibilité de prix accord avec les meilleures mesures technologiques disponibles par l'Agence Américaine de la protection de l'environnement pour une mise à exécution en l'on 1984. Les alternatives sont les suivantes: (1) Ameliorer une système de traitement de la lagune déjà existant en prenant les dispositions nécessaires pour recycler les eaux usées et les ré-utiliser; (2) Construire une nouvelle installation pour le traitement actif du fange avec déversement dans le fleuve Ohio; ou (3) Construire une nouvelle installation pour le traitement du fange avec déversement dans un système de captation et de traitement des eaux etant proprieté publique. La première alternative a été choisie car elle présentait le coût annuel total le plus bas, 20 ans étant nécessaires à l'amortiser, plus les avantages de recyclage des eaux usées en eaux purifées et elle évitait aussi le déversement de ces eaux dans le fleuve. Un graphique d'écoulement et une description du système proposé sont présentés daus cet écrit. Les résultats du coût final pour les alternatives des trois traitements sont donnés par rapport au coût annuel total et à l'accroissement par unité des coûts de production.

RESUMEN

Este estudio presenta un análisis de factibilidad y un proyecto para mejorar el tratamiento existente de la descarga de aguas servidas en la tenería de George Moser Leather Company en New Albany. Las tres alternativas mas viables para el tratamiento de las aguas servidas han sido analizadas en base al costo y de acuerdo con las normas tecnológicas establecidas por la Agencia para la Protección Ambiental de los Estados Unidos de Norteamérica propuestas para el año de 1984. Estas tres alternativas incluyen lo siguiente: (1) Mejorar un sistema de tratamiento de laguna existente con provisiones para reusar el flujo de agua en futuros procesos; (2) Construir una nueva planta de tratamiento de cieno activado con flujo de descarga a el Rio Ohio; ó (3) Construir una nueva planta de tratamiento de cieno activado con flujo de descarga a un sistema público de colección y tratamiento. La alternativa (1) fue seleccionada en base a que tiene el más bajo costo anual, usando un período de amortización de 20 años, más la ventaja del reuso del agua en futuros procesos evitando una descarga adicional hacia el río. Un diagrama de flujo y descripción del sistema propuesto son presentados en este documento. El costo final de la tres alternativas de tratamiento está dado en términos del costo total anual y del incremento unitario de los costos de producción.

GENERAL DESCRIPTION OF EXISTING TANNERY FACILITIES

THE TANNERY AND PLANT facilities of the George Moser Leather Company were established in the year 1874 and are located in New Albany, Indiana, near the Ohio River. Both chrome- and vegetable-tanning operations are carried out in the tanning of raw cattle hides for the production of leather, sold to other companies for the manufacture of horse saddles, horse bridles, waist belts, oil seals for trucks, gaskets for water wells, shoes, etc.

The total property is comprised of approximately 45 acres, including two existing waste-water treatment lagoons totaling 19 acres in area. The company has a special flooding problem in that the waste-water treatment lagoons are subject to flooding from backwaters of the Ohio River during rather infrequent, high-water periods in the river, although the tannery facilities are well protected with a flood wall. Process water is supplied at a temperature around 60°F from three water wells located on company property; the well-water at this temperature is considered to be quite desirable for certain tannery operations.

As is the case with most tanneries in the U.S.A., the company is hard pressed to remain competitive with relation to world markets because of rising costs including those requiring extensive treatment facilities to meet stringent limitations on waste water.

WASTE WATER & WASTE-WATER TREATMENT SYSTEMS

Current and Future Tannery Production

The basic tannery production operation is 5 days per week, Monday through

Friday. Current average production is as follows:

3 packs cattle hides/day @ 80/pack = 240 hides/day

3 packs hides/day @ 4600 lb. = 13,800 lb/day raw stock

The same production is intended for the foreseeable future.

Water Usage per Pound of Stock at Average Production

Current Water Usage $= \dfrac{120,000 \text{ gpd}}{13,800 \text{ lb/day}} = 8.7$ gpd/lb stock at average production

(Note: gpd = gallons/day; lb = pounds)
Future Water Usage—8.7 gpd/lb stock—same as current at average production
By comparison, the EPA-proposed tannery industry standards for plants discharging waste waters to receiving streams, are as follows:

Best Practicable Technology (BPT) = approx. 5.5 gpd/lb stock (intended practice by year 1981)

Best Available Technology (BAT) = approx. 3.7 gpd/lb stock (intended practice by year 1984)

These water-usage standards are intended as a basis for evaluating the concentrations and strengths of waste waters where effluents are discharged to receiving waters. However, they would not apply in a case where effluent waters are recycled, as considered in this paper.

Waste-water Discharge: Current and Future

The current average waste-water discharge from the tannery is approximately 120,000 gpd and this is intended for the future. Many years of company operations have shown this level of water usage to produce a high quality leather product and therefore, it is intended as a continuing practice along with waste-water effluent recycling.

Pollutant constituents of main concern, existing and proposed, are listed in Table 1 along with the limits proposed by the U.S. Environmental Protection Agency. The proposed waste-water limits were published in the U.S. Federal Register/Vol. 44, No. 128, July 2, 1979, entitled "Leather Tanning and Finishing Point Source Category Effluent Limitation Guidelines, Pretreatment Standards and New Source Performance Standards". Certain of these limits may change as a result of discussions with tanning-industry representatives but currently they remain as guidelines.

In the future, the raw waste-water discharges, including both quantity and

Table 1. Waste-water pollutant concentrations—existing and proposed alternative 1

Pollutant or Property	Existing & Future Raw Wastewater Average	Existing Treated Effluent	Prop. Tertiary Recirc. Avg.	Prop. Tertiary Recirc. Max.	Prop. Treated Reuse Avg.	Prop. EPA 1984 BAT Limits Avg.	Prop. EPA 1984 BAT Limits Max.	Prop. EPA BAT (1984) Effluent Limits	Proposed Treated Reuse Water	Prop. System Effluent To Stream
	mg/1	mg/1	mg/1	mg/1	mg/1	mg/1	mg/1	lb/1000 lb Raw Material		mg/1
BOD$_5$	355	35	7	8*	4**	21	74	0.65	0.0003	0
COD	1782	250	50	56*	39***	200	325	6.2	2.8	0
TSS	1086	70	14	16*	4**	24	84	0.74	<0.2	0
Oil/Grease	64	7	1	5*	<1	9	32	0.28	<0.1	0
Total Chromium	1	0.5	<0.1	<0.1*	<0.1	0.5	1.8	0.015	<0.004	0
TKN	136	20	<3	3*	<3**	23	79	0.69	<0.3	0
Ammonia	136	<15	<2	2*	<2	7.5	26	0.23	<0.2	0
Nitrate	0.01		5		5**	—	—			0
Phenol	0.01	<0.01	<0.01	<0.01	<0.01	0.15	0.53	0.0046	<0.00072	0
Sulphide		2	0.0	0.0	0.0	0.0	0.0			0
pH	7.5 (5.5–12.9)	7.5 (6.9–8.0)	7.5	8	7.5	(within 6–9 at all times)		6–9	6.9–8	—

* Gloyna, Earnest F. (1971) *Waste Stabilization Ponds.* World Health Organization, pp. 60–62.

* *Manual of Practice No. 8; Wastewater Treatment Plant Design.* Water Pollution Control Federation, 1977, pp. 16.

** Estimates based on data from *Cost & Performance Estimates for Tertiary Wastewater Treating Processes,* Robert A. Taft Water Research Center Report No. TWRC-9, Federal Water Poll. Control Admin., Cincinnati, 1969.

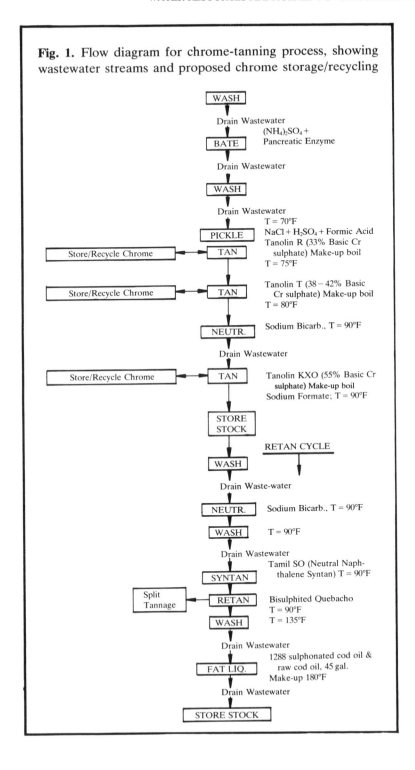

Fig. 1. Flow diagram for chrome-tanning process, showing wastewater streams and proposed chrome storage/recycling

quality, are expected to closely approximate those currently discharged, except for chromium, and therefore, the concentrations are shown as the same in Table 1. Actually, this assumption is conservative from a treatment removal viewpoint because the trend and attitude of the company are to implement waste reduction practices wherever possible.

Although the George Moser Leather company carries out both vegetable- and chrome-tanning operations, the chrome stream is of particular concern from a waste-water standpoint because of the difficulty in treating chrome with ordinary biological methods. Therefore, in the future, it is intended that chrome will be removed from the waste waters to a large extent through in-plant recycling, as illustrated in Figure 1. Through storage and recycling in the plant operations, it is expected that the total chromium will be reduced by 90 to 100 per cent from the current practice.

ALTERNATIVE METHODS OF WASTE-WATER TREATMENT

Three alternative methods of waste-water treatment were analyzed for comparison purposes, including:

Alternative 1—Waste-water Treatment Lagoons With Effluent Reuse

Alternative 2—New Waste-water Treatment Plant With Effluent to the Ohio River

Alternative 3—New Waste-water Treatment Plant With Effluent to Publicly Owned Treatment Works

As will be seen later from a summary of cost results, Alternative 1 was found to be the most economically feasible and therefore, we shall concentrate on its description only.

Alternative 1: Waste-water Treatment Lagoons With Effluent Reuse

This system is an extension and improvement of the existing waste-water treatment lagoons and will provide for complete reuse of the treated waste-water, with no effluent discharge to any stream except during highly unusual emergency conditions. Since there normally would be no discharge to any stream, the system would be in complete compliance with the proposed EPA 1984 effluent requirements for the tanning industry. Even during any emergency period, such as a malfunction of mechanical equipment or river flooding, any brief effluent discharge is calculated to be in compliance with the proposed EPA 1984 effluent requirements. A schematic flow plan of this system is shown in Figure 2 and a general description of the proposed system is outlined below.

(1) Chrome-reuse System: The flow diagram in Figure 1, including proposed tannery operations, will provide for the reuse of chrome. It is estimated that current tanning operations take up 70 per cent of the process chrome, with 30 per cent being discharged in the waste water and solids. With the proposed recovery, the discharge would be reduced to approximately 10 per cent, and ultimately, it is planned that no chrome would be discharged to the lagoons, with essentially full recovery.

(2) Screening and Grit Removal: Mechanical screening will be provided for coarse material in an addition to be located on the easterly side of the tannery. One mechanical screening unit with openings of the range of $\frac{1}{4}$ to $\frac{1}{2}$ inch will be provided. This range of opening would eliminate the coarse material from the waste-water discharge but would avoid the collection of the finer sludge material. Screenings would be dewatered and disposed of by hauling to a secure land fill.

(3) Flow Measurement: An open channel venturi flume will be installed in the waste collection chamber for raw waste-water flow measurement, with automatic recording equipment.

(4) Primary Treatment Lagoon: The existing 10.5-acre primary lagoon will be utilized with certain modifications. These modifications include:
  (a) Changing the influent discharge location so as to allow a longer flow path;
  (b) Re-directing the storm drainage to eliminate flow into the lagoon; and
  (c) Construction of a median divider curtain to lengthen the flow path.
The lagoon has an average depth of approximately 1.75 ft. (varies from 1.5 to 2.0 ft. or more) and provides a detention period of 50 days based on the future design flow of 120,000 gallons per day (gpd).

(5) Aerated Lagoon: The existing secondary lagoon will be utilized as an aerated treatment lagoon with the following modifications:
  (a) Existing lagoon would be excavated and enlarged with an increase in the height of the dikes by approximately 2 ft.;
  (b) A median divider curtain will be installed to lengthen the flow path; and
  (c) Two floating aerators, of approximately 30 H.P. each, would be installed for aeration treatment.
The existing lagoon is approximately 4.2 acres in area with an average depth of 3.0 ft. and a detention period of 34 days. This will be enlarged to provide for depths of approximately 8 ft. in the aerated areas, with a corresponding increase in detention based on the design flow of 120,000 gpd.

(6) Tertiary Lagoon: A third lagoon for tertiary treatment will be constructed

Fig. 2. Flow diagram for tannery waste-water effluent recycling system

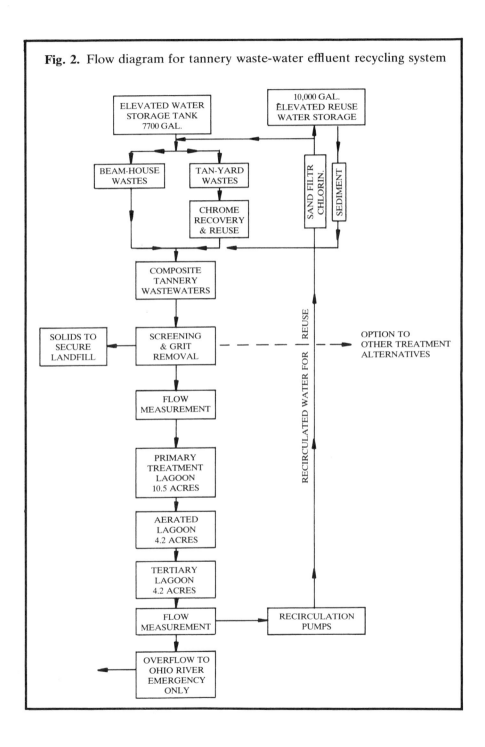

with dimensions of approximately 450 ft. × 400 ft. and a depth of 3.0 ft. The total area will be 4.2 acres, with a detention time of 34 days based on the 120,000 gpd. design flow.

(7) Recirculation Pumps (Submersible): Two alternating, submersible-type pumps will be provided to recirculate the treated tertiary effluent back to the tannery for reuse. Each pump would be of 125 gallons/minute (gpm) capacity so that each pump would have sufficient capacity to recirculate the 120,000 gpd. flow during a daily 16-hour period. This recirculation capacity will adequately provide for the normal operation of the tannery which is 8 hours per day for 5 days a week.

(8) Recirculation Structure: The recirculation structure will receive the final effluent from the tertiary lagoon and will provide a sump for installation of the recirculation pumps. For flow measurement, a V-notch weir with automatic recording will be provided. An overflow from the structure to the Ohio River will be provided for emergency purposes.

(9) Pressure Sand Filtration: The total suspended solids in the tertiary lagoon effluent are estimated to average 14 mg/1; therefore, a pressure-type sand filter, approximately 5 ft. in diameter and a 5 ft. bed depth, will be provided in the recirculation system. Filtration would be at a rate of 6.4 gpm/sq. ft. of filter area with this design which would yield an effluent suspended solids concentration of approximately 4 mg/1 or less for the water to be stored for reuse. Backwash water will be provided at a rate of 15 gpm/sq. ft. from the treated, elevated, 10,000-gallon storage tank. The existing compressed air system in the building would be utilized in connection with the backwashing. Discharge of the backwash waste waters would be to the emergency storage reservoir, with drainage back to the primary lagoon.

(10) Chlorination: An automatic hypochlorinator will be provided for chlorination of the discharge from the sand filter, prior to storage in the 10,000-gallon, elevated, treated water storage tank to be provided for the recirculated water. The purpose of the chlorination will be to provide for disinfection and as an algae-inhibitor in the storage tank. Since the water will be for process purposes, the rate of chlorination will be comparatively low and is anticipated at less than 5 mg/1 available chlorine.

(11) Elevated Reuse Water Storage: A 10,000-gallon storage tank will be located at the third-story roof level, for treated reuse water to be received from the pressure sand filter/hypochlorinator.

(12) Emergency Waste-water Storage Reservoir: A 300,000-gallon, ground storage reservoir is to be provided for emergency waste-water storage during infrequent periods when the Ohio River may flood the lagoons. The operational plan during these periods would be as follows;

(a) When a rising Ohio River reaches the normal, water level stage in the tertiary lagoon, all raw waste-water discharge to the primary lagoon would be stopped and all waste water would be discharged at a reduced operation rate to the 300,000-gallon, emergency storage reservoir. Aeration will be provided.

(b) Tannery operations during this period would be reduced to an average waste-water discharge of approximately 30,000 gpd so that up to 10 days emergency storage can be received. If the full capacity of the emergency storage is reached, the tannery will suspend any waste-water discharge.

(c) When the falling Ohio River again reaches the normal, tertiary lagoon, water level stage, normal waste-water operations would be resumed. The waste-waters stored in the emergency storage reservoir would be drained to the primary lagoon for treatment and the reservoir would be flushed.

(13) Proposed Treated Waste-water Quality: The expected treated water qualities are given in Table 1 for the resulting tertiary, recirculated effluent and the treated reuse waters, following sand filtration and chlorination. These estimates have been based on results with similar lagoon facilities and tertiary treatment, as noted in Table 1.

From a comparison of the proposed pollutant concentrations with the EPA 1984 BAT limits, it can be seen that the treated reuse water and the tertiary treated recirculation water are expected to be well within the EPA 1984 BAT limitations. Actually, these limits would apply only to effluents to a receiving stream, and since there would be no such effluent in this case, except possibly under extreme emergency conditions, the proposed Alternative 1 recirculation waters would be in complete compliance with the proposed limitations.

(14) Comparison of Existing and Proposed Waste-water Pollutants Based on Raw Material Stock: Since the proposed 1984 BAT limitations by EPA refer to limitations based on the lb. of pollutant per lb. of raw material, Table 1 also includes these data compiled for reference. It will be noted that the proposed treated reuse water, in all cases of the various pollutants, is well within the indicated limits. Actually, since the limits are intended to apply where an effluent is discharged to a stream, the limits do not apply because there will be no effluent except possibly during an unusual emergency condition. Therefore, the proposed Alternative 1 system would be in complete compliance with the proposed EPA 1984 BAT limitations.

FEASIBILITY ANALYSES

THE TOTAL ANNUAL COST (based on a capital recovery over a 20-year period at 14 per cent interest) for Alternative 1 is estimated at $72,500, as compared with $114,700 and $138,500 respectively for Alternatives 2 and 3. In terms of the unit production of leather, this translates into an incremental cost of $0.0275/sq. ft. for Alternative 1 and costs $0.0435/sq. ft. and $0.0527/sq. ft. respectively for Alternatives 2 and 3.

CONCLUSIONS

ANALYSES have been carried out for proposed waste-water treatment system improvements at the George Moser Leather Company.

Alternative 1, which includes extensive improvements in the existing waste-water lagoon treatment system plus complete recirculation of the treated waters, has been determined to be the most cost-effective system of the three alternative systems analyzed. The proposed system would provide for complete reuse of the waste waters with no effluent to any stream and would be in full compliance with the expected U.S. EPA 1984 waste-water discharge regulations, as applicable to the tanning industry.

ACKNOWLEDGEMENTS

Considerable information and data for this paper have been provided by a number of principals from the George Moser Leather Company, including James M. Thornton, President; Donald J. Moser, Vice President; James J. Thornton, Vice President; and Ray Hauck, Chemist. Their contributions are gratefully acknowledged.

Municipal Waste Water Reuse: A Perspective

Takashi Asano

*Office of Water Recycling, California State Water
Resources Control Board, P.O. Box 100, Sacramento,
California 95801, USA*

SYNOPSIS

*The solution to the anticipated future water shortages involves both
development of increased freshwater sources and more efficient use
of the existing water supplies. Included in the latter category are the
alternatives of municipal waste-water reclamation and reuse, and
waste-water recycling. Among present and future freshwater withdrawals, it is estimated that agriculture and steam-electric plants
continue to use over 75 per cent of all freshwater withdrawn in the
United States. These categories of water use can be supplemented
or supplied by reclaimed municipal waste water in large quantities.
Use of reclaimed municipal waste water in these applications are also
the least sensitive to public health hazards and public acceptance,
thus relatively easier to implement. This paper discusses general views
on these two, large-volume applications of reclaimed water, namely
in agricultural irrigation and industrial cooling.*

RÉSUMÉ

*La solution aux pénuries d'eau envisagées dans le futur, implique à
la fois un développement accru des approvisionements en eau*

douce et une utilisation plus éfficace des ressources actuellement existantes. La récupération, le recyclage et la réutilisation des eaux municipales usées font partie de cette seconde catégorie. Aux Etats-Unis les besoins actuels et futurs de l'agriculture et des centrales thermo-électriques sont estimès à plus de 75% de la consommation totale. Dans ces domaines l'utilisation d'eaux municipales recyclées peut fournir un apport considérable. Il s'agit également de secteurs où les risques pour la santé publique sont les plus faibles et où l'accueil par le public est le plus favorable, ce qui devrait permettre une mise en oeuvre relativement facile. Cet article discute des problèmes généraux de l'utilisation d'eau recyclée dans les deux importants domaines de l'irrigation en agriculture et du refroidissement industriel.

RESUMEN

La solución inmediata a futuros problemas con agua consiste en comenzar a desarrollar e incrementar recursos de agua "dulce" y la utilización más eficiente de las aguas de suministro. El segundo punto contempla la posibilidad de aprovechamiento y reuso de aguas municipales incluyendo el reciclo de estas aguas. De las actuales y futuras disponibilidades de agua "dulce" en Los Estados Unidos más del 75% es estimado por propósitos de agricultura y plantas electricas de vapor. Grandes cantidades de estas aguas pueden ser suplementados o suplidas de aguas que previamente han sido usadas con propositos municipales. El uso de estas aguas para tales fines trae un minimo riesgo en la salud del público y en su aceptación y como consecuencia una facil implementacion. En este trabajo se discuten los puntos de vista generales en relacion a dos grandes aplicaciones del agua que puede ser reusada en irrigacion agricola y enfriamiento industrial.

INTRODUCTION

THE SOLUTION to the anticipated future water shortages involves both development of increased freshwater sources and more efficient use of the existing water supplies. Included in the latter category are the alternatives of municipal waste-water reclamation and reuse, and waste-water recycling.

The waste-water reclamation and reuse imply existence of a pipe, or other conveyance facilities, for delivering the first user's effluent to the second users or uses. Indirect reuse, through discharge of an effluent to a receiving water for assimilation and withdrawal downstream, is recognized to be important but does not generally constitute planned reuse. In contrast to direct reuse, the waste-water recycling or recirculation involves only one user or use, and the effluent from the user is captured and redirected back into that use scheme. In this context, waste-water recycling is predominantly practised in industry such as in steam-electric, manufacturing and mineral industries.

ROLE OF MUNICIPAL WASTE-WATER REUSE

WASTE WATERS potentially available for reuse include discharges from municipalities, industries and agricultural return flows. Among them, return flows from agricultural irrigation are usually collected and reused without further treatment. The degree of waste-water treatment and requirements for treatment-process reliability will depend on the categories of planned reuse, as identified in Table 1. These categories of municipal waste-water reuse are arranged in descending order of anticipated future volume of use.

Table 1. Categories of Municipal Waste-water Reuse

1. Agricultural and Landscape Irrigation
2. Industrial Process and Cooling Water
3. Impoundment for Recreational Facilities
4. Stream Flow Augmentation
5. Ground Water Recharge
6. Direct Consumptive Use

The quantities of freshwater requirements and waste-water discharges in the U.S.A. are summarized in Table 2. The data indicate that freshwater requirements, as represented by withdrawals for agriculture, steam-electric plant, and manufacturing, are expected to decrease substantially by the year 2000 (2, 10, and 62 per cent, respectively). The freshwater requirement for municipal purposes and waste-water discharge from municipalities are projected to increase in the future.

Among present and future freshwater withdrawals reported in Table 2, it is estimated that agriculture and steam-electric plants continue to use over 75 per cent of all freshwater withdrawn in the United States. Freshwater use in industries is primarily for three purposes: (1) cooling, (2) boiler feed and (3) processing.

Table 2. Summary of Freshwater Withdrawal and Waste-water Discharge in the USA [1, 2]

Use Category	Freshwater Withdrawal				Waste-water Discharge			
	1975 10^6 m³/day	(%)	2000 10^6 m³/day	(%)	1975 10^6 m³/day	(%)	2000 10^6 m³/day	(%)
Agriculture	699.2	(50.9)	682.5	(54.5)	320.6	(34.6)	272.5	(39.5)
Steam-Electric	337.3	(24.6)	303.2	(24.2)	332.0	(35.9)	263.1	(38.1)
Manufacturing	193.8	(14.1)	74.6	(6.0)	171.1	(18.5)	18.9	(2.7)
Municipal	100.0	(8.0)	140.4	(11.2)	81.0	(8.8)	104.5	(15.1)
Minerals	26.9	(1.9)	42.8	(3.4)	18.5	(2.0)	29.1	(4.2)
Public Lands	4.5	(0.3)	6.4	(0.5)	0	(0)	0	(0)
Fish Hatcheries	2.3	(0.2)	2.6	(0.2)	2.3	(0.2)	2.6	(0.4)
Total	1,373.0	(100)	1,252.6	(100)	925.5	(100)	690.7	(100)

About 70 per cent of all industrial water use is for cooling and this represents a potential for municipal waste-water reuse and recycling. Industrial water recycling is projected to increase substantially by the year 2000 and there is potential for using reclaimed municipal waste water to supply a significant part of the requirement for makeup water. Boiler-feed water and process water in general require higher quality and stricter public health regulations. The potential for these applications is, therefore, more limited.

Table 3 represents a summary of current and projected municipal waste-water reuse and industrial water recycling in the U.S.A. The data in Table 3 help in placing municipal waste-water reuse in perspective on a national scale. The relatively small municipal waste-water reuse fraction in 1975 is expected to remain the same in the future, even though the actual quantity of reuse is expected to increase seven-fold.

Table 3. Summary of Municipal Waste-water Reuse and Industrial Water Recycling [1, 2]

Category	Quantity, 10^6 m³/day		
	1975	1985	2000
Freshwater Withdrawals	1,373.0	1,348.7	1,252.6
Industrial Water Recycle	526.5	1,463.8	3,276.3
Municipal Waste-water Reuse	2.6	7.9	18.2

The data presented in Tables 2 and 3 are based upon realistic evaluations of available waste waters, future water needs, availability of other water sources, geographic and climatic factors and conformance to national waste-water dis-charge standards [3]. In many water-short areas, however, waste-water reuse in agriculture and in industrial process and cooling may provide essential alternatives to potable and non-potable municipal reuse which could have a considerably greater impact on supplementing existing water supplies.

Most of the water volume (62 per cent) and the largest number of projects are for agricultural irrigation and there were only 29 large projects which supply industrial cooling and process waters. The majority of reuse projects, accounting for the largest volume of reclaimed water, are located in the south-west and south-central regions of the United States, primarily in Arizona, California and Texas. A summary of municipal waste-water reuse projects developed by Gulp *et al* [2] is shown in Table 4.

Among water-short regions of the country, California has the most active and ambitious waste-water reclamation and reuse programme. As a result of the severe drought in 1976–77, the use of reclaimed water has steadily increased and, today, some 727×10^3 m³/day of reclaimed municipal waste water are used in California for agricultural and landscape irrigation, groundwater recharge, industry and other purposes.

The Federal Clean Water Construction Grant Programme has provided the

Table 4. Existing Municipal Waste-water Reuse Projects in the USA [2]

Category	No. of Projects		10^3 m^3/day	
Irrigation	470		1,589	
Agriculture		(150)		(753)
Landscape		(60)		(124)
Not Defined		(260)		(712)
Industrial	29		814	
Process				(250)
Cooling				(538)
Boiler Feed				(26)
Groundwater Recharge	11		129	
Other (Recreation, etc.)	26		38	
Total	536		2,570	

most construction costs of waste-water reclamation projects, consisting of 75 per cent by U.S. Environmental Protection Agency, and in the case of California, 12.5 per cent each by State of California and municipality. However, due to the limited financial resources available in the Construction Grants Programme, only waste-water reclamation projects which also proved to be cost-effective, water-pollution control options are being funded. Because the need to expand the use of the reclaimed water is clearly evident, several financial assistance programmes are being planned or implemented; for example, Calfornia Clean Water and Water Conservation Bond Law of 1978—State Assistance Programme (16 million dollars financing five waste-water reclamation projects), Renewable Resources Bill, State Water Project, and local and regional financing of waste-water reclamation projects.

PLANNING METHODOLOGY FOR WASTE-WATER REUSE

THERE ARE A NUMBER of factors which affect implementation of municipal waste-water reclamation and reuse. Historically, the impetus for waste-water reuse has risen from three prime motivating factors:
(1) Availability of high quality effluent:
(2) Increasing cost of freshwater development;
(3) Desirability of establishing comprehensive water resources planning, including water conservation and waste-water reuse.
In industrialized nations, the applicable water-pollution control regulations

are such that, in general, secondary treatment of municipal waste water and, in some instances, advanced waste-water treatment are required to meet effluent discharge standards. As a consequence, a unique opportunity for reuse with higher quality, reclaimed water has been in existence. Thus, in this context, discharging high quality effluents to oceans may be considered a waste of limited water resources. The availability of reclaimed water for reuse at relatively low incremental cost, the increasing cost of freshwater and the demonstrated need for additional water form a basis for incorporating waste-water reclamation and reuse as an integral and complementary part of water resources. Reclaimed municipal waste water is a reliable source of water supply even in a drought year.

The general factors affecting waste-water reuse decisions include: (1) local and regional water supply conditions, (2) water-quality requirements for intended water-reuse applications, (3) existing or proposed waste-water treatment facilities and degree of treatment process reliability, and (4) potential health risks mitigation and public acceptance.

Facilities planning for municipal waste-water reclamation and reuse projects that involve primary benefits in the area of water supply require additional steps which are not a common part of water-pollution control planning. Although waste-water reclamation and reuse may be justified on the basis of a least-cost alternative to water-pollution control projects, much of the efforts in waste-water reclamation projects focus on the market assessment, or actual marketing, of reclaimed water as a basis for facilities planning. Thus, the facilities planning should consist of the following three primary steps:

(1) Preliminary and detailed market assessment and analysis;
(2) Engineering analyses of treatment facilities, conveyance facilities and distribution systems;
(3) Economic and financial analyses of the project.

These steps should result in the development of a recommended facilities plan for municipal waste-water reclamation and reuse, including reclaimed water-pricing policy and financial plans for the project.

WASTE-WATER REUSE IN AGRICULTURE AND INDUSTRIAL COOLING

AMONG THE SIX CATEGORIES of municipal waste-water reuse identified in Table 1, (a) agricultural and landscape irrigation, and (b) industrial process and cooling water constitute the largest volume applications of reclaimed water. These categories of municipal waste-water reuse are also the least sensitive to public health hazards and public acceptance, thus relatively easier to implement.

Agricultural Irrigation

Application of waste-water to agricultural land can be designed for two different objectives: (1) primarily for waste-water treatment and disposal, or (2) to maximize crop production by irrigation. The first objective is accomplished most cost-effectively at the highest possible waste-water application rate by keeping land requirements to a minimum. Such a system may, however, be disruptive to agricultural production with potential pollution consequences to surface water and ground water. Alternatively, the second objective deals with agricultural irrigation that requires more land and a lower application rate of reclaimed water, consistent with crop water demand. This alternative, of course, is more compatible with existing agricultural practice.

The motivation for agricultural irrigation with reclaimed water generally arises from (1) the unavailability of a freshwater supply at à competitive price, (2) potential use of plant nutrients contained in reclaimed water, (3) the desire to free higher quality water for other beneficial uses, (4) the requirement to treat waste water to high levels prior to discharge to surface waters, and (5) the prohibition of effluent discharges to surface waters.

When reclaimed waste water is used for agricultural irrigation, a number of possible disadvantages must also be evaluated: (1) integration of supply and demand may be difficult as the supply of reclaimed water is continuous throughout the year, while agricultural irrigation is seasonal and dependent on crop water demands, (2) reclaimed water may plug nozzles in sprinkler or trickle irrigation systems or clog capillary pores of heavy soils, (3) some soluble waste-water constituents may be present in concentrations injurious to plants, (4) health regulations may restrict applications of reclaimed water to certain crops, and (5) when waste water is not properly treated or managed, it may be a nuisance to the environment.

There are many instances where reclaimed municipal waste water is supplied directly to an agricultural land via pipelines or other conveyance facilities, without benefit of the assimilative capacity of a receiving water. Therefore, the most important requirements for the use of reclaimed water in irrigated agriculture are the capability of a waste-water reclamation plant to produce consistent water quality meeting irrigation requirements and the capacity of holding reclaimed water *in situ* for peak irrigation water demand.

Historically, the quality of irrigation water had been evaluated by the concentration of certain dissolved salts that may be present in irrigation water and their impact upon soils and crops. The water analyses to determine the suitability of an irrigation water should include: (1) electrical conductance or total dissolved solids, (2) chemical analyses for sodium, calcium, magnesium, chlorides, sulphates and bicarbonates, and (3) other specific chemical constituents such as boron, nitrates, pH and other phytotoxic substances. Although the availability of this information is essential for the successful application of reclaimed water in agricultural irrigation, more often than not water-quality parameters besides biochemical oxygen demand (BOD), suspended solids and coliform bacteria are difficult to obtain in practice. The discrepancy exists because municipal waste-water treatment facilities have not been planned or constructed for the production of reclaimed water; therefore, the detailed chemical analyses of the effluent are not normally required for the discharge permits.

The primary health concerns regarding the use of reclaimed water are the elimination of health hazards and the control of environmental pollution. The health aspects of reclaimed water use have been the subject of much recent research and the prime concern for the safe use of reclaimed water in agricultural irrigation. A summary of the California Waste-water Reclamation Criteria for agricultural irrigation is given in Table 5.

In recent years there has been a trend to reuse treated effluent for purposes such as landscape and food-crop irrigation and for recreational impoundments, while uses requiring lower quality effluents have increased only moderately. These changes have brought about a significant increase in the probability of public exposure to reclaimed water.

Table 5. Treatment Requirements for Agricultural Irrigation with Reclaimed Water [4]

Type of Irrigation Use	Treatment Required	Bacteriological Quality Required (MPN/100 ml)
Food Crops—Spray Irrigation	Disinfection, Oxidation, Coagulation, Clarification, Filtration	7-day median value not to exceed 2.2; nor exceed 23 in any 30-day period
Food Crops—Surface Irrigation	Disinfection, Oxidation	7-day median value not to exceed 2.2
Orchards and Vineyards—Surface Irrigation	Primary	No contact of fruit with water or ground
Fodder, Fibre, Seed Crops—Spray or Surface Irrigation	Primary Treatment	No Requirement
Pasture for milking animals	Disinfection, Oxidation	7-day median value not to exceed 23

Industrial Cooling

Since industrial process and cooling water constitute the largest water-use category after agricultural irrigation, it is logical to evaluate the use of reclaimed municipal waste water for industrial cooling systems. Industrial cooling systems are common to most industries and are less sensitive to health restrictions. The impetus for most users has been a lack of available water supplies particularly in northern Texas and Oklahoma where the availability of natural resources makes industrial development attractive. There have been over 29 installations of cooling systems in the U.S.A. using reclaimed municipal waste water which include Southeastern Public Utilities, Lubbock, Texas; El Paso Products, Odessa, Texas; and Glendale Power Plant, Glendale, California.

Feasibility analysis for reclaimed municipal waste water for industrial cooling systems can be accomplished in the following three categories: (1) water quality and treatment, (2) institutional and (3) economics. Reclaimed water quality differs from that of freshwater in general in its greater potential for product contamination in direct contact cooling applications, and for corrosion, scaling, biological growth and fouling in non-contact heat exchanger/condenser cooling systems.

There are significant variations among large, industrial cooling systems. The range includes once-through, non-contact cooling such as at large power-generating facilities or petroleum refineries near the ocean; direct contact cooling of relatively inert material as in the primary metal industry; and non-contact, recirculating cooling at large inland industries with limited water resources.

Depending on the quality of the treated municipal waste-water effluent, its intended use and the relative costs, external treatment possibilities include: (1) no treatment, (2) lime/lime-soda clarification, (3) alum treatment, (4) ferric chloride precipitation, (5) ion exchange (sodium ion exchange, weak acid ion exchange, split stream strong acid-sodium ion exchange), and (6) reverse osmosis [5].

The 'no treatment' option is exercised by a few facilities, where the lack of pretreatment can be compensated for, to a certain extent, by internal chemical treatment. At the City of Burbank power plant, for example, tertiary filtered municipal effluent is fed straight into the cooling tower. Sulphuric acid is added to control the pH in the towers to around 6.5 and to reduce the incoming alkalinity. In addition, polyphosphates are added for corrosion control, phosphonates are utilized for calcium phosphate destabilization, polyacrylates are used for suspended solids dispersion, chlorine dioxide for biological control, and antifoaming agents are used for dispersion of foam caused by phosphates and organic molecules. Even with this regime, however, they have the additional benefit of being able to mix fresh, lake water with the effluent if the latter is unsuitable for use. The usual treatment is lime clarification, although alum treatment is being utilized in one California power plant, and a sodium ion exchange system is constructed and slated for operation to provide cooling water for several Contra Costa County industries.

An analysis of the feasibility of using reclaimed municipal effluent in cooling systems must also include consideration of institutional factors. These factors can be broken down into three parts: (1) supply and delivery, (2) use regulations and (3) blowdown and sludge disposal. In the simplest supply scenario, reclaimed water is sold directly from the city or agency running the reclamation plant to the industrial user. User regulations primarily consist of health regulations, i.e., back flow prevention and operator safety. Blowdown disposal and sludge disposal are regulated by a series of regulations and agencies. These do not differ when using reclaimed effluent or potable supplies; however, the types or concentrations of regulated constituents in the industrial waste stream may differ for the two sources. This may make compliance more difficult and costly.

In the final analysis all of the above technical and institutional considerations are brought to a financial basis. The specific cost components consist of the base price of water, delivery costs, pretreatment capital and O&M costs, internal chemical and O&M costs, disposal costs and regulatory compliance costs (over and above those obtained when using freshwater supplies). Without political considerations, the financial analysis will determine whether or not an industry goes to reclaimed water supplies. With political considerations, an industry may be forced to use reclaimed water, whether or not it is financially attractive. In this latter case, it is possible that some form of subsidy will compensate the industry for its extra costs.

CONCLUSIONS

THE ROLE of municipal waste-water reuse in two potentially large users, namely, agricultural irrigation and industrial cooling, is discussed. Planning methodology and factors affecting waste-water reuse decisions are also discussed in the context of water resources development.

References

1. U.S. Water Resources Council (December 1978) *The Nation's Water Resources, 1975-2000, Vol. 1: Summary.* U.S. Government Printing Office, Washington, D.C.
2. Culp/Wesner/Culp (July 1979) *Water Reuse and Recycling, Vol. 1.* Office of Water Research and Technology, U.S. Department of the Interior, Washington, D.C.
3. Asano, T. and Madancy, R.S. (1981) Water Reclamation Efforts in the U.S.A., in *Wastewater Reuse—State-of-the-Art* (E.J. Middlebrooks, Ed.) Ann Arbor Science Publishers Inc., Woburn, MA.
4. State of California (1978) *Water Reclamation Criteria.* California Administrative Code, Title 22, Division 4, Environmental Health, Department of Health Services, Berkeley, CA.
5. Office of Water Recycling (November 1980) *Evaluation of Industrial Cooling Systems Using Reclaimed Municipal Wastewater.* California State Water Resources Control Board, Sacramento, CA.

Water Pollution Control in the
Wisconsin Fox River Valley

Harold J. Day
*Professor, College of Environmental Science, University
of Wisconsin—Green Bay, Green Bay, Wisconsin, USA*

and

Richard E. Fedler
*Vice-President, Donohue & Associates, Inc.,
Sheboygan, Wisconsin, USA*

SYNOPSIS

*There is a long history of serious water pollution problems in the
Lower Fox River in north-eastern Wisconsin. Pollution has been
caused primarily by industrial waste-water discharges, especially
from the numerous pulp and paper mills along the river, and by the
municipal waste-water discharges. However, a dramatic improvement in river water quality has occurred since 1975. This very
beneficial improvement in the quality of the river is the result of
substantial investment in pollution-abatement projects by both the
pulp and paper mills and the municipalities. Social and institutional pressures and constraints played a major role in shaping
this improvement. These pressures and constraints have included
federal legislation and grant programmes; state, regional and local
mandates and timetables for improved water quality; economic
incentives or the lack thereof; and a very strong sense of local
independence. While much has been accomplished to data, the task
is not yet finished. Even the massive, pollution-abatement projects
already completed will not provide a total clean-up of the river to*

achieve the goals of a stream safe for fishing and bathing. The desire to achieve this goal at the least overall cost has resulted in investigation of non-traditional, water-quality management practices. Practices being investigated include wasteload allocations, flow re-regulation, discharge permits relating allowable discharges to river flow and temperature, transferable discharge permits and instream aeration. Regional management organizations, required for the implementation of some of the proposed practices, are also being investigated. Experience gained in the Wisconsin Fox River Valley indicates that pollution abatement can be accomplished quickly and effectively, provided that there are adequate incentives.

RÉSUMÉ

Depuis longtemps il y a de graves problèmes de pollution des eaux dans la partie inférieure de la rivière Fox au nord est de l'état du Wisconsin. C'est le débit des eaux usées, surtout celles provenant des villes et des nombreuses usines de l'industrie des pâtes à papier qui longent la rivière, qui en est principalement la cause. Pourtant, depuis 1975 on a vu une nette amélioration de la qualité des eaux fluviales, que l'on peut attribuer aux efforts importants conçus par les communes et les sociétés pour réduire la pollution. Ont joue un rôle majeur dans cette amélioration, des pressions sociales et des contraintes industrielles, parmi lesquelles figurent des règlementations et des subventions du gouvernement fédéral ainsi que des mandats mis en place par les gouvernements de l'état et des communes qui ont établi un calendrier pour effectuer les améliorations désirées. A tout ceci viennent s'ajouter des tentatives de motivation économique, soit positives soit negatives, et enfin les sentiments profonds d'indépendance qui se manifestent dans la région. Cependant, bien qu'on ait beaucoup avancé dans ce domaine, il ne faut pas croire que la tâche soit accomplie. Même les programmes colossaux déjà mis au point pour diminuer la pollution ne peuvent assurer un assainissement complet permettant de nouveau d'utiliser la rivière pour se baigner et pêcher; ce qui représente en fin de compte le but que l'on cherche à atteindre. Et pourtant c'est précisément le désir de réussir ce projet, aux frais les moins élevés possibles, qui a provoqué les recherches sur des moyens non-traditionnels pour garantir la qualité des eaux. Faisant l'objet des recherches on compte plusieurs moyens. Parmi eux: la répartition de la quantité des eaux usées; des contrôles en amont du courant de l'eau; des permis variables qui règlent le débit des eaux usées selon la vitesse et la température de la rivière; des permis transférables; l'aération de l'eau fluviale. On étudie également la possibilité de mettre en place des organisations régionales pour surveiller les programmes en cours d'étude. L'experience acquise dans la vallée de la rivière Fox dans le Wisconsin démontre la possibilité de réduire de façon effective la pollution, à condition de fournir une stimulation économique et sociale suffisante.

RESUMEN

Hay una larga historia de los muy serios problemas de la contaminación del agua en la parte baja del Río Fox situado en el nor-este de Wisconsin. La contaminación ha sido producida principalmente por las evacuaciones de las aguas con desechos, especialmente los de las numerosas fábricas de pulpa de madera y de papel que se encuentran a lo largo del Río, y por las evacuaciones de las aguas con desechos del municipio. Sin embargo, un mejoramiento dramático en la calidad del agua del río ha occurrido desde 1975. Este beneficioso mejoramiento de la calidad del río es el resultado de las considerables inversiones en proyectos para la mitigación de la contaminación efectuadas por ambas, las fábricas de pulpa de madera y papel y las municipalidades. Las presiones y los coñstrenimientos sociales e institucionales desempeñaron un papel principal en la formulación de esta mejora. Entre las presiones y los constreñimientos se han incluido legislaciones federales, programas de subvenciones, mandatos estatales, regionales y locales y horarios para que se mejore la calidad del agua, incentivos económicos o la falta de ellos, y un fuerte sentido de independencia local. En tanto que se ha logrado mucho hasta la fecha, todavía la tarea no se ha terminado. Aun los amplios proyectos para la mitigación de la contaminación que ya se han completado no proporcionan una limpieza total del río para lograr la meta de un río en cuya corriente se pueda pescar, nadar. El deseo de obtener esta meta al menos costo posible ha estimulado la investigación de prácticas no tradicionales para el control de la calidad del agua. Las prácticas que se están investigando incluyen el establecimiento de cuotas a la cantidad de desperdicio contenida en el agua, regulación del fluir, permiso de evacuación relacionado a la evacuación admisible en el fluir del río y la temperatura, permisos de evacuación transferibles y ventilación dentro de la corriente. También se están investigando las organizaciones de control regional para la implementación de algunas de las prácticas propuestas. La experiencia obtenida en el Valle del Río Fox de Wisconsin indica que la mitigación de la contaminación se puede lograr rápida y eficazmente siempre que haya incentivos adecuados.

INTRODUCTION

WATER-POLLUTION control is an important part of society in north-eastern Wisconsin today. Although the State of Wisconsin has been known for many years as an area with many freshwater lakes and rivers, water pollution concerns have not become dominant until the past decade. The Wisconsin Fox River Valley is an industrial area dependent upon the extensive nearby forest lands. Many pulp and paper mills are located along the shores of the river. The expansion of pulp and paper mills during the last thirty years has resulted in severe water pollution in the downstream river and Green Bay areas [1]. During the past five to ten years, major capital improvement programmes in both industrial and municipal waste-water treatment, have been underway. Today, the local aquatic ecosystem is regaining some of its former health. Fish have begun to return to those areas where they were before World War II. In general, the local, surface-water quality is much better than a few years ago. Much more needs to be done, though, in the areas of microcontaminants such as PCBs and nutrients such as phosphorus and nitrogen in both urban and rural runoffs. How did this clean-up occur so quickly? Who paid for it? What is likely to happen next? What can be learned as a result of this success story for other industrialized and polluted river systems?

THE PHYSICAL SETTING

THE LOWER FOX RIVER is at the downstream end of a 16,000 square kilometer catchment area. As shown in Figure 1, most of the catchment (about 90%) is located upstream of Lake Winnebago. Two major river systems exist in this upstream area—the Upper Fox River and the Wolf River. They both flow into Lake Winnebago, the largest lake in the State of Wisconsin, with a surface area of approximately 550 square kilometers and an average depth of 4 meters. The lake

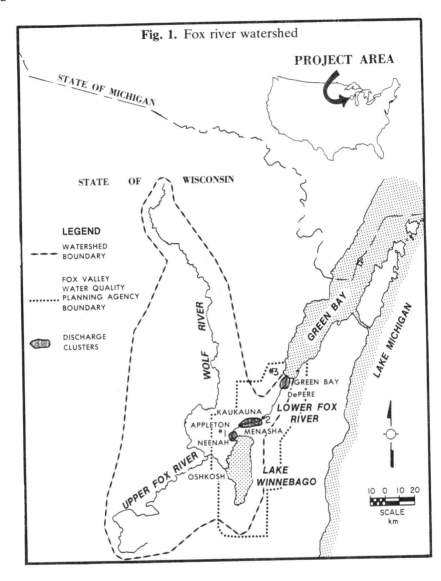

Fig. 1. Fox river watershed

is very susceptible to eutrophication. Warm summer water temperatures and excessive levels of nutrients, primarily from upstream cropland soil erosion, combine to produce luxuriant growths of blue-green algae. The average annual flow out of Lake Winnebago to Green Bay is 116 cubic meters per second. Typical annual maximum and minimum flows are 340 and 55 cubic meters per second respectively. This stable and relatively large flow, when combined with the elevation drop of 51 meters over the 64-kilometer distance from the lake to the bay, offered the combination of a dependable hydropower source and shoreline industrial sites for the early entrepreneurs in the area. These desirable natural resources served as the basis for what today is the highest concentration of paper industry in the world. Fifteen mills discharge treated waste water directly to a 64-kilometer stretch of the river.

In addition, seven municipal waste-water treatment plants release their effluent into the river in this same area. The river's ability to assimilate these biochemical, oxygen-demanding wastes is hindered by a series of pools behind the thirteen dams along the river. Each of these dams is associated with a navigation lock, built before 1860 during the period when water-based navigation for commercial purposes was dominant.

POLLUTION ABATEMENT DURING THE PAST DECADE

WHY DID POLLUTION abatement occur during the past decade? There is no simple answer to this question but some evidence is apparent. New federal and state laws, requiring action by both industries and municipalities polluting the river, is certainly an important reason. However, other reasons exist for the action. The public attitude has supported pollution-abatement investments during recent years. People from all walks of life became increasingly aware that the local surface waters were not healthy and that something must be done.

Action by the United States Government and passage of Public Law 92-500, Federal Water Pollution Control Act Amendments of 1972, served without question as a major incentive for action. This legislation indirectly established water-quality standards for the river and effluent limitations for the industrial and municipal dischargers to the river. Two sections within the bill, Sections 201 and 208, had a direct influence on the Fox River Valley in Wisconsin. Section 201 provided grants for construction of municipal treatment works. Through it, up to 75% of the construction cost of a municipal waste-water treatment facility was paid for with federal funds. Local municipalities, however, were required to pay 100% of the operation and maintenance costs, so care was exercised to design and construct plants suited to the local situation.

INDUSTRIAL AND MUNICIPAL RESPONSE TO POLLUTION ABATEMENT NEEDS

RESPONSES during the past decade by communities and industries in the Fox River Valley to pollution abatement have varied up and down the river. In two of the communities, several of the pulp and paper mills have joined with the community and entered into contracts for the construction and operation of a single treatment plant, to handle both municipal and industrial waste water. In other communities along the river, the mills have constructed their own separate waste-water treatment facilities and the municipal facilities have been expanded to treat the residential, commercial and other industrial waste waters.

There are several key reasons for the two different responses to meeting the industrial and municpal water-pollution abatement needs. Historically, many of the pulp and paper mills along the river have been self-sufficient in meeting their own utility needs, including pollution abatement. With few exceptions, they have decided to continue that policy. Some mills were concerned with a potential loss of control over the adequacy of, and cost of, treatment of their waste water if it was treated in a single plant, handling both industrial and community waste water and operated by the community.

However, probably the single most important factor in the decision by the various mills to either treat their waste waters separately or jointly with the community was economic consideration. Several mills determined that it would be better for them to join with the community in a single waste-water treatment facility than to provide their own. The economies occurred in these cases both due to economies of scale involved in constructing and operating a single, large treatment plant versus two smaller plants, and due to the economic incentives available to the community in the form of state and federal grants-in-aid for the construction of a waste-water treatment facility. No grants-in-aid were available for separate industrial waste-water treatment facilities.

Up until several years ago, grants-in-aid to cover from 55% to 75% of the construction cost of municipal waste-water treatment facilities, including the capacity to handle industrial waste-water, were available for communities along the river. Thus, if an industry were to participate with a municipality in a single treatment plant, the industry would benefit from the grant that the community would receive by paying substantially less for construction of that portion of the treatment plant to handle the industrial waste-water.

Other mills found that their costs would be higher if they participated jointly with the community than if they built their own separate treatment facility. In addition, industries faced potential penalties and fines if they did not have treatment facilities, adequate to meet their effluent limits, in operation by certain dates. While the municipalities had similar dates with which to comply, enforcement of these dates by the state and federal regulatory agencies was generally more stringent in the case of industries.

The net result of the interaction of these various factors was that about one-third of the mills along the river joined with the communities in constructing and operating joint municipal-industrial, waste-water treatment facilities, while the other two-thirds of the mills constructed separate treatment facilities.

WHAT CAN BE EXPECTED TO HAPPEN NEXT?

NOW THAT A SUBSTANTIAL reduction in organic waste discharge to Fox River and to Green Bay has occurred, what can we expect to happen? Water-quality monitoring of the river during the past several years has confirmed the prediction that waste treatment levels beyond conventional secondary will be necessary occasionally during the high temperature, low-flow, summer months. This fact, together with a goal to achieve suitable water quality at the least cost, has resulted in the development of a waste-load allocation [2]. In other words, the reduced natural assimilative capacity of the river must be rationed to maintain both the river and bay's dissolved oxygen level (5.0 mg/l), deemed necessary to keep the waters suitable for fishing and bathing.

The twenty-two major dischargers to the river downstream of Lake Winnebago are geographically clustered into three groups. The first is located in the Neenah-Menasha area as shown on Figure 1. The second is located between Appleton and Kaukauna and the third is located between DePere and Green Bay. Extensive dissolved oxygen computer modelling, conducted cooperatively by the State and by the Regional agency, demonstrated that the first cluster would have to increase the treatment level from approximately 85% to approximately 90%, while the second cluster would have to be treated at a level of approximately 93%. Modelling results for the downstream cluster are not yet available. As shown in Table 1 [3], the extremely high projected costs to provide these treatment levels in a conventional manner, (i.e., the construction of tertiary treatment facilities at each outfall) provided a special motivation for each cluster of dischargers to work with the State and Regional agencies to find more economical procedures to maintain the river at a satisfactory dissolved oxygen level most of the time. Both short-term and long-term activities have been proposed to achieve this goal.

The short-term activities are the development of a non-traditional discharge permit which allows the amount of waste released to the river to vary according to the river's assimilative capacity. This permit, called a Temperature Flow Permit, would allow each discharger within a cluster to discharge more waste water when the assimilative capacity is greater. An example of a Temperature Flow Permit is shown in Table 2 Another short-term activity is the development of a procedure to adjust steady state model results to match the randomly fluctuating discharge conditions actually present. Since the probability of each discharger within a cluster releasing the maximum amount at the same time is very remote, a statistically based correction has been calculated for each of the two upstream clusters. Use of this procedure will reduce the discrepancy between the true level of organic waste released to the river and that assumed to be released in the model.

Longer term, water-quality management activities, designed to maintain higher dissolved oxygen levels at lower costs, include both instream aeration and flow re-regulation.

Table 1. Estimated annual costs for added pollution-abatement facilities in clusters one and two (see Figure 1 for location of clusters)

		Alternative Actions			
1	2	3	4	5	6
Conventional Additional End-of-Pipe Treatment	Stream Temperature and Flow Variable Permits	Instream Aeration	Transferable Discharge Permits	Upstream Flow Re-regulation	Combination of Alternatives 2, 3, and 4
$15 to $20	$6 to $7	$8 to $9	$6 to $8	$11 to $12	$1 to $3

Note: All dollar amounts are millions of dollars.

Table 2. Sample Temperature Flow Permit

Maximum Daily BOD in kilograms
from one discharger during August

		Stream Flow in Cubic Meters Per Second						
°F	°C	27 or Less	27.1 to 34	34.1 to 42	42.1 to 57	57.1 to 71	71.1 to 85	85.1 or More
84	28.9	1,905	1,905	2,346	2,626	3,067	3,384	3,880
80	26.7	1,983	2,169	2,399	2,701	3,165	3,726	4,356
76	24.4	1,976	2,193	2,451	2,782	3,441	4,144	4,910
72	22.2	1,950	2,216	2,492	2,948	3,778	4,608	5,602
68	20.0	1,962	2,264	2,650	3,223	4,192	5,190	5,602
64	17.8	2,006	2,404	2,927	3,612	4,755	5,602	5,602
60	15.6	2,110	2,714	3,370	4,207	5,602	5,602	5,602

(Left axis label: Stream Temperature)

The close proximity of many dischargers on the lower river provides the opportunity for non-traditional economic incentives to reduce costs while maintaining the social amenities of the river. Transferable discharger permits have been proposed for the area. These permits are based on the concept that individual dischargers could contract with upstream or downstream neighbours within the cluster for the maintenance of their share of the river's assimilative capacity. For example, one discharger with an older, more expensive treatment facility might pay an upstream neighbour to treat at a higher level in order to allow the downstream discharger to release wastes at a level higher than normal. Such an arrangement could be carried out at a reduced total cost and without degradation of the receiving waters.

The first steps toward regional, water-quality management have recently occurred. The waste-load allocation process has stimulated the development of ideas for area-wide, water-quality management organizations. Most dischargers expect to find smaller cost increases to achieve higher treatment levels within a regional management framework than they would have to pay as individual, independent dischargers. Many view this situation with strong, mixed emotions. On one hand, the economics of regional involvement are appealing, while on the other hand, the potential reduction of independence and freedom of action is repulsive. Three alternatives have been proposed and discussed at length [6]:

(1) The Fox River Basin Authority
(2) The Fox River Dischargers Association
(3) Maintaining the *status quo*

The Fox River Basin Authority would be a rather broadly based organization, both geographically and institutionally, to which county government elected leaders, and both municipal and industrial sewage-treatment officials, would belong. The scope of management activities would include the monitoring of river water quality for day-to-day maintenance of river and bay dissolved oxygen levels, as well as other water-quality-related planning and management functions, such as urban and rural runoff problems caused by various land management practices.

The Fox River Dischargers Association would be restricted in scope to the collection and distribution of river water-quality information necessary for each discharger to function within the law, in releasing the appropriate volume and strength of waste water to the river. Membership in the Dischargers Association would be restricted to the public and private organizations that own and operate waste-treatment facilities along the river.

The third alternative would include continuing into the future with the same combination of regulatory agencies, state and federal, with no significant changes. This alternative is judged by most dischargers to be unacceptable, since the new discharge permits under this arrangement would not include the flexibility of the Temperature Flow Permit discussed earlier.

As might be expected, the Fox River Dischargers Association has received the strongest level of support. It provides the economic advantages of the Temperature Flow Permit while creating the minimum level of increased inter-institutional co-operation and involvement.

IMPLICATIONS FOR THE FUTURE

THE OVERALL IMPLICATION of the experience gained in the Wisconsin Fox River Valley is that pollution abatement can be accomplished relatively quickly, with a significant improvement in water quality. However, for this result to be achieved in a relatively short timeframe, certain incentives may need to be provided. These incentives may be either positive, in the form of grants-in-aid or similar types of economic incentive, or they may be negative, in the form of penalties and fines for failure to achieve a certain level of pollution abatement by a certain date. Experience in the valley has indicated that equally effective improvements in water quality can be obtained regardless of whether the major industries treat their own waste waters, join with the communities in constructing and operating a single treatment plant, or a combination of the two methods. A benefit that has been gained in the Fox River from the decision by approximately two-thirds of the pulp and paper mills to construct their own treatment facilities is that the discharge of treated waste water to the river occurs in smaller amounts at more locations along the river than if all of the mills had joined with the communities. This results in a better utilization of the assimilative capacity of the stream and also provides a certain degree of protection against major, water-quality problems caused by an upset in the operation of any one treatment facility.

New pollution-abatement issues, both technical and economic, are certain to arise in the near future. The technical issues will probably centre around three stresses to the river and bay not judged in the past as important—nutrients, suspended solids and microcontaminants [7]. Attention will probably shift away from the BOD-producing organic wastes of the municipalities and mills and shift toward some new regions of the watershed. Nutrients (primarily nitrogen and phosphorus) are entering the surface water system in significant amounts from farmland runoff (barnyards and cropland) upstream of Lake Winnebago. Improved rural land management, such as soil conservation and animal-manure-spreading practices, will naturally be stressed.

The suspended solids entering Green Bay from upstream sources, and the bottom sediments of the bay that are periodically resuspended by wind-driven wave action, will also receive attention. Offshore construction projects, such as islands and peninsulas designed to reduce the fetch and create more quiet water, can be expected. Increased attention to the microcontaminants, such as PCBs, will involve the segment of society in the watershed that is active now—municipalities and major wet industries.

The economic issues will naturally center on the people and organizations with primary interests in the control of these stresses. Farmers from upstream portions of the watershed and fishermen in the lower bay can be expected to join pulp and paper-mill managers and municipal leaders in developing plans to reduce the impact of nutrients, microcontaminants and suspended solids that prevent the river and bay from becoming a healthy aquatic ecosystem, serving many and diverse elements of society. This broadened scope of water-quality management, both geographically and institutionally, will heighten the awareness of citizens to the importance of a watershed as a land and water unit with important interlocking activities.

The future of water-pollution control in the Fox River Watershed is full of uncertainty. However, several specific predictions can be made. The focus on industrial and municipal organic wastes will shift to include a wider range of stresses to the aquatic ecosystem. Strong candidates for those stresses likely to move into the spotlight are nutrients, microcontaminants and suspended solids. An increasily diverse, both geographically and vocationally, group of people will become actively involved in water-pollution abatement. The wider understanding of upstream/downstream interdependencies in the watershed will motivate the creation and operation of new political and institutional linkages within the watershed.

References

1. Anonymous, Editorial article in the *Green Bay Press Gazette*, Green Bay, WI, December 7, 1970.
2. Elman, W., *Wasteload Allocation Recommendations and Summary of Public Involvement*, Fox Valley Water Quality Planning Agency, Neenah, WI, December, 1979.
3. David, E., "Cost Effective Management Options for Attaining Water Quality," presented at Wisconsin Section AWRA, February 20, 1981.
4. David, E., Personal communication, November 20, 1980.
5. Eheart, J., Joeres, E., and David, M., "Distribution Methods For Transferable Discharge Permits," *Water Resources Research*, Vol. 16, No. 5, October, 1980.
6. Elman, W., *Management Structure To Implement Wasteload Allocation For The Lower Fox River*, Fox Valley Water Quality Planning Agency, Neenah, WI, September, 1980.
7. Day, H., and Harris, H., "Toward the Integrated Management of the Fox River Green Bay System," presented at AWRA National Symposium, May, 1980.

Rejection of Industrial Effluents in the Tagus Basin and their Influence on the Lisbon Regional Water Supply

César Ferreira Antunes
Head, Water Treatment Sector of EPAL

Rui Manuel Carvalho Godinho
Head, Technical Bureau, Water Treatment Sector of EPAL

and

José Domingos Maria Rosa
Head, Department of Weak Currents, Electricity and Lifting Sector of EPAL

SYNOPSIS

A brief sketch is given of the history of the use of the surface waters of the Tagus for the water supply of the Lisbon region since the beginning of the present century. The main sources of pollution of the waters of the Tagus River are pointed out, these being both direct and indirect through its tributaries: the Nabão, Almonda and Alviela. The characteristic factors defining the quality of the water for public supply are studied and the way they have evolved since 1963 is indicated. On the other hand, the trend of the same factors is analysed and the conclusion is reached that although the Tagus River, in the area where water is obtained to supply Lisbon, still shows only a low degree of pollution, there is nevertheless a tendency for the factors studied to deteriorate. Finally, with regard to the control of the waters of the Tagus at the EPAL level, a summary is given of the plans to be carried out within the scope of the General Telecontrol System for the installations making up the Lisbonne depuis le début du siecle en cours. On souligne les principaux sources de pollution des eaux du Tage, soit directes, soit quantitative terms and for its insertion in the General Telecontrol System to be established.

RÉSUMÉ

On fait l'histoire résumée de l'utilization des eaux superficielles du Tage en vue de l'approvisionnement d'Eaux dans la Région de Lisbonne depuis le début du siècle en cours. On souligne les principaux sources de pollution des eaux du Tage, soit directes, soit indirectes, par ses affluents: le Nabão, l'Almonda et l'Alviela. On étudie les paramètres caractéristiques définissant la qualité des eaux pour l'approvisionnement public, en indiquant de quelle manière ils ont évolué depuis 1963, et par ailleurs, quelle est la tendance d'évolution de ces derniers, en arrivant à la conclusion que bien que le Tage, près de la Zone de la prise d'eau destinée à l'approvisionnement de Lisbonne, soit encore peu pollué, il existe une tendance allant vers une dégradation des paramètres étudiés. On fait référence à les actions qui, à l'avis des auteurs, serait indispensable mettre en oeuvre envisageant le contrôle et la gestion de la qualité de l'eau du Tage en amont de Valada do Ribatejo.

Finalement, en ce qui concerne le contrôle des eaux du Tage au niveau d'EPAL, l'on fait un résumé de ce qui est programmé en matière de réalisation dans le cadre du Système Général de Télécontrôle des installations qui constituent le Système d'Approvisionnement d'Eau de la Région de Lisbonne; en présentant le schéma prévue pour la mise en oeuvre effective de ce contrôle, tant sur le plan de la qualité que de la quantité ainsi que son insertion dans le Schéma Général de Télécontrôle à installer.

RESUMEN

Se hace la historia resumida del aprovechamiento de las aguas superficiales del Tejo para el Abastecimiento de Aguas à la Région de

Lisboa desde principios de siglo. Se apuntan las principales fuentes contaminantes de las aguas del río Tejo, sea directa sea indirecta a través de sus afluentes: Nabão, Almonda, Alviela.

Se estudian los parámetros característicos definidores de la calidad de las aguas para el abastecimiento público, indicando como evolucionarían desde 1963 y cual sería la tendencia que presentan en cuanto à su evolución, concluyendo que aunque el río Tejo en la zona de captación de agua del abastecimiento de Lisboa se presenta todavia poco contaminado, hay mientras tanto la tendencia para la degradación de los parámetros estudiados. Finalmente en eo que concierne al control de las aguas del río Tejo por parte de EPAL se hace un resumen de lo que se planea realizar en el ámbito del Sistema General de Telecontrol de las Instalaciónes que forman el Sistema de Abastecimiento de Agua a la Región de Lisboa, presentando el esquema previsto para efectuar ese control sea cualitativo sea cuantitativo y su inserción en el Esquema General de Telecontrol a instalarse.

INTRODUCTION

THE LISBON WATER SUPPLY system is intended to supply about half a million cubic metres of drinkable water per day to a population of approximately one and a half million people distributed over an area of about one thousand five hundred square kilometres; this water is impounded over approximately one hundred kilometres.

At the beginning of the next century, the orders of magnitude will probably be the following: one and a half million cubic metres of drinkable water per day; a population of three million people distributed over two thousand five hundred square kilometres and a water production area about a hundred and fifty kilometres long.

Attempts to use the Tagus surface water date back to the beginning of this century (1906 to 1918), when a project was presented which consisted in installing slow filters upstream from Santarém, taking into account the disadvantage resulting from the fact that the sewage of this town (50,000 people) is discharged directly into the river, totally untreated.

This project was revised in 1932, in connection with the contract entered into between the Government and the concessionnaire for the supply of water to Lisbon. The solution then adopted also included the use of the Tagus alluvial waters, considering that they could be easily caught and were very pure as compared with surface water.

One of the great disadvantages then pointed out concerning the Tagus surface water was doubtless its chloride and sulphate contents during the summer droughts, resulting from the fact that the tributaries of the Tagus in Spain, the rivers Tajuña and Henares, in the Jarrama drainage basin, flow through "keuper", i.e., a region of acid earth and gypsiferous clays which account for the high sulphate contents found in the water of the rivers flowing through this area.

It has been found out that there is a relationship between the sulphate contents and the Tagus water flow rates, the former varying between 20 and 100 mg/l from October to December; 100 and 250 mg/l from January to July, and 250 and 400 mg/l from August to September.

Thanks to the construction of large hydro-electric power stations, both in Portugal (on the Zezere and on the Tagus itself, at Belver), and Spain (such as the Alcantara dam), the sulphate problem has been mitigated by the new regularity of the water flow rates and mainly by the accumulation of the water for long periods in the huge lake formed by the Alcantara dam.

The effective utilisation of the Tagus surface water to supply the Lisbon area dates back to 1963, when an intake was installed in the area of Valada do Ribatejo and a Water Treatment Station was set up in a non-flooding nearby zone, situated near a small village called Vale da Pedra, approximately 50 km away from Lisbon.

Nowadays, the main problem connected with the Tagus surface water is that of the deterioration of its quality due to increased industrial pollution caused by the factories that discharge their effluents and wastewater directly into the Tagus, or into its main tributaries.

POLLUTION IN THE TAGUS

THERE IS NO INTEGRATED study of pollution, either industrial or otherwise, in the Portuguese section of the Tagus upstream from the water catchment station for water supply to the Lisbon area, set up at Valada do Ribatejo.

With the exception of the data existing at EPAL's offices since the Tagus surface water began to be used to supply the population of Lisbon (1963) there have been only studies of pollution in the most polluted tributaries of the Tagus, namely the rivers Alviela, Almonda and Nabão plus miscellaneous data obtained during other analyses carried out outside EPAL and the results of the GEMS (Global Environmental Monitoring system) for 1980. All these data have been made available by the Direcção dos Serviços de Controlo da Poluição of the DGRAH (Ministry of Housing and Public Works).

The facts mentioned above, together with an almost complete ignorance of what is happening in the Spanish section of the Tagus and its tributaries, with regard to wastewater discharges, make it impossible to objectively estimate or assess the degree of pollution in the section under analysis, and the way in which it reflects on the quality of the water impounded at Valada.

In any case, we shall not neglect to comment on the available data, and express our opinion about the evolution of the water quality at Valada do Ribatejo, with particular reference to the drought that has lately been felt, with certain relationships and conclusions drawn from the available data.

MAIN SOURCES OF INDUSTRIAL POLLUTION

THE MAIN SOURCES of industrial pollution situated in the Portuguese territory that affect the quality of the Tagus water upstream from Valada are to be found on the banks of the rivers Nabão, Almonda, Alviela and on the Tagus itself.

On the basis of the studies already referred to about pollution in these tributaries, we can list the following sources of pollution:

Nabão

The Nabão is a tributary of the Zezere, joining this river at a place near its mouth, at Constância. One hundred and thirty nine sources of industrial pollution have been listed, comprising three pulp mills—middle-sized companies—a wood agglomerate plant—also a middle-sized company—seven small and middle-sized distilleries, two textile plants, seven middle-sized animal raising farms, and a hundred and seven olive oil factories. We have also identified 15 sources of nonindustrial pollution (sewage) of which the town of Tomar (40,000 inhabitants) is the most important.

All these industrial units discharge their wastewaters without adequate treatment into the nearest stream of the Nabão drainage basin, thus contributing to the high degree of pollution carried by this river into the last section of the Zezere upstream from the Castelo do Bode dam, and hence into the Tagus.

Table 1 shows data taken from the Pollution Control Study for this river, carried out in 1977, and covering some important parameters. These figures have been obtained at the sampling station nearest where this river flows into the Zezere.

The more recent data stated hereunder (1981), obtained in a non-systematic way on the same river, during the recent drought show that pollution in this river has not decreased, and has even increased under certain aspects: BOD—6.6 mg/l; COD—26 mg/l; oxidability in the presence of $KMnO_4$—7.00 mg/l; Dissolved oxygen (%) 45%; Alkalinity ($CaCO_3$)—195 mg/l; Bicarbonates (HCO_3)—238 mg/l; Albuminoid nitrogen—0.400 mg/l; Nitrites—0.600 mg/l NO_2.

Table 1. Maximum, Medium and Minimum Values of Certain Significant Variables

Variables Values	Conductivity $\times 10^{-6}$	pH	Dissolved Oxygen %	BOD_5 (mg/l)	Nitrites (mg/l)	Nitrates (mg/l)
Maximum	1085	8.0	95%	24.6	0.23	8.5
Medium	500	7.6	65%	6.8	0.06	4.5
Minimum	425	6.8	28%	3.8	0.03	0.5

Almonda

On the Almonda drainage basin there are 50 sources of industrial pollution, namely two middle-sized pulp mills, two large textile plants, two food processing plants and seven small and middle-sized distilleries, besides the thirty-six olive presses, whose activity is seasonal. The study referred to above concludes that this river is highly polluted in terms of industrial pollution, aggravated by the uncontrolled discharge of untreated sewage coming from the town of Torres Novas (25,000 people).

In research carried out by the Direcção dos Serviços de Controlo da Poluição in 1974, the values obtained for some significant variables at different points along this river, near the outfalls of industrial effluents, were extremely high, as follows: Temperature—39°C; Turbidity—652 mg/l of SiO_2; Colour—360 (Pt–Co); BOD_5 (20°C)—2900 mg/l; Dissolved oxygen (DO)—0 mg/l, at least at 10 points along the river; Oxidability ($KMnO_4$)—842.6 mg/l of O_2; Phenol—260 mg/l; Sulphates—937.8 mg/l; Chlorides—213 mg/l; Alkalinity—3200 mg/l; pH—12.5; Conductivity—11,980 × 10⁶. This pollution is also carried into the Tagus.

Alviela

Of the three tributaries considered as polluted upstream from the water catchment of Valada do Ribatejo, this is the one that shows the largest number of sources of pollution, and about which we possess the least data.

During the studies recently carried out by the Direcção dos Serviços de Controlo da Poluição, 355 sources of pollution have been identified on this river or its tributaries. Special mention should be made here of the highly polluting 107 small and middle-sized tanning plants scattered about the drainage basin of the Alviela, and of the 120 cattle raising farms which are also highly polluting.

This river is therefore in a highly polluted condition, and it also carries its pollution into the Tagus.

Other sources

Besides the polluting agents of industrial origin carried mainly by these three tributaries into the Tagus, there are numerous non-discriminated sources of pollution on the banks of the Tagus itself, among which are the pulp mills of PORTUCEL at Vila Velha de Ródão, and those of Companhia de Celulose do Caima, SARL, at Constância. The former has a production capacity of 260 tons of raw pulp per day, and the amount of polluting agents discharged by this plant directly into the Tagus has been estimated at 5,200 kg/day, expressed in terms of Biochemical Oxygen Demand (BOD_5—20°C). With regard to the other pulp mill, situated opposite the mouth of the river Zezere at Constância, the amount of polluting agents discharged by it into the Tagus has been estimated at about 2600 kg/day, expressed in terms of BOD_5, for a production capacity of 170 tons of bleached pulp per day. In terms of concentration of polluting agents, we can find values in the order of 3,500 mg/l of COD (Chemical Oxygen Demand) and 1000 mg/l of BOD_5. This plant is equipped with a wastewater treatment station which is not always in operation, but capable of reduction of the above values by approximately 50 per cent on average.

A campaign recently carried out by EPAL and the Direcção dos Serviços de Controlo da Poluição (1981) with the purpose of determining the effects of the recent drought on the quality of the water taken from the Tagus, has made it possible to obtain the data stated in Table 2.

Worthy of mention among the data concerning the various sections of the river, from its source to its mouth, are the high COD and the troubles regarding Dissolved Oxygen (DO). Furthermore, we should emphasise the results obtained at the Ponte de Constância Station, situated about 500 m downstream from the outfall of untreated wastewater discharged by Cellulose Caima Pulp.

With regard to the DO (dissolved oxygen) obtained, it is interesting to make a comparison with Klein (1959) *River Pollution—Vol. 1*, confirmed by Nemerow (1974) *Scientific Stream Pollution Analysis*, according to whom saturation values exceeding 90 per cent indicate good conditions for utilisation, values between 75 and 90 per cent acceptable conditions, values between 50 and 75 per cent medium pollution, and doubtful utilisation and values lower than 50 per cent high pollution.

We would like to point out the existence in Spain of at least two Nuclear Power Stations on the banks of Spanish section of the Tagus, of which one, the Almaraz Power Station, has recently been put into operation. These two units may pollute the Tagus water which flows towards Portugal. EPAL is monitoring the level of radioactivity of the Tagus water near the intake of Valada in terms of α and β radiation; nothing abnormal has been detected so far.

Indeed, the maximum values obtained in 1980 were 1.1 pCi/l and 9.8 pCi/l for α and β radiation, respectively; in most cases, however, the values obtained for both types of radiation did not exceed 0.0 pCi/l.

It should not be forgotten that for drinkable water, the World Health Organization recommends radioactivity levels not exceeding 3.0 pCi/l for α radiation and 30.0 pCi/l for β radiation.

Table 2. Quality of the Tagus Water (March–August 1981): Certain Significant Parameters

Parameters	Mouth of Nabão			Constância			Mouth of Almonda			Mouth of Alviela			Mouth of Vala Alpiaza		
	Max.	Med.	Min.	Max.	Med.	Min.	Max.	Med.	Min.	Max.	Med.	Min.	Max.	Med.	Min.
pH	8.10	7.54	7.30	8.25	6.79	5.00	7.60	7.50	7.40	7.60	7.30	6.80	8.45	7.63	7.20
Dissolved Oxygen (% saturation)	100	81.7	9 (*)	80	49.7	0	94	65.4	33	100	72.1	39	100	91.4	65
BOD_5 (20°C) (mg/l O_2)	13.5	6.7	2.2	103.5	30.0	2.6	6.9	4.0	1.1	9.0	4.6	1.8	8.3	4.5	1.4
COD (mg/l O_2)	152.9	32.7	7.0	1923.6	441.2	19.4	53.8	29.3	11.7	31.0	19.2	7.7	61.4	24.9	7.7
Mercury (mg/l Hg)	(*) —	—	—	—	—	—	1.1	0.85	0.70	—	—	—	1.4	0.93	0.70
Oxidability KMnO₄ (mg/l O_2)	160 (*) 176 (**)	39.3	2.24	824.0	198.2	14.0	33.6	14.5	5.8	14.4	8.3	4.6	13.1	7.1	5.1

(*)(**) Samples taken on 2.4.81 and 8.4.81 after discharges into the river Nabão of great quantity of industrial effluents from a wood factory. Many dead fish found in river.

CHARACTERISTICS OF THE TAGUS WATER AT VALADA DO RIBATEJO

In order to control the water quality and consequently determine the degree of treatment to be carried out at the Vale da Pedra treatment station, we have used water samples taken from the river on a weekly basis since 1963. These water samples are then submitted to physico-chemical, biological and bacteriological analysis in the laboratory.

Considering that our main concern is industrial pollution, we will only mention the physico-chemical parameters which define the quality of the water to be used for public supply, as well as the way in which such parameters have evolved since 1963. We have chosen the following parameters: pH, alkalinity, oxidability in the presence of $KMnO_4$, conductivity, sulphates and chlorides. For this purpose we are using all the data that have been filed at the Water Treatment Service since 1963 (with the exception of 1964), and which correspond to the weekly analysis of the samples referred to above. At a rate of 45–50 samples per year, this corresponds to about 800 values for each of the parameters under analysis, whose variation is shown in Table 3 and in Figure 1.

In order to evaluate more objectively the development of the quality of the water caught at Valada, and the possible problems and/or deterioration caused by pollution upstream from this station, particularly industrial pollution, we have prepared Figure 1. This figure shows the maximum, minimum and average annual oxidability in the presence of $KMnO_4$ (measurement of the amount of organic matter) during this period. As in the case of the other parameters shown in Table 3, we can see that there are considerable annual and interannual fluctuations as regards oxidability. However, Figure 1 shows a certain tendency towards a slight increase, mainly as from 1975 the year in which yearly averages started regularly to exceed the average of yearly averages, which is 4.09 mg/l; it also shows a sharp rise in maximum yearly values in 1976. The average value referred to is, however, still lower than the 5 mg/l allowed by the EEC.

Taking the oxidability parameter as a basis, we have drawn up Figure 2, which shows the variation of this parameter throughout 1980, on the basis of weekly measurements.

This allows us to conclude that in 72% of the cases the oxidability exceeds 4.09 mg/l, which confirms the tendency shown in Figure 1. Another aspect to be noted is the frequency of steep rises between April and September.

As a complementary study, we have also analysed the evolution of the amounts of dissolved oxygen corresponding to the oxidability shown in Figure 2 (using the samples taken in 1980). We have found out that in 81 per cent of the cases, saturation exceeded 90 per cent, and that in all the other cases it was between 70 and 90 per cent. With regard to industrial pollution of an inorganic nature, no significant increase has been found. Some steep rises have however been detected, as shown by the values obtained for chloride content.

Table 3. Summary of the most significant values of the parameters under analysis (1963 to 1980)

Parameters	Average of yearly averages (1)	Maximum yearly maximum (2)	Minimum yearly minimum (3)	Maximum yearly average (4)	Minimum yearly average (5)	Max. difference (2) − (3)
pH	7.60	8.85(1968)	6.69(1976)	8.24(1968)	7.12(1976)	2.16(24.4%)
Alkalinity (mg/l)	66.3	135(1963)	20(1965)	84(1980)	52(1969)	115(82.2%)
Conductivity (n × 10⁻⁶ mhm)	379	840(1963)	90(1969)	470(1980)	234(1969)	800(90%)
Oxidability in the presence of KMnO₄ (mg/l O₂)	4.09	8.80(1976)	0.80(1966)	4.53(1977)	3.63(1969)	8(91%)
Sulphates (mg/l)	96	338(1965)	9.5(1969)	126(1965)	45(1969)	328.5(97%)
Chlorides (mg/l)	23.9	126(1966)	8.9(1963)	38.9(1976)	20.5(1969)	117.1(93%)

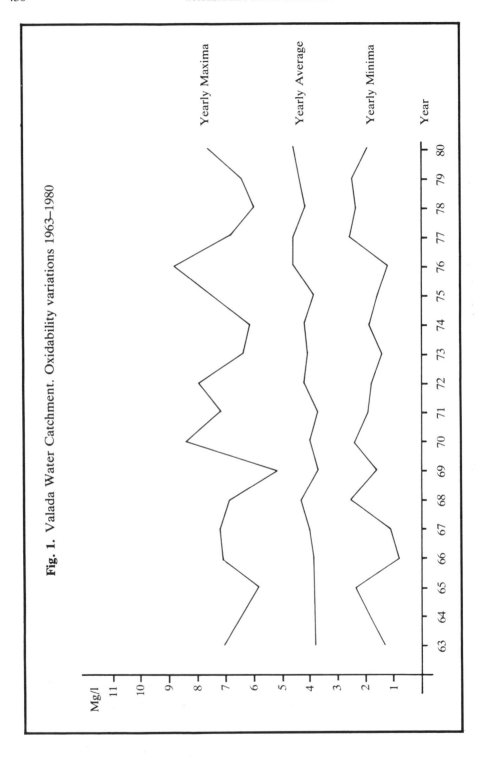

Fig. 1. Valada Water Catchment. Oxidability variations 1963–1980

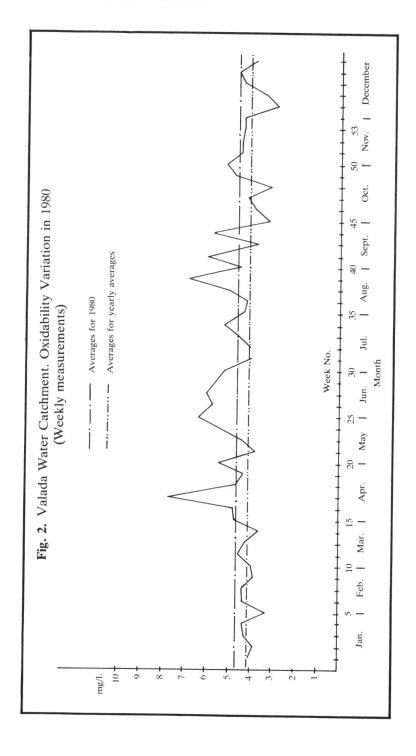

Fig. 2. Valada Water Catchment. Oxidability Variation in 1980 (Weekly measurements)

—————— Averages for 1980

—··—··— Averages for yearly averages

As has already been said, during the first half of 1981, Portugal was affected by a drought which had negative effects on the quantity and quality of the Tagus water (see Table 2), therefore considerably affecting the Valada Catchment.

Thus, in connection with smaller upstream flow rates, there occurred pollution peaks at Valada during the first three months of the year, expressed by high colour, oxidability and COD values. Values as high as 40° Hazen have been reached in the first case; the oxidability was higher than 8 mg/l of O_2 during the month of February and in March, it reached a maximum value of 12.6 mg/l of O_2. As to the COD, values of 36.8 mg/l have been reached.

If we compare these data with the information obtained since 1963, we must come to the conclusion that no such values had been detected until the beginning of 1981. We can refer to Figure 3 to have an idea of the oxidability values obtained during the months of January, February and March, as compared with those obtained every year, from 1963 to 1981.

It is reasonable to suppose that the high oxidability measured at Valada at the beginning of this year is already the result of the uncontrolled discharge of industrial effluents into the Tagus and its tributaries. From the information quoted above we can conclude that the Tagus is not yet very polluted at Valada do Ribatejo, although it shows a slight but already clear tendency to a certain degradation. Though in average terms, such a tendency is not yet preoccupying, particular attention should start to be given to the occurrence of pollution peaks and their frequency.

The self-purifying capacity of the section of the Tagus upstream from Valada is improved in our opinion, among other factors, by the frequent addition of good quality water discharged by the dams, mainly by the Castelo do Bode dam, and by the large oxygen exchange surface it possesses, due to the fact that in this section of its course, the Tagus is what could be called a plain river. It should be pointed out that at the beginning of 1981, during the drought, the Castelo do Bode dam did not discharge the amounts of water it usually discharges as a result of the power production process; this has also contributed to aggravating the situation of the river, which has continued to receive the same amounts of industrial wastewater and sewage in a medium showing much smaller flow rates and a worse quality.

More recent data obtained at the Valada water catchment from the beginning of April to the end of August 1981 have enabled us to draw Figure 4, which shows the evolution of the water quality with regard to organic matter (oxidability $KMnO_4$) and Dissolved Oxygen (DO) in the first eight months of 1981 (35 weeks).

In our opinion, the situation in the months of July and August is particularly worrying, and, in spite of the drought that has affected Portugal, we cannot deny the negative influence of the industrial wastewater discharged into the Tagus (see Table 2), and, consequently, the increased degradation of the quality of the Tagus water at the Valada water catchment. The average of oxidability averages has already increased from 4.60 mg/l O_2 (1980) to 6.90 mg/l O_2 in 1981, and the frequency of pollution peaks is also rising steeply. However, the physico-chemical characteristics of the water supplied to consumers have not yet exceeded the required safety levels.

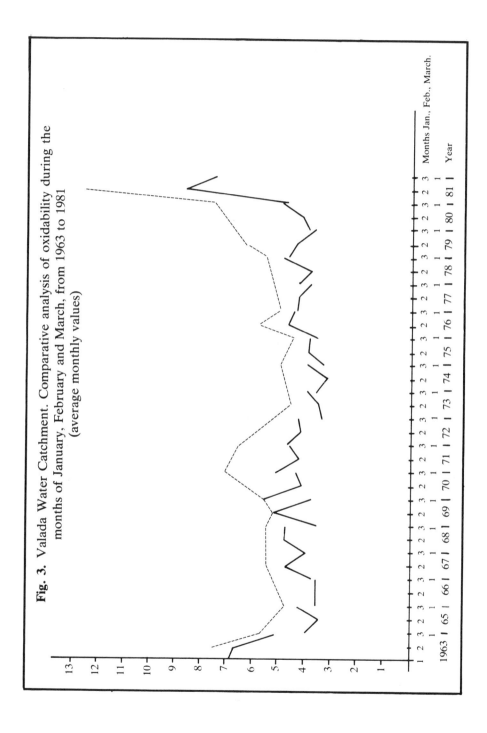

Fig. 3. Valada Water Catchment. Comparative analysis of oxidability during the months of January, February and March, from 1963 to 1981 (average monthly values)

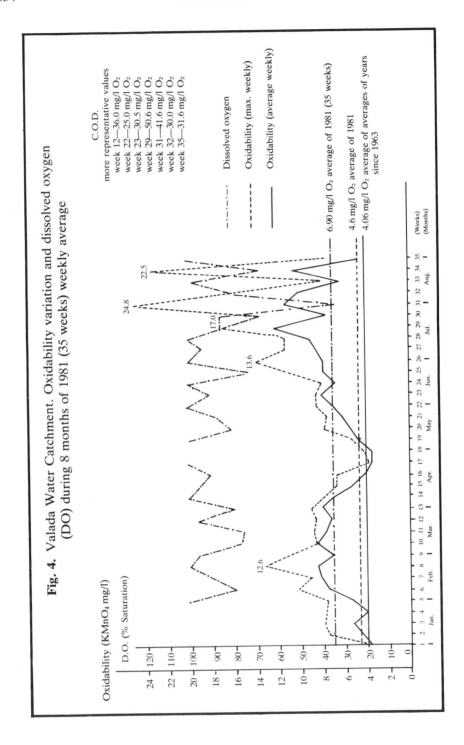

Fig. 4. Valada Water Catchment. Oxidability variation and dissolved oxygen (DO) during 8 months of 1981 (35 weeks) weekly average

STEPS TO BE TAKEN

THE EXISTING STUDIES and the campaigns in progress, due to their limited scope, their lack of co-ordination and the fact that they are not inserted in a comprehensive plan for the management and quality control of the Tagus water in the Portuguese section of the river upstream from Valada, can hardly make it possible to predict the future relationship between the quality of the water caught at Valada and the characteristics and flow rates of the wastewater discharged into the river.

At present, besides the pollution studies mentioned hereabove and the regular weekly sampling carried out by EPAL at Valada for control purposes, there is but one project in progress in Santarém, within the scope of the international project of the WHO/PNUD, called GEMS (Global Environmental Monitoring System). The six series of samples taken within the scope of this Project in 1980 have revealed nothing new about the Tagus.

Thus, it seems imperative to intensify the qualitative study of the Tagus drainage basin, particularly with regard to the Portuguese section of this river upstream from Valada; such a study should, as much as possible, be integrated with actions extendable to the whole drainage basin of this river. Indeed, any partial decisions that can be made on the basis of such a study shall take into account the fact that basic solutions suppose the unified control of the whole basin.

Thus, considering that the noblest use of the Tagus water is to supply the Lisbon Area, it would be important to establish a co-ordinated management and control system limited to the section of the river and its tributaries between the Spanish border and Valada do Ribatejo, with particular emphasis on the industrial zones.

Initially, this system would constitute a pilot zone—like that of the Tagus Estuary—which would make it possible to build a "hydraulic-sanitary" physical model enabling the formation of an opinion about the behaviour of the river on the basis of real or simulated situations.

In order that the above mentioned objective can be pursued, it will be necessary to take certain actions, namely:

(1) To set up a sampling system, intended to provide samples for analysis, using automation systems.
(2) To continually collect and analyse all the data obtained in the meantime.
(3) To evaluate the current situation of the Tagus and its tributaries in the section under analysis, trying to forecast the evolution of the quality of their waters.
(4) To study the dispersion and diffusion of industrial polluting agents, in order to find out the transformations and degradation of such polluting agents that result from the self-purifying capacity of the river itself.
(5) To try to evaluate the self-purifying capacity of the Tagus and its main tributaries.

(6) To develop and select the most adequate sewage and industrial waste-water treatment processes and technologies, and adapt them to local conditions.

Furthermore, certain precautions shall be taken in the first phase followed by an adequate planning in some domains in the next phase, in order to safeguard the national section of the Tagus against the effects of pollution beyond the Portuguese border, including radioactive pollution. These points and others connected with quality shall be dealt with in the Portuguese-Spanish Agreement regarding the use of the water in international rivers, which has not been ratified so far.

As far as EPAL is concerned, studies are being carried out to provide the Company with water storage units near the surface impoundment, install automatic control mechanisms and to set up alarm stations on the Tagus intended to prevent the occurrence of unexpected peaks of industrial pollution.

Thus, when the general principles of operation of the main remote control system of the units that make up the Lisbon areas water supply system were laid down in 1978, it was immediately decided to include the monitoring of the Tagus water quality parameters upstream from the Valada intake and at the Vale da Pedra Treatment Station, completed by the monitoring of the treated water quality, during its transport to the supply network. For reasons connected with the geographic location of the plants and the possibilities of transmission, and due to the philosophy of operation that has been adopted, the Remote Control System has been laid out on the basis of Regional Control Stations which are individually responsible for one zone, and will be connected to a Central Decision Station.

Two of these RCSs shall be set up, one at the Vale da Pedra Station, which treats the Tagus water caught at Valada, and the other at the Asseiceira Water Treatment Station, which will treat the Zezere water caught at Castelo do Bode; they shall carry out the qualitative and quantitative analysis of the water of these two rivers down to Vila Franca de Xira, whose RCS will be situated in the Pumping Station, which is the pivot of the whole water delivery system to Lisbon; after this Pumping Station the water quality will only be checked in the Lisbon reservoirs. The delivery of water to the city with its mains, tanks and water castles, and to the suburbs will be controlled from the Decision Station to be set up in Lisbon; the whole system will be supervised from this Station, with regard to catchment, treatment, transport and delivery.

Automatic stations for the continuous monitoring of untreated water characteristics (pH, turbidity, dissolved oxygen, conductivity, total organic carbon and redox potential) will be set up on the Tagus, in places still to be fixed, and will be connected to the Vale da Pedra RCS by remote measuring systems assisted by radio links. A Process Control Computer, in continuous operation, will process these data together with other introduced on-line river characteristics (e.g. amount of water being treated, water quality upon treatment, etc); or previously stored on the basis of relevant data (e.g. periodicity, cost of chemicals and electric power, etc). This computer will control the treatment process on a technical-economic and critical basis, to ensure the required water quality at minimum cost.

Quantitative and qualitative data regarding the Tagus water will regularly be sent by the computer of the Vale da Pedra RCS to the Lisbon Decision Station through the RCS of Vila France de Xira, where such data will be processed and despatched together with similar information about water from other sources.

The Computer of the Decision Station, which is more powerful than that of the RCSs and is provided with mass storage devices and adequate terminals, will ensure, among other things, the processing and storage of data concerning the Tagus water, and produce multipurpose loggings and records, which can be used as work data to monitor the characteristics of the Tagus.

Taking into account the know-how it already possesses, the studies in progress, and the fact that it is the major user of Tagus water, EPAL is ready to integrate a number of organizations, which would make up the central organization for execution and co-ordination of the actions proposed above. Furthermore, and as a logical consequence of this, EPAL will also play an active part in the development of the institutional bodies which will have to be created to execute the management policy suggested by the results of the studies mentioned above.

Drainage and Treatment of Wastewater on Industrial Estates in Portugal

João Quinhones Levy
Project Director, Consultores de Engenharia
Sanitária, Lda. (CESL), Lisbon, Portugal

and

Arnaldo Sá Frias
Engineer, Consultores de Engenharia
Sanitária, Lda. (CESL), Lisbon, Portugal

SYNOPSIS

Industrial estates started in Portugal in 1973. Being the result of a new policy and because the industrial profile of each estate was unknown beforehand, there was no previous experience on the selection and values of the parameters that are important for the design of the sewer networks, nor on the treatment schemes and final disposal of the wastewater. The authors present in this paper the parameters that were used for the design of the sewer networks of the industrial estates of Beja, Covilhã, Évora and Guimarães and consider the treatment schemes and the final disposal methods that were adopted.

438

RÉSUMÉ

Les parcs industriels ont vu son début au Portugal en 1973. Etant une politique nouvelle, on n'avait aucunne expérience dans le choix et la valeur des paramètres qui régissent le calcul des réseaux d'égout ainsi que son traitement et rejet, parce que au début on ne connaissait pas le profit industriel de chacun des parcs. Les auteurs présentent dans cet article les paramètres qui ont été suivis dans le calcul des réseaux d'égout des parcs industriels de Beja, Covilhã, Évora et Guimarães et font quelques considérations sur le traitement et le type de rejet adoptés.

RESUMEN

Los parques industriales en Portugal empezaron en 1973. Como consistía en una nueva politica no habia ninguna experiencia para elegir y dar valor a los parametros que pudiesen regular el cálculo del alcantarillado así como del tratamiento de las águas residuales, pues no se conocía el perfil industrial de cada parque. Los autores presentan en este articulo los parametros que fueron seguidos para el cálculo del alcantarillado de los parques industriales de Beja, Covilhã, Évora y Guimarães y describen también el tratamiento y el tipo de evacuación adoptados.

INTRODUCTION

AN INDUSTRIAL ESTATE is generally considered as an industrial urbanization in which fundamental services are guaranteed by a central administration. Its objective is the industrial development of the region where it is located and the reorganization of existing industries which should be removed from the cities. These estates should serve, above all, the industries that do not need a great covered area.

The development of industrial estates in Portugal began in 1973, with these objectives. Since that year the EPPI (Public Enterprise of Industrial Estates) developed the estates of Beja, Braga, Covilhã, Évora and Guimarães and is developing the Faro estate.

Being an entirely new idea in Portugal, the main difficulties found in the design of the sewerage systems and treatment plants were the evaluation of the parameters to be used as the industrial profile of the estate was unknown.

CHARACTERISTICS OF THE INDUSTRIAL ESTATES IN PORTUGAL

Beja Estate

This estate will be built near Beja-Serpa road, in the vicinity of Beja. The total area will be about 282,500 m² and the covered area 53,475 m². The total number of workers will be 1,780. The main industries will be agricultural and food industries. The EPPI usually defines for each estate a list of the industries which can be established without special authorisation.

Covilhã Estate

This estate is already under construction and it is located 2 km from Covilhã, near the road to Guarda. Its total area will be about 315,000 m², with a covered area of 54,000 m². The total number of workers will be 2,000. This estate was designed in order to help woolen manufacturing and development of the agricultural and food industries. This objective does not prevent the installation of other industries, such as the optical, pharmaceutical and cosmetics industries which have already applied for a place in the estate.

Évora Estate

This estate was built in a region where there were no industries, and its objective was to create agricultural and food manufacturing industries and to solve the problem of unemployment in the region. This estate is comprised of very different industries, such as:

Canned meat
Dairy products
Food and agricultural products
Nourishing oils
Flours
Bread and sweetmeats
Chocolates
Drinks
Wood

Pharmaceutic products
Mechanical constructions
Its total area will be about 500,000 m² and its covered area will be 145,000 m². The total number of workers will be 4,825. This estate is also under construction.

Guimarães Estate

Located 4 km from Guimarães, this estate was an alternative to the Braga estate. Built in 1976, its total area will be, after the second phase, about 280,000 m² with a covered area of 75,350 m². The total number of workers will be 3,000. Its industrial profile comprises food and agricultural manufacturing, canned products and paper and milk industries.

ESTIMATION OF THE FLOW OF WASTEWATER

THE ESTIMATION of the design flow for the sewerage system was obtained by evaluating the needs of the factories, administrative services and social areas. The water drained from the industries is dependent on several factors:
the kind of industries;
the manufacturing process;
the degree of reutilization of the water.
It is only possible to fix average values for the drained water, in the known industries.

In the industrial estates, though the profile is not known, there is a list of the possible industries, and the sewerage system may be designed. For the evaluation of the sewerage flow a large bibliography was consulted. However the majority of the authors only present values for specific industries and not for an entire industrial estate. Studies that have been done in other countries tend to admit values of about 35–40 m³/day/ha of the total area. For the four estates the value of 40 m³/day/ha of covered area was used and so an average consumption of 12 l/day/m² was obtained.

As each estate has an industrial and domestic consumption it was considered that 10 l/day/m² was due to industries and 2 l/day/m² to the domestic uses. The rate between the peak flow and the medium flow adopted is 4, because the consumption of some industries is only important during 5 or 6 hours, although the working time is generally 8, 12 or 16 hours a day.

These values correspond only to the general profile of the estates, because if there is a great consumption, the flow mentioned before must be increased by the quantity necessary to this specific industry. This is the case of the industrial estate of Covilhã, to which was added to the medium flow, a flow of 100 m³/day because of woolen manufacturing industry.

The design flow of the sewerage system is evaluated, adding the infiltration flow to the peak flow multiplied by a reduction coefficient, which is a function of the characteristics of the soil of each estate and generally equal to 0.8 l/s/km. Sometimes, a quantity evaluated as a certain percentage of the industrial flow is added to the last sum in order to meet extraordinary needs.

DESIGN OF THE SEWERAGE SYSTEMS

THE SEWERAGE SYSTEMS of the four estates were designed in order to avoid stagnation and to assure good ventilation of the pipes. The time of retention must be very short and turbulence and shocks must be avoided. The plan of each sewerage system was also designed to permit easy extension. The pipes are placed at the middle of the roads with the necessary works for the operation of the system.

The profile of the pipes is designed, in addition to the usual criteria established in the "Regulamentos Gerais das Canalizações e Esgotos", to assure self-cleaning. So, a shear stress minimum of $0.2 \, kgf/m^2$ is imposed in all the branches of the industrial sewerage system and of $0.4 \, kgf/m^2$ in the storm-water networks.

So-called "automatic flush tanks" were not used because damage in the tap can lead to an important loss of water. Besides that, they can lead to contamination of the water supply network from the sewerage system. Furthermore, their action is only applied over a short distance.

In order to assure good aeration in every branch, the depth of water inside the pipes must not exceed 0.5D (D = diameter) for pipes whose diameter is less than 700 mm and 0.7D for the others in the sewerage systems. In the storm-water network the maximum height must be equal to the diameter.

CONSIDERATIONS ABOUT THE TREATMENT AND THE DISCHARGE OF THE USED WATER

THE MAIN DIFFICULTY in choosing the type of treatment for wastewater is due to the nonexistence of information on the profiles of the estates. Usually, the treatment plant is built before the installation of the first industries. Its design must allow for great flexibility in the types of treatment catered for. This happened in Covilhã where the wastewater treatment plant is composed of a flow equalization basin, a flocculation tank, and a primary sedimentation tank in its primary phase, the sludges being dried in dry beds.

The treatment plants of the Guimarães and Beja estates are still under study. In the latter, the municipality is studying the possibility of treating the wastewater from the neighbouring villages in the treatment plant of the estate.

The wastewater treatment from the Évora estate as initially designed was abandoned, because of the permission granted by the municipality of Évora to treat the wastewater of the estate in the Évora treatment plant, which is under construction. The dimension of this treatment plant with trickling filters will allow the treatment of the wastewater of the estate. However, the municipality imposes limits to some of the characteristics of the wastewater of the estate drained to the treatment plant (see Table 1).

Table 1. Maximum values for some characteristics of the wastewater of the Évora estate, imposed on admission to the town treatment plant

Characteristics	Maximum Values
Aluminium	50 mg/l
Arsenic	5 mg/l
Barium	50 mg/l
Cadmium	5 mg/l
Copper	5 mg/l
Hexavalent chromium	1 mg/l
Lead	2,5 mg/l
Tin	10 mg/l
Magnesium	1,000 mg/l
Mercury	0,5 mg/l
Nickel	12,5 mg/l
Zinc	25 mg/l
Cyanide	5 mg/l
Phenolic compounds	200 mg/l
Sulphates	1,200 mg/l
Fluorides	50 mg/l
Oil and grease	400 mg/l
Hydrocarbons	60 mg/l
Anionic detergents	40 mg/l
BOD	1,500 mg/l
COD	2,500 mg/l
Temperature	45°C
pH	between 5 and 40

CONCLUSIONS

THE SEWERAGE SYSTEMS and the treatment plants of the industrial estates in Portugal are under construction or under study, and so it is not yet possible to analyse the results of these works. However, the evolution of the development of each estate as well as of its industrial profile allow us to conclude that the sewerage system and the treatment plants must be designed in order to make them sufficiently flexible.

The sewerage systems must always assure the drainage of wastewater from the beginning of their operation and must be designed to make expansion to all the future building sites possible.

The treatment plants, with primary or secondary treatment in the beginning, must always allow, after knowledge of the industrial profile of the estate, the expansion to secondary and tertiary treatment, if necessary.

The study of the industrial wastewater treatment with the sewerage system of the neighbouring municipalities should be considered, because it can carry important investment and operational economies.

Tanning Effluents: Characterisation and Treatment

J. Santos Oliveira
Professor, Universidade Nova de Lisboa, Lisbon

M. Conceição R. Santos
Lecturer, Universidade Nova de Lisboa, Lisbon

and

Leonor Cartaxo
Engineer, Direcção Geral dos Serviços de Controle da
Poluição, Lisbon, Portugal

SYNOPSIS

The effluents of a tannery plant near Lisbon have been studied in order to analyze them in terms of pollutant load and concentration of a few particular substances. The presence of important quantities of chromium and the irregularity of flows of the waste liquors led to physico-chemical treatment of the effluents. The efficiency of several products in flocculation has been tested (lime, aluminium sulphate, ferric sulphate, ferric chloride). The influence of sand filtration and ion exchange resins has also been studied. This study will be continued in order to determine the biodegradability of substances present in the supernatant and the efficiency of a mixed treatment with domestic waste water.

445

RÉSUMÉ

Les effluents d'une usine de tannage de peaux, près de Lisbonne, ont été étudiés de façon à les charactèriser du point de vue de la charge polluante et la concentration de quelques substances particulières. La présence d'importantes quantités de chrome et l'irrégularité des décharges indique la possibilité de traitement physicochimique des effluents. Des essais ont été realisés pour étudier l'efficacité de quelques floculants (chaux, sulfate d'aluminium, sulfate ferreux, chlorure ferrique).

On a étudié aussi l'influence de la filtration sur sable et l'échange d'ions. Ce travail doit être continué de façon à determiner la biodégradabilité des substances en presence dans le surnageant et le rendement d'un traitement biologique sur un mélange des effluents avec des eaux residuelles domestiques.

RESUMEN

Los despojos de una fábrica de curtidos de las cercanías de Lisboa, han sido estudiados con miras a caracterizarlos del punto de vista de la carga de polucion y de la concentración de algunas substancias particulares. La presencia de importantes cantidades indica la posibilidad de tratamiento físicoquímico de los despojos. Se realizaron ensayos para estudiar la eficacia de algunas substancias (cal, sulfato de aluminio, sulfato ferroso y cloruro férrico).

Ha sido estudiada tambien la influencia de la filtración de arena y el cambio iónico. Este trabajo debe ser continuado para poder determinar la biodegradabilidad de las substancias que se encuentran en la superficie y el rendimiento de un tratamiento biológico sobre la mezcla de estos despojos con residuos de águas domésticas.

INTRODUCTION

THE TANNING INDUSTRY is one of the oldest industrial activities in the world. The objective of leather treatment is to break down the proteins of the skin in order to increase its resistance and durability and avoid putrefaction. Historically this operation was first made by sun drying. Later tanning was performed using vegetable tannins, especially some tree barks like oaks. More recently, tanning has been carried out by the action of some inorganic products, namely chromium salts (or their mixtures with vegetable tannins).

Leather treatment comprises:

(a) Cutting and preservation
(b) Washing to eliminate different solids and salt
(c) Liming in vats aided by sodium sulphite
(d) Neutralization by organic acids, ammonium salts, calcium acetate or chemicals of similar behaviour
(e) Tanning by action of inorganic products or vegetable tannins
(f) Dyeing and washing
(g) Drying of tanned and dyed leather and other finishing procedures such as cutting and thinning of leathers.

From each of these steps, very important liquid effluents result, averaging $13.6\,cm^3$ per 100 Kg of leather. Water consumption depends on raw material and industrial processes used.

DESCRIPTION OF THE PLANT UNDER STUDY

THE PLANT whose effluents are described herein is located in Cacém, Alto da Bela Vista, near Lisbon, producing 1600 square feet of leather each day and discharging $160\,m^3$/day, five days a week, using a small river (Jamor) as a final sink. The treatment of leather in this particular factory plant comprises:

(a) Washing of leather;
(b) Liming aided by sodium sulphite;
(c) Neutralization by organic acids, ammonium salts and calcium acetate;
(d) Tanning by chromium salts;
(e) Dyeing.

Domestic sewage from the sanitary installations of the plant are added to the industrial effluent. The resulting effluents are rich in organic and inorganic matter, very basic in pH, and with a very high five-day Biochemical Oxygen Demand (BOD_5).

EFFLUENT CHARACTERISTICS. TREATMENT POSSIBILITIES

SAMPLES FROM the final effluents were collected from an equalization tank, in June 1976 (sample A) and September 1976 (sample B). Table 1 presents the results of

Table 1. Results of Analyses

	Samples	
	Average June	Average September
pH	8.95	10.60
Color (un. Pt-Co)	2500	4000
Turbidity (FTU)	800	1300
Alkalinity (mg/l Ca CO_3)	1776.2	750.0
Acidity (mg/l Ca CO_3)	0	0
Sulphide (mg/l)	217.6	256.0
Chromium (mg/l)	13.6	10.3
Conductivity (μmhos/cm)	28,000	26,000
Total solids (g/l)	14.15	14.28
Suspended solids (g/l)	1.99	2.02
Oxidability (mg O_2/l)	630	824
BOD_5 (mg O_2/l)	1000	1320
COD (mg O_2/l)	5165	5913
BOD_5/COD	0.19	0.22

the analyses performed on those samples. Only colour, turbidity and alkalinity present some variations.

The relative importance of the contribution of this industry to the amount of industrial pollution in Portugal had been studied by some Portuguese and others. In the inventory published by Ribeiro [1] the most polluted rivers due to this type of effluent are Leça and Alviela.

According to Figueiredo [2], tannery and leather finishing, with an annual production of 14,499 tons, represents a load equivalent to 270,819 inhabitant-years and corresponds to 2 per cent of total industrial pollution.

In effect, tanning industry effluents present:
(a) high alkalinity;
(b) important contents of suspended and dissolved solids;
(c) toxic substances such as sulphides and chromium salts;
(d) high contents of oxygen-demanding substances.

The impact of these effluents on the ecological equilibrium of the receiving river is obviously dramatic. Characteristics of river water changes markedly, in terms of colour, turbidity, pH and total solids. Degradation of water quality to be used by the community, contamination of underground water and soil, problems with the liberation of H_2S and other volatile products that cause bad odours, must also be mentioned.

It is obvious that effluent characteristics will change with the type of industry process and the type of effluents discharged, because they have a very different polluting capacity. Effluents from liming and tanning are the most polluting of all.

Different methods are used to treat these effluents:
   (a) Physical treatments (straining);
   (b) Physico-chemical treatments (addition of chemical substances and sedimentation);
   (c) Biological treatments (activates sludge, biological filters or stabilization ponds, in general after physical or physico-chemical treatment).
   To treat the present effluent a physico-chemical treatment was chosen, as follows:
   (1) Addition of $Ca(OH)_2$;
   (2) Addition of a flocculant, $Al_2(SO_4)_3$, $FeSO_4$ or $FeCl_3$;
   (3) Sand filtration;
   (4) Ion exchange resins filtration.

RESULTS

VARIOUS TESTS were performed to determine the most convenient dosage of $Ca(OH)_2$ to be added to the effluent. Table 2 presents the results obtained for

Table 2. Determination of the most Convenient Dosage of $Ca(OH)_2$ on Sample A

$Ca(OH)_2$	Colour (un. Pt-Co)	Turbidity (FTU)	Conductivity (umhos/cm)	pH	Total Solids g/l	Oxidability (mg O_2/l)
A+ 22 g/l	320	135	18,000	12.30	12.76	450
A+ 24 g/l	280	85	18,000	12.30	12.54	450
A+ 26 g/1	340	100	25,000	12.30	12.63	480
A+ 28 g/1	190	75	18,000	12.30	12.48	430
A+ 30 g/1	160	75	18,000	12.30	12.35	400
A+ 32 g/1	150	50	18,000	12.35	12.14	400
A+ 34 g/1	70	30	17,000	12.35	11.60	320
A+ * 36 g/1	50	25	15,000	12.35	11.24	320
A+ 38 g/1	50	30	15,000	12.35	11.40	320
A+ 40 g/1	50	30	15,000	12.40	11.58	320

* The most convenient dosage.

Table 3. Determination of the most Convenient Dosage of $Al_2(SO_4)_3$, on Sample A, after $Ca(OH)_2$ Treatment

g/l $Al_2(SO_4)_3$	Colour (un. Pt. Co)	Turbidity (FTU)	Conduct. (umhos/cm)	pH	Total Solids (g/l)	Oxidab. (mg O_2/l)	Sulphides (mg S^{2+}/l)	Chromium (mg Cr/l)
A +36 g/l $Ca(OH)_2$	50	25	15,000	12.35	11.24	320	217.6	0.5
A + $Ca(OH)_2$ +0.1 g/l	60	18	28,000	12.2	14.03	352	89.6	0.5
A + $Ca(OH)_2$ +0.2 g/l	45	18	25,000	12.1	13.74	352	89.6	0.5
A + $Ca(OH)_2$ +0.3 g/l	45	16	21,000	12.1	13.20	344	89.6	0.5
A + $Ca(OH)_2$ +0.4 g/l	35	16	21,000	12.0	12.60	328	89.6	0.5
A + $Ca(OH)_2$ +0.5 g/l	20	16	20,000	12.0	11.54	296	89.6	0.25
A + $Ca(OH)_2$ +0.6 g/l	20	16	20,000	12.0	11.14	200	89.6	0.25
A + $Ca(OH)_2$ +0.7 g/l	20	16	20,000	12.0	10.47	130	89.6	0.25
A + $Ca(OH)_2$ +0.8 g/l	20	16	20,000	12.0	10.18	100	89.6	0.25
A + $Ca(OH)_2$ +0.9 g/l	30	16	20,000	12.0	10.06	120	89.6	0.15
A + $Ca(OH)_2$ +1 g/l	40	16	20,000	12.0	9.46	150	89.6	0.08

Table 4. Determination of the most Convenient Dosage of FeSO$_4$, in Sample A, after Ca(OH)$_2$ Treatment

g/l FeSO$_4$	Colour (un. Pt. Co)	Turbidity (FTU)	Conduct. (umhos/cm)	pH	Total Solids (g/l)	Oxid. (mg O$_2$/l)	Sulphides (mg S^{2-}/l)	Chromium (mg Cr/l)
A +36 g/l Ca(OH)$_2$	50	25	15,000	12.35	11.24	320	217.6	0.5
A+Ca(OH)$_2$ +0.1 g/l	60	16	28,000	12.2	13.75	320	89.6	0.5
A+Ca(OH)$_2$ +0.2 g/l	50	16	25,000	12.2	12.67	296	89.6	0.5
A+Ca(OH)$_2$ +0.3 g/l	50	12	23,000	12.2	11.64	304	89.6	0.5
A+Ca(OH)$_2$ +0.4 g/l	40	12	23,000	12.2	11.51	272	89.6	0.5
A+Ca(OH)$_2$ +0.5 g/l	30	12	23,000	12.2	11.18	272	89.6	0.25
A+Ca(OH)$_2$ +0.6 g/l	20	10	20,000	12.0	10.77	150	89.6	0.1
A+Ca(OH)$_2$ +0.7 g/l	20	10	20,000	12.0	10.24	140	89.6	0.1
A+Ca(OH)$_2$ +0.8 g/l	20	10	20,000	12.0	10.00	140	89.6	0.1
A+Ca(OH)$_2$ +0.9 g/l	20	10	20,000	12.0	9.92	140	89.6	0.1
A+Ca(OH)$_2$ +1 g/l	20	10	20,000	12.0	9.29	130	89.6	0.05

Table 5. Determination of the most Convenient Dosage of $FeCl_3$ on Sample A, after $Ca(OH)_2$ Treatment

g/l Fe Cl₃	Colour (un. Pt. Co)	Turbidity (FTU)	Conduct. (umhos/cm)	pH	Total Solids (g/l)	Oxid. (mg O₂/l)	Sulphides (mg S²⁺/l)	Chromium (mg Cr/l)
A +36 g/l Ca(OH)₂	50	25	15,000	12.35	11.24	320	217.6	0.5
A +Ca(OH)₂ +0.1 g/l	40	18	30,000	11.5	15.78	320	89.6	0.035
A +Ca(OH)₂ +0.2 g/l	40	16	30,000	11.5	14.70	320	89.6	0.02
A +Ca(OH)₂ +0.3 g/l	80	23	30,000	11.5	13.62	320	89.6	0.019
A +Ca(OH)₂ +0.4 g/l	40	14	30,000	11.7	13.04	320	89.6	0.018
A +Ca(OH)₂ +0.5 g/l	40	10	25,000	11.7	12.12	320	89.6	0.009
A +Ca(OH)₂ +0.6 g/l	40	8	25,000	11.7	11.28	296	89.6	0.008
A +Ca(OH)₂ +0.7 g/l	40	7	25,000	11.7	11.20	296	89.6	0.01
A +Ca(OH)₂ +0.8 g/l	30	6	22,000	11.7	10.14	296	89.6	0.012
A +Ca(OH)₂ +0.9 g/l	20	5	20,000	11.7	10.01	296	89.6	0.02
A +Ca(OH)₂ +1 g/l	20	10	20,000	11.7	9.47	296	89.6	0.006

some parameters from supernatant analysis. The appropriate dosage was found to be in the range of 34 to 40 g/l.

After $Ca(OH)_2$ treatment, the effluent still had a very high amount of total solids, so we studied the effect of the addition of $Al_2(SO_4)_3$ on an effluent treated with a convenient dosage of $Ca(OH)_2$ (36 g/l). Table 3 presents the results of this study: the determination of the most efficient dose is doubtful, but 0.5 g $Al_2(SO_4)_3$/l was chosen. The pH reduced by 0.35 units after addition of $Ca(OH)_2$. We also studied the effect of $FeSO_4$ after addition of 36 g/l of $Ca(OH)_2$. Results are presented in Table 4. We also carried out tests using $FeCl_3$, adding it to the effluent already treated with 36 g/l $Ca(OH)_2$. The results are presented in Table 5. Table 6 presents the percentage reductions attained after addition of convenient dosages of $Ca(OH)_2$ and each one of the studied coagulants.

Comparing data we can see that the addition of 1 g/l of $FeCl_3$, $FeSO_4$ or $Al_2(SO_4)_3$ in relation to 0.5 g/l of each coagulant did not increase the reduction of sulphides but reduced chromium to 99.96 per cent of its initial value. In sample B we also studied the effect of $Ca(OH)_2$, $Al_2(SO_4)_3$, $FeSO_4$ and $FeCl_3$ addition. The most convenient addition of $Ca(OH)_2$ was found to be 38 g/l as can be seen in Table 7. Table 8 presents the percentage reductions obtained in relation to the initial Sample B.

Figure 1 represents the decrease in polluting of sample A, after flocculation and coagulation treatment.

Similarly as for sample A, sample B presents very high colour, turbidity and chromium reductions, after treatment. The decrease of total solids, oxidability, sulphides and conductivity is good but relatively less marked.

This observation, valid for both samples, justified a complementary study of physico-chemical treatments, such as filtration on sand and ion exchange.

Table 9 presents the results obtained with sample A after complete treatment.

Table 6. Percentage Reductions on Sample A, after Flocculation-Coagulation Treatment

	36 g/l $Ca(OH)_2$	36 g/l $Ca(OH)_2$ +0.5 g/l $Al_2(SO_4^2)_3$	36 g/l $Ca(OH)_2$ +0.5 g/l $FeSO_4$	36 g/l $Ca(OH)_2$ +0.5 g/l $FeCl_3$
Colour	98.00	99.20	96.25	98.40
Turbidity	96.25	98.00	98.50	98.75
Conductivity	46.29	40.00	10.71	10.71
Total Solids	20.57	18.45	20.99	14.35
Oxidability	49.21	41.21	56.83	49.21
Sulphides	25.00	0	58.82	58.85
Chromium	99.02	98.16	98.16	99.93

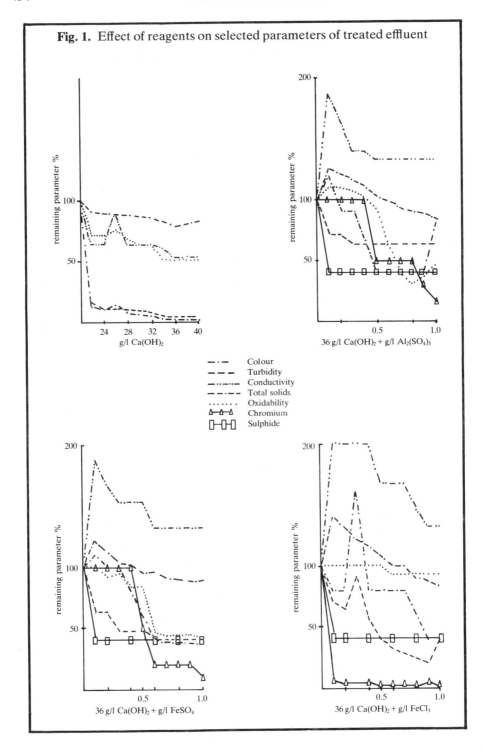

Fig. 1. Effect of reagents on selected parameters of treated effluent

Table 7. Determination of the most Convenient Dosage of Ca(OH)$_2$
(Sample A)

	Colour (un. Pt-Co)	Turbidity (FTU)	Conductivité (umhos/cm)	pH	Total Solids g/l	Oxidability (mg O$_2$/l)
B + 32 g/l	450	118	19,900	12.0	13.70	820
B + 34 g/l	380	118	19,900	12.0	12.45	800
B + 36 g/l	200	60	20,000	12.0	11.72	800
* B + 38 g/l	160	50	20,000	12.0	11.34	780
B + 40 g/l	180	60	20,000	12.0	11.96	800

* The most convenient dosage.

The reductions observed in total solids, conductivity, oxidability and sulphides have been very significant in relation to those obtained after flocculation-coagulation.

Table 10 presents data from sample B after the same type of treatment. The pH of final effluents is very low, about 1.5 to 2.2, making it objectionable to discharge into river courses. They must be diluted first with other effluents or then, the cation exchange step must be eliminated, because the effluents resulting from sand filtration and anion exchange are already satisfactory.

The BOD$_5$ and COD after complete treatment present a big reduction in relation to the initial values, as can be seen in Table 11.

Table 8. Percentage Reductions Obtained on Sample B

	B + 38 g/l Ca(OH)$_2$	B + 38 g/l Ca(OH)$_2$ + 0.5 g/l Al$_2$(SO$_4$)$_3$	B + 38 g/l Ca(OH)$_2$ +0.5 g/l FeSO$_4$	B + 38 g/l Ca(OH)$_2$ +0.5 g/l FeCl$_3$
Colour	96.80	97.75	98.25	97.25
Turbidity	96.15	97.31	98.46	97.08
Conductivity	3.00	34.62	34.62	34.62
Total Solids	20.59	31.02	30.67	28.99
Oxidability	5.34	19.42	12.62	23.30
Sulphides	25.00	40.00	40.00	40.00
Chromium	99.02	99.75	99.71	99.71

Table 9. Sample A after complete treatment

		Colour (un. Pt-Co)	Turbidity (FTU)	Conduct. (umhos/cm)	pH	Total Solids (g/l)	Oxid. (mg O$_2$/l)	Sulphide (mg S^{2-}/l)	Chromium (mg Cr/l)
A +36 g/l Ca(OH)$_2$	(1)	50	25	15,000	12.35	11.24	320	217.6	0.5
A +36 g/l Ca(OH)$_2$ +0.5 g/l Al$_2$(SO$_4$)$_3$	(2)	20	16	20,000	12.0	11.54	296	89.6	0.25
A +36 g/l Ca(OH)$_2$ +0.5 g/l FeSO$_4$	(3)	30	12	23,000	12.2	11.18	272	89.6	0.25
A +36 g/l Ca(OH)$_2$ +0.5 g/l FeCl$_3$	(4)	40	10	25,000	11.7	12.12	320	89.6	0.009
1 + filtration on sand	1'	40	22	10,000	7.9	7.42	320	32.0	0.02
2 + filtration on sand	2'	10	15	15,000	7.5	7.45	240	32.0	0.019
3 + filtration on sand	3'	20	10	13,000	7.9	8.14	240	32.0	0.01

4 + filtration on sand								
1' + exchange of anions	4'	30	10	19,000	6.2	8.03	300	32.0	0.017
2' + exchange of anions	1"	4	0	9,000	11.6	3.58	290	0	0.009
3' + exchange of anions	2"	4	0	11,000	11.7	1.62	220	0	0.008
4' + exchange of anions	3"	4	4	15,000	9.6	4.60	230	0	0.005
1" + exchange of cations	4"	10	10	16,000	9.7	5.85	280	0	0.007
2" + exchange of cations	1‴	0	0	10,000	2.0	0.57	200	0	0.001
3" + exchange of cations	2‴	0	0	13,000	2.2	0.34	180	0	0.009
4" + exchange of cations	3‴	10	5	18,000	1.5	1.72	180	0	0.009
	4‴	10	2	20,000	1.5	3.87	200	0	0.009

Table 10. Sample B after complete treatment

	Colour (un. Pt-Co)	Turbidity (FTU)	Conduct. (umhos/cm)	pH	Total Solids (g/l)	Oxid. (mg O_2/l)	Sulphides (mg S^{2-}/l)	Chromium (mg Cr/l)
B+38 g/l Ca(OH)$_2$ (1)	160	50	20,000	12.0	11.34	780	192	0.1
B+38 g/l Ca(OH)$_2$ +0.5 g/l AlSO$_4$ (2)	90	35	17,000	12.0	9.85	664	153.6	0.025
B+38 g/l Ca(OH)$_2$ +0.5 g/l FeSO$_4$ (3)	70	20	17,000	12.0	9.90	720	153.6	0.03
B+38 g/l Ca(OH)$_2$ +0.5 g/l FeCl$_3$ (4)	110	38	17,000	12.0	10.14	632	153.6	0.05
1+filtration on sand 1'	120	40	17,500	8.0	10.14	710	108.8	0.05
2+filtration on sand 2'	55	18	16,000	7.7	8.96	616	108.8	0.02
3+filtration on sand 3'	50	18	16,000	7.9	8.53	672	108.8	0.03

4 + filtration on sand	4'	90	30	16,000	7.8	9.24	568	108.8	0.03
1' + exchange of anions	1"	19	9	13,500	9.6	10.76	520	0	0.015
2' + exchange of anions	2"	8	5	8,200	9.6	6.86	480	0	0.015
3' + exchange of anions	3"	10	5	8,100	9.6	6.26	520	0	0.015
4' + exchange of anions	4"	22	10	9,800	11.2	6.79	416	32	0.014
1" + exchange of cations	1'''	99	30	22,000	1.7	3.30	400	0	0.018
2" + exchange of cations	2'''	25	8	18,100	1.7	1.71	216	0	0.015
3" + exchange of cations	3'''	35	12	17,500	1.7	2.61	296	0	0.015
4" + exchange of cations	4'''	35	12	22,200	1.7	4.25	264	0	0.015

Table 11. Samples BOD$_5$ and COD after Treatments.

		BOD$_5$	COD
	Ca(OH)$_2$ + filtration + ion exchange	900	2100
	Ca(OH)$_2$ + Al$_2$(SO$_4$)$_3$ + filtr. + ion exch.	400	1290
Sample A	Ca(OH)$_2$ + FeSO$_4$ + filtr. + ion exchange	450	1900
	Ca(OH)$_2$ + FeCl$_3$ + filtr. + ion exchange	450	1925
	Ca(OH)$_2$ + filtration + ion exchange	1200	2511
	Ca(OH)$_2$ + Al$_2$(SO$_4$)$_3$ + filtr. + ion exch.	600	2019
Sample B	Ca(OH)$_2$ + FeSO$_4$ + filtr. + ion exchange	700	2178
	Ca(OH)$_2$ + FeCl$_3$ + filtr. + ion exchange	600	2212

Table 12. Percentage Reductions after Treated Sample Filtration on Sand and Ion Exchange

% Treatment Reduction		(1)	(2)	(3)	(4)
Colour	A	100	100	99.6	99.6
	B	97.5	99.4	99.1	99.1
Turbidity	A	100	100	99.4	99.8
	B	97.7	99.4	99.1	99.1
Conductivity	A	64.3	53.6	35.7	28.6
	B	15.4	30.4	32.7	14.6
Total Solids	A	96.0	97.6	87.8	72.6
	B	76.9	88.0	81.7	70.2
Oxidability	A	68.3	71.4	71.4	75.0
	B	51.5	73.8	64.1	68.0
Sulphides	A	100	100	100	100
	B	100	100	100	100
Chromium	A	100	100	100	100
	B	99.8	99.9	99.9	99.9

CONCLUSION

COMPARING RESULTS obtained with the two samples, a very important reduction on some characteristics of tanning effluents can be observed, namely a decrease of sulphides and chromium that eliminate the toxic effects on living organisms, and avoid H_2S odours.

Even if we could consider the quality of final effluent good enough, its aggressivity is very reduced and biological treatment of these effluents in a mixture with domestic sewage, in classic treatment plants adapted to the socio-ecological conditions of each country region, can be performed.

References

1. Ribeiro, S. *Inventário realizado sobre a poluição do meio aquático*, in *I Simpósio Nacional sobre poluição das águas interiores* 1971.
2. Figueiredo, J.M.A. *Intervenção administrativa no problema da poluição das águas por efluentes industriais e tentativa de avaliação dos custos desta poluição em Portugal*, Lisboa, I.N.I.I., 1973, 102 p.

Authors' Index